Math
Matters

Understanding the Math You Teach

Grades K–8

Second Edition

Math Matters

Understanding the Math You Teach
Grades K–8

Second Edition

Suzanne H. Chapin

Art Johnson

Math Solutions Publications
Sausalito, CA

Math Solutions Publications
A division of
Marilyn Burns Education Associates
150 Gate 5 Road, Suite 101
Sausalito, CA 94965
www.mathsolutions.com

Library of Congress Cataloging-in-Publication Data
Chapin, Suzanne H.
    Math matters : understanding the math you teach, grades K–8 /
Suzanne H. Chapin, Art Johnson.—2nd ed.
        p. cm.
    Includes bibliographical references and index.
    ISBN-13: 978-0-941355-71-1 (alk. paper)
    ISBN-10: 0-941355-71-3 (alk. paper)
    1. Mathematics—Study and teaching (Elementary)   I. Johnson, Art.   II.
Title.
    QA135.6.C473 2006
    372.7—dc22
                                                                    2006001876

Editor: Toby Gordon
Production: Melissa L. Inglis
Cover design: Isaac Tobin
Interior design: Angela Foote Book Design
Composition: Interactive Composition Corporation

Printed in the United States of America on acid-free paper
10 09 08 07   ML   2 3 4 5

To our daughters

> Catherine Ann Chapin
> Elizabeth Jane Chapin
> Candace Raven Johnson
> Alexa Brit Johnson

who with smiles on their faces shared their understanding of mathematics with us. Thank you. We learned so very much!

For my uncle Nicholas Sideris.

> His integrity and enthusiasm for life have always inspired me.
> —AJ

A Message from Marilyn Burns

We at Math Solutions Professional Development believe that teaching math well calls for increasing our understanding of the math we teach, seeking deeper insights into how children learn mathematics, and refining our lessons to best promote students' learning.

Math Solutions Publications shares classroom-tested lessons and teaching expertise from our faculty of Math Solutions Inservice instructors as well as from other respected math educators. Our publications are part of the nationwide effort we've made since 1984 that now includes

- more than five hundred face-to-face inservice programs each year for teachers and administrators in districts across the country;
- annually publishing professional development books, now totaling more than fifty titles and spanning the teaching of all math topics in kindergarten through grade 8;
- four series of videotapes for teachers, plus a videotape for parents, that show math lessons taught in actual classrooms;
- on-site visits to schools to help refine teaching strategies and assess student learning; and
- free online support, including grade-level lessons, book reviews, inservice information, and district feedback, all in our quarterly *Math Solutions Online Newsletter*.

For information about all of the products and services we have available, please visit our website at *www.mathsolutions.com.* You can also contact us to discuss math professional development needs by calling (800) 868-9092 or by sending an email to *info@mathsolutions.com.*

We're always eager for your feedback and interested in learning about your particular needs. We look forward to hearing from you.

Math Solutions®
PUBLICATIONS

Contents

Preface to the Second Edition

The ideas and activities in *Math Matters* have a long history. They are based on our work in mathematics education with undergraduate and graduate students and our involvement in many professional development programs and presentations over the past twenty years. First, funding for the Partners in Change Project (#R215J40072, U.S. Department of Education, 1994–1997) enabled us to articulate the activities we found most helpful in our previous work with educators—activities that teachers found valuable in extending and deepening their current mathematical knowledge. Second, with support from Marilyn Burns, we were able to take the activities from the Partners in Change Handbook and create a resource to help K–6 teachers deepen their understanding of the mathematics they have to teach.

Many teachers who are responsible for teaching math in grades K–8 haven't studied mathematics in depth. The assumption has long been that the mathematics taught in elementary and middle school deals with topics that aren't suitable for advanced study. Unfortunately, this means that many teachers have had extremely limited opportunities to study the mathematics they have to teach. Their knowledge, in large part, is based on their own early schooling, which typically focused on computation skills, not understanding. Based on the belief that teachers can't teach well what they don't understand, the first edition of *Math Matters* addressed several fundamental questions:

▲ What math concepts and skills are important in the elementary grades?
▲ What does a teacher need to understand in order to teach these concepts and skills well?
▲ What can we learn from research about teaching and learning these ideas so that we can bridge the gap between research and practice?

Our work with teachers has continued to evolve, expand, and change, and we're pleased to share new insights and content in this second edition.

There are fourteen chapters in the book, each focusing on an important math topic that's studied in the elementary or middle grades. Each chapter begins with a brief introduction, followed by numbered sections that address different aspects of the topic. The chapter on number sense, for example, has three sections: Classifying Numbers, Understanding Numbers, and Our Place Value Numeration System. The chapter on measurement has four sections: Learning to Measure, The Metric Measurement System, The English Measurement System, and Measurement Relationships.

Each section explains the mathematical concepts basic to that particular aspect of the topic and introduces and defines related terms. When available, the results of research on children's learning provide insights into why particular topics are included in the curriculum and why some students have difficulty understanding specific ideas or learning particular skills.

Also, very important, interspersed throughout each chapter are activities directly linked to the mathematical information presented. There are 116 activities in the book, and they can be done alone, with a colleague, or with a study group. Some activities are investigations and others are problems to be solved; some use materials to provide concrete experiences with concepts and skills. Following each activity is a thorough discussion of the mathematics involved (with answers!), as well as information about how the particular math ideas fit into the larger framework of elementary and middle school mathematics. Not only do the activities enhance learning, they also suggest useful ways for expanding students' knowledge.

What is new in this second edition? Classroom teachers, district math coordinators, school math coaches, college and university professors, and in-service providers have all asked that we include more mathematics. Topics that are typically explored in upper elementary and middle school grades were mentioned again and again. Responding to this feedback, we've broadened the scope of the chapters to address the topics important to the K–8 mathematics curriculum: integers, exponents, similarity, the Pythagorean Theorem, Platonic solids, box-and-whisker plots, and more. Also, because ratios, proportions, and proportional reasoning are such important middle school topics, we've added a new chapter devoted to understanding ratios and rates and applying them to a range of situations. And we've expanded the chapter on algebra to focus on how teachers might enhance students' abilities to reason algebraically through generalizing, formalizing, and justifying ideas.

In another effort to make *Math Matters* a more effective resource, we have elaborated on some of the topics taught in the elementary grades. For example, the book now deals with operations with decimal numbers and informal strategies and algorithms for solving fraction and percent problems.

We've also made use of the World Wide Web. Certain Web sites (but not all) have the potential to support the understanding of mathematics by both teachers and students. We have directed our readers to sites that we believe meet this criterion. For example, manipulating "virtual" fraction pieces can help build an understanding of equivalence, and repeatedly reflecting objects can help clarify the concept of lines of symmetry.

Throughout this second edition, the emphasis continues to be on making sense and reasoning about relationships. One of the ways people learn is through firsthand experiences that promote thinking and reasoning. To this end, we've continued to intersperse throughout each chapter activities that help bring meaning to the mathematical ideas presented. Another way that most people learn involves reflecting on ideas. Knowing this, we've now added at the end of each chapter questions for reflection and discussion. These questions ask the reader to make connections among ideas, to think about similarities and differences among concepts, and to consider how students might come to understand the mathematics presented.

Math Matters can be a resource for math teaching no matter what instructional program is being used. Teachers preparing to teach a new topic will find the chapter addressing that particular content extremely helpful. The information will not only help them become more comfortable with the important underlying ideas but also prompt them to ask better questions of students, explain ideas more accurately or clearly, and stress important relationships and concepts.

Teaching children mathematics is both challenging and rewarding. We hope that changes made to this second edition of *Math Matters* contribute to your sense of mathematical power and your ability to help students understand this wonderful subject!

Number Sense

Number concepts and skills form the core of elementary school mathematics. Thus, a great deal of instructional time is devoted to topics related to quantity. One of the goals of instruction in arithmetic is for students to become numerically powerful and proficient. There are a number of components that are involved in numerical proficiency: conceptual understanding, procedural proficiency, strategic competence, adaptive reasoning, and productive disposition (Kilpatrick, Swafford, and Findell 2001). Being numerically proficient goes far beyond being able to compute accurately and efficiently; it entails understanding and using various meanings, relationships, properties, and procedures associated with number concepts and operations. It also involves the capacity to explain and justify one's actions on numbers and to use strategies appropriately and efficiently. How do we promote the development of children's numerical power? Certainly the instructional tasks we set for students have a bearing on what students learn. Equally important, however, is what we ourselves understand about numbers and number systems, for this knowledge contributes to our ability to ask students questions and provide learning experiences that are mathematically significant.

1. Classifying Numbers

We use numbers in many ways, for many purposes. Numbers can represent quantities— 13 apples, 6 eggs. They can indicate relative position—the 5th person in line. They can define measurements—the distance between two towns, the temperature on a thermometer. Numbers can also be identifiers; we think of a telephone number or the number on a football jersey as "labels."

In addition to these everyday uses of numbers, we classify numbers in sets. For example, consider the set of whole numbers—0, 1, 2, 3, 4, and so on. When we add or multiply whole numbers, the answer is always a whole number. But what happens when we subtract whole numbers? Certainly problems such as $32 - 14$ and $5 - 3$ result in whole number answers. But we run into trouble when we try to record a drop in the outside temperature to below 0° or calculate $3 - 8$, because the answer isn't in the set of whole numbers. We need a broader set of numbers that includes negative numbers. Similarly, solving problems like $7 \div 2$ or $10 \div 3$ calls for a set of numbers that includes fractions. Defining different sets of numbers in mathematics becomes more important as our questions about how much and how many become more complex.

A third way to classify numbers is to examine particular characteristics of numbers. Within the set of whole numbers, for example, some numbers are even and some are odd. This characteristic is obvious to us as adults but not so clear to young children. Some numbers are divisible by 2, some by 3, and some by both 2 and 3. There are triangular numbers and square numbers, prime numbers and composite numbers. When the set of numbers includes decimals, there are some decimals that can be written as fractions and some that do not have a fractional representation. Classifying numbers by characteristics helps us make generalizations about sets of numbers and can provide insights into the relationships among numbers. For example, the number 36 is even so it is divisible by 2; we can arrange 36 beans in pairs. It is also a composite number, divisible by 1, 2, 3, 4, 6, 9, 12, 18, and 36. It is a square number, which means that 36 objects can be arranged in a rectangular array to make a square. Some of the characteristics of 36 are related—its being even and its being divisible by two. Other characteristics of 36 are not connected—its being even has nothing to do with its being a square number. Figuring out the why and why not of these relationships leads to a deeper understanding of specific numbers as well as of sets of numbers.

Classifying Numbers by Use

There are six different ways that we use numbers: for rote counting (saying numbers in sequence), for rational counting (to count objects), as cardinal numbers (to name "how many" objects are in a set), as ordinal numbers (to name the relative positions of objects in sets), for measurements (to name "how much" when we measure), and as nominal or nonnumeric numbers (for identification).

When numbers are verbally recited without referring to objects, they are being used in sequence. This is often referred to as *rote counting*. When we state that the number 5 comes after 4 and before 6, we are referring to numbers as part of a sequence. Adults sometimes consider rote counting a simple mechanical task. However, for very young children, counting in sequence is not at all simple—at least not at the outset. Children must learn the names of the numbers in the proper order and make sense of the patterns. In addition, a child's ability to count aloud well does not mean that he or she can correctly count a set of objects. Later, when the quantity meaning of numbers has been established, rote counting can be used to find answers to computations such as 16 + 3: by counting on from 16, saying 17, 18, 19. Number in the context of sequence can also be used to compare quantities—some children use counting to determine whether 25 or 52 is the larger quantity, knowing that the larger number will be said after the smaller number.

In *rational counting*, objects or events are matched with a number name. For example, when someone asks, *How many candies did you eat?*, you point to the last candy in the box and say, *This will be number 5*. It is through rational counting and matching number names and objects one-to-one that children start to understand the concept of quantity. Young children benefit from repetitively counting objects such as pennies, blocks, stones, acorns, and beans—they not only are learning the number names in sequence but also associating those numbers with specific amounts. Repetition appears necessary for children to develop effective strategies for counting items once and only once and to invent advanced strategies such as grouping. Many teachers introduce a weekly counting activity in which every student in the class counts and records the number of objects in a set. When the quantity is large (two- and three-digit amounts), students can be asked to group the objects and then to count the groups.

A *cardinal number* describes how many there are in a set; it can be thought of as a quantifier. In the statement *I ate 5 candies*, the number 5 is used to tell how many candies were eaten. Children gradually grasp the idea that the last number stated in a rational counting sequence names the amount in that set, but you can help students understand this meaning by using labels in a cardinal context (*I have 4 dogs*, not *I have 4*). When children consistently use numbers to tell "how many," even if the quantity is inaccurate, they are displaying an understanding of cardinality.

An *ordinal number* indicates the relative position of an object in an ordered set. Most children learn the initial ordinal numbers—*1st*, *2nd*, and *3rd*—in the context of ordinary situations. They construct the others from sequence, counting, and cardinal contexts. Understanding ordinal numbers is based on counting but lags behind: 95 percent of five-year-old children can say the first eight number words, but only 57 percent can say the first five ordinal names; only about 25 percent of entering kindergarten students can point to the third ball, but about 80 percent can create a set of three objects (Payne and Huinker 1993). Pointing to objects while using the word number (*number 1*, *number 2*, *number 3*) and linking these names with the ordinal numbers (*1st*, *2nd*, *3rd*) are techniques for helping students learn the ordinal numbers.

Number as a *measure* is used to indicate the size, capacity, or amount obtained by measuring something—how many units along some continuous dimension are being considered. We use number as a measure when we say that a kitchen has 14 feet of counter space. (Did you visualize one counter 14 feet long or 14 separate feet of counter space?) The idea of a continuous quantity—one in which the units run together and fractional values make sense—is difficult for students, since most of their other number experiences have involved whole numbers and counting individual items. Measurement tasks give you a chance to discuss different ways to represent a quantity (e.g., as a length or as separate objects) and what kinds of numbers are useful for describing how much instead of how many (e.g., dividing 17 feet of rope to make two jump ropes, each $8\frac{1}{2}$ feet long, makes sense; dividing 17 cars into two equal groups of $8\frac{1}{2}$ cars does not).

Nominal or nonnumeric numbers, such as telephone numbers, numbers on license plates, house numbers, bus numbers, numbers on athletes' jerseys, and social security numbers, are used for identification. Confusion arises for children because nominal numbers rarely correspond with other number meanings. For example, house number 5 does not have to be the fifth house on the street nor do there even have to be five houses on the street.

Classifying Numbers by Sets

Historically, the development of number systems closely followed the development of how numbers were used and manipulated. As people asked and then solved more and more sophisticated problems, they had to expand their ideas about number. For example, the first numbers used were the *counting numbers* (1, 2, 3, 4, 5, . . .), also known as the *natural numbers*. Some of the earliest written records of ancient cultures include numerical symbols in reference to counting people and animals. The development of trade and agriculture brought with it new needs for numbers: civilizations needed to be able to divide such things as land or goods. More than four thousand years ago, both the Egyptians and the Babylonians developed the idea of fractional portions so that they could represent quantities less than one in division.

While zero was used as a place holder by the Babylonians, the concept of zero as a number was not documented until the seventh century when it was credited to Hindu mathematicians. However, the work of an Arabian mathematician, Al-Khowarizmi, around A.D. 825, who also used zero as a number, was of greater importance to the development of mathematics in Western Europe. The translation of Al-Khowarizmi's work in the thirteenth century contributed to our use today of the Hindu-Arabic numerals. While the counting numbers as a set do not include zero, both the *whole numbers* (0, 1, 2, 3, 4, . . .) and the rational numbers do.

Europeans began to use negative numbers during the Renaissance, expanding the set of whole numbers to the set of integers, although the concept of having less than zero was used by both the Hindus and Arabs centuries earlier. The widespread use of negative and positive numbers came about because of increased commerce and the need to keep records of both gains and losses. Today, upper elementary or middle school students learn about *integers*—a set of numbers that includes zero, the counting numbers, and their opposites (the opposite of a number is the number that is the same distance from zero on the number line, only in the opposite direction). For example, . . . $^-5$, $^-4$, $^-3$, $^-2$, $^-1$, 0, 1, 2, 3, 4, 5, . . . are all integers. There are also negative fractions and decimals, but they are not classified as integers because they are not opposites of natural (counting) numbers.

Throughout history, different sets of numbers have been defined and then used to answer questions of how much and how many. In school, students must learn about and use different types of numbers to answer these same questions. In the early grades, children deal primarily with whole numbers. However, elementary-age children also use numbers from other sets. Children who live in cold climates are more likely to be introduced to integers at an early age, since the weather is an important topic of conversation. Temperatures of 5 below zero ($^-5$) or a wind chill of $^-20$ have meaning for these children!

When students learn about fractions, they have to deal with a new set of numbers—*rational numbers*. Rational numbers enable us to answer questions about how many and how much using whole amounts and parts of whole amounts. Numbers that can be expressed as a ratio of two integers are *rational* numbers, hence the name. More formally, all rational numbers can be written in the form $\frac{a}{b}$ (a ratio) where a and b represent integers and b does not equal zero. The set of rational numbers includes whole numbers and negative numbers. The rational number set also includes all fractions and some of the decimal numbers that are between integers, $^-26\frac{1}{3}$, $^-4.35$, $\frac{7}{8}$, and 1.75, for example.

Why are some decimal numbers rational numbers? Many decimals can be represented as a fraction ($0.5 = \frac{1}{2}$ and $3.7 = 3\frac{7}{10}$). All repeating decimals such as $0.333\ldots$ and $0.277\ldots$ are classified as rational numbers; they also can be represented as fractions ($\frac{1}{3}$ and $\frac{5}{18}$, respectively). Not all decimals, however, are rational numbers. Many decimals cannot be written as a ratio of two integers because they have decimal expansions that do not terminate or become periodic (repeat in some way). These are known as the *irrationals* (not ratios, hence the name). Many irrational numbers are found by taking the roots of rational numbers. The root of a number, N, is a number that can be multiplied by itself a given number of times to produce N. For example, the square root of 25 ($\sqrt{25}$) is 5 since $5 \times 5 = 25$. The cube root of 8 ($\sqrt[3]{8}$) is 2 since $2 \times 2 \times 2 = 8$. Both of these numbers are rational. However, the square root of 2 is $1.414213562\ldots$ and this number is irrational. The square root of other numbers that are not perfect squares, such as $\sqrt{3}$, $\sqrt{11}$, and $\sqrt{24}$, are also irrational. The decimal expansion of these numbers cannot be written as a fraction. But taking the roots of rational numbers is not the only way to find an irrational number. There are an infinite number of irrational numbers that are not roots, such as π, e, and numbers like $0.34334333433334333334\ldots$. The irrational and rational number sets are infinite sets but, surprisingly, the irrational set has more elements.

Together the sets of rational and irrational numbers form the set of *real numbers*. Real numbers are used in all applications: measuring, comparing, counting, or determining quantities. Not all numbers in mathematics are real numbers, however ($\sqrt{^-7}$, for example, isn't a real number). These "imaginary" numbers belong to the set of complex numbers and are studied in high school and college.

It may help to visualize the different sets of numbers using a Venn diagram:

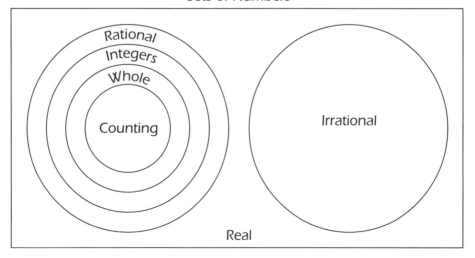

Sets of Numbers

Notice how most of these sets of numbers nest within each other. As numerical questions and answers become more complicated, students move from using "inside" sets of numbers to the full range of numbers in the real number system.

Activity

Exploring Irrational Numbers

Objective: explore lengths of line segments that are classified as irrational numbers.

If irrational numbers represent decimal expansions that do not terminate and do not repeat, can they be used to indicate measurements?

1. Use geoboards or sheets of dot paper similar to those in the picture below and construct or draw fourteen line segments of different lengths with dots as endpoints.
2. Determine the lengths of the line segments in units without using a measuring tool.
3. Which of the lengths represent rational numbers and which of the lengths represent irrational numbers? Explain how you know.
4. Without using the square root key on your calculator, use your calculator to determine the approximate length of one of the irrational number line segments to three decimal places.

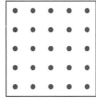 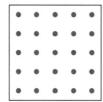 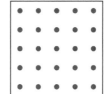 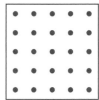

Things to Think About

In order to find all fourteen line segments of different lengths on the geoboard, consider starting at one point and systematically connecting it to other points horizontally, vertically, or diagonally. Make sure each line segment is a unique length and not a duplicate of previously drawn segments. The orientation or placement of the line segment is not of interest in this activity, simply the length of the segment.

How do we determine the length of a diagonal line segment? One way is to apply the Pythagorean Theorem. First, draw a right triangle so that the diagonal segment is the hypotenuse of the triangle. (The hypotenuse is the side of a right triangle opposite the right angle.) The legs or sides of the triangle will be perpendicular to each other. The Pythagorean Theorem ($a^2 + b^2 = c^2$) enables us to find the length of the hypotenuse of a right triangle, given the lengths of the legs of the triangle. In the equation, a and b represent the lengths of the legs and c represents the length of the hypotenuse. Next, substitute values into the formula $a^2 + b^2 = c^2$. For example, the line segment shown on page 7 forms a right triangle with legs 1 unit and 3 units long. Applying the Pythagorean Theorem, we can determine that the value of c is $\pm\sqrt{10}$:

$$a^2 + b^2 = c^2$$
$$1^2 + 3^2 = c^2$$
$$1 + 9 = c^2$$
$$10 = c^2$$
$$\pm\sqrt{10} = c$$

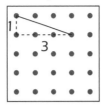

So what is the length of this segment? Every positive number has two square roots, a positive and a negative one. The symbol for the positive square root is $\sqrt{}$. Using a calculator, we find that $\sqrt{10}$ is approximately 3.16. The negative square root of 10 is shown by placing the negative sign outside the square root symbol ($^-\sqrt{10}$). The value of $^-\sqrt{10}$ is about $^-3.16$. Lengths of line segments are positive values, so the negative square root does not make sense in this situation. The length of this segment can be recorded as either $\sqrt{10}$ or about 3.16 units.

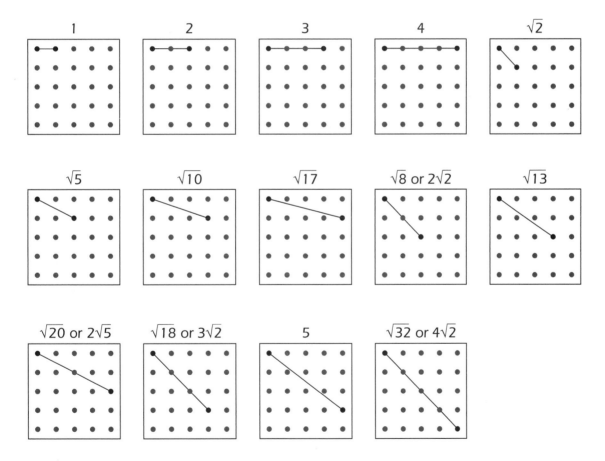

Five of the fourteen lengths can be classified as rational numbers (1, 2, 3, 4, and 5 units). These lengths can be represented as fractions or put another way as the ratio of two integers (can you determine what these ratios are?). The other nine line segments represent lengths that are classified as irrational numbers ($\sqrt{2}$, $\sqrt{5}$, $\sqrt{8}$, $\sqrt{10}$, $\sqrt{13}$, $\sqrt{17}$, $\sqrt{18}$, $\sqrt{20}$, $\sqrt{32}$ units). Notice that all of the irrational numbers in this problem are square roots. Irrational numbers can represent the measure of distances.

Every irrational number can be represented by a nonrepeating decimal expansion. Since the expansion continues forever, if we represent a length such as $\sqrt{10}$ units using the radical (root) sign, the answer is exact. But if we represent the length as a decimal, such as 3.162 units, the answer is approximate. Why? Because 3.162 is an estimate of the square root of 10. If you multiply 3.162 times itself (3.162 × 3.162), the product is close to 10 but not 10 exactly (9.998244). We can obtain a closer estimate of the square root of 10 by using a calculator or a computer to refine our estimate (3.162277 × 3.162277 = 9.999995824729), but no matter what number we try, we will never find a number that when multiplied by itself has a product of exactly 10. This fact is what makes the square root of 10 an irrational number. By leaving the length as $\sqrt{10}$ units, we are giving an exact answer even though we cannot physically measure it exactly.

So how do we estimate the value of a square root without using the calculator's square root function? Let's use $\sqrt{5}$ as an example. First, think about numbers that when multiplied by themselves are close in value to 5. The numbers 2 and 3 (2 × 2 = 4 and 3 × 3 = 9) fit the bill; we use these to estimate that the square root of 5 will be between them. It will be closer to 2 than 3 since 5 is much closer to 4 than 9. If we try 2.2 as the estimate, we find it is too small: 2.2 × 2.2 = 4.84. The number 2.3 is too large since 2.3 × 2.3 = 5.29. Using this information, make another estimate to two decimal places—perhaps 2.25. This estimate is too large, as is 2.24, but 2.23 is too small. Continuing with this guess-and-check strategy eventually leads us to 2.236 as an approximation to three decimal places for the square root of 5.

Another method for approximating the square root of a number dates back to the Babylonians and is often referred to as the "divide and average" method. Let's again use $\sqrt{5}$. Use what you know about multiplication to find a number that when multiplied by itself is close to 5 (2 or 3). Make a first estimate for the square root that is between these two numbers (say, 2.2). Using a calculator, divide 5 by 2.2 (5 ÷ 2.2 = 2.27272727). Now average the original estimate (also known as the divisor) and quotient [(2.2 + 2.272727273) ÷ 2 = 2.23636363]. Use this average as the new estimate and repeat the process. In other words:

$$5 \div 2.2 = 2.27272727 \qquad \text{divide by estimate}$$
$$(2.2 + 2.27272727) \div 2 = 2.23636363 \qquad \text{average estimate and quotient}$$
$$5 \div 2.23636363 = 2.23577236 \qquad \text{divide by new estimate}$$
$$(2.23636363 + 2.23577236) \div 2 = 2.236067995 \qquad \text{average new estimate and quotient}$$

Since the square root of 5 using the square root function on the calculator is 2.236067977, this method works quite well. Any ideas why?

You may wonder whether eventually, by trying numbers with more and more decimal places, you'll ever find a number that when multiplied by itself produces exactly 5. The answer is no, but the proof of this is beyond the scope of this book. Elementary and middle school students might enjoy examining the decimal expansion of a particular irrational such as $\sqrt{5}$, which they can find on the Web, to see for themselves that it does not repeat or terminate in the given number of decimal places. While an example does not prove that the irrational number's decimal expansion does not terminate or repeat, it still can be a powerful way to help students understand the complexity of this set of numbers. ▲

Classifying Numbers by Particular Characteristics

Certain characteristics are specific to certain sets of numbers. For example, whole numbers can be separated into even and odd numbers, but that categorization doesn't make sense when considering rational numbers, because all rational numbers can be divided by 2 and result in a rational answer. With whole numbers, only those that can be divided by 2 and result in another whole number are even. Likewise, fractions can be classified into one of two groups depending on whether their decimal representation terminates or repeats, but that classification doesn't have any relevance when thinking about counting numbers.

Classifying numbers by certain characteristics helps identify number patterns (e.g., the last digit in an odd number is either 1, 3, 5, 7, or 9) and leads to generalizations about numbers. The more students know about a set of numbers, the more powerful they are in making sense of numerical situations. Since a great deal of time in the elementary grades is spent using whole numbers, this section focuses on some of the characteristics of those sets of numbers.

An important characteristic of numbers is whether they are even or odd. (We often think only of whole numbers as being even or odd, but technically negative numbers may also be classified this way.) There are a number of ways for students to check whether a number is even or odd. One is to take counters corresponding to the quantity designated by the number (e.g., 12) and try to divide them into two equal groups. If there is one extra counter left over, the number is odd; if not, the number is even. Taking counters and putting them into two equal groups is equivalent to dividing a number by 2. If the result has no remainder when divided by 2, the number is even. Using multiplication to represent this relationship, even numbers can be written in the form $2 \times n$ where n is an integer ($12 = 2 \times 6$ since $12 \div 2 = 6$; $184 = 2 \times 92$ since $184 \div 2 = 92$). But if the result when divided by 2 has a leftover or remainder, then the number is odd. Again using multiplication to represent this relationship, odd numbers can be written in the form $(2 \times n) + 1$. For example, $11 \div 2 = 5$ r 1 and $11 = (2 \times 5) + 1$, and $185 \div 2 = 92$ r 1 and $185 = (2 \times 92) + 1$. A third way to explain evenness is by using the analogy of dancing partners—when you have an even number of people everyone has a partner or can form pairs. If even and odd numbers are represented using objects, the idea of partners can be shown concretely:

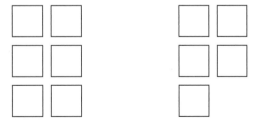

Knowing that the ones digit of all even numbers is either 0, 2, 4, 6, or 8 lets students quickly identify even numbers, but the pattern in itself does not help students understand the concept of evenness. They need many experiences in which they either separate counters into two equal groups or form "partners" with them and then decide whether the number quantity the counters represent is even or odd.

Is the number 0 even or odd? This confuses students since if they have 0 counters, how are they to check if the counters can be separated into two equal groups? They can't so we must use another method for checking: divide by 2 and see if the result has a remainder. When we divide 0 by 2, the quotient is 0 with no remainder ($0 \div 2 = 0$). Furthermore, we can represent 0 as ($2 \times n$) where $n = 0$ ($2 \times 0 = 0$). Notice that there is no value for n that works to make ($2 \times n$) + 1 equal to 0. Thus, 0 is an even number. Most second graders can simply be told that 0 is even, but older students (and some precocious second graders) should be asked to make sense of why.

Activity

Even and Odd Numbers, Part 1

Objective: investigate sums of even and odd numbers.

Consider the following questions:

1. Is the sum of two even numbers even or odd?
2. Is the sum of two odd numbers even or odd?
3. Is the sum of one odd number and one even number even or odd?

Using words, drawings, symbols, or concrete materials, explain why these types of sums occur.

Things to Think About

Why is the sum of two even numbers an even number? If a number is even, it can be represented using "partners," or pairs. Combining two numbers that are each separable into groups of two results in a third number (the sum) that is also separable into groups of two. Another way of stating the relationship is that the sum can be divided into two equal groups:

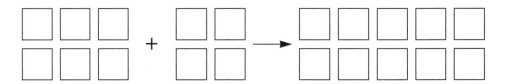

The sum of two odd numbers is also an even number. An odd number has what we can refer to as a "leftover"—when an odd number of counters is divided into two equal groups or into groups of two, there is always one extra counter. When we combine two odd numbers together, the "leftovers" from each odd number are joined and form a pair:

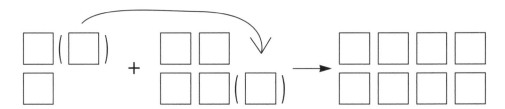

Using this same line of reasoning, it follows that the sum of one even and one odd number will always be an odd number. ▲

Activity

Even and Odd Numbers, Part 2

Objective: investigate products of even and odd numbers.

Consider the following questions:

1. Is the product of two even numbers even or odd?
2. Is the product of two odd numbers even or odd?
3. Is the product of one odd number and one even number even or odd?

Using words, drawings, symbols, or concrete materials, explain why these types of products occur.

Things to Think About

Why is the product of two even numbers an even number? One way to interpret multiplication is as a grouping operation. For example, 2 × 4 can be interpreted as two groups of four. Since there are an even number in each group (4) and an even number of groups (2), the total amount is always going to be an even number:

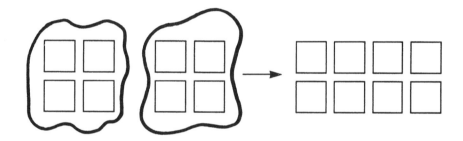

By generating examples, you discovered that the product of two odd numbers is an odd number. Why? In this case, think of multiplication as repeated addition. Using 3 × 5 to illustrate, we can interpret this multiplication as 5 + 5 + 5—and we notice we are adding an odd number an odd number of times. Since every two odd numbers when added together will total an even number, the extra odd number will remain without a partner and will affect the total by making it odd:

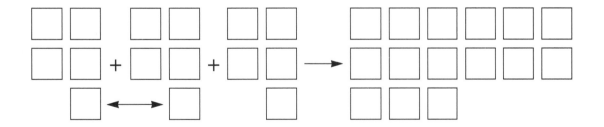

The third case, an even number multiplied by an odd number, always gives an even product. Both interpretations of multiplication, grouping and repeated addition, can be used to explain why. ▲

Another important classification of numbers is based on factors. A factor of a number divides the number evenly—there is no remainder. The numbers 2, 3, 4, and 6 are factors of 24, but 5 and 7 are not. Mathematicians have been intrigued for centuries by prime numbers: a prime number has exactly two unique factors, 1 and itself. Composite numbers have more than two factors.

Activity

Rectangular Dimensions and Factors

Objective: use rectangular arrays to visualize the differences among prime numbers, composite numbers, and square numbers.

Materials: graph paper.

Draw on graph paper as many different-shape rectangles as possible made from 1 square, 2 squares, 3 squares, . . . 25 squares. What are the dimensions of your rectangles? When you use 6 squares there are four whole number dimensions possible—1 and 6, and 2 and 3—but when you use 7 squares there are only two whole number dimensions—1 and 7. The whole number dimensions of these rectangles are also called *factors* of these numbers. Use the dimensions of rectangles formed from each number to list the factors of the numbers from 1 through 25. Remember that a square is a special kind of rectangle. Sort the numbers based on the number of factors.

Things to Think About

Does the orientation of the rectangles matter? Is a 2-by-5 rectangle the same as a 5-by-2 rectangle? The rectangles are different in that they show two distinct arrays, but they cover the same area: a 2-by-5 rectangle can be rotated to represent a 5-by-2 rectangle. For this activity we are interested in the dimensions of the rectangles (or the factors of the numbers), not in their vertical or horizontal orientation. What is important to note is that 2 and 5 are both factors of 10.

What did you find out about the number of factors? The number 1 has one factor (itself) and forms one rectangle (a 1-by-1 square); it is classified by mathematicians as a special number and is neither prime nor composite. Many numbers have only two factors and make just one rectangle: 2, 3, 5, 7, 11, 13, 17, 19, and 23. These numbers are the prime numbers. Prime numbers are defined as having exactly two unique factors. All the other numbers are composite numbers and have more than two factors; composite numbers can be represented by at least two unique rectangular arrays.

NUMBER	FACTORS	NUMBER OF RECTANGLES	PRIME OR COMPOSITE
1	1	1	Neither
2	1,2	2	Prime
3	1,3	2	Prime
4	1,2,4	3	Composite
5	1,5	2	Prime
6	1,2,3,6	4	Composite
7	1,7	2	Prime

8	1,2,4,8	4	Composite
9	1,3,9	3	Composite
10	1,2,5,10	4	Composite
11	1,11	2	Prime
12	1,2,3,4,6,12	6	Composite
13	1,13	2	Prime
14	1,2,7,14	4	Composite
15	1,3,5,15	4	Composite
16	1,2,4,8,16	5	Composite
17	1,17	2	Prime
18	1,2,3,6,9,18	6	Composite
19	1,19	2	Prime
20	1,2,4,5,10,20	6	Composite
21	1,3,7,21	4	Composite
22	1,2,11,22	4	Composite
23	1,23	2	Prime
24	1,2,3,4,6,8,12,24	8	Composite
25	1,5,25	3	Composite

Examine the rectangles representing the numbers 1, 4, 9, 16, and 25. Did you notice that in each case one of the rectangles that can be formed is also a square? Ancient Greek mathematicians thought of number relationships in geometric terms and called numbers like this square numbers, because one of the rectangular arrays they can be represented by is a square. The square numbers have an odd number of factors, whereas the other numbers examined have an even number of factors. Numbers that are not square always have factor pairs. For 12, for example, the factor pairs are 1 and 12, 2 and 6, and 3 and 4. But square numbers always have one factor that has no partner other than itself. For 9, for example, 1 and 9 are a factor pair, but 3 is its own partner because $3 \times 3 = 9$. The factor of a square number that has no partner—3 for the square number 9—isn't listed twice. Therefore, the factors of 9 are 1, 3, and 9, and the factors of 16 are 1, 2, 4, 8, and 16—an odd number of factors.

The square numbers between 25 and 200 are 36, 49, 64, 81, 100, 121, 144, 169, and 196. The terminology *squaring a number*—eight squared (8^2), for example—comes from the fact that when you multiply 8 by 8, one way to represent this amount geometrically is in the form of a square array with eight unit squares on each side. ▲

One of the earliest mathematicians to study prime and composite numbers was Eratosthenes (Era-toss'-the-neez), a Greek. He is known for a method of identifying prime numbers, the Sieve of Eratosthenes. Since the time of Eratosthenes, the hunt for prime numbers has occupied many mathematicians. A French mathematician from the early Renaissance, cleric Marin Mersenne (1588–1640), proposed the following formula for generating prime numbers: $2^n - 1$, where n is a prime number. Substitute the numbers 1 through 7 for n in his formula. Which of your results were prime numbers? Did you find that when n was a prime number, another prime number was generated by the formula? If $n = 2$, then the Mersenne Prime is 3 ($2^2 - 1 = 3$), and if $n = 3$, a Mersenne Prime, 7, is created ($2^3 - 1 = 7$). For $2^5 - 1$, the Mersenne Prime is 31. The next Mersenne Prime is $2^7 - 1$, or 127, and there are several prime numbers between 31 and 127. Over the course of the last three hundred years, as mathematicians worked on finding primes using Mersenne's formula, they discovered that Mersenne's formula does not generate all possible prime numbers. But by 1947 it was determined that if $n = $ 2, 3, 5, 7, 13, 17, 19, 31, 61, 89, 107, or 127, the formula does produce another prime number.

As counting numbers become larger, it becomes increasingly arduous to determine whether they are prime or not. Even high-speed computers have a difficult time examining extremely large numbers to determine whether they are prime. Therefore the current search for prime numbers examines only Mersenne Primes, because those numbers have the potential to be prime numbers. As of 2005, the largest prime number was a Mersenne Prime: $2^{254,964,951} - 1$. It contains over seven billion digits!

Other mathematicians fascinated by primes include Pierre de Fermat (1601–1665), Leonhard Euler (1707–1783), and Christian Goldbach (1690–1764). In a letter dated June 7, 1742, Goldbach presented his now famous conjecture to Euler, namely that any even number can be represented as the sum of two prime numbers. Test Goldbach's conjecture by finding sums for several even numbers using prime numbers as addends: $6 = 3 + 3, 8 = 5 + 3, 12 = 7 + 5, 20 = 13 + 7$ are all examples that support Goldbach's conjecture. Students enjoy learning about prime numbers and investigating Goldbach's conjecture. (No one has ever found an even number greater than 2 that cannot be written as the sum of two prime numbers.)

The exploration of number characteristics is sometimes purely recreational. One interesting classification scheme involves labeling counting numbers as *perfect*, *abundant*, or *deficient*. These classifications are related to the factors of the numbers. A perfect number is equal to the sum of all its factors other than itself (e.g., 28 is perfect, since $28 = 1 + 2 + 4 + 7 + 14$). If the sum of the factors of a number (other than itself) is greater than the number, then it is classified as abundant (e.g., 18 is an abundant number, since $1 + 2 + 3 + 6 + 9 = 21$). Finally, a deficient number is one whose factors (other than itself) sum to less than the number (e.g., 16 is a deficient number, since $1 + 2 + 4 + 8 = 15$). Factors of a number other than itself are sometimes referred to as proper factors.

Activity

Perfect Numbers

Objective: learn about perfect, abundant, and deficient numbers.

Pick a number. List the proper factors. Find the sum of the proper factors, and then classify the number as perfect, abundant, or deficient. Pick another number, list the proper factors, find their sum, and classify the number. Can you find one number of each type?

Things to Think About

Were you able to find a perfect number? There aren't a lot of perfect numbers, only two that are smaller than 30: 6 and 28. Some abundant numbers are 12, 18, 20, 24, and 30. Examples of deficient numbers include 8, 9, 10, 14, 15, 21, and 25. All prime numbers are deficient numbers. Can you think of a reason that explains why? A prime number has only two factors, 1 and itself, so the only proper factor is 1. Therefore, the "sum" of the proper factors is also 1 and is always less than the number. Exposing students to a variety of classification schemes broadens their appreciation of the many roles numbers play in society. ▲

2. Understanding Numbers

Students' understanding of quantity is based on their understanding of number meaning and number relationships and develops over time. Young children use counting to make sense of quantity both by recognizing where numbers are in the counting sequence and by connecting counting and cardinality to actual objects. Their understanding is extended when they are able to consider sets of objects as parts of wholes and can conceptualize a number as comprising two or more parts. They eventually establish anchor quantities like 5 and 10 and realize that these groups can themselves be counted (e.g., 60 can be thought of as 6 groups of 10 not just 60 units). As students' understanding of number progresses, they establish relationships that link prime factors, factors, and multiples in numerous ways.

Counting is very important in developing students' early understanding of quantity. Rational counting progresses from objects that can be touched to objects that are only seen to the mental image of a group of objects. Learning to count by rote involves both memorization and identification of patterns. The first twelve numeral names are arbitrary and must be memorized. The numerals 13 through 19 follow a "teens" pattern—a digit name followed by *teen*, which represents a ten. Then the pattern shifts so that the tens value is presented first (twenty, thirty, . . .) followed by the ones digits. The transition at decades (e.g., counting on from 79 to 80 or on from 109 to 110) is especially difficult for children, in part because the decade names break the tens-ones pattern (we don't say twenty-ten, twenty-eleven) and require students to have learned the order of the decade names. Interestingly, the Chinese numerals for the decades are much more orderly and systematic—one-ten represents the number ten, two-ten is equivalent to twenty, three-ten represents thirty, and so on. Thus, 42 is read four-ten-two, and 89 is read eight-ten-nine.

Some children enter kindergarten being able to count to 10 or 20; this ability is strongly affected by opportunities to practice. Other children are unable to count when they come to school, because they have had limited or no practice. Furthermore, many early childhood programs don't include counting activities with quantities greater than 20. As a result it is very difficult for students to identify counting patterns, learn the decade names, and generalize how these patterns continue. Teachers need to increase the number of counting activities for children whose counting skills are weak so that they learn the number names in sequence. Asking students to discuss patterns in counting and to reflect on how numbers are said also promotes the development of these skills.

In order for students to attach quantitative meaning to number words, however, they must do a great deal of counting of things. This is sometimes referred to as "meaningful counting," "counting with understanding," or "rational counting." Young children work hard to master counting objects one by one and with time develop strategies for counting things accurately. Most mistakes occur because students don't count each member of the relevant set once and only once, perhaps because they are moving too many objects at a time or not attending to what they are doing. If you notice students who do not coordinate their verbal counting with their actions with regard to objects, you can show these students how to keep track of their counts by moving an object from the uncounted pile to the counted pile as you say each number (it helps to use a mat with a line down the center or a shoe box lid divided into two sections with string). In addition it helps children make generalizations about quantity if you vary the arrangement of objects to be counted (in a row, a circle, or a random pattern) and if you ask children to share their own strategies for keeping track of what they have counted (Ginsburg 1989). Counting pictures or things that can't be moved is a different skill. If possible, have children cross off each picture as it is counted.

An important milestone occurs when children connect counting and cardinality—they understand that the last number counted indicates how many are in a set. Some children grasp the cardinal meaning of number as young as age two or three. When children start school without this understanding, teachers may be explicit: *The last number you say when counting tells how many objects you have. Watch me. One, two, three, four, five. Five. There are five marbles. Watch again.*

In addition to using counting to make sense of quantities, children also use imagery. In general, children are interested in developing more efficient ways to count, and over time they learn to "see" small numbers without counting. They instantly recognize ◆◆◆ as three. The identification of small quantities without counting is known as *subitizing* and appears to develop after children have had repeated practice in counting such sets. Sometimes students recognize only particular arrangements of objects such as the dots on a die. In order for students to extend their use of subitizing, it helps to vary the arrangement of the objects. For example, the number 4 can be shown using many different dot patterns:

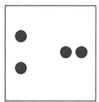 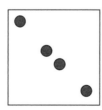 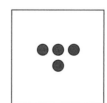 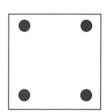

Furthermore, when students identify without counting that there are four dots, they tend to think about this quantity as a group instead of as individual dots. Visualizing a set of objects as a "group" is an important step toward being able to decompose quantities into small groups (e.g., 5 can be thought of as a group of 2 and a group of 3). Dot cards, dominoes, and dice are often used in instruction because they present a variety of arrangements of dots (or pips) for small numbers.

The ten-frame (a 2-by-5 array of squares) is a tool used to help students organize visual patterns in terms of 5 and 10. As students count objects, they place each counted object into a cell of the ten-frame. It is important in terms of visualization that students first fill the top row of the ten-frame (5) and then move to the second row. This helps them see that a quantity such as 8 can be thought of as a group of 5 and a group of 3.

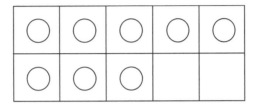

A ten-frame can be used in spatial relationship activities that focus on identifying groups of objects. For example, you can place eight pennies on a ten-frame and cover it with a sheet of paper. Quickly uncover the ten-frame and observe which students count and which students "see" the parts (5 and 3) and/or the whole group (8). Exposure to this type of activity will help students develop visual images of specific-size groups. The ten-frame also helps students visualize and quantify 10. In the ten-frame above, eight cells are filled and two cells are empty—leading us to consider 10 as 8 plus 2 and as 5 plus 3 plus 2.

Understanding Part-Whole Number Relationships

Recognizing small groups or quantities is a skill students use to develop more sophisticated understanding about number. A major milestone occurs in the early grades when students interpret number in terms of part and whole relationships. A part-whole understanding of number means that quantities are interpreted as being composed of other numbers. For example, the number 6 is both a whole amount and comprises smaller groups or parts such as 1 and 5 or 2 and 4. Research indicates that students instructed using a part-whole approach do significantly better with number concepts, problem solving, and place value than those students whose instruction focuses just on counting by ones. Students first learn about part-whole relationships for the numbers 0 through 10. Solid understanding of the many relationships inherent to number takes time. Therefore it is not unusual for some second graders to have limited part-whole constructs for the numbers 7 through 12.

There are many instructional activities that encourage part-whole thinking. For example, you can show students a tower of interlocking cubes and ask them to determine all the ways they can divide the tower into two parts. Be sure to ask students to link numerical symbols with the concrete manipulations; when dividing a set of cubes into two groups, students should record their findings on paper. After they finish, they should reconnect the blocks in order to revisualize the "whole" amount. Or give your students six objects, ask them to put some in one hand, the rest in their other hand, and to put their hands behind their backs. Then ask each child how many objects are in one hand (for example, 4), how many are in the other hand (2), and how many objects he or she had to start with (6). It may appear that these activities are teaching addition, and they do provide a strong conceptual base for addition and subtraction. However, the focus is actually on the meaning of the quantity in terms of composition/decomposition.

Activity

Exploring Part-Whole Relationships

Objective: explore patterns when numbers are decomposed additively into two parts.

A number can be broken into two parts in different ways. Eleven, for example, is made up of 4 and 7, among other combinations. Order matters, because we are looking at the number of combinations, not the actual addends: 4 and 7 is different from 7 and 4. Zero is an acceptable part. How many different two-part combinations of whole numbers are possible for 11? 7? 12? 35? n? What patterns do you notice in the combinations? What generalizations can you make?

Things to Think About

For 11, there are 12 two-part combinations; for 7, there are 8 two-part combinations; for 35, there are 36 two-part combinations; and for *n*, there are *n* + 1 two-part combinations. What patterns did you observe in the combinations? For the number 7, the combinations are 7 and 0, 6 and 1, 5 and 2, 4 and 3, 3 and 4, 2 and 5, 1 and 6, and 0 and 7; as one number decreases, the other number increases. The reason there are *n* + 1 two-part combinations becomes clear if you look at the actual combinations. Since zero (0) is a part, there are actually eight different numbers (0 through 7) that can be combined with other numbers: any of the eight numbers 0, 1, 2, 3, 4, 5, 6, or 7 can be the first part, and the corresponding quantity that creates 7 is the second part. ▲

Activity

Exploring Combinations

Objective: explore patterns when numbers are decomposed additively into more than two parts.

Materials: Cuisenaire rods.

A purple Cuisenaire rod is 4 units long. There are eight different ways to combine other Cuisenaire rods to create a rod that is the same length as the purple rod:

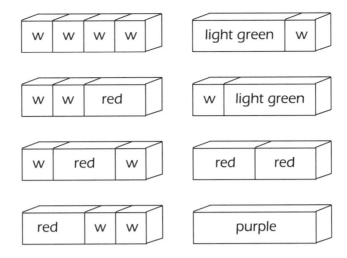

You can use four rods (1-1-1-1), three rods (1-1-2; 1-2-1; 2-1-1), two rods (3-1; 1-3; 2-2), or one rod (4). The order of the parts matters: 1-1-2 is different from 1-2-1. How many different ways are there to create each of the other Cuisenaire rods? You may wish to list the different combinations in a table.

ROD (LENGTH)	PARTS THAT MAKE THE ROD	NUMBER OF COMBINATIONS
White (1)		
Red (2)		
Light Green (3)		
Purple (4)	1 + 1 + 1 + 1, 1 + 1 + 2, 1 + 2 + 1, 2 + 1 + 1, 3 + 1, 1 + 3, 2 + 2, 4	8
Yellow (5)		
Dark Green (6)		

Things to Think About

For the smallest rod, white, there is only one way to show that length—with a white rod. The length of the next rod, red, can be made using two white rods or one red rod. There are four combinations that equal the length of the light green rod—light green; red and white; white and red; and white, white, and white. There are eight combinations for the purple rod, sixteen combinations for the yellow rod, and thirty-two combinations for the dark green rod.

ROD (LENGTH)	PARTS THAT MAKE THE ROD	NUMBER OF COMBINATIONS	
White (1)	1	1	2^0
Red (2)	1 + 1, 2	2	2^1
Light Green (3)	1 + 1 + 1, 1 + 2, 2 + 1, 3	4	2^2

Continued

ROD (LENGTH)	PARTS THAT MAKE THE ROD	NUMBER OF COMBINATIONS	
Purple (4)	1 + 1 + 1 + 1, 1 + 1 + 2, 1 + 2 + 1, 2 + 1 + 1, 3 + 1, 1 + 3, 2 + 2, 4	8	2^3
Yellow (5)	1 + 1 + 1 + 1 + 1, 1 + 1 + 1 + 2, 1 + 1 + 2 + 1, 1 + 2 + 1 + 1, 2 + 1 + 1 + 1, 2 + 2 + 1, 1 + 2 + 2, 2 + 1 + 2, 3 + 1 + 1, 1 + 3 + 1, 1 + 1 + 3, 1 + 4, 4 + 1, 3 + 2, 2 + 3, 5	16	2^4
Dark Green (6)	1 + 1 + 1 + 1 + 1 + 1, 1 + 1 + 1 + 1 + 2, 1 + 1 + 1 + 2 + 1, 1 + 1 + 2 + 1 + 1, 1 + 2 + 1 + 1 + 1, 2 + 1 + 1 + 1 + 1, 1 + 1 + 2 + 2, 1 + 2 + 1 + 2, 1 + 2 + 2 + 1, 2 + 2 + 1 + 1, 2 + 1 + 1 + 2, 2 + 1 + 2 + 1, 1 + 1 + 1 + 3, 1 + 1 + 3 + 1, 1 + 3 + 1 + 1, 3 + 1 + 1 + 1, 1 + 2 + 3, 2 + 1 + 3, 2 + 3 + 1, 1 + 3 + 2, 3 + 1 + 2, 3 + 2 + 1, 1 + 1 + 4, 1 + 4 + 1, 4 + 1 + 1, 3 + 3, 4 + 2, 2 + 4, 1 + 5, 5 + 1, 2 + 2 + 2, 6	32	2^5

What patterns did you observe in the number of combinations? As the rods got longer, by one centimeter each time, the number of combinations doubled. These numbers, 1, 2, 4, 8, 16, 32, . . . , are referred to as powers of two, since each of the numbers can be represented as 2 to some power: $1 = 2^0$, $2 = 2^1$, $4 = 2^2$, $8 = 2^3$, $16 = 2^4$, and $32 = 2^5$. Another pattern can be seen in the exponents; each exponent is one less than the length of the rod. For example, the yellow rod is 5 cm long and there are 2^4, or 16, ways to make a rod this length. The patterns observed in the number of combinations can be used to generalize the relationship to rods of any length; the number of combinations for each rod is $2^{(n-1)}$, where *n* is the length of the rod in units. Thus, there are 2^6, or 64, ways to make a black rod; 2^7, or 128, ways to make a brown rod; 2^8, or 256, ways to make a blue rod; and 2^9, or 512, ways to make the 10-centimeter orange rod. Notice how quickly the number of combinations increases. ▲

Understanding Multiplicative Number Relationships

So far in this section we have examined number from a counting and a part-whole (or additive) perspective. As students' understanding of number expands and as they move through formal schooling, they are introduced to multiplicative number relationships. One multiplicative relationship involves *factors* and *products*. For example, because 3 times 8 equals 24, 3 and 8 are factors and 24 is a product. Factors that are prime numbers are called *prime factors*. Factors are also called *divisors*, since they divide the number evenly with a zero as the remainder. Knowledge of factors and divisors is used when applying the rules of divisibility, determining the least common denominator, and finding common multiples.

Integers greater than 1 can always be expressed as the product of prime factors in one and only one way. The number 12 can be factored using the following primes: $2 \times 2 \times 3$. Twelve is unique in its composition of prime factors. Thus, changing one of the prime factors (e.g., $2 \times 2 \times 5$) results in a different product and thus a different number (20). The relationship between a number and its prime factors is so important that there is a theorem about it, the Fundamental Theorem of Arithmetic, which states that every integer greater than 1 can be expressed as the product of a unique set of prime factors. The order of the factors does not matter. For example, $2 \times 3 \times 5$ is the same as $3 \times 5 \times 2$. Each set of these prime factors equals 30, regardless of which factor is listed first, second, or third.

Activity

Prime Factors

Objective: understand how prime factors are combined multiplicatively to form numbers.

Determine the prime factors for 120. Then list all factors of 120. How can you use the prime factors of 120 to determine all the factors of 120? Is 120 divisible by 2, 3, 4, 5, 6, 7, or 8? How are the prime factors of 120 related to whether or not 120 is divisible by any of these numbers? Pick another composite number and determine its prime factors. What are the factors of your new number? What numbers divide evenly into your new number or, put in another way, are divisors of your new number?

Things to Think About

There are a number of ways to factor a number, but the most common approach is to use a factor tree. In a factor tree, the factors are represented on branches and the next-lower line of branches presents factors that produce the number above as a product. The tree continues until no number on the bottom line can be factored further. Here are two factor trees for 120. Notice that while the upper parts of the trees use different factors, the prime factors at the bottom of the trees ($2 \times 2 \times 2 \times 3 \times 5$) are the same:

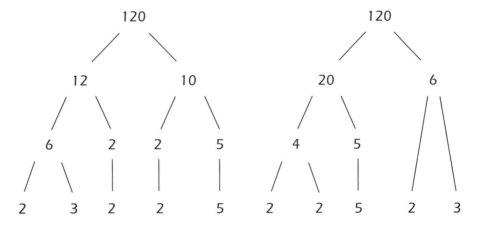

How can the prime factors be used to determine all the factors of 120? First, it is important to remember that all the prime factors of 120 must be used; otherwise you will end up with a different number than 120. Using the commutative and associative properties, the prime factors of 120 can be combined in different ways to find all other factors. For example, multiplying two of the prime factors,

2 and 3, gives a product of 6, which is one factor. That leaves 2 × 2 × 5, or 20, as the other factor that pairs with the 6. Some of the factors of 120 are:

$$4 \times 30 \text{ or } (2 \times 2) \times (2 \times 3 \times 5)$$
$$8 \times 15 \text{ or } (2 \times 2 \times 2) \times (3 \times 5)$$
$$10 \times 12 \text{ or } (2 \times 5) \times (2 \times 2 \times 3)$$
$$120 \times 1 \text{ or } (2 \times 2 \times 2 \times 3 \times 5) \times 1$$

Continuing with this method, 16 factors of 120 can be found. They are 1, 2, 3, 4, 5, 6, 8, 10, 12, 15, 20, 24, 30, 40, 60, and 120.

The number 120 is divisible by 1, 2, 3, 4, 5, 6, 8, 10, 12, 15, 20, 24, 30, 40, 60, and 120, because each of these numbers is a factor of 120. Numbers that are not factors of 120, such as 7 and 9, do not divide evenly into 120. ▲

Understanding Negative and Positive Number Relationships

In the middle grades, students' experiences with numbers are expanded to include negative numbers. The topic is difficult for a number of reasons. Students not only must make sense of negative values with which many have little experience, but also are introduced to new symbols and vocabulary. Computations with negative and positive numbers are especially problematic, as the operations and algorithms are rarely understood and easily confused.

What are the important characteristics of this group of numbers? One is *direction*, which indicates whether a number is to the right of zero, and therefore positive, or to the left of zero, and therefore negative. We can use the concept of direction to compare numbers, since the farther a number is to the right on the number line, the greater it is. For example, which is greater, ⁻4 or ⁻9? Both are negative and are to the left of zero, but ⁻4 is greater than ⁻9 since ⁻4 is to the right of ⁻9 on the number line.

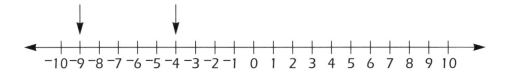

The other important characteristic when thinking about positive and negative numbers is the *magnitude* of the number. Magnitude is the distance of a number from 0. Five is 5 intervals from 0 and ⁻2 is 2 intervals from 0. We refer to the magnitude of a number as its absolute value. Put another way, the absolute value of a number is its distance from 0. This concept is so important that there is a particular symbol, |n|, to represent when we are referring to a number's magnitude or absolute value. The absolute values of both ⁻6 and 6 are the same (|⁻6| = 6 and |6| = 6) since both ⁻6 and 6 are 6 intervals from 0, yet these numbers are in opposite directions from 0. Numbers that are the same distance from 0 but on opposite sides of 0 are known as *opposites*. What do we now know about the number ⁻467? It is a negative number and thus its direction is to the left of 0. It is less than 0 and is 467 intervals away from 0. It is a small number, because it is so far from 0 to the left. The opposite of ⁻467 is 467. Both numbers are the same distance from 0.

When we combine the two characteristics of direction and magnitude, we have powerful information to help us interpret, compare, and order all numbers, but in particular, negative numbers.

The language associated with comparisons is particularly important when working with negative numbers: we compare numbers using the terms *greater than*, *less than*, and *equal to*. Informal language used to compare quantities, such as *bigger*, *smaller*, and *larger*, can cause significant confusion when dealing with negative numbers. In the early elementary grades, when students work with positive numbers, there is general agreement on the meaning of comparative terms; students understand that if a number is "bigger" or "larger" than another, it is another positive number. Their knowledge comes from counting; the last number you say when counting is the greatest. But when students start working with negative numbers, informal language can be problematic. For example, which is larger, ⁻8 or ⁻2? Since when we count, 8 comes after 2, students often think ⁻8 is greater than ⁻2. Furthermore, the magnitude or distance from 0 to ⁻8 is greater than ⁻2, so again students think ⁻8 is greater. Also, a common model to help students think about negative numbers uses red chips for negative values and black chips for positive values. Eight red chips representing ⁻8 is physically more than two red chips representing ⁻2, even though ⁻8 is actually less than ⁻2.

One way to help students avoid these types of errors is to link the concepts of distance and magnitude to comparisons on the number line. Numbers to the right of other numbers are greater; 25 is greater than ⁻47 because it is to the right of ⁻47. Likewise, since ⁻2 is to the right of ⁻8 on the number line, ⁻2 is greater than ⁻8 (or we can say that ⁻8 is less than ⁻2). Which negative number is closer to 0 (⁻2 is closer to 0 than ⁻8, for example) is another way of determining which of them is greater. However, which number is closest to 0 is not enough when comparing negative and positive numbers. For example, ⁻1 is closer to 0 than 5 but ⁻1 is not greater than 5; 5 is farther to the right on the number line. Students need to learn that the placement of a number on the number line is important when comparing the size of negative numbers, in particular. In addition, we should try to use only the proper terminology, *greater than* and *less than*, in order to eliminate any possible confusion about which characteristics we are considering. We want these comparison words to be correctly associated with the related concepts.

Positive numbers can be written in three ways: 35, +35 or ⁺35. A positive number does not have to have a plus sign; it is required only when there may be confusion as to the sign of the number. Sometimes the plus sign is raised, but it doesn't have to be. Negative numbers always have a negative sign in front of them (raised or not) and are often put in parentheses in number sentences where a subtraction sign is used and the negative sign is not raised (e.g., $5 - (-3)$) to help us differentiate between the negative sign and the subtraction sign. When using positive and negative numbers it is tempting to refer to them using the terms *plus* and *minus*. However, if we say *plus 20* instead of *positive 20* or *minus 7* instead of *negative 7*, it is easy to become confused: do we mean the positive and negative numbers or do we mean the operations of addition and subtraction?

Two other terms are also applied to negative and positive numbers: *signed numbers* and *integers*. *Signed numbers* is an informal name for the set of negative and positive real numbers. It is usually used when we want to let others know we are talking about negative and positive numbers, including negative and positive fractions and decimals (and irrationals). *Integers*, on the other hand, are numbers that are formally defined as the whole numbers and their opposites—they do not include negative and positive fractions and decimals. Thus, some signed number are integers (⁻23 and 149), but other signed numbers are not (⁻2.5 and 13⅝).

Activity

The Number Line

Objective: create a number line and generalize its important features.

1. Draw a blank number line (without numbers indicated). Make two marks anywhere along the line. Label the marks ⁻3 and 5. Where is 0? Where is 1?

2. Place the following numbers on your number line: A) ⁻2.3; B) $-\frac{1}{5}$; C) $\sqrt{23}$; D) $-3\frac{3}{4}$; E) $|^-2|$; F) the opposite of $^-5\frac{1}{4}$; G) $^-\sqrt{13}$; H) x when $|x| = 4$.
3. Is 0 a positive number, a negative number, or neither? What is the opposite of 0? Explain your thinking.

Things to Think About

The number line is an important representation that pictures numbers as points on a line. Every point on the real number line corresponds to exactly one real number, and every real number corresponds to exactly one point on the number line. Although we refer to a number as a point, this is not actually the case—a point really represents the magnitude of the number or its distance from zero.

What did you have to consider in order to construct your number line? First, determining the placement of 0 is essential, since numbers to the right of 0 represent positive values (values greater than 0) and numbers to the left of 0 represent negative values (or values less than 0). Second, the number line is symmetrical around 0 (namely, pairs of numbers are the same distance from 0). Thus both ⁺5 and ⁻5 are 5 intervals away from 0 and are 10 intervals apart. The idea that the line folds onto itself around 0 may be an image that helped you in numbering the line. Third, the intervals between consecutive integers must be the same but the actual length of the interval is arbitrary. There are 8 intervals between ⁻3 and 5, so we can make 7 equally spaced hash marks to represent the numbers ⁻2, ⁻1, 0, 1, 2, 3, and 4. The size of the intervals on your number line may be different from the one here because of where you originally placed ⁻3 and 5. Each interval represents one unit.

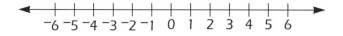

Constructing number lines and placing points on the line focuses our attention on both the size and direction of each number. Where do $\sqrt{23}$ and $^-\sqrt{13}$ belong? The square root symbol, often called a radical, indicates that the operation of evaluating the square root is to be performed. Thus the approximate values are 4.8 and ⁻(3.6), respectively, which can then be placed on the number line. The absolute value symbol indicates that we must evaluate the absolute value of the number |⁻2|, which is 2 (since it is 2 units from 0), and place 2 on the number line. The absolute value of a number is always positive since it is a distance (the number of intervals from 0). What is x when $|x| = 4$? In this case, x has two values. Both 4 and ⁻4 have an absolute value of 4.

Students always have questions about 0. Is it positive? Is it a number? Does it have an opposite? Zero is neither a positive number nor a negative number since there is no change in direction and it has no magnitude. The opposite of 0 is 0: numbers with the same absolute value are opposites, and opposites are numbers that are the same distance from 0 but on opposite sides of 0. ▲

3. Our Place Value Numeration System

In order to communicate ideas related to number, we must have a way of representing numbers symbolically. A numeration system is a collection of properties and symbols that results in a systematic way to write all numbers. We use the Hindu-Arabic numeration system, which was developed around A.D. 800.

One of the important features of the Hindu-Arabic numeration system is that it is a positional system: there are place values. Equally important is that it is based on repeated groupings of ten. For this reason the Hindu-Arabic system is also referred to as the *base ten* or *decimal numeration* system.

These two characteristics, place value and groupings by ten, require students to interpret numerals within numbers on two levels: place value and face value. The 5 in 58 has a place value representing the tens place; the face value of the 5 must therefore be interpreted to mean that five groups of ten, not five ones, are being considered. Sometimes students interpret numbers by considering only the face values of the digits. For example, students who have little understanding of place value might incorrectly assume that 58 and 85 represent the same quantity, since each numeral contains both a 5 and an 8. Likewise, when dealing with decimal fractions, students often state that 0.4 and 0.04 are equivalent if they consider only the face values (both numerals have a 4 in them) and not the place values.

Larger numbers are read by naming the period of each group of three digits. The three digits in each period represent the number of hundreds, tens, and ones making up that period. The periods to the left of hundreds are thousands, millions, billions, trillions, quadrillions, quintillions, and so on. Zillions, though used a great deal in literature, are not a mathematical period! The numeral 23,456,789 is read "twenty-three million, four hundred fifty-six thousand, seven hundred eighty-nine." It provides us with a great deal of information—there are 2 groups of ten million and 3 groups of one million (which is equivalent to 23 groups of one million); 4 groups of one hundred thousand, 5 groups of ten thousand, and 6 groups of one thousand (which is equivalent to 456 groups of one thousand); plus 7 hundreds, 8 tens, and 9 ones. While we say the quantity in each period as if we are only focusing on face value ("four hundred fifty-six thousand"), students must be able to interpret the place value meaning of each digit within the periods (which involves more than simply identifying the place value of each digit).

Helping Students Understand Our Place Value System

How can we help students understand our place value system? First, students must be able to organize objects into specific-size groups (tens, hundreds, thousands, . . .) and realize that they can count these groups. Many teachers use grouping activities to help their students think of quantities as groups of hundreds, tens, and ones. For example, students might count 147 beans by grouping the beans into sets of ten. Counting reveals that there are 14 groups of ten plus 7 additional beans. The notion that 147 can be represented by single units and by a variety of groups of tens and hundreds doesn't always makes sense to children; counting helps young students verify that the quantities, despite the different groupings, are equal. With sufficient experiences and guidance from a teacher, students internalize these relationships.

Second, students must apply their understanding of the part-whole relationship to partitioning numbers into groups based on powers of ten (e.g., hundreds, tens, and units). For example, 123 is equivalent to 1 group of a hundred plus 2 groups of ten plus 3 ones. Note that if students aren't quite sure that they can count groups or that these groupings are equivalent to a number of units, they will have difficulty decomposing a number into place values. Students' understanding of these notions is gradual and appears to develop first with two-digit numbers and then with three-digit numbers. Students often partition numbers into place values when they devise their own algorithms for adding and subtracting numbers, because this allows them to deal with the component parts separately.

Other ideas related to place value that students must make sense of involve the relationships among the groups. There is growing evidence from research and national assessments that many young students do not understand to any depth the multiplicative relationship among groups and thus have difficulty comprehending, for example, that there are 32 hundreds in 3,289 or that ten hundredths equals one tenth. Decomposing numbers into equivalent parts using place values other than the face values is another problematic area for students; many students can identify that 78 is equal to 7 tens and 8 ones but are not so sure that 78 can be represented with 6 tens and 18 ones, or 5 tens and 28 ones. The standard subtraction algorithm is an example of using equivalent representations—to subtract 38 from 62 using the standard algorithm we have to think of (or regroup) the 62 as 5 tens and 12 ones.

Activity

Analyzing a Different Numeration System

Objective: group and record quantities using a different number base system.

A factory packages chocolate truffles in cartons that hold 27 truffles, in trays that hold 9 truffles, in 3-packs, and in individual boxes:

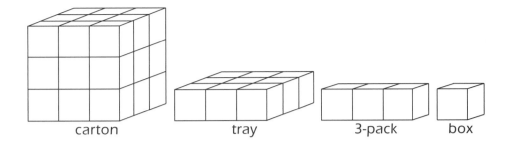

carton   tray   3-pack   box

When an order for truffles arrives at the factory, workers package the truffles in as few boxes as possible: that is, they never use three packaging units of the same size (e.g., three trays) but instead always repack the truffles into the next-larger unit (e.g., one carton). Thus, an order for 38 truffles would be filled using one carton (27), one tray (9), and two single boxes (2). The factory's method for recording this shipment is $1102_{truffles}$: each digit corresponds to the number of cartons (1), trays (1), 3-packs (0), and singles (2).

You have just begun work at the truffle factory. Determine the packaging for orders of 10, 49, 56, 75, and 100 truffles. (You may want to make sketches of the packages.)

Now record shipments of 1 to 20 truffles. You start with 1, which you record as $1_{truffles}$; 2 truffles you record as $2_{truffles}$; 3 truffles would be packaged in a 3-pack and recorded as $10_{truffles}$. Continue recording the packaging of 4 through 20 truffles.

Things to Think About

The record entry for 10 truffles is one tray and one single ($101_{truffles}$), since $9 + 1 = 10$. The record entry for 49 truffles is one carton, two trays, one 3-pack, and one single ($1211_{truffles}$), for 56 truffles it is two cartons and two singles ($2002_{truffles}$), and for 75 truffles it is two cartons, two trays, one 3-pack, and zero singles ($2210_{truffles}$). Did you notice that the groupings in the truffle factory are based on threes? When there are three singles they are regrouped into a 3-pack, three 3-packs are regrouped into a tray, and three trays are regrouped into a carton. Each package is three times as large as the next smallest package. The truffle factory record system is similar to our numeration system in that it uses groupings, but it is dissimilar in that the groupings are based on threes rather than tens.

Was your record entry for 100 truffles $321_{truffles}$? What happens when we have three cartons? Because the factory regroups whenever there are three of any-size package, we need to regroup and make a new package that is equivalent to three cartons and holds 81 truffles. Let's call it a crate! Thus, following the packaging rules, when packaging 100 truffles we use one crate (81), zero cartons, two trays (18), zero 3-packs, and one single—$10201_{truffles}$.

Packaging truffles in groups of three provides you with some insight into the difficulties students have making sense of grouping by tens. The chocolate factory uses a base three numeration system. To make sense of the symbols—$21012_{truffles}$, for example—you have to understand the place values of the digits and the grouping relationships among the place values associated with base three. Just as you had to clarify packaging by threes, students have to master base ten relationships. Pictures and models can help students make sense of our base ten system.

The record entries for packaging 1 through 20 truffles are 1, 2, 10, 11, 12, 20, 21, 22, 100, 101, 102, 110, 111, 112, 120, 121, 122, 200, 201, and 202. Notice that only the digits 0, 1, and 2 are used to represent all the packaging options. Whenever there are three of any package, the numeral three isn't used to represent this quantity because the truffles are repackaged (regrouped) into a larger package. That is, the number after 212 is not recorded as 213 but as 220, since the three singles are repackaged into another 3-pack. The packaging notation for the truffle factory is identical to counting in base three. Our base ten numeration system has ten digits—0, 1, 2, 3, 4, 5, 6, 7, 8, and 9. Whenever there are ten of any item, we regroup (repackage) the quantity and record the amount using the next place value. Thus, in base ten when we have 19 items and add one additional item, we don't record that we have one ten and ten ones but regroup to show that we have two tens (20). ▲

So far we have examined place value concepts using quantities greater than one. Grouping whether in base ten or base three enables us to represent large quantities efficiently and with only a few symbols. But what about when we have to represent quantities less than one? How do we apply the idea of groups of 10 with small quantities? When dividing up quantities we can partition groups into 10 equal pieces. In other words, in our numeration system we divide (or partition) groups by 10 when representing quantities less than one.

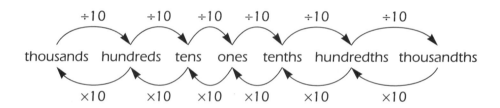

Let's start with 5 brownies that we want to share evenly with 4 people. How much will each person receive? We can represent the 5 brownies using squares.

Each person will receive one full brownie and a part of a brownie. To determine the part of the one brownie that each person gets, we must follow our dividing rule—cut the extra brownie into 10 equal pieces called *tenths*. Distribute 2 of these tenths to each person, leaving 2 pieces left over.

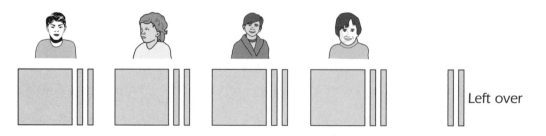

Left over

Following the dividing rule again, we cut the 2 tenths into 10 pieces each. We now have 20 pieces, each one-hundredth of the original square. These 20 hundredths can be distributed evenly to the four people—each person receiving 5 hundredths.

Therefore, each person receives 1 whole brownie, and 2 tenths plus 5 hundredths of a brownie, for a total of 1.25 brownies.

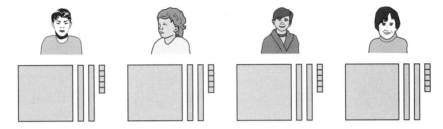

Activity

Place Values Less than One

Objective: understand decimal place values.

Materials: graph paper cut into 10-by-10 squares.

Try the cutting activity yourself to help you better understand how decimal place values are created. For example, explore sharing 1 brownie equally among 6 people and 17 brownies equally among 8 people.

Things to Think About

In order to share 1 square (brownie) equally among 6 people, we have to cut the brownie. Following the dividing rule, we cut it into 10 pieces called tenths. Each of the 6 people gets one-tenth with 4 tenths left over. Divide each of the 4 pieces by 10 and we have 40 hundredths. These can be distributed to the 6 people, each receiving 6 hundredths (40 ÷ 6 = 6 with 4 left over). Take these 4 hundredths and cut each of them into 10 pieces, forming 40 thousandths. Again the 6 people each receive 6 thousandths with 4 thousandths left over. When one brownie is shared equally among 6 people, they each receive 0.166 brownie and there is 4 thousandths of the brownie left over. Notice that if we keep cutting the leftovers, the process will never end. Repeating decimals result when there are leftovers from the dividing process no matter how many times we divide.

When 17 brownies are shared equally among 8 people, each person gets 2.125 brownies. This decimal does not repeat but terminates, since there are no leftovers from the cutting process. ▲

Teaching Number Sense

Promoting the development of children's number sense is a complex and multifaceted task. Students' early understanding of number involves making sense of counting, decomposition, and place value. These ideas are the foundation of mathematics.

As students progress through school they build on the additive nature of number and consider multiplicative relationships involving factors, products, divisors, and multiples. Students in middle school expand their use of number to different sets of numbers such as rational numbers and irrational numbers. They must be aware of both the similarities and differences among sets of numbers.

Teachers play an important role in helping students develop number sense. Tasks that highlight relationships and properties as well as that focus on skills are essential. Reexamine your curriculum materials in light of some of the discussions in this chapter. Decide how you might incorporate some of these ideas into appropriate instructional tasks for your students.

Questions for Discussion

1. Numbers are classified in many ways. Which classification system do you find most useful? Why?
2. Why is the concept of evenness and oddness so important? How might a fourth grader explain that the sum of two odd numbers must be an even number?
3. How does a young child's concept of quantity develop? Discuss activities that will promote students' understanding and help them reach important milestones.
4. Numbers can be decomposed both additively and multiplicatively. What does it mean to understand number concepts from these two perspectives?
5. What features of signed numbers are essential for students to explore?
6. Using what you know about our base ten system, explain why the decimal expansion of $\frac{1}{12}$ is $0.08\overline{3}$. (See Chapter 6, page 133.)

2

Computation

Whole number computation—adding, subtracting, multiplying, and dividing—has always been a major topic in the elementary school curriculum. And this focus is still justifiable, even in today's technological age. First, being able to compute is a practical skill that lets us answer questions such as how much? how many? how many times greater? We use computation every day—when verifying that a store clerk has given us the correct change, figuring the tip to leave in a restaurant, or determining how much it will cost to buy the required number of party favors for a birthday celebration. Second, whole number computation is the foundation of arithmetic. It can help students make sense of mathematical relationships and prepare them for later work with fractions, signed numbers, and algebra. Whether computations involve "naked" numbers or are embedded in word problems, students need to know how to solve them. They must be able to determine when to use mental math, paper and pencil, or the calculator. Most important, their methods must make sense, both to themselves and to others.

1. Mathematical Properties

All of us use the commutative, associative, and distributive properties when working with whole numbers, fractions, and decimals. Yet many teachers consider properties to be "too mathematical for young students" and "not especially relevant to what we teach in the elementary grades." The opposite is closer to the truth. These properties, together with the operations of addition, subtraction, multiplication, and division, are the foundation of arithmetic. We use mathematical properties when performing computations and recalling basic facts. We use them to reduce the complexity of equations and expressions and to perform mental calculations more easily. Children often notice the relationships on which these properties are based (e.g., the order of the addends does not affect the sum) and use them when computing. The goal is for elementary students to build upon their understanding of these properties using whole numbers, fractions, and decimals and in the middle grades to be able to represent these properties symbolically with variables. Mathematical properties are an avenue to higher-level thinking, because they illustrate general cases and can lead to mathematical generalizations.

The Commutative Property

The commutative properties of addition and multiplication state that the order of two addends (e.g., $12 + 9$ or $9 + 12$) or two factors (e.g., 3×7 or 7×3) does not affect the sum or product, respectively. The root word of commutative is *commute*, which means to interchange—we can reverse the order of two addends or two factors without changing the result. These powerful properties reduce the number of basic facts students need to memorize: having learned that $5 + 6 = 11$ or $3 \times 4 = 12$, they also know that $6 + 5 = 11$ and $4 \times 3 = 12$.

But not all students recognize on their own that the order of the addends or factors doesn't matter in terms of the sum or product. One reason is that when they first learn basic addition or multiplication, they focus on the operation and on obtaining an answer that ideally makes sense. They don't reflect on the outcome of the operation in relation to the order of the numbers. Often teachers decide to introduce the idea of the commutative property after students have become familiar with either addition or multiplication. They might help students discover that when adding $3 + 9$ in their head, for example, it is easier to start with the 9 and count on three numbers (10, 11, 12) than to start with the 3 and count on nine numbers. However, this still doesn't necessarily mean students will generalize that the order of the addends doesn't matter. Teachers can then present a number of examples of the commutative property of addition ($6 + 8 = 14$ and $8 + 6 = 14$, $23 + 57 = 80$ and $57 + 23 = 80$, etc.), ask students to identify any patterns in the number pairs and make a generalization about the pattern, and then ask them to investigate whether their generalization holds true for other numbers.

The commutative property of multiplication can be especially confusing to students. In an addition operation, the addends represent subgroups comprising the same things: if $2 + 3$ is expressed as $3 + 2$, only the order of the subgroups changes. In the grouping interpretation of multiplication, 3×4 and 4×3 represent different groupings—three groups of four versus four groups of three—and do not look the same.

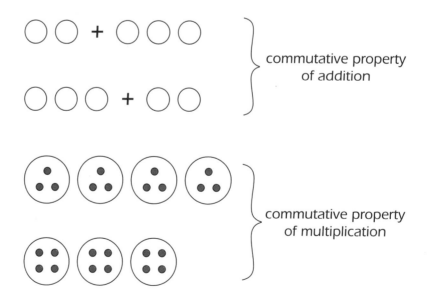

commutative property of addition

commutative property of multiplication

Students need to model many multiplication equations in order to see that the products are identical. A rectangular array (consisting of rows and columns) often helps students make sense of multiplication's commutative property, because the dimensions of an array can be depicted in different orders (5 by 8 and 8 by 5, for example) but each arrangement consists of the same number of squares. Rotating an array bearing row and column labels also provides a strong visual image of commutativity.

The commutative property of multiplication can also be confusing since switching the factors switches the relationships in some word problems. Sometimes the switched relationships are similar and still make sense; other times they change the problem completely. For example, running 3 miles at 10 minutes a mile is quite different from running 10 miles at 3 minutes per mile, even though total running time in each case is 30 minutes. The first rate is within normal ranges, but someone running 10 miles in 30 minutes would be making history! Instruction therefore also needs to focus on how the relationships in multiplication problems change when the numbers are switched even though the products are still equal.

Activity

How Does Order Affect Differences?

Objective: learn how order affects differences and identify and explain the resulting patterns.

Pick a simple subtraction equation such as $6 - 2 = 4$. Now reverse the two numbers and perform the new subtraction, $2 - 6 = {}^-4$. Pick another equation and reverse the numbers. Do this a number of times. Examine the pairs of differences (e.g., 4 and $^-4$). What patterns do you see in the differences? Why does this pattern occur?

Things to Think About

Students are told often that the order of the numbers doesn't matter in addition but does in subtraction. While it is true that most of the time order does matter in subtraction, there is an exception. When both numbers are identical, order doesn't matter ($20 - 20 = 20 - 20$).

Even though subtraction is not commutative, there are interesting relationships in the differences of numbers when their order is reversed for subtraction. When the two numbers are not the same (e.g., 2 and 6), the pair of differences are opposites: one difference is a positive number (e.g., 4) and the other is its negative mirror image (e.g., $^-4$). This can be represented formally as: $a - b = c$ and $b - a = {}^-c$ if $a \neq b \neq 0$. This pattern holds for fractions, decimals, and integers, as shown in the examples below:

$$\frac{5}{8} - \frac{2}{8} = \frac{3}{8} \qquad 1.4 - 1.2 = 0.2 \qquad 7 - (^-4) = 11$$
$$\frac{2}{8} - \frac{5}{8} = \frac{-3}{8} \qquad 1.2 - 1.4 = {}^-0.2 \qquad {}^-4 - 7 = {}^-11$$

Did you notice that the pairs of differences sum to zero (e.g., $^+4 + {}^-4 = 0$)? The number 0 is the identity element for addition. You can add 0 to any other number and the sum will be the original number. Why does this pattern of opposites occur when we change the order of the numbers in a subtraction problem? The difference between two numbers can be represented on a number line as an interval—the distance between two points. Since a distance is something we can measure, the interval is either a positive value or zero. Thus the distance between

2 and 6 is 4. But we can also think of this interval in terms of a direction (see Chapter 1, page 22). If we start at 2 and move to the right toward the positive numbers, we represent this action as adding a positive 4 and we land at 6. However, if we start at 6 and move to the left toward the negative numbers, this action is represented as adding a negative 4.

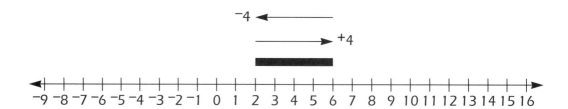

Interestingly, once we include negative numbers in the set of numbers with which we are working (for example, the real number set), the operation of subtraction is technically unnecessary. Instead of subtracting, we can obtain the same answer by adding the opposite of the subtrahend (the number we are taking away). One reason we refer to relationships as "additive" instead of "additive and subtractive" is because in the set of real numbers, by using opposites, it is possible to rewrite all subtraction expressions and equations as equivalent addition expressions and equations. For example, we can solve $10 - 4$ by adding the opposite of 4, or $^-4$ ($10 + {}^-4$) and we can solve $10 - (-2)$ by adding the opposite of $^-2$, or 2 ($10 + 2$). Examine the steps below that show why these pairs of expressions ($10 - 4$ and $10 + {}^-4$; and $10 - {}^-2$ and $10 + 2$) are equivalent.

$10 - 4$	$10 - {}^-2$
$10 + (^-4 + 4) - 4$	$10 + (2 + {}^-2) - {}^-2$ Add 0
$10 + {}^-4 + (4 - 4)$	$10 + 2 + (^-2 - {}^-2)$ Associative property
$10 + {}^-4 + 0$	$10 + 2 + 0$ Add 0
$10 + {}^-4$	$10 + 2$

Students whose instruction has focused on examining differences on number lines or hundred charts sometimes use this understanding of differences in their mental calculations. For example, one technique for computing $34 - 19$ involves thinking of both numbers in terms of tens and ones ($30 + 4$ and $10 + 9$). The numbers in each place are subtracted separately without regrouping ($30 - 10$ and $4 - 9$), with the ones place resulting in a negative value. The tens and ones values are then combined—$20 + (-5)$—for an answer of 15.

$$\begin{array}{r} 34 \\ -\ 19 \\ \hline 20 \\ +\ (-5) \\ \hline 15 \end{array}$$ *Think:* $30 - 10 = 20$
  $4 - 9 = {}^-5$

  $20 + (-5) = 20 - 5 = 15$

Young students' explanations rarely acknowledge that they are using negative numbers, but they often comment that $4 - 9$ is "5 below zero" or they might mention that they are "5 in the hole" or "owe 5." They may either subtract the 5 from the 20 or add $^-5$ to 20. Teachers are encouraged to revisit these ideas with older students as a way of expanding their understanding of properties and operations. ▲

How Does Order Affect Quotients?

Objective: explore patterns in the quotient when the dividend and divisor are reserved.

Pick a simple division equation such as 10 ÷ 2 = 5. The number 10 is the *dividend*, 2 is the *divisor*, and 5 is the *quotient*, or answer. Next reverse the dividend and the divisor and perform the new division, $2 \div 10 = \frac{1}{5}$. Pick another equation and reverse the dividend and divisor. Do this a number of times. Examine the pairs of quotients (e.g., 5 and $\frac{1}{5}$). What patterns do you see in the different quotients? Do these patterns hold for all types of numbers?

Things to Think About

Division is also not commutative, but did you notice that when you reverse the order of the dividend and the divisor, the resulting quotients are reciprocals? Reciprocals are pairs of numbers that when multiplied together, give a product of 1. For example, 5 and $\frac{1}{5}$ are reciprocals, since $5 \times \frac{1}{5} = 1$. The number 1 is called the *identity element* for multiplication—when you multiply by 1, the value of the expression stays the same. This same pattern holds true for fractions and integers—in fact, for all real numbers. Here are a few examples:

$$\frac{1}{2} \div \frac{1}{4} = 2 \qquad {}^-18 \div 6 = {}^-3$$

$$\frac{1}{4} \div \frac{1}{2} = \frac{1}{2} \qquad 6 \div ({}^-18) = {}^-\frac{1}{3}$$

$$2 \times \frac{1}{2} = 1 \qquad {}^-3 \times \left({}^-\frac{1}{3}\right) = 1$$

What happens when the dividend and the divisor are the same number? In this case, for example, 6 ÷ 6, the quotient is 1. Reverse the 6s and the quotient stays the same—it's 1 in both instances. Likewise, 1 × 1 = 1, so 1 is its own reciprocal.

What happens when at least one of the numbers is 0? Consider the situation in which the dividend is 0 and the divisor is 4 (0 ÷ 4 = ☐). If we think of the operation of division as repeated subtraction, we can ask ourselves, "How many groups of four can I subtract from zero?" The answer of 0 makes sense. Using a missing-factor interpretation of division, find the factor that when multiplied by 4 equals 0 (4 × ☐ = 0). Again, the answer, 0, makes sense. To generalize, if the dividend is 0 and the divisor is another number (0 ÷ *a* when *a* ≠ 0), then the quotient is 0. Now reverse the dividend and divisor: 4 ÷ 0 = ☐. How many times can you subtract a group of 0 from 4? Once, twice, an infinite number of times? There isn't a unique answer that makes sense using this interpretation of division. Let's try the missing-factor interpretation: 0 × ☐ = 4. There is no solution, because 0 × 0 = 0 and 0 times any other number also equals 0.

For 0 ÷ 0, you can subtract 0 from 0 any number of times and still get 0, so again there isn't a unique answer that makes sense using a repeated subtraction interpretation of division. Using the missing-factor interpretation ask, 0 times what number equals 0? Any number works. Therefore, for 0 ÷ 0, there is also no unique answer. Because there isn't an answer to expressions that are divided by 0 (*a* ÷ 0), mathematicians have agreed that division by 0 is "undefined." When you try to divide by 0 on a calculator, the readout displays ERROR or E—the operation is undefined and thus has no solution.

The patterns in this activity are related to the fact that multiplication and division are inverse operations—to undo multiplication we divide and to undo division we multiply. In fact, if we multiply the dividend (the 6 in 6 ÷ 2) by the reciprocal of the divisor (the divisor is 2, the reciprocal of 2 is $\frac{1}{2}$), we have an equivalent operation (6 ÷ 2 = 3, $6 \times \frac{1}{2} = 3$). The relationship between reciprocals and undoing multiplication and division is very powerful and is used in algebra. One more point: the reason we refer to operations that are based on multiplication and division only as multiplicative is because all divisions can be rewritten as multiplications times the reciprocal of the divisors. ▲

The Associative Property

The associative properties of addition and multiplication relate to how we group numbers in order to find sums and products. These properties are often used in conjunction with the commutative properties for these operations because we regularly change the order of addends or factors prior to regrouping. Addition and multiplication are often referred to as *binary* operations: we can operate on only two numbers at a time (e.g., $3 + 4$, 7×8). If a computation involves three addends, we first add two of the numbers and then add the third to the previous sum—for example, $(3 + 4) + 5 = 7 + 5 = 12$. The associative properties of addition and multiplication state that the way in which three or more addends or factors are grouped before being added or multiplied does not affect the sum or product.

The associative and commutative properties are used to compute mentally. For example, when adding a list of single-digit numbers, many people group digits together that sum to 10—given, for example, $3 + 6 + 7 + 2 + 4$, they might think $(3 + 7) + (4 + 6) + 2$, or $10 + 10 + 2 = 22$. They use the commutative property of addition to switch the order of some addends and then use the associative property of addition to regroup the numbers to simplify the calculations by forming compatible numbers. Compatible numbers, often referred to as "friendly" numbers, are numbers whose sums and products are easy to calculate mentally. For example, 25 and 4 are compatible because $25 \times 4 = 100$, and 35 and 65 are compatible because $35 + 65 = 100$. In general, numbers that can be combined to form multiples of 10 (e.g., 10, 50, 100, 200, 1,000) are compatible.

Too often, students operate on numbers strictly in the order in which they are encountered. Teachers can help students make sense of the associative properties of addition and multiplication by specifically focusing on grouping—asking them to experiment with adding or multiplying numbers in different orders and reflecting on the results and the relative ease or difficulty of the calculations. For example, students might be asked to rewrite expressions like the ones below to show different groupings of the same numbers and to decide which grouping produces the easiest calculation. Notice that the last expression in each list groups compatible numbers—$(24 + 36)$ and (4×5)—and can be computed quickly without paper and pencil.

Using 17, 24, and 36, form three addition expressions	Using 4, 5 and 17, form three multiplication expressions
$(24 + 17) + 36$	$(4 \times 17) \times 5$
$24 + (17 + 36)$	$4 \times (17 \times 5)$
$(24 + 36) + 17$	$(4 \times 5) \times 17$

Through experimentation with specific cases, students will realize that the sums and products are the same regardless of which two numbers are operated on first. They may also observe that some calculations (e.g., addends that sum to 10 or its multiples, multiplication involving a factor that has a zero in the ones place) are easier than others. Once students have started to notice patterns and shortcuts, conduct whole-class discussions about what they observe about the mathematical relationships as a way to help all students understand how they can use these properties when computing.

Many procedures students invent when learning to add and subtract make use of both the commutative and associative properties in conjunction with knowledge of place value. For example, how do you mentally compute 76 + 89? One way is to break the numbers down into tens and ones—70 + 6 + 80 + 9—and then add the tens and the ones separately:

$$
\begin{array}{r}
76 \\
+\ 89 \\
\hline
150 \quad (70 + 80) \\
+\ 15 \quad (6 + 9) \\
\hline
165 \\
\end{array}
$$

When computing mentally we often work left to right rather than right to left—first adding the tens (150), then the ones (15), and then performing a final calculation to get 165. The order in which we add (i.e., ones then tens or tens then ones) does not matter in terms of the final sum. Many adults learned the rule that with all computations except division you start on the right and are not aware that there are many efficient methods for computing that don't follow this rule.

A mental math technique called *compensation* involves reformulating a sum, product, difference, or quotient so that it is easier to work with. For example, rewriting addition computations to form compatible numbers doesn't change the value of the expression. Addends can be decomposed and then recomposed using the commutative and/or associative property to create easier computations. The addition 9 + 5 can be changed to an equivalent addition, 10 + 4, by decomposing 5 into 1 + 4 and adding the 1 and 9. In the computation 76 + 89, the 76 can be decomposed into 75 + 1; using the associative property, the 1 can then be recomposed with the 89 (1 + 89 = 90) to form the equivalent expression of 75 + 90.

For	Think	How it works
9 + 5	10 + 4	9 + (1 + 4) = (9 + 1) + 4
76 + 89	75 + 90	(75 + 1) + 89 = 75 + (1 + 89)

Subtraction expressions can also be adjusted without changing the final value (difference). But in the case of subtraction, a quantity is added to (or subtracted from) both numbers in the expression.

For	Think	How it works
13 − 9	14 − 10	(13 + 1) − (9 + 1) = (13 − 9) + (1 − 1)
62 − 28	64 − 30	(62 + 2) − (28 + 2) = (62 − 28) + (2 − 2)

In the examples above, either 1 or 2 is added to both numbers (which does not affect the difference) so that the number subtracted is a friendly, compatible number. The numbers added (in these cases, 1 and 2) are not arbitrary—they were chosen so that both of the subtrahends (9 and 28) would be multiples of 10 (9 + 1 = 10 and 28 + 2 = 30). The reason we can either add or subtract a set quantity to both numbers in a subtraction problem can be illustrated using the concept of the difference as an interval on the number line. We know that 10 − 6 = 4, because the interval between 10 and 6 is 4. If we move the interval along the number line, say to 7 and 3 by subtracting 3 from both 10 and 6, the interval or difference hasn't changed. Many subtraction problems have a difference of 4 and we can create these problems by moving the interval along the number line, adding or subtracting the same amount each time.

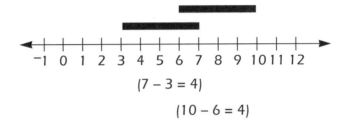

(7 − 3 = 4)

(10 − 6 = 4)

Multiplication and division expressions can also be adjusted using the commutative and associative properties of multiplication as well as the fact that a number can be expressed as a product of its factors. The computation 306 × 5, for example, can be rewritten as 153 × 10. Because 306 has 153 and 2 as factors, the expression can be restated as 153 × 2 × 5. Using the associative property of multiplication, the multiplication 2 × 5 is calculated first, followed by 153 × 10.

For	Think	How it works
306 × 5	153 × 10	(153 × 2) × 5 = 153 × (2 × 5)

Even though how we group addends or factors does not change the final sums or products, these properties cannot be generalized to number sentences that involve more than one operation. So what happens when we have number sentences with more then one operation? Is grouping important? For example, what is the answer to 2 + 6 × 3? Did you get 24 or 20? When there is more than one operation in a computation, how we group the numbers makes a difference in terms of the answer!

Remember that the operations of addition, subtraction, multiplication, and division are binary operations. Namely, we perform these operations on two numbers at a time. So when we consider the order in which to perform computations, we are always working with two numbers and one operation at a time. Rules for the order of operations developed gradually over hundreds of years. Some of the rules evolved naturally, such as the use of parentheses to clarify the intent of the writer of a number sentence, but other rules are somewhat arbitrary and were agreed on by mathematicians as the need for consistency became greater. In particular, with more and more computations being performed by calculators and computers, it became important that everyone agree on a specific order in situations that might be interpreted in many ways. Looking back at 2 + 6 × 3, the order of operations indicates that we first multiply 6 times 3 and then add 2 for an answer of 20!

How Do Grouping and Order Affect Answers?

Objective: explore how the order of operations affects answers.

When does it matter which operation is performed first in a problem? Pick two operations to investigate—say addition of 5 and division by 2. Choose four numbers to perform the operations upon (1, 9, 12, and 20) and then switch the operations and record the results in a table. Compare the results. What patterns do you notice?

Starting Number	Add 5, Divide by 2	Divide by 2, Add 5
1		
9		
12		
20		

Try this with the following operations:

▲ Addition and subtraction.

▲ Multiplication and division.

▲ Multiplication and subtraction.

Things to Think About

Examining the two columns that have + 5 followed by ÷ 2 and ÷ 2 followed by + 5, we see that the order of these two operations does matter.

Starting Number	Add 5, Divide by 2	Divide by 2, Add 5
1	3	5.5
9	7	9.5
12	8.5	11
20	12.5	15

The answer is always greater when you divide first and then add. In fact, the difference is exactly 2.5. Why? Let's use x to stand for any number. We can represent "add 5, divide by 2" as $\frac{x+5}{2}$ and "divide by 2, add 5" as $\frac{x}{2} + 5$. Before proceeding, take a minute and decide why the symbolic representations of these two expressions are different. It may help to be explicit about the actions: "add 5 to a number and divide the new sum by 2" compared with "take a number and divide it by 2 and then add 5 to the result." Next represent each expression as the sum of two fractions: $\frac{x+5}{2} = \frac{x}{2} + \frac{5}{2}$ and $\frac{x}{2} + 5 = \frac{x}{2} + \frac{5}{1}$.

Notice that we divide the number, x, by 2 in both expressions ($\frac{x}{2}$), but when we add 5 first, that 5 also gets divided by 2, which gives us 2.5. When we add the 5 after the division, that 5 is unaffected by the division. The difference between 5 and 2.5 is 2.5.

When a computation only has the operations of addition and subtraction, the order in which we perform the operations doesn't matter in terms of the answer. For example, in $3 + 9 - 2$ we can either add $3 + 9$ first or subtract $9 - 2$ first. The answer in both cases is 10.

$$
\begin{array}{cc}
(3 + 9) - 2 & 3 + (9 - 2) \\
12 - 2 & 3 + 7 \\
\mathbf{10} & \mathbf{10}
\end{array}
$$

When we have both the operations of multiplication and division or the operations of multiplication and subtraction, it does matter which operation we perform first.

$$
\begin{array}{cc}
30 \div (2 \times 5) & (30 \div 2) \times 5 \\
30 \div 10 & 15 \times 5 \\
\mathbf{3} & \mathbf{75} \\[6pt]
(25 - 12) \times 2 & 25 - (12 \times 2) \\
13 \times 2 & 25 - 24 \\
\mathbf{26} & \mathbf{1}
\end{array}
$$

The answers are quite different, depending on which operation is performed first. Explore the relationships between the answers based on which operation is performed first using algebra. Let x represent the starting value. Explain why the answer to $(x - 12) \times 2$ is different from the answer to $x - (12 \times 2)$.

In order to avoid errors, when there are more than two operations in a number sentence, we use the Order of Operations: first do any calculations that are grouped together (often shown with parentheses or the fraction bar), then calculate exponents, then multiply and divide from left to right, and finally add and subtract in order from left to right. Teachers sometimes provide students with the mnemonic PEMDAS (parentheses, exponents, multiplication, division, addition, subtraction) as a way to remember the order of operations. However, many educators believe this mnemonic causes more harm than good. If students have not had opportunities to explore what happens when the order of operations is reversed, they may apply the rules blindly or misinterpret what the letters in PEMDAS represent. For example, instead of performing the operations of multiplication and division in the order they occur from left to right, students sometimes first do all the multiplications followed by all divisions, regardless of order. ▲

The Distributive Property

The distributive property of multiplication over addition allows us to "distribute" a factor, a, to two different addends (or in more math terms, "over" two different addends), b and c: $a(b + c) = ab + ac$. It is used extensively when computing mentally. For example, how would you mentally multiply 3 times 58? One approach is to think of the 58 as 50 + 8 and use the distributive property of multiplication over addition:

$$3 \times 58 \Rightarrow 3 \times (50 + 8) \Rightarrow (3 \times 50) + (3 \times 8) \Rightarrow 150 + 24 \Rightarrow 174$$

The distributive property is often used in connection with compensation; that is, to calculate 3×58, we adjust it to make an easier calculation. In the example above, we can round 58 to 60 and then subtract 2. This quantity is then multiplied by 3 ($3 \times (60 - 2)$).

But can the distributive property of multiplication be applied to subtraction? Yes, since we can decompose a number into the sum of two addends and the addends can be negative or positive. For example, think of the subtraction $60 - 2$ as equivalent to $60 + {}^{-}2$, since adding $^{-}2$ is equivalent to subtracting 2. Thus, we can distribute multiplication over the $(60 - 2)$, which is equivalent to distributing multiplication over $(60 + {}^{-}2)$:

$$3 \times 58 \Rightarrow 3 \times (60 - 2) \Rightarrow (3 \times 60) - (3 \times 2) \Rightarrow 180 - 6 \Rightarrow 174$$
$$3 \times 58 \Rightarrow 3 \times (60 + {}^{-}2) \Rightarrow (3 \times 60) + (3 \times {}^{-}2) \Rightarrow 180 + {}^{-}6 \Rightarrow 174$$

The distributive property may also be applied to division expressions. Consider the expression $132 \div 12$. An equivalent expression using multiplication is $132 \times \frac{1}{12}$. If we rewrite 132 as $(120 + 12)$, we can distribute the multiplication by $\frac{1}{12}$ over both addends.

$$132 \times \tfrac{1}{12} \Rightarrow (120 + 12) \times \tfrac{1}{12} \Rightarrow (120 \times \tfrac{1}{12}) + (12 \times \tfrac{1}{12}) \Rightarrow 10 + 1 \Rightarrow 11$$

Because we can rewrite all division (except by 0) as multiplication, we can also apply the distributive property of multiplication over addition to the problem:

$$132 \div 12 \Rightarrow (120 + 12) \div 12 \Rightarrow (120 \div 12) + (12 \div 12) \Rightarrow 10 + 1 \Rightarrow 11$$

Not only is the distributive property useful when computing mentally, but it also is applied in our standard multiplication and division algorithms. When students study algebra, they learn how to apply the distributive property when multiplying polynomials.

Properties of whole numbers are used extensively when computing. The particular numbers involved in a calculation determine when it makes sense to use the commutative, associative, or distributive property or some combination of them. Although it's not important for young students to be able to identify these properties by name, it is extremely important that teachers understand how these properties enable students to compute accurately. Thus, teachers can highlight the essential components of students' solution methods (e.g., multiplying by one, changing the order, grouping different numbers together, undoing an operation, or decomposing and recomposing) in order to help students analyze why procedures work to produce correct answers. In middle school, students revisit these properties in preparation for algebra. If they have a solid grasp of when and how these properties are used in arithmetic, they will be better able to generalize the relationships and represent them with variables.

2. Basic Facts

The basic facts in addition and multiplication are all possible sums and products of the digits 0 through 9. Although technically there are 100 addition facts and 100 multiplication facts, because of the commutative property there are actually only 55 unique basic facts for each operation:

+	0	1	2	3	4	5	6	7	8	9
0	0	1	2	3	4	5	6	7	8	9
1	1	2	3	4	5	6	7	8	9	10
2	2	3	4	5	6	7	8	9	10	11
3	3	4	5	6	7	8	9	10	11	12
4	4	5	6	7	8	9	10	11	12	13
5	5	6	7	8	9	10	11	12	13	14
6	6	7	8	9	10	11	12	13	14	15
7	7	8	9	10	11	12	13	14	15	16
8	8	9	10	11	12	13	14	15	16	17
9	9	10	11	12	13	14	15	16	17	18

addition basic facts

×	0	1	2	3	4	5	6	7	8	9
0	0	0	0	0	0	0	0	0	0	0
1	0	1	2	3	4	5	6	7	8	9
2	0	2	4	6	8	10	12	14	16	18
3	0	3	6	9	12	15	18	21	24	27
4	0	4	8	12	16	20	24	28	32	36
5	0	5	10	15	20	25	30	35	40	45
6	0	6	12	18	24	30	36	42	48	54
7	0	7	14	21	28	35	42	49	56	63
8	0	8	16	24	32	40	48	56	64	72
9	0	9	18	27	36	45	54	63	72	81

multiplication basic facts

Furthermore, adding 0 or multiplying by 1 poses no problems for memorization because of the identity properties of addition and multiplication ($a + 0 = a$ and $a \times 1 = a$). Thus, there are even fewer than 55 facts to learn.

Since knowledge of the addition facts can be applied to subtraction and knowledge of multiplication facts can be applied to division, there is no need to learn subtraction and division facts as isolated procedures. However, this assumes that the relationships between inverse operations (operations that "undo" each other—addition and subtraction, and multiplication and division) have been thoroughly explored, discussed, and internalized. When students understand the inverse relationship between operations, you can encourage them to use what they know about multiplication, for example, to learn about division. If they need to solve $36 \div 9$, suggest that they think, 9 *times what number is equal to 36?* After generating equations that use the numbers 36, 9, and 4, they can then discuss how and why these multiplication and division equations are related. You might also ask them to write two stories (one multiplication, one division) that use the numbers 36, 9, and 4 and then to reflect on how the stories are similar and different. You can also introduce activities that feature division "near facts." For example, if we convert $50 \div 8$ to a multiplication problem, 8×7 is too large, 8×5 is too small, and 8×6 is still too small but closer. Using this information, students can then determine that $50 \div 8 = 6$ with a remainder of 2.

Students need to know the basic facts in order to be both efficient and accurate, whether their calculations are performed mentally or by applying paper-and-pencil algorithms. Instruction involving basic facts should focus on making sense, highlight strategies for remembering facts, and be connected to all other work with number.

This instruction might include activities that ask students to explore relationships between operations (e.g., addition and subtraction) or to explore properties and then apply the properties to learning other facts. For example, students might determine 8×7 by decomposing 7 into $3 + 4$ and using their knowledge of 8×3 and 8×4 ($24 + 32 = 56$). This strategy works because of the distributive property ($8 \times (3 + 4)$). Likewise, students can further their knowledge by writing word problems that use the facts in a meaningful context, using concrete objects to connect these situations with symbols, and discussing relationships within fact families.

Learning facts is a gradual process that for most students takes a number of years. (See Chapter 3 for specifics on how skills develop in addition and subtraction.) Eventually, however, students need to commit the basic facts to memory. Naturally, the exact age when a particular student masters these facts varies. In general, however, most students have mastered addition/subtraction facts by the end of third grade and multiplication/division facts by the end of fifth grade. "Mastery" does not imply that students are human calculators able to perform at lightning speed. It means that they know the facts well enough to be efficient and accurate in other calculations.

3. Algorithms

Algorithms, as the term is applied to the arithmetic procedures students traditionally have learned in school, are systematic, step-by-step procedures used to find the solution to a computation accurately, reliably, and quickly. Algorithms, whether performed mentally or with paper and pencil, a calculator, or a computer, are used when an exact answer is required, when an estimate won't suffice. Because they are generalizations that enable us to solve classes of problems, they are very powerful: we can solve many similar tasks ($1,345,678 - 987,654$ and $134 - 98$, for example) using one process. In the best of circumstances, algorithms free up some of our mental capacity so that we can focus on interpreting and understanding a solution in the context of a problem. In the worst of circumstances, algorithms are used when a task could be done mentally or are applied by rote with little understanding of the bigger mathematical picture—why the calculation is important and how the answer will be used.

There are many different algorithms for performing operations with numbers. Some of these algorithms are now referred to as *standard* or *conventional* simply because they have been taught in the majority of U.S. classrooms over the past fifty years. For example, you may have learned (or taught) the standard addition algorithm shown below, in which you "carry" from the ones column to the tens column to the hundreds column:

$$
\begin{array}{r}
{\scriptstyle 1\,1} \\
456 \\
+899 \\
\hline
1355
\end{array}
$$

Interestingly, some of the conventional algorithms in the United States are not the standard algorithms in Europe or South America. Children around the world learn different computational procedures in school.

Other algorithms are known as *alternative* algorithms—they differ from the standard algorithms for adding, subtracting, multiplying, and dividing. Alternative algorithms also are accurate, reliable, and fast. Alternative algorithms such as the lattice method for multiplication have sometimes been used in schools as enrichment activities. Today many alternative algorithms are part of the elementary mathematics curriculum. Making sense of algorithms can be instructive; students figure out why certain procedures work, which leads them to insights into important ideas such as place value and the distributive property of multiplication over addition.

In the 1990s many researchers and mathematics educators began to question the wisdom of the rote teaching of conventional algorithms to students in the elementary grades. Research has shown that when children simply memorize the steps to complete the standard addition and subtraction algorithms, they lose conceptual understanding of place value. In contrast, students who invent their own procedures or algorithms for solving addition and subtraction problems have a much better understanding of place value and produce more accurate solutions (Kamii 1994; Kamii and Dominick 1998; Narode, Board, and Davenport 1993). Many mathematics educators now suggest that instead of teaching students standard algorithms as the only or best ways to compute with paper and pencil, we provide many opportunities for students to develop, use, and discuss a variety of methods. Having students invent algorithms leads to enhanced number and operation sense as well as flexible thinking (Burns 1994b; Carroll and Porter 1997, 1998).

Many elementary curriculums are designed so that children initially use logical reasoning and their understanding of number (e.g., that 36 can be decomposed into 30 + 6), place value, and mathematical properties to invent their own algorithms and procedures to solve addition and subtraction problems. The purpose of this type of instruction is to extend and expand students' understanding of number, place value, decomposition, and recomposition (see Chapter 1 for elaboration) as they learn to compute. Student-invented or student-generated procedures sometimes are algorithms; that is, they can be generalized to classes of problems and they enable the student to produce accurate answers. (They many not be efficient or easy to use, however.) Other procedures are not algorithms; they may enable a child to calculate a correct answer, but they cannot be generalized to other problems.

However, as students progress through the grades, they need to acquire efficient ways to compute, and student-generated methods may not suffice. Thus, after students have experimented with developing their own methods, teachers often introduce standard and alternative algorithms as a focus of study. When these algorithms are examined and analyzed, not taught in a rote way, students have the opportunity to build on their already established understanding of number and place value to expand their repertoire of efficient, reliable, and generalizable methods.

In schools we often associate the study of algorithms with paper-and-pencil procedures. One useful by-product of paper-and-pencil algorithms is that they provide a written record of the processes used to solve a problem. Students can use this record to refine procedures, share what has been accomplished, and reflect on solutions. Keeping a record of the steps in an algorithm is especially important when students are trying to make sense of the reasoning involved in the computation. The activities in this section examine a variety of algorithms and student-invented procedures for whole number computations. The goal is for you to understand why these methods work and to consider the mathematics that students have made sense of in order to use them.

Analyzing Students' Thinking, Addition

Objective: learn some common addition strategies.

Examine the following examples of students' procedures for solving addition problems. First, explain what the student did to obtain a correct answer. Then use the student's algorithm to solve the problem 1367 + 498.

Kelly	Rudy	Andy

567	567	567 ⇒ 600
+ 259	+ 259	+ 259 + 226
700		826
110	200 − 567, 667, 767	
16	50 − 777, 787, 797, 807, 817	259
826	9 − 818, 819, 820, 821, 822	− 33
	823, 824, 825, 826	226

Things to Think About

Kelly's algorithm is sometimes called the partial sums method. She added the digits in the problem by place value, starting with the largest place value (hundreds)—500 + 200 = 700, 60 + 50 = 110, 7 + 9 = 16. After calculating the partial sums, Kelly added them (700 + 110 + 16 = 826). Kelly is able to decompose numbers into hundreds, tens, and ones, add like units, and then recompose the three subtotals to produce the final sum. Since her use of this algorithm implies that she understands place value through hundreds, she would probably be able to generalize this approach to four-digit and larger sums. To solve 1367 + 498 using Kelly's method you would figure this way:

$$
\begin{array}{r}
1367 \\
+ \ 498 \\
\hline
1000 \\
700 \\
150 \\
15 \\
\hline
1865
\end{array}
$$

How did Rudy solve 567 + 259? It appears that he started with 567 and either counted on or added on, first by hundreds, then by tens, finally by ones. He started with the hundreds, writing 567, 667, 767. Then he continued with five tens: 777, 787, 797, 807, 817. Finally he finished with the ones: 818, 819, 820, 821, 822, 823, 824, 825, 826. While this procedure works, it is prone to error, especially when an increase in one grouping necessitates an increase in the next one up (797 to 807, for example). To solve 1367 + 498 using Rudy's method, round 498 up to 500, count on by hundreds (1467, 1567, 1667, 1767, 1867), and then count backward by ones (1866, 1865). Sometimes students use an invented procedure for a short period of time and then move on to another, more efficient procedure or algorithm. The importance of classroom discussion about solution procedures cannot be overemphasized—students often learn about other approaches when their classmates describe their method.

Andy used an approach different from the other two students in that he did not decompose the numbers based on hundreds, tens, and ones. Instead, he changed both numbers to other numbers that he thought would be easier to use. He started by adding 33 to 567 to get 600. He then subtracted the 33 from 259 to get 226. Finally, he added his two adjusted numbers: 600 + 226 = 826. Andy's method works because of the associative and commutative properties. The identity property of addition also comes into play: adding zero—33 + (−33) = 0—doesn't change the sum:

$$567 + 259 = (567 + 259) + (33 + {}^-33)$$
$$= (567 + 33) + (259 + {}^-33)$$
$$= (567 + 33) + (259 - 33)$$
$$= 600 + 226$$
$$= 826$$

Andy's procedure is very efficient with an addition such as 1367 + 498, because it's easy to "see" how to change 498 to 500 and compensate by subtracting two from 1367. However, this approach may not be all that ideal with problems such as 2418 + 1725 (though it will work), since the additions and subtractions leading to the adjusted numbers may require a lot of mental energy. ▲

Activity

Analyzing Students' Thinking, Subtraction

Objective: learn some common subtraction strategies.

Examine the following examples of students' procedures for solving the same subtraction problem. What did each student do to obtain a correct answer? Why does the student's algorithm work?

Caitlin	*Louis*	*Kenley*

```
   Caitlin              Louis         Kenley

                          13
     63                   6̸3            63
   − 18    10 + 8       −²1̸8          −18
  ─────               ─────          ─────
  63 − 10 = 53          45            28    10⎫
  ─────────                           38    10⎬
  52, 51, 50, 49,                     48    10⎪
  48, 47, 46, 45                      58    10⎭  or    40
                                    + 5                  5
                                    ─────              ─────
      45                              45                 45
```

Things to Think About

Caitlin solved this computation by inventing a procedure based on her understanding of place value and counting back. First she decomposed 18 into 10 + 8, then she removed the 10 from 63 (63 − 10 = 53), and finally she counted back 8 from 53 to 45. This procedure is commonly seen in second-grade classrooms in which children have been encouraged to invent their own procedures that make sense to them. Let's try Caitlin's procedure with 152 − 39.

```
        152
      − 39    30 + 9
     ─────
        100
        52 − 30 = 22
        122
     ─────────
122, 121, 120, 119, 118, 117, 116, 115, 114, 113
```

While it is unlikely that you would use this procedure for larger multidigit subtraction problems, adults do use a combination of methods including counting back with simple calculations such as determining elapsed time (e.g., *for how many hours do I pay the baby-sitter if it is now 12:45 A.M. and I left at 4:30 P.M.?*). Depending on the context and the numbers in a problem, simple counting procedures can be quick and efficient.

Louis moved to the United States when he was eleven and learned this algorithm in school in Italy. What are the steps in Louis's algorithm? First, Louis noticed that there were not enough ones in the ones place (3) to subtract 8, so he changed the 3 to a 13. Because he added 10 to the 63 (63 + 10 = 60 + 13), he had to add 10 to the 18 (10 + 18 = 28) in order not to change the problem. Louis recorded the 10 added to the 18 by changing the 1 in the tens place to a 2. He then subtracted the ones (13 − 8 = 5) and the tens (6 − 2 = 4) to obtain the answer of 45. This algorithm uses compensation (see page 37 in this chapter)—if you add (or subtract) the same number to both the minuend and the subtrahend in a subtraction problem, the difference is not affected.

$$
\begin{array}{rcl}
63 + 10 \;\Rightarrow\; 73 & \quad 63 + 10 = 60 + 13 \\
-\,18 + 10 \quad\; -\,28 & \quad -18 + 10 = 20 + 8 \\
\hline
45 \qquad\quad 45 & \quad 40 + 5
\end{array}
$$

What is interesting about Louis's algorithm is that the 10 is added to different place values, which simplifies the computation. Let's try his procedure with 81 − 58:

$$
\begin{array}{r}
^{11} \\
8\cancel{1} \\
-\,^{6}\cancel{5}8 \\
\hline
23
\end{array}
$$

Kenley understands the inverse relationship between addition and subtraction and used an approach sometimes referred to as "adding on" or "counting up." It is often used by students for subtraction word problems involving money when making change. For example, to solve the problem, "How much change should you receive from a $5.88 purchase if you give the clerk a $10 bill?," you can add on from $5.88 to $10.00 ($.12 makes $6.00 plus $4.00 makes $10.00, the change is $4.12). The amount Kenley added on to 18 to reach 63 was her answer. She counted by tens until she was close to but not above 63: 28, 38, 48, 58. She recorded that she had added four tens, or 40. When she realized that five more ones would bring her to 63 (58 + 5 = 63), she had her final answer of 45. Let's use Kenley's method to solve 81 − 58:

$$
\begin{array}{rl}
& 58 \qquad 68, 78 \\
81 & +\boxed{20} \qquad \Leftarrow \\
-\,58 & \overline{78} \qquad 79, 80, 81 \quad \boxed{23} \\
& +\boxed{3} \qquad \Leftarrow \\
& \overline{81}
\end{array}
$$

The standard subtraction algorithm is the one that most adults were taught when students. It is an efficient method that is based on decomposition and regrouping. Let's examine how Juan solves 152 − 39.

$$
\begin{array}{r}
^{4\,12} \\
1\cancel{5}\cancel{2} \\
-\,39 \\
\hline
113
\end{array}
$$

Juan's actions are based on the fact that numbers can be decomposed into hundreds, tens, and ones (152 = 100 + 50 + 2) and recomposed in less efficient groupings (152 = 100 + 40 + 12) that can be used in certain types of problems. He notes that since there are only 2 ones in the ones place and he wants to subtract 9 ones, he needs to regroup 1 ten from the tens place and combine these 10 ones with the 2 ones for a total of 12 ones. This leaves only 4 tens in the tens place. Now he can subtract by place value (12 − 9 = 3, 40 − 30 = 10, 100 − 0 = 100). In the most abbreviated version of this algorithm, Juan subtracts 4 − 3 and 1 − 0 as if these numbers represented ones, but knows that by their placement in the tens and hundreds columns, respectfully, they represent 40 − 30 and 100 − 0. As with many algorithms, this one can be applied by rote. If students solve problems such as this one using a memorized procedure, they usually are unable to explain their actions. For example, they can't tell you what the 4 or the 12 above the tens and ones places represent and why those numbers are being used. Students who are unclear on the purpose of regrouping sometimes record answers that make no sense. Or, if students report that "this is how you do it" when asked to explain their steps, it is a signal that they may have memorized the procedures to execute the algorithm without understanding them. However, if students understand the relationships involved, they will have a solid grasp of place value and decomposition/recomposition and will find this algorithm very useful.

The application of the standard algorithm is more difficult when the minuend contains one or more zeroes. Teachers and students alike agree that in these situations the standard algorithm is confusing and hard to use! The regrouping process involves many steps and requires that students understand the relationships between larger place values. Let's take a look at 5009 − 836.

$$
\begin{array}{r}
{}^{9} \\
{}^{4\,\cancel{1}\cancel{0}10} \\
\cancel{5}\cancel{0}\cancel{0}9 \\
-\ 836 \\
\hline
4173
\end{array}
$$

When we decompose the number 5009 into place values, there are no tens or hundreds to regroup in different ways. This means that we must decompose the 5000 into 4000 + 1000 and regroup the 1000 as 10 hundreds. This is shown in the algorithm by crossing out the 5 (5 thousand), replacing it with a 4 (4 thousand) and putting a 10 over the hundreds to indicate the regrouping of 1000 as 10 hundreds. Then we decompose the 10 hundreds into 900 + 100 and regroup the 100 as 10 tens. Using symbols, this is recorded by crossing out the 10 above the hundreds place and writing a 9 (9 hundred) and placing a 10 above the tens place (10 tens). Finally, we are ready to subtract place by place (9 − 6 ones, 10 − 3 tens, 9 − 8 hundreds, and 4 − 0 thousands).

Whereas the standard algorithm can be quite efficient, some students find it easier to use compensation when subtraction involves numerous zeroes in the minuend. For example, subtract 9 from both numbers (5009 − 9 and 836 − 9). The equivalent subtraction problem of 5000 − 827 can be solved in a variety of ways. Using Kenley's "adding on" method, students might count on from 827 starting at the ones place (827 ⇒ 3 + 70 + 100 + 4000). Or they might add 173 to both numbers (5000 + 173 = 5173, 837 + 173 =1000) and perform the simpler calculation, 5173 − 1000 = 4173. Take a minute and think about what students need to understand in order to be able to use a variety of solution methods. ▲

Analyzing Students' Thinking, Multiplication

Objective: learn some common multiplication strategies.

Examine the following examples of students' procedures for solving the same two multiplication problems. What did each student do to obtain a correct answer? Why does the student's algorithm work?

Sasha		Emily

Sasha:

```
    12          43
  × 13        × 62
  -----      -----
     6           6
    30          80
    20         180
 + 100       +2400
  -----      -----
   156        2666
```

Emily:

$$12 \times 13$$
$$10 \times 13 = 130$$
$$2 \times 13 = \underline{26}$$
$$156$$

$$43 \times 62$$
$$20 \times 62 = 1240$$
$$20 \times 62 = 1240$$
$$3 \times 62 = \underline{186}$$
$$2666$$

Tabitha

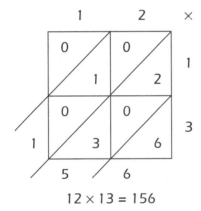

$$12 \times 13 = 156$$

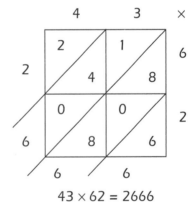

$$43 \times 62 = 2666$$

Things to Think About

Sasha's algorithm, the partial product algorithm, is often taught to help students understand the steps in a multiplication problem prior to learning the standard multiplication algorithm. To solve 12 × 13, Sasha decomposed both numbers into tens and ones—(10 + 2) × (10 + 3)—and completed four multiplications (3 × 2, 3 × 10, 2 × 10, and 10 × 10) to obtain partial products. He then added these partial products together to obtain the answer. The partial product algorithm works because of the distributive property: 12 × 13 is equivalent to 12 × (10 + 3), which is also equivalent to (10 + 2) × (10 + 3). Students revisit this application of the distributive property in algebra (where it is known as the "foil method") when they multiply polynomials such as $(x + 3)(x + 2)$. The partial product algorithm is sometimes presented using a rectangular array to help students visualize multiplication in terms of the area of a region. A rectangle with the length and width of the factors in the multiplication problem (12 by 13, in this case) is first constructed on graph paper. Each side is partitioned into tens and ones. Lines are drawn to show the different regions, and the area of each region is determined.

These areas are then added together. (Base ten blocks—hundreds, tens, and ones—can be used to fill in the regions to represent the areas concretely.)

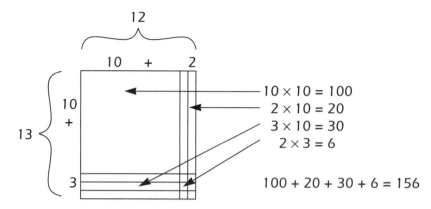

Try the rectangular array approach with Sasha's second problem, 43 × 62. One side of the 43 by 62 rectangle can be marked to show 40 + 3, or 10 + 10 + 10 + 10 + 3. The other side can be marked to show 60 + 2, or 10 + 10 + 10 + 10 + 10 + 10 + 2.

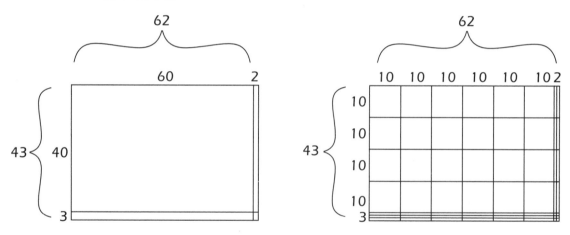

Emily broke down 12 × 13 into computations simple enough to do in her head. She used a method similar to the partial product algorithm in that she found some partial products and then added. Her method also relies on the distributive property, distributing 13 across the 10 and the 2: (13 × 10) + (13 × 2).

12 × 13   ⇒   10 × 13 = 130   ⇒   2 × 13 = 26   ⇒   130 + 26 = 156

Emily's solution to 43 × 62 again uses the distributive property, but in order to keep the calculations easy enough to do in her head she first thought of 43 as (20 + 20 + 3) and then calculated the partial products of each of these multiplied by 62. Since there were many steps in this calculation, she jotted them down:

$$20 \times 62 = 1240$$
$$20 \times 62 = 1240$$
$$3 \times 62 = 186$$
$$1240 + 1240 + 186 = 2666$$

Notice that the individual procedures produce individual partial products, which are then added to find the final product. Clearly, Emily understands what happens when one multiplies and is ready to learn a quicker, more efficient algorithm.

Tabitha used the *lattice* method of multiplication. It is an alternative algorithm students almost never invent on their own; it is taught because analyzing it can help students make sense of the role of regrouping in multidigit multiplication. To multiply 43 × 62, Tabitha wrote the two factors, 43 and 62, above and to the right of the lattice and recorded partial products in cells with the tens value above the diagonal line and the ones value below the diagonal line (see 3 × 6 and 3 × 2 in the figure on page 49). After she had done this for 4 × 6 and 4 × 2 as well, she extended the diagonal lines and added the numbers in each diagonal. If the sum in a diagonal was greater than 9 (such as the second diagonal from the right), she regrouped the 10 tens as 1 hundred into the next diagonal to the left. The final product is read starting from the left side of the lattice. The product of 43 × 62 is 2666.

Why does the lattice method of multiplication work? While it looks very different, this algorithm is similar to the standard multiplication algorithm. The number 43 is multiplied by 2 (the bottom row) and by 60 (the top row) for a total of 62 times. While it appears that you are only multiplying by 6, notice how the numbers in the cells in the top row are all shifted over one place because of the diagonals. This has the effect of placing the numbers in positions that represent multiplication by 60, not 6. In the standard multiplication algorithm we also shift the placement of digits (often using a zero as a place holder) in order to represent multiplying by 60:

$$
\begin{array}{r}
43 \\
\times\, 62 \\
\hline
86 \\
2580 \\
\hline
2666
\end{array}
$$
⟸ shift over or place a 0 in the ones place

One feature of the lattice algorithm that makes it especially appealing to some students is that multiplication and addition within the algorithm are kept separate. Basic facts are used to fill the cells but adding only occurs when determining the sums of the diagonals. ▲

Activity

Analyzing Students' Thinking, Division

Objective: learn some common division strategies.

Examine the following examples of students' procedures for solving division problems. What did each student do to obtain a correct answer? Why does the student's algorithm work?

Doug	Nancy	Madelaine

Doug:
$$
\begin{array}{r}
137\ \text{r}\ 4 \\
5\overline{)689} \\
-\,500 \quad 100 \cdot 5 \\
\hline
189 \\
50 \quad 10 \cdot 5 \\
\hline
139 \\
50 \quad 10 \cdot 5 \\
\hline
89 \\
50 \quad 10 \cdot 5 \\
\hline
39 \\
35 \quad 7 \cdot 5 \\
\hline
4 \quad 137 \cdot 5
\end{array}
$$

Nancy:
$$
\begin{array}{r}
137\ \text{r}\ 4 \\
5\overline{)689} \\
5 \\
\hline
18 \\
15 \\
\hline
39 \\
35 \\
\hline
4
\end{array}
$$

Madelaine:
$$
\begin{array}{rl}
500 \div 5 = & 100 \\
100 \div 5 = & 20 \\
50 \div 5 = & 10 \\
30 \div 5 = & 6 \\
9 \div 5 = & 1\ \text{r}\ 4 \\
\hline
689 \div 5 = & 137\ \text{r}\ 4
\end{array}
$$

Things to Think About

Doug's method is sometimes referred to as the scaffold algorithm, which uses repeated subtraction to find quotients. For example, in 689 ÷ 5, multiples of 5 are subtracted successively until a remainder less than 5 is obtained. Doug was able to calculate the products of 5 times 100 and 5 times 10 mentally. He then subtracted these amounts from the quotient. Doug was unclear on how many groups of 5 he could subtract at a time so he repeatedly subtracted 10 groups of 5, or 50. Another student solving this problem using the same algorithm might estimate first and subtract out the 30 groups of 5 at one time:

$$
\begin{array}{r|l}
5\overline{)689} & \\
\underline{500} & 100 \cdot 5 \\
189 & \\
\underline{150} & 30 \cdot 5 \\
39 & \\
\underline{35} & \underline{\quad 7 \cdot 5} \\
& 137 \cdot 5
\end{array}
$$

While this algorithm can be somewhat slow and cumbersome, accuracy is fairly high. Furthermore, this method is faster if an individual uses estimation to remove multiples of the divisor. (The algorithm can help students improve their estimation skills, since a teacher can highlight the relationship between the divisor, partial quotient, and subtracted amount.)

Nancy used the standard long division algorithm to find the quotient. She has learned the four steps in this algorithm: estimate, multiply, subtract, and bring down. But what is happening in each of these steps, and why does the standard algorithm work? When Nancy estimated the number of groups of 5 she could remove from 6 (1), she actually estimated the number of 5s she could remove from 600 (100) but suppressed the zeroes in the quotient and in the dividend. She then multiplied the 5 and the 1 to obtain the amount she would subtract. Since she had suppressed the zeroes, she simply brought down the next digit (the 8) as if she had subtracted zero:

$$
\begin{array}{r}
1 \\
5\overline{)689} \\
\underline{5} \\
18
\end{array}
\qquad \Rightarrow \qquad
\begin{array}{r}
100 \\
5\overline{)689} \\
\underline{500} \\
189
\end{array}
$$

In the next step, in which she estimated the number of 5s in 18 (3), she really estimated the number of 5s in 189 (30), but she again suppressed the zero and ignored the 9 (ones):

$$
\begin{array}{r}
13 \\
5\overline{)689} \\
\underline{5} \\
18 \\
\underline{15} \\
3
\end{array}
\qquad \Rightarrow \qquad
\begin{array}{r}
130 \\
5\overline{)689} \\
\underline{500} \\
189 \\
\underline{150} \\
39
\end{array}
$$

When she finally brought down the 9 and estimated the number of 5s in 39, she recorded that seven 5s can be subtracted from 39 with 4 left over:

$$
\begin{array}{r}
137 \text{ r } 4 \\
5\overline{)689} \\
\underline{5} \\
18 \\
\underline{15} \\
39 \\
\underline{35} \\
4
\end{array}
$$

After students have made sense of the scaffold algorithm, in which hundreds of 5s and tens of 5s are subtracted, they often have no trouble understanding the steps in the standard long division algorithm. They can explain what is happening and why we can use the shortened version. Students often become much more proficient at long division when they understand why it works.

Madelaine used the distributive property to distribute the division across many subtraction substeps. She subtracted numbers from 689 that were divisible by 5 and recorded the results in a linear fashion. For example, she first subtracted 500 from 689 since 500 is divisible by 5. She then continued by subtracting 100 from 689 (since 500 + 100 = 600) and dividing it by 5. She then subtracted multiples of 10 that were divisible by 5 (50 and then 30), and finally a group of ones. Like Doug, she could have subtracted different amounts that also were divisible by 5 to obtain the correct answer. Madelaine's invented method is based on her understanding that she can decompose 689 and that it is most efficient first to consider the number of hundreds that can be subtracted, then the tens, and finally the ones. Use Madelaine's method to divide 378 by 3.

Division algorithms are not used all that often in today's world. We may use division when we calculate our gasoline mileage or when we eat out with friends and divide the bill evenly. Most of the division we do involves small dividends and single-digit divisors. For more complicated division problems, we reach for the calculator. When using a calculator, however, students should have a ballpark estimate in mind as a check that they have selected keys correctly. And they need to be able to do divisions with paper and pencil. However, practicing long division algorithms with large divisors and even larger dividends has limited value. Much more important is providing students with opportunities to make sense of division situations and procedures. ▲

Teaching Computation

One reason algorithms were invented and codified is so that we can compute accurately and efficiently without having to expend a great deal of mental energy. Yet which algorithm or procedure we use depends on the level of precision needed and whether we are computing mentally or with paper and pencil. (Calculators and computers use programmed algorithms and are by definition quick and accurate.) Students need to understand a variety of approaches to solving problems in order to choose the most appropriate method based on the numbers involved and the complexity of the procedure.

Another factor that affects our choice of algorithms or procedures involves the context of the problem. The context indicates whether we need an accurate answer or if an approximate value will suffice. Sometimes an accurate answer isn't necessary. For example, when checking to see whether we have enough cash for the groceries in our cart we might adjust prices up ($1.89 to $2.00) but not bother to compensate later by subtracting the added amount (11¢) from the final sum. However, when a situation requires a precise answer, we will want to choose a solution method that guarantees accuracy.

Students' facility with the different operations and algorithms develops slowly over time. With experience they become flexible in using a variety of procedures and algorithms based on the numbers in the computations. They also learn to apply their knowledge of contexts to determine when an exact answer is required and when an estimate will suffice. As they progress through the grades, students learn a variety of algorithms for performing computations with rational numbers and integers quickly and easily. Ideally they will understand how the mathematical properties they are familiar with are used with all numbers and how these new algorithms are related to ones they have already encountered.

Questions for Discussion

1. Explain how understanding mathematical properties helps students compute mentally or make sense of operations.
2. A number of commercially available mathematics curriculums are designed so that students invent addition and subtraction algorithms. Why is this considered important?
3. Should students be taught more than one algorithm for an operation? Should all students know the "standard algorithms"? Explain.
4. What might a teacher do when a child explains a procedure for solving a problem but no one in the class seems to understand it, not even the teacher?

3

Addition and Subtraction

In order to use addition and subtraction effectively, children must first attach meaning to these operations. One way for young children to do this is by manipulating concrete objects and connecting their actions to symbols. However, this is not the only way. They extend their understanding of situations involving addition and subtraction by solving word problems.

In this chapter we investigate how children solve addition and subtraction word problems involving small quantities and address several questions: How do children decide which operation is called for? (Is it an addition or subtraction situation?) How do children represent the mathematics symbolically? (Can they write an appropriate number sentence or equation to represent the situation?) How do children think numerically to perform the needed computation?

As students progress through our educational system, they are introduced to the set of integers and to addition and subtraction of signed numbers. In order to make sense of these operations, students must start to work with formal mathematical systems and expand their definitions of addition and subtraction to include directions of movements on the number line.

1. Types of Addition and Subtraction Word Problems

Students extend their understanding of and skill with addition and subtraction of whole numbers by solving word problems based on different meanings or interpretations of these operations. For example, consider these two subtraction problems:

> *I have seven apples and Carla has four apples. How many more apples do I have than Carla?*

> *I had seven apples and ate four apples. How many apples are left?*

Both situations can be expressed with the same number sentence: $7 - 4 = \square$. However, the first problem requires a "comparison" interpretation, the second, a "take away" interpretation. When an operation is reduced to symbols, it is impossible to determine which meaning or interpretation is being represented. So that students can learn that there are multiple interpretations of an operation and expand their repertoire of situations that model the operation, we need to give them a variety of problems to solve.

Evidence suggests that the general meaning of a problem rather than specific words or phrases determines both the difficulty of the problem and the processes students use to solve it. In other words, it is how the operation is expressed and, by extension, a student's ability to make sense of that meaning rather than grammatical considerations such as the sequence of information and the presence of cue words that make problems easier or harder. In general, difficulties with word problems do not occur because students cannot read the words but because they cannot make sense of the mathematical relationships expressed by these words. Students' understanding of the different kinds of relationships in word problems is improved by solving and discussing problems.

A common classification scheme identifies four broad categories of addition and subtraction based on the type of action or relationship in the problems: join, separate, part-part-whole, and compare (Carpenter, Fennema, and Franke 1994; Carpenter, Fennema, Franke, Levi, and Empson 1999). Within these four broad categories, there are a total of eleven problem types. (Many of these problems use the same key words, even though their structure is different.) Often, textbooks include only one or two types of addition and subtraction problems. However, to become proficient and competent users of mathematics, students need to be able to solve all types of problems.

Join Problems and Separate Problems

Join problems and separate problems involve actions that increase or decrease a quantity, respectively. In both categories, the change occurs over time. There is an initial quantity that is changed either by adding something to it or by removing something from it, resulting in a larger or smaller final quantity. There are three subsets of each of these problem types, depending on which quantity the solver is being asked to determine: the result, the amount of change, or the initial quantity.

JOIN	EXAMPLE PROBLEM
Result Unknown	Laina had four dolls. She bought two more. How many dolls does she have now? $4 + 2 = \square$
Change Unknown	Laina had four dolls. She bought some more dolls. Now she has six dolls. How many dolls did Laina buy? $4 + \square = 6$
Initial Quantity Unknown	Laina had some dolls. She bought two more dolls. Now she has six dolls. How many dolls did Laina have before she bought some more? $\square + 2 = 6$

SEPARATE	EXAMPLE PROBLEM
Result Unknown	Rodney had ten cookies. He ate three cookies. How many cookies does Rodney have left? $10 - 3 = \square$
Change Unknown	Rodney had ten cookies. He ate some of the cookies. Now he has seven cookies left. How many cookies did Rodney eat? $10 - \square = 7$
Initial Quantity Unknown	Rodney had some cookies. He ate three cookies. Now he has seven cookies left. How many cookies did Rodney have to start with? $\square - 3 = 7$

In join problems and separate problems, the action of adding or subtracting is explicit. You can help students solve both types of problems by asking them to model these actions with objects. For example, using the join/amount-of-change-unknown problem above (*Laina had four dolls. She bought some more dolls. Now she has six dolls. How many dolls did Laina buy?*), students first can represent the four dolls using four blocks. Mimicking the action in the problem, students add some more blocks (dolls) until there are a total of six blocks. By then asking your students to explain how they determined the number of blocks to add, you help them form mental models of this type of situation as well. After solving many problems of this type, students eventually no longer need the physical model and can deal with the relationships symbolically.

Which quantity in a problem is unknown contributes to the overall difficulty of the problem. In general, when the result is unknown, students are more likely to be able to make sense of the relationships. Students are most familiar with result-unknown problems, because they encounter many similar problems in their everyday lives. These types of problems are also more heavily represented in textbooks.

Join problems and separate problems in which the initial quantity or the amount of change is unknown are more difficult for students. One reason is that these problems are often presented in language that suggests one action (e.g., separating) but require using the opposite action (e.g., joining) to find the answer. For example, take the following separate problem in which the initial quantity is unknown: *Rodney had some cookies. He ate three cookies. Now he has seven cookies left. How many cookies did Rodney have to start with?* There is a separating action in the problem, but a child can solve it using addition, or by counting on from seven: "Eight, nine, ten. Rodney started with ten cookies." Similarly, some join problems are solved by subtracting. It's important to notice whether a child is able to recognize the operation that matches the situation, can represent the number sentence or equation correctly, and then can think numerically to find the answer. It is useful for teachers to talk with students about each aspect of problem solving: *What is the problem describing? How can you write that down? How can you find the answer?*

Part-Part-Whole Problems

Part-part-whole problems do not use action verbs—action neither occurs nor is implied. Instead, relationships between a particular whole and its two separate parts are established. There are two types of part-part-whole problems. In one type, the sizes of both parts are given and the student is asked to find the size of the whole. In the other type, the size of one part and the size of the whole are provided and the student is asked to find the size of the other part.

PART-PART-WHOLE	EXAMPLE PROBLEM
Whole Unknown	Five boys and three girls are on the basketball team. How many children are on the basketball team? $5 + 3 = \square$
One Part Unknown	Eight children are on the basketball team. Five are boys and the rest are girls. How many girls are on the basketball team? $5 + \square = 8$

Part-part-whole problems involve a comparison of "parts" (subsets) with the "whole" (set). While the part-part-whole problems above could be modeled with manipulatives, the language in the problems does not suggest any action joining the "parts," or subsets. This static relationship between subsets is the subtle difference that distinguishes these problems from join problems involving action.

Compare Problems

Compare problems involve a comparison of two distinct, unconnected sets. Like part-part-whole problems, compare problems do not involve action. However, they differ from part-part-whole problems in that the relationship is not between sets and subsets but between two distinct sets. There are three types of compare problems, depending on which quantity is unknown: the difference (the quantity by which the larger set exceeds the smaller set), the quantity in the larger set, or the quantity in the smaller set. A relationship of *difference*, *more than*, or *less than* is found in compare problems.

COMPARE	EXAMPLE PROBLEM
Difference Unknown	Ahmed has two brothers. Christine has three brothers. Christine has how many more brothers than Ahmed? $3 - 2 = \square$ or $2 + \square = 3$
Larger Quantity Unknown	Ahmed has two brothers. Christine has one more brother than Ahmed. How many brothers does Christine have? $2 + 1 = \square$
Smaller Quantity Unknown	Christine has one more brother than Ahmed. Christine has three brothers. How many brothers does Ahmed have? $\square + 1 = 3$ or $3 - \square = 1$

Compare and part-part-whole problems exemplify that the operations of addition and subtraction are based on the relationships between two sets or between a set and its subsets. One reason to ask students to solve a variety of problem types is so that they will generalize the meaning of these operations beyond "actions" to relationships between sets.

Students' ability to solve the various problem categories is related to their ability to recognize the distinctions among them. Contexts and wording that indicate the actions or relationships in a problem can make a problem easier or more difficult. For example, consider these two problems:

There are five boys and eight hats. How many more hats than boys are there?

There are five boys and eight hats. If each boy puts on a hat, how many hats are left over?

Carpenter, Fennema, and Franke (1994, 10) found that the second problem is easier for students because the action is more explicit. The magnitude of the numbers in a problem also affects its level of difficulty. The following problems are both separate problems in which the change is unknown, but the second one is more difficult for young students because the numbers are larger:

Liz had twelve pennies. She gave some pennies to Caitlin. Now she has eight pennies. How many pennies did Liz give Caitlin?

Liz had 45 pennies. She gave some pennies to Caitlin. Now she has 28 pennies. How many pennies did Liz give Caitlin?

However, after students solve many separate/amount-of-change-unknown problems that involve small quantities, they are more likely to be able to answer similar problems with larger quantities.

Students' ability to translate the words in a problem to an operation that represents the relationships presented by the words takes time and many experiences. Teachers need to present all problem types throughout the school year so that students have the opportunity to develop meaning and fluency for word problems.

Activity

Classifying Addition and Subtraction Word Problems

Objective: identify join, separate, part-part-whole, and compare problems.

Before reading further, discuss with a colleague the four types of addition and subtraction problems. Next classify each of the following problems as join, separate, part-part-whole, or compare. Indicate which quantity is unknown and write a number sentence that represents the relationships expressed in each problem.

1. Carlton had three model cars. His father gave him four more. How many model cars does Carlton have now?
2. Juan has nine marbles. Mary has six marbles. How many more marbles does Juan have than Mary?
3. Janice has three stickers on her lunch box and four stickers on her book bag. How many stickers does she have in all?
4. Catherine had a bag of four gummy bears. Mike gave her some more. Now Catherine has seven gummy bears. How many gummy bears did Mike give her?
5. A third grader has seven textbooks. Four textbooks are in his desk. The rest of his textbooks are in his locker. How many textbooks are in his locker?
6. Vladimir had some baseball cards. Chris gave him 12 more. Now Vladimir has 49 baseball cards. How many baseball cards did Vladimir have before he received some from Chris?

7. Keisha had some crayons. She gave two crayons to Tanya. Now Keisha has nine crayons. How many crayons did Keisha have in the beginning?

8. Anthony had nine library books on his bookshelf. He returned six books to the library. How many books are left on his bookshelf?

9. There are nine board games in Joyce's room. Mariah has six fewer board games than Joyce. How many board games does Mariah have?

10. Eric weighed 200 pounds. During the summer, he lost some weight. Now he weighs 180 pounds. How many pounds did Eric lose?

11. Eli had some money. He gave his brother Johannes $5.50. Now Eli has $18.50 left. How much money did Eli have to begin with?

12. Graziella has four CDs. Fadia has eight more CDs than Graziella. How many CDs does Fadia have?

Things to Think About

Sometimes it's difficult to distinguish part-part-whole problems from join problems and separate problems. The main difference is that in part-part-whole problems the relationship between entities is static (as in Question 3 above), whereas the relationships in join problems or separate problems are always described using combining or separating action verbs. The different addition and subtraction problems are not equally easy (or difficult) for students. In general, students find result-unknown problems in the join and separate categories, whole-unknown problems in the part-part-whole category, and difference-unknown problems in the compare category easier than problems in the remaining categories. Furthermore, the types of quantities used in problems can make them easier or more difficult; crayons are easy to model and count, whereas pounds are a more abstract quantity to represent.

Some of the problems (1 and 3, 8 and 9) can be represented by the same number sentence. You might want to write a few number sentences and then make up different types of problems that fit each sentence. This is another way to extend your own understanding of the different types of problems.

Three of the problems in this activity (1, 4, and 6) are "join" problems. In number 1, the result is unknown ($3 + 4 = \square$), in number 4 the amount of change is unknown ($4 + \square = 7$), and in number 6 the initial quantity is unknown ($\square + 12 = 49$). There are four "separate" problems: 7, 8, 10, and 11. In number 8, the result is unknown ($9 - 6 = \square$); in number 10, the amount of change is unknown ($200 - \square = 180$); and in numbers 7 and 11, the initial quantity is unknown ($\square - 2 = 9$ and $\square - 5.50 = 18.50$). The two "part-part-whole" problems are 3 and 5. In number 3, the whole is unknown ($3 + 4 = \square$), and in number 5, one of the parts is unknown ($4 + \square = 7$). Finally, problems 2, 9, and 12 are "compare" problems. In number 2, the difference is unknown ($9 - 6 = \square$); in number 9, the smaller quantity is unknown ($9 - \square = 6$ or $\square + 6 = 9$); and in number 12, the larger quantity is unknown ($4 + 8 = \square$). ▲

2. Solution Strategies

Young children use informal knowledge and different types of strategies to solve word problems and perform computations (Carpenter, Fennema, and Franke 1994; Carpenter, Fennema, Franke, Levi, and Empson 1999). Some of the strategies that students use are based on the structure and semantics of the problem. Other strategies are related to students' growing sense of number and their understanding of mathematical properties and place value. In order to plan instruction that helps students develop increasingly sophisticated and efficient problem-solving strategies, it is important to recognize a variety of strategies and to understand how students' strategies develop.

Students tend to use three types of strategies when solving simple addition and subtraction word problems:

1. Strategies based on direct modeling with fingers or physical objects.
2. Strategies based on counting sequences.
3. Strategies based on number sense.

These strategies are hierarchical: students progress from modeling to counting to using number sense. However, this does not mean that students use only one strategy type for all problems; students apply different types of strategies to different types of problems. For example, when solving a separate word problem in which the amount of change is unknown, a student might use a modeling strategy. When solving a separate problem in which the result is unknown, the same student might use a counting strategy. And when solving a join problem involving numbers less than five in which the result is unknown, this student might use her knowledge of number facts, although she might revert to using less sophisticated strategies in join problems involving larger numbers.

Modeling Strategies

In modeling strategies, students use physical objects such as blocks, counters, and fingers to model the actions and/or relationships in a problem. They then count some or all of these objects to obtain an answer. Many young students use modeling strategies when they first start to solve addition and subtraction problems. Older students unfamiliar with a particular problem type often use a modeling strategy to make sense of the problem. There are five common modeling strategies: joining all, separating from, separating to, adding on, and matching.

Joining all. In this addition strategy, students use physical objects to represent each of the addends in a problem. The answer to the problem is found by joining the sets of objects and counting them all, starting with one. Sometimes students first join the sets and then count all the items, sometimes they count one set followed by the other set. Interestingly, students don't seem to differentiate whether or not they physically join the sets, as long as they have modeled each set.

> *Katie had two stickers. She bought five more stickers. How many stickers does Katie have now?*

Using objects or fingers, the student makes a set of 2 objects and a set of 5 objects. Then he counts the union of the two sets, starting with one.

Separating from. In this subtraction strategy, students use concrete objects to model the action of separating out the smaller quantity given in the problem. Usually the student counts the remaining objects to arrive at the answer.

> *There were seven boys playing tag. Two boys went home. How many boys were still playing?*

Using objects or fingers, the student makes a set of 7 objects. She removes 2 objects. The number of remaining objects is the answer.

Separating to. This subtraction strategy is similar to the separating-from strategy except that objects are removed from the larger set until the number of objects remaining is equal to the smaller number given in the problem. Counting the number of objects removed provides the answer. This strategy involves some trial and error in that a student has to keep checking to see whether the appropriate amount still remains. Students often use this strategy to solve separate problems in which the change is unknown.

> *There were 7 boys playing tag. Some went home. Now there are 2 boys playing tag. How many boys went home?*

The student counts out a set of 7 objects. Then he removes objects until only 2 remain. The number of objects removed is the answer.

Adding on. This strategy involves an addition action and is used by students to solve both addition and subtraction problems. A student sets out the number of objects equal to the smaller given number (an addend) and then adds objects one at a time until the new collection is equal to the larger given number. Counting the number of objects "added on" gives the answer. This strategy also involves some trial and error in that a student has to check regularly to see whether the larger number has been reached.

> *Liz had two apples. Lyman gave her some more. Now Liz has five apples. How many apples did Lyman give her?*

The student makes a set of 2 objects. Then she adds objects to the set one at a time until there is a total of 5 objects. She finds the answer by counting the number of objects added.

Matching. This concrete strategy is used by many students to solve comparison problems in which the difference is unknown. The student puts out two sets of objects, each set representing one of the given numbers. The sets are matched one to one. Counting the objects without matches gives the answer.

> *Tom has five brothers. Juan has two brothers. How many more brothers does Tom have than Juan?*

The student creates a sets of 5 objects and a set of 2 objects. He matches the objects in each set one to one and counts the number of unmatched objects.

Counting Strategies

Counting strategies are more advanced solution processes than modeling strategies, because they are more abstract and there is more flexibility in which one to choose. The shift from modeling to counting depends on the development of certain number concepts and counting skills. Students must understand the relationship between counting and the number of elements in a given mathematical set (*cardinality*), must be able to begin counting at any number, and must be able to count backward. For some situations, students must also be able to keep track of how many numbers they have counted and at the same time recognize when they have reached the appropriate number. Activities that focus on these counting skills and relationships will further students' ability to apply counting strategies to the solution of problems.

There are six common counting strategies: counting all, counting on from first, counting on from larger, counting down from, counting down to, and counting up from given (this list isn't exhaustive—don't be surprised if your students invent new ones!). In helping students use these strategies, it is important to realize that counting strategies are not mechanical techniques that students can simply memorize. Counting strategies are conceptually based and build directly on modeling strategies. Thus students need opportunities to connect modeling strategies with counting strategies. Many counting strategies have direct links to specific modeling strategies:

MODELING STRATEGIES	COUNTING STRATEGIES
Joining all	Counting all
Separating from	Counting down from
Separating to	Counting down to
Adding on	Counting up from given
Matching	None
None	Counting on from first
None	Counting on from larger

One way to help young students link strategies is to have them discuss how they got their solution. After students have presented their processes, teachers can highlight the similarities between two related strategies (e.g., separating from and counting down from). Furthermore, teachers can encourage the use of counting strategies and provide opportunities for students to practice them.

Counting all. This addition strategy is similar to the joining-all modeling strategy except that physical models or fingers are not used to represent the addends. As the name implies, students start the counting sequence with one and continue until the answer is reached. This strategy requires that students have a method of keeping track of the number of counting steps in order to know when to stop. Most students use their fingers to keep track of the number of counts. (Fingers here play a different role than in the joining-all modeling strategy; they are used to keep track of the number of steps rather than to model one of the addends.)

> *Katie had two stickers. She bought five more stickers. How many stickers does Katie have now?*

The student begins the counting sequence with 1 for 2 counts (1, 2) and then continues on for 5 more counts (3, 4, 5, 6, 7). The answer is the last term in the counting sequence.

Counting on from first. With this addition strategy, the student recognizes that it is not necessary to reconstruct the entire counting sequence and begins "counting on" from the first addend in the problem.

> *Katie had two stickers. She bought five more stickers. How many stickers does Katie have now?*

The student begins the counting sequence at 2 and continues on for 5 counts. The answer is the final number in the counting sequence.

Counting on from larger. This addition strategy is identical to the counting-on-from-first strategy except that counting begins from the larger of the two addends. This is a more sophisticated counting-on strategy, since implicit in its application is that the student understands that the order of the addends does not matter in addition problems.

> *Katie had two stickers. She bought five more stickers. How many stickers does Katie have now?*

The student begins the counting sequence at 5 and continues on for 2 counts. The answer is the final number in the counting sequence.

Counting down from. This subtraction strategy is the parallel counting strategy to the separating-from modeling strategy. In this strategy students initiate a backward counting sequence beginning at the given larger number. The counting sequence contains as many numbers as the given smaller number.

> *There were seven boys playing tag. Two boys went home. How many boys were still playing?*

The student begins a backward counting sequence at 7. She continues the sequence for 2 counts (i.e., 6, 5). The last number in the counting sequence (5) is the answer.

Counting down to. This subtraction counting strategy is parallel to the separating-to modeling strategy. Students use a backward counting sequence until the smaller number is reached. How many numbers there are in the counting sequence is the solution. Students often use their fingers to keep track of the counts, but they are not actually modeling the situation.

> *There were seven children playing tag. Some went home. Now there are two children playing tag. How many children went home?*

The student starts a backward counting sequence at 7 and continues until 2 is reached (i.e., 6, 5, 4, 3, 2). The answer is how many numbers there are in the counting sequence (5).

Counting up from given. This counting strategy is parallel to the adding-on modeling strategy. The student initiates a forward counting strategy from the smaller number given. The sequence ends with the larger number given. The student keeps track (often using his or her fingers) of how many numbers there are in sequence.

> *Liz had two apples. Lyman gave her some more. Now Liz has five apples. How many apples did Lyman give her?*

The student starts counting at 2 and continues until 5 is reached (i.e., 3, 4, 5). The answer is how many numbers there are in the sequence (3).

Activity

Matching Problems and Strategies

Objective: link problem types with strategies that students typically use in solving them.

Understanding the relationships within problems will help you link problem structure to students' solution strategies. Analyze each problem in Activity 1 in terms of which strategies could be used to model the actions or relationships in the problem. Indicate both a modeling strategy (with objects) and a counting strategy. Many problems can be solved using a number of different strategies or by using a strategy not presented here.

Things to Think About

Students' strategy choices are influenced by a number of factors. First, students are most likely to pick a solution strategy that matches the structure of a problem. Whether the strategy chosen is a modeling, counting, or number sense strategy depends in part on students' familiarity with the type of problem (can they make sense of which operation to use?) and on students' understanding of number and counting. When students have not made sense of the relationships in a problem and have not yet connected these relationships to specific operations, they are more likely to use a modeling strategy.

Problems are much more difficult if students do not have a process available to model the actions or relationships. For example, a compare problem in which the difference is unknown is difficult if students have never considered or seen a matching strategy. You can help students learn new strategies by creating specific problems for them to solve and then having them discuss their various solution strategies in pairs and as a whole class. New approaches and strategies are often introduced this way. While occasionally you may wish to model a solution strategy for students, it is important that students don't just observe the strategy but use and discuss it. Students also need many opportunities to apply new strategies. After a strategy has been introduced, you should assign problems that enable students to practice and refine the particular strategy.

Some strategies are not as widely used as others (counting down is not used as much as counting up from given, for example), and some students never use some of the strategies. In many cases, students don't even differentiate between strategies (some look at counting on and counting up from given as the same strategy). Likewise, as students mature, they often change which strategies they use (the matching strategy is abandoned after the early grades, for example).

Finally, remember that it is not necessary for students to label their solution strategies (e.g., counting on). But it is important for you to recognize the different types of strategies in order to choose future instructional activities that support students' developing proficiencies.

Here are the most likely ways to solve the problems in Activity 1:

1. Counting all; counting on from larger.
2. Matching; counting up from given.
3. Counting all; counting on from larger.
4. Adding on; counting up from given.
5. Separating from; counting down from.

6. Adding on; counting up.
7. Counting all; counting on from larger.
8. Separating from; counting down from.
9. Separating from; counting down from.
10. Separating to; counting down to.
11. Counting all; counting on from larger.
12. Separating from; counting down from. ▲

Number Sense Strategies

Students eventually replace modeling and counting strategies with number sense strategies. To do so they must (1) understand whether the relationships and actions in a problem require them to add or subtract, and (2) be able either to recall number facts or to use known number facts to derive new facts.

The relationship between counting and mental strategies is not clear. We do know that students' previous use of counting strategies helps them recall number facts. Certainly, the ability to move to this level of abstraction depends in part on being able to make sense of the relationships in many types of problems, and this means students must have solved many different kinds of problems.

Being able to use known number facts to derive new facts is linked to an understanding of part-whole relationships (not to be confused with the part-part-whole problem type described in Section 1). Quantities can be interpreted as comprising other numbers. For example, a set of eight objects can be represented using two or more parts such as 0 and 8; 1 and 7; 2, 2, and 4; eight 1s; and so on. Eight is the "whole," the numbers making up eight are the "parts." If students do not understand number in terms of part-whole relationships, they are not able to decompose wholes and recombine parts flexibly. For example, to find the answer to $6 + 8$, some students decompose 8 into two parts (6 and 2) and reinterpret the calculation as $6 + 6 + 2$. If they already know that $6 + 6 = 12$, they can use that information to determine that $6 + 8 = 14$. Some researchers believe that the most important conceptual achievement in the early grades occurs when students interpret number in terms of part-whole relationships. It must be emphasized that the use of part-whole reasoning to find the answers to basic facts is not limited to superior students.

Students' solutions involving part-whole relationships are often based on number facts that sum to 10. For example, a student might calculate $4 + 7$ like this: *three plus seven is ten, and four plus seven is just one more, so the answer is eleven.* This student knows that the number fact for $3 + 7$ is 10 and understands that 4 can be thought of as 3 and 1 even though that relationship is not explicitly stated. Doubles facts are also used by many students to derive new facts. For example, to solve $7 + 8$ a student might respond: *eight plus eight is sixteen, and seven plus eight is just one less than sixteen, so the answer is fifteen.*

Other factors that contribute to students' ability to use mental strategies based on number sense are their knowledge and understanding of addition and subtraction properties and relationships. Knowing about the commutative property, which states that the order of the addends (e.g., $9 + 4$ or $4 + 9$) does not affect the sum, lets students transpose a problem to an easier form. The inverse relationship between addition and subtraction can also help students find answers (e.g., knowing that $6 + 7 = 13$, it follows that $13 - 6 = 7$) or develop new strategies (e.g., counting up).

The time needed before students consistently use mental strategies to solve problems varies, but for some students it can take a number of years. Mathematical tasks that highlight part-whole relationships in general and that focus on doubling and numbers summing to ten in particular provide a foundation on which students can build. Likewise, instruction that highlights the relationship between addition and subtraction and enables students to reflect on properties also contributes to children's number and operation sense.

Activity

Observing How Students Solve Problems

Objective: use knowledge of problem types and solution strategies to understand students' thinking.

Write one or two problems that fit the classification scheme described in Section 1 and are appropriate for the students you teach. (You may want to begin with join problems in which the result is unknown and separate problems in which the amount of change is unknown.) In individual five-minute interviews, ask students to solve the problems. Record each student's solution strategy for each problem. When you have all your data, group students' solution strategies by type. How many students are using modeling, counting, or number sense strategies? How might you use this information to further students' understanding?

Things to Think About

When watching students solve problems, it isn't always easy to determine what strategy they are using, since they may be unable to articulate their thinking. You may have to ask probing questions or watch for overt behavior in order to hypothesize about students' thought processes. Furthermore, when a child uses his fingers, is he using a modeling strategy or a counting strategy? It's a modeling strategy if the fingers are used to show the quantities in the problem; it's a counting strategy if the fingers are used to keep track of how many numbers are in a counting sequence.

You may find that students use different strategies for join problems in which the result is unknown than they do for separate problems in which the amount of change is unknown. This may be partly because they haven't had much experience with the latter type of problem.

If students are using modeling strategies, you may wish to include mathematical tasks and sequences in your instruction that support the development of counting strategies. Providing students with many opportunities to practice counting forward and backward (especially starting in the middle of a sequence), identify patterns when counting (e.g., when we count by 100s, what changes with each increase? what doesn't change with each increase?), and connect a modeling strategy with a counting strategy will help. If students are using any of the counting strategies, you can focus on instruction that supports the use of more sophisticated methods. Activities that enable students to grapple with part-whole relationships; that emphasize number combination strategies such as doubles, doubles plus one, and doubles minus one (e.g., 5 + 6 can be thought of as 5 + 5 + 1 or as 6 + 6 − 1); and that have students exploring the relationship between addition and subtraction will all contribute to your goal. ▲

3. Addition and Subtraction of Signed Numbers

Addition and subtraction of negative and positive numbers, also known as signed numbers, are most often introduced in middle school. These are complex topics for a number of reasons. First, there are relatively few situations that are represented using negative values: temperature, wind-chill, position (elevator), debt (owing money), and loss (sports yardage, game points) are the best known. Second, while these situations lend themselves to using negative numbers to represent an amount the opposite of something ($^-$$10 represents a debt of $10, the opposite of having money) or a location relative to zero (the temperature is $^-7°$, 7 below zero), they also have mathematical limitations when it comes to using them to make sense of operations such as modeling the subtraction of a negative number. As a result, instruction on the addition and subtraction of signed numbers is often devoid of context.

There are a number of ways that students can come to understand addition and subtraction of signed numbers. One way deals with negative numbers as quantities that mirror the behavior of ordinary positive quantities but that can be "canceled out" in relation to them. The "red and black chip" model uses this interpretation. Imagine black chips representing positive numbers (shown with a $+$) and red chips representing negative numbers (shown with a $-$). One positive chip and one negative chip cancel, or "zero," each other out; the numbers they represent sum to zero. Likewise, three positive chips and three negative chips when combined equal zero, but three positive chips and four negative chips are equivalent to $^-1$.

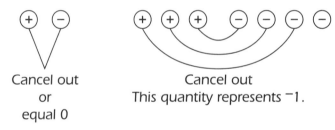

Cancel out
or
equal 0

Cancel out
This quantity represents $^-1$.

Addition using this chip model involves combining chips that represent positive and negative quantities and then "zeroing out" any chips that add to 0. The chips that are left represent the sum. This red/black chip model makes use of the relationship between additive inverses ($^+1 + {}^-1 = 0$) to justify what we refer to as zeroing or canceling. Notice that when modeling $^-2 + {}^-3$, there are no positive chips and thus no way to form a sum of 0, which leaves a sum of $^-5$. When adding $^-1 + 3$, it is possible to combine chips to add to 0 ($^-1 + {}^+1$), leaving two positive chips or a sum of $^+2$.

$^-2 + {}^-3 = {}^-5$

Cancel
$^-1 + 3 = 2$

Subtraction of integers is generally problematic for children and adults. Many of us use rules that make little sense and are easily forgotten. How does this model work when subtracting? First, the separate meaning of subtraction is used and chips are physically removed. So when modeling $^-5 - ^-1$, five red chips are shown and one red chip is removed, leaving four red chips, or $^-4$, as the answer.

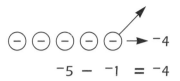

$$^-5 - ^-1 = ^-4$$

But what do we do when the amount we are to take away is not represented ($^-2 - ^+1$)? Here is an example of where the concept of the additive identity element (e.g., the additive identity is 0, since any number plus 0 is the number: $\square + 0 = \square$) is used to form an equivalent expression. In this problem we are starting with 2 red chips and we do not have any black chips to remove. We want to have a quantity that is equivalent to $^-2$ but that somehow has black chips represented. We know that 1 red and 1 black chip cancel each other out ($^-1 + ^+1 = 0$), and since these values are opposites, they sum to 0. By adding 1 red and 1 black chip (which represents a quantity of 0) to the 2 red chips, we have not changed the value of the initial quantity ($^-2$) but we have represented it differently (3 red chips and 1 black chip is equivalent to 2 red chips).

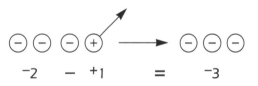

Each set of chips represents the quantity $^-2$.

Now since there is a positive black chip that can be removed, we can show that -2 subtract $^+1$ is $^-3$.

$$^-2 - ^+1 = ^-3$$

Activity

Using a Chip Model to Add and Subtract Integers

Objective: understand how to model addition and subtraction of integers using the red/black chip model.

Materials: red and black chips or slips of paper with + and − signs.

Use the chip model to add and subtract. What mathematical properties (see Chapter 2) are used to find sums and differences? Explain why the answers make sense.

$^+2 + ^-4 = $ _____	$^+13 + ^-5 = $ _____	$^-3 + ^-9 = $ _____
$^-4 - ^-7 = $ _____	$^+2 - ^+5 = $ _____	$^+1 - ^+6 = $ _____
$^-5 + ^+9 = $ _____	$^+4 - ^-7 = $ _____	$1 - ^+2 = $ _____
$0 - ^-2 = $ _____	$^-16 + ^-5 = $ _____	$^-9 + ^+9 = $ _____

Things to Think About

Did this model for addition and subtraction of signed numbers help you generalize and explain your results? Let's examine addition first. When adding two numbers with the same sign, we are not able to cancel out any chips. That is, we can't use the additive inverse property since there is only one type of chip. Students often state that if the sign of the addends is the same ($^-3 + {}^-9$), simply combine the addends as if they were positive numbers. Another way of saying this is to add the absolute values of the addends ($|^-3| + |^-9| = 12$) and the sum has the same sign as the addends ($^-12$).

When the addends have different signs ($^+2 + {}^-4$ and $^+13 + {}^-5$), we find that we use the idea of canceling red and black chips to form chip combinations that equal zero (additive inverse property: $^+1 + {}^-1 = 0$). We form as many red/black pairs as we can and count the leftovers to find the sum. If we aren't using chips, most adults find the difference between the absolute values ($4 - 2 = 2$ and $13 - 5 = 8$). The sign of the answer is the same as the addend with the greatest absolute value. Notice in $^+2 + {}^-4$ that $|^-4| > |2|$; the answer will have a negative sign. But in $^+13 + {}^-5$ the answer will have a positive sign since $|13| > |^-5|$. Why? Use the chips to help you think about what is happening with the model. For example, in $^+2 + {}^-4$ when we cancel 2 black chips and 2 red chips ($^+2 + {}^-2 = 0$) there are still red chips left over! In fact, there are 2 red chips left ($4 - 2 = 2$), so the answer is $^-2$ ($^+2 + {}^-4 = {}^-2$).

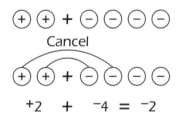

How did you model the subtraction problems? Let's take the example of a positive number minus a positive number ($^+2 - {}^+5$). Starting with 2 black chips we want to remove 5 black chips but there are not enough. So we represent $^+2$ another way. Three black and 3 red chips cancel each other out and are equivalent to zero. When we add 3 black and 3 red chips to the 2 black chips ($^+2 + ({}^+3 + {}^-3)$), we are adding zero to $^+2$, which enables us to then represent this amount with 5 black chips and 3 red chips. Using this equivalent expression ($^+2 = {}^+5 + {}^-3$), we are able to physically remove $^+5$ from ($^+5 + {}^-3$) to get $^-3$.

We use these same fundamental ideas when subtracting all integers using the chip model. For example, in $^-1 - {}^+2$ we start with 1 red chip. In order to create an equivalent expression to $^-1$, we add chips that equal zero (2 black and 2 red, or $^+2 + {}^-2$), and then remove the 2 black chips.

$$\ominus = \ominus \quad \underbrace{\oplus \ominus} \quad \underbrace{\oplus \ominus}$$
$$^-1 = {}^-1 + 0 + 0 = {}^-3 + {}^+2$$

$$\ominus \ominus \ominus \underbrace{\oplus \oplus}\nearrow$$
$$^-1 - {}^+2 = {}^-3$$

The difference is $^-3$ ($^-1 - {}^+2 = {}^-3$). Notice how we use the additive inverse property ($a + (^-a) = 0$) and the identity element for addition ($a + 0 = a$) to form equivalent expressions when subtracting signed numbers. The answers to the problems are:

$^+2 + {}^-4 = {}^-2$	$^+13 + {}^-5 = 8$	$^-3 + {}^-9 = {}^-12$
$^-4 - {}^-7 = 3$	$^+2 - {}^+5 = {}^-3$	$^+1 - {}^+6 = {}^-5$
$^-5 + {}^+9 = 4$	$^+4 - {}^-7 = 11$	$1 - {}^+2 = {}^-3$
$0 - {}^-2 = 2$	$^-16 + {}^-5 = {}^-21$	$^-9 + {}^+9 = 0$

While the chip model helps us make sense of the computations many of us learned by rote as students, there are problems with it. Simply by representing negative values with objects, it is easy to see how students might erroneously think that $^-7$ is greater than $^-1$. There are 7 red chips compared with 1 red chip; these physical representations of the magnitude component of negative numbers give the wrong message about size! This model also does not take into account both features of signed numbers, magnitude and direction. As teachers what do we do? If you use the chips model in instruction, you most likely will want to have students discuss the dilemma of $^-7$ being less than $^-1$ even though with $^-7$ there are more red chips. You might also want to introduce a more formal definition of negative numbers using a number line (see Chapter 1) that includes direction and magnitude. ▲

The operations of addition and subtraction can also be modeled as movements on the number line. Adding signed numbers is like moving forward and backward on a football field. If a team gains 3 yards on one play and then loses 5 yards on the next play, the net result is a 2-yard loss, $3 + (^-5) = {}^-2$. On the number line, start at 0 and move in the direction of the positive numbers, 3 units. Next, to show that you are adding what amounts to a loss of 5 yards $^-5$, move in the direction of the negative numbers, 5 spaces to the left. You end up at $^-2$, so $3 + {}^-5 = {}^-2$. Notice that we use the concept of magnitude to determine how many units to move and the concept of direction to help us decide in which direction to move.

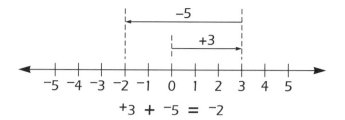

$$^+3 + {}^-5 = {}^-2$$

When using the number line to model subtraction of signed numbers, it helps to first recognize that the minus sign ($-$) can be interpreted in three ways: (1) as an operation sign for subtraction; (2) as a sign to indicate a negative number; and (3) as an operation sign meaning "the opposite of." Thus, -4 can be interpreted as "subtract positive 4 from some number," "the negative number located four units to the left of 0," and "the opposite of positive 4." The idea of using the minus sign to indicate movement in the "opposite" direction is especially useful when modeling subtraction of negative numbers on a number line. For example, consider $3 - 7$. Start at 0 and move to the right 3 units since 3 is a positive number.

If we were adding positive 7, we would move 7 additional spaces to the right toward the positives. But since we are subtracting, use the idea of "opposites" and move in the opposite direction from positive 3 toward the negative numbers.

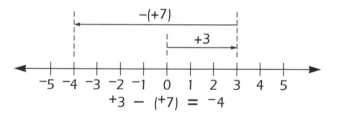

$$^+3 - ({}^+7) = {}^-4$$

We end at $^-4$, so $3 - 7 = {}^-4$.

Here is another example: $3 - {}^-7$. Again start at 0 and move to the right 3 units. If you were adding $^-7$ we would go 7 spaces to the left toward the negative numbers, but because we are subtracting $^-7$, we move in the opposite direction, or right toward the positive numbers.

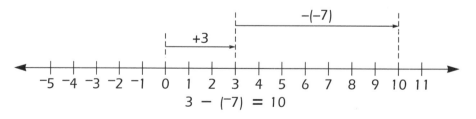

$$3 - ({}^-7) = 10$$

This time we end at 10, so $3 - {}^-7 = 10$.

Instead of using rules to compute with signed numbers, try to reason out the answer using the concept of movement and direction. When adding positive numbers we move to the right, and when adding negative numbers we move to the left. When subtracting, we move in the opposite direction from that indicated by the number: subtracting a positive number means we move to the left toward the negatives, and subtracting a negative number means we move to the right toward the positive numbers!

Activity

Using a Number Line to Add and Subtract Integers

Objective: become familiar with how to model addition and subtraction of signed numbers on a number line.

Draw a number line to illustrate the following addition and subtraction problems.

1. ⁻4 + 3
2. ⁻5 + ⁻3
3. ⁻1 − ⁻4
4. ⁻1 − 4

How did you interpret the minus sign? Did this interpretation help you in using the number line to model these operations?

Things to Think About

When we add on the number line, we use the concept of direction. Namely if an addend is positive we move that number of intervals or units to the right in the direction of the positive numbers. And if the addend is negative we move that specified number of units left in the direction of the negative numbers. The diagrams below illustrate the number lines for the addition problems.

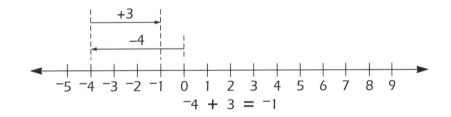

$$⁻4 + 3 = ⁻1$$

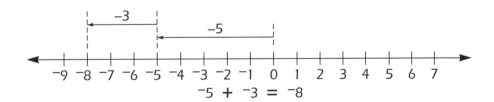

$$⁻5 + ⁻3 = ⁻8$$

One way to make sense of subtraction on the number line is to realize that the minus symbol has more than one meaning and to use the opposite interpretation. Thus, in the problem ⁻1 − ⁻4, we start by drawing an arrow from 0 to ⁻1. This arrow goes left as the negative sign in $^-1$ indicates this direction. From $^-1$, draw an arrow to represent moving the opposite of $^-4$. The opposite of negative 4 is positive 4 so we draw an arrow to the right for 4 intervals or spaces. We end at 3 so $^-1 - {^-4} = 3$. Notice how taking the opposite of $^-4$, that is, $- {^-4}$, is equivalent to adding 4.

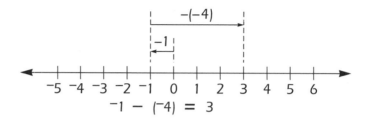

The final problem, $^-1 - 4$, is solved using the same reasoning. Start at 0 and move to the left to $^-1$. The opposite of 4 (notice this is a positive 4) is $^-4$ so we move toward the negatives 4 intervals. The answer to $^-1 - 4$ is $^-5$.

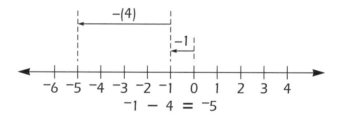

Many students need to model addition and subtraction of positive numbers on the number line before working with signed numbers. This preliminary work sets the stage for thinking of subtraction as the "opposite" of addition. For example, to perform $7 - 3$ on the number line, we first move from 0 to 7 (to the right, since 7 is positive). Then instead of moving 3 more units to the right (since 3 is a positive number) we go in the opposite direction, or left, because subtraction is the opposite of addition. It is not too great a leap to $7 - {^-3}$: instead of moving from 7 left toward the negative numbers (because it is negative 3), go in the opposite direction, or right, 3 units toward the positive numbers. Many students find that by focusing on the direction and magnitude of numbers, they are able to generate the rules for operating on both positive and negative numbers. ▲

Teaching Addition and Subtraction

Students' understanding of addition and subtraction forms the foundation for more advanced work with these operations in upper elementary and middle school. As they progress through the grades, students learn a variety of methods to perform multidigit computations quickly and easily. They learn to solve problems that involve multiple steps, rational numbers, integers, and unnecessary data. Many of their initial strategies are abandoned as their ability to deal with symbols and generalizations increases. However, students often revert to using simpler strategies when they are presented with problems that contain larger numbers, decimals, or fractions.

Questions for Discussion

1. Examine a textbook series to see which types of addition and subtraction word problems are included. Assuming you were using the series to teach children, what insights did this chapter provide in how to use the textbook series effectively?

2. Students often use different strategies to solve similar problems. Create three "separate" problems with three different unknowns and describe strategies that might be used to solve each.

3. If a child is predominantly using modeling strategies to solve simple addition and subtraction problems, what might you do as a teacher to help the child start using some counting strategies?

4. Which of the addition and subtraction problem counting strategies do you find confusing? Explain these strategies in your own words using different examples.

5. Explain, using both a chips model and a number line model, how it is possible to have a positive difference when subtracting two negative numbers—e.g., $^-2 - {}^-7$.

4

Multiplication and Division

Multiplication and division have always been important topics in elementary school mathematics. However, in the past, instruction has focused primarily on helping students develop procedural competency with basic facts and paper-and-pencil algorithms. This procedural competency is an important goal (and suggestions for helping students become competent with multiplication and division facts and algorithms are included in Chapter 2), but recent research makes it clear that students also need to develop deep conceptual knowledge of multiplication and division in order to apply and use these operations to solve problems. The National Council of Teachers of Mathematics recommends that students in grades 3 through 5 should "develop a stronger understanding of the various meanings of multiplication and division, encounter a wide range of representations and problem situations that embody them, learn about the properties of these operations, and gradually develop fluency in solving multiplication and division problems" (NCTM 2000, 149). In middle school, students solve a wide range of problems using these operations and learn to multiply and divide signed numbers in preparation for algebra.

1. Types of Multiplication and Division Problems

Think back to the childhood instruction you received in multiplication and division. The focus may have been on performing multidigit calculations accurately. Students' ability to "do" multiplication and division calculations—to apply step-by-step procedures that result in correct solutions—implies that they have procedural knowledge of these operations. However, simply being able to perform calculations does not necessarily mean that students understand these operations. Conceptual knowledge is based on understanding relationships—in this case, relationships that represent multiplication and division. These relationships can be expressed using pictures, graphs, objects, symbols, and words. For example, when students encounter a word problem and are asked to translate the relationship into symbols, their conceptual knowledge of the situation helps them do so. Since everyday mathematics is almost always applied in the context of words, not symbols, it is important for students to understand the relationships inherent in multiplication and division problems. In addition, students' understanding of these relationships helps them generalize their knowledge and apply it to related concepts in algebra.

Likewise, the language of multiplication and division situations must be understood. In a multiplication equation such as $3 \times 2 = 6$, the 3 and the 2 are *factors*. The 6, which is the solution to this equation, is the *product*. In division we sometimes convert the operation to a multiplication equation ($2 \times \square = 6$, if we are dividing 6 by 2) and refer to the unknown as the missing factor, but more often we use separate labels. In the equation $6 \div 2 = 3$, for example, the 6 is the *dividend*, the 2 is the *divisor*, and the 3 (the answer) is the *quotient*. In some division expressions ($7 \div 2$, for example), there is also a remainder, which can be expressed in a number of different ways: as a whole number, a decimal, or a fraction. In the example given, the quotient can be represented as 3 remainder 1, 3.5, or $3\frac{1}{2}$. The relationship between these terms can be expressed generically this way: *factor* $\times$ *factor* = *product* and *dividend* $\div$ *divisor* = *quotient* + *remainder*. Middle school student who have difficulty rewriting division sentences with and without remainders as multiplication sentences may not be secure in their understanding of the inverse relationship between the two operations. For example, the sentence $7 \div 2 = 3$ r 1 is related to $(2 \times 3) + 1 = 7$, and $7 \div 2 = 3\frac{1}{2}$ is related to $2 \times 3\frac{1}{2} = 7$.

Researchers have defined and classified multiplication and division problems in a number of different ways based on their semantic structure—that is, how the relationships are expressed in words. The semantic structure of problems differs with regard to the nature of the quantities used and the quantity that serves as the unknown. The semantic structure of multiplication and division problems has two broad categories: asymmetrical and symmetrical problems. In asymmetrical situations, the quantities play different roles. For example, in the problem *There are 15 cars in the parking lot and each car has 4 tires. How many tires are there in all?*, 4 represents the amount in one group, 15 represents the number of groups and also acts as the multiplier. These roles are not interchangeable. If you switch the numbers (4 cars with 15 tires each) you have a different problem: the number of things in one group is 15 and the number of groups is now 4. (In an asymmetrical problem the answer is the same regardless of the role of the quantities, but that is not obvious to children.) In symmetrical situations, on the other hand, the quantities have interchangeable roles. In symmetrical multiplication problems it is not clear which factor is the multiplier. For example, in the problem *What is the area of a room that is 10 feet by 12 feet?*, either number can be the width or the length and either can be used as the multiplier.

There are three subcategories of asymmetrical problems: (1) equal grouping, (2) rate, and (3) multiplicative compare. There are two subcategories of symmetrical problems: (1) rectangular array and (2) Cartesian product. Each subcategory includes both multiplication and division problems, depending on which quantity is unknown. Students need to work with all types of multiplication and division problems in order to make sense of the relationships inherent to each type and to extend their understanding of these operations beyond mere procedures. As a teacher you need to guide students in discerning the role of the quantities within problems.

Equal Grouping Problems

Usually when we think of the operation of multiplication, an equal grouping problem comes to mind. In equal grouping multiplication problems, one factor tells the number of things in a group and the other factor tells the number of equal-size groups. This second factor acts as a multiplier. For example, in the problem *There are four basketball teams at the tournament and each team has five players. How many players are at the tournament?*, the factor 5 indicates the number of players in one group and the factor 4 indicates the number of equal groups of 5. In this case, the 4 acts as the multiplier. Equal grouping problems are easy to model with pictures or by using repeated addition:

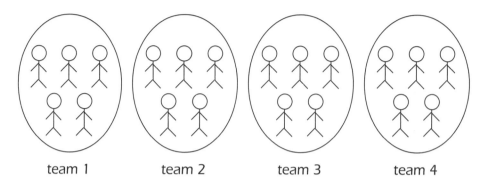

team 1   team 2   team 3   team 4

Two situations result in a problem's being classified as an equal grouping division problem—either the number of groups is unknown or the number in each group is unknown. These two types of division situations are referred to as *quotitive division* and *partitive division*, respectively.

Here is a partitive division problem:

Twenty-four apples need to be placed into eight paper sacks. How many apples will you put in each sack if you want the same number in each sack?

The action involved in partitive division problems is one of dividing or partitioning a set into a predetermined number of groups. If students model this situation, 24 objects are evenly distributed into 8 different paper sacks or groups.

When teaching division, teachers often choose partitive division examples to highlight equal sharing. For example, students are instructed to divide a set number of counters into four equal groups by distributing the counters one at a time into four piles:

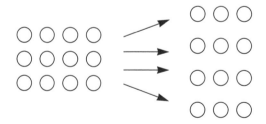

Yet if partitive division problems are used exclusively in instruction, students often have difficulty making sense of quotitive division problems. Their mental model of what division is all about does not include this other meaning.

In quotitive division problems (sometimes referred to as *repeated subtraction* problems) the number of objects in each group is known, but the number of groups is unknown. For example: *I have 24 apples. How many paper sacks will I be able to fill if I put*

3 apples into each sack? The action involved in quotitive division is one of subtracting out predetermined amounts. If asked to model this problem, students usually repeatedly subtract 3 objects from a group of 24 objects and then count the number of groups of 3 they removed (i.e., 8). (In partitive division, on the other hand, they "divide" the 24 objects into 3 groups.)

The standard long division algorithm uses the quotitive interpretation of division: the divisor represents the number in one group, and this amount is repeatedly subtracted from the dividend. The number of multiples (or groups) of the divisor that are subtracted from the dividend is the answer. Students benefit from exposure to both types of division examples so that they internalize that two actions, subtracting and partitioning, are used to find quotients.

Rate Problems

Rate problems involve a rate—a special type of ratio in which two different quantities or things are compared. Common rates are miles per gallon, wages per hour, and points per game. Rates are frequently expressed as unit rates—that is, one of the quantities in the ratio is given as a unit (e.g., price per single pound or miles per single hour). In rate problems, one number identifies the unit rate and the other tells the number of sets and acts as the multiplier. For instance, in the problem *Concert tickets cost seven dollars each. How much will it cost for a family of four to attend the concert?*, the unit rate is seven dollars per single ticket (seven to one) and the multiplier is four. Rate problems can also be expressed as division situations. Here is a partitive division rate problem (size of one group is unknown): *On the Hollingers' trip to New York City, they drove 400 miles and used 12 gallons of gasoline. How many miles per gallon did they average?* Quotitive division problems (number of equal groups is unknown) are also common in this category: *Jasmine spent $108 on some new CDs. Each CD cost $18. How many did she buy?*

Many students have had little experience with rates other than prices. As a result, they often are unsure of how to approach, interpret, and solve these types of problems. One way to help students understand rate multiplication problems is to have them calculate a unit rate (e.g., the number of feet they can walk or jog in one minute, the number of words they can read or write in one minute) and then apply this unit rate to various unit groupings (if I can read 45 words in one minute, I can read 90 words in two minutes, 135 words in three minutes, . . .). Through experiences, students learn which rates are extendable (the proportional relationship can be applied to all cases: if one bag of sugar costs $2.59, we can predict the cost of 5 or 12 or 80 bags) and which rates are limited (the proportional relationship does not extend beyond a certain domain: if you can run 1 mile in 4 minutes, how long will it take to run a marathon [26 miles]?). Especially difficult for young students are rates involving speed and distance. Not only are the ideas somewhat hard to grasp, but we refer to these two concepts in a number of different ways—by using a rate (miles per hour or miles per gallon) or by using words and phrases such as *speed, distance, how fast,* and *how far.*

Multiplicative Compare Problems

The third type of asymmetrical problem is multiplicative compare, also called a *scalar problem.* Here, one number identifies the quantity in one group or set while the other number is the comparison factor. For example, in the problem *Catherine read twelve books. Elizabeth read four times as many. How many books did Elizabeth read?*, the number 12 tells us the amount in a group and the number 4 tells us how many of these groups are needed. In multiplicative compare division problems, either the amount in each group or the comparison factor is missing. The following problems are multiplicative compare division problems:

> *Elizabeth read 48 books during summer vacation. This is four times as many as Catherine. How many books did Catherine read during summer vacation?*

> *Elizabeth read 48 books during summer vacation. Catherine read 12 books during summer vacation. How many times greater is the number of books Elizabeth read compared with the number of books Catherine read?*

The relational language in multiplicative compare problems (e.g., *times as many, times greater*) is difficult for all students, especially so for those for whom English is a second language. Students make sense of both the language and the relationships the language implies by discussing and modeling these problems. Comparing and contrasting the language of additive relationships (*more than, less than*) with that of multiplicative relationships (*times more than, times as many*) may also be helpful to students. Despite the complex nature of these problems, the consensus among researchers is that early experience with multiplication and division should involve problems of this type.

Rectangular Array Problems

The rectangular array problem, a subcategory of symmetrical problem commonly known as an area problem, is often used to introduce the idea of multiplication. Students are presented with an array (e.g., three by four) and asked to label the two sides of the array and determine the total number of square units in the array:

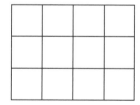

In rectangular array problems the role of the factors is interchangeable. For instance, when finding the area of the array above, neither the three nor the four is clearly the multiplier.

Cartesian Product Problems

The other subcategory of symmetrical problems, known as Cartesian product problems, involves two sets and the pairing of elements between the sets. These problems entail a number of combinations. For example: *Pete's Deli stocks four types of cold cuts and two types of cheese. How many different sandwiches consisting of one type of meat and one type of cheese are possible?* In these problems, like the rectangular array problems, neither of the two factors is clearly the multiplier.

Students tend to use tree diagrams to solve Cartesian product problems, in order to help them find all the combinations. For example, for the problem above, a student might use a diagram like this:

Meats	Cheese	Sandwich Combinations
turkey	swiss	turkey swiss
turkey	cheddar	turkey cheddar
ham	swiss	ham swiss
ham	cheddar	ham cheddar
bologna	swiss	bologna swiss
bologna	cheddar	bologna cheddar
roast beef	swiss	roast beef swiss
roast beef	cheddar	roast beef cheddar

However, this diagram doesn't highlight how multiplication can be used to determine the number of combinations. Teachers often have to point out the relationship between the number of objects to be combined (4 and 2) and the final number of combinations ($4 \times 2 = 8$).

Another way to solve Cartesian product problems is to construct a rectangular array like the one below. The number of columns (4) and the number of rows (2) are the factors in the problem.

	Ham	Turkey	Salami	Roast Beef
Swiss	Swiss/Ham	Swiss/Turkey	Swiss/Salami	Swiss/RB
Cheddar	Cheddar/Ham	Cheddar/Turkey	Cheddar/Salami	Cheddar/RB

This representation shows how finding the number of combinations of 4 luncheon meats and 2 cheeses is similar to finding the area of a rectangle that is 4 units by 2 units.

Both rectangular array and Cartesian product problems have related division problems called *missing factor division problems*. For example: *Susan has 24 different outfits consisting of a blouse and a pair of pants. She has four pairs of pants. How many blouses does she own?*

Although this problem can be solved by dividing 24 by 4, the relationship can also be expressed as $4 \times \square = 24$. Many students convert combination division problems to the inverse operation of multiplication, hence the name *missing factor*.

The diagram below shows how the different multiplication and division problems are related:

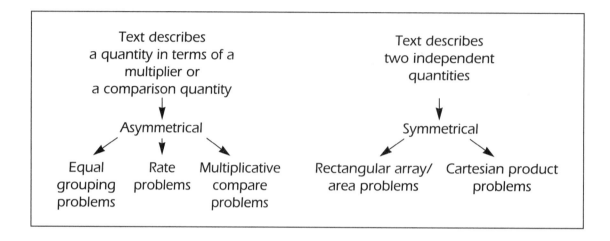

All the problem types should be used with students in order to help them extend their understanding of multiplication and division. Although it isn't essential to make the categories explicit for students or for them to learn the labels, categorizing problems can promote memory and understanding. Teachers should therefore be able to identify the different problem types and make them part of their instruction.

Activity

Identifying and Classifying Problems

Objective: differentiate among the different types of multiplication and division word problems based on the role of the factors within the problems.

Determine whether the following problems are asymmetrical or symmetrical. Then decide on the category in which the problem belongs (equal grouping, rate, multiplicative compare, rectangular array, or Cartesian product). Finally identify whether each problem is a multiplication or a division problem. (For the equal grouping division problems, also decide if the problem might be modeled using partitioning or repeated subtraction.)

1. Five children are planning to share a bag of 53 pieces of bubble gum. How many will each get?
2. Pies cost $7.50 each. Paula bought 5 pies. How much did they cost in all?
3. Peter bicycled 36 miles in 3 hours. How fast did Peter bike?

4. A restaurant offers 5 appetizers and 7 main courses. How many different meals can be ordered if a meal consists of one appetizer and one main course?

5. This year Mark saved $420. Last year he saved $60. How many times as much money did he save this year than last year?

6. This year Maddie saved 4 times as many dollars as she saved last year. Last year she saved $18. How many dollars has she saved this year?

7. Each jar holds 8 ounces of liquid. If there are 46 ounces of water in a pitcher, how many jars are needed to hold the liquid?

8. Leroy has a 1,440-square-inch piece of fabric that is 60 inches wide. How long is the fabric?

9. Sam Slick is really excited about his new clothing purchases. He bought 4 pairs of pants and a number of jackets, and they all can be mixed and matched. Sam can wear a different outfit consisting of jacket and pants 12 days in a row. How many jackets did he buy?

10. Liana walked 12 miles at a rate of 4 miles per hour. How many hours did it take Liana to walk the 12 miles?

11. Maria earned $24. She earned 4 times as much as Jill. How much did Jill earn?

12. The foundation of the house measures 70 feet by 25 feet. What is the square footage of the ground floor of the house?

Things to Think About

How did you proceed in classifying problems? Many adults first sort the problems into two groups, either multiplication problems or division problems, and then identify the subcategories. Students usually have a difficult time sorting problems, since it requires a deep understanding of problem structure. This understanding develops gradually over time after extensive involvement with problems. How do you think students might react to Problem 3? It is a rate problem, and the question asks how fast Peter biked. Many students do not realize that miles per hour and speed (how fast) represent the same idea and are confused by this problem. Discussion is one way to address this discrepancy. ▲

Are you surprised by the variety of multiplication and division problems that students have to be able to solve? Being able to make sense of and solve multiplication and division word problems is one aspect of understanding these operations. Research suggests that children in the elementary grades need experiences with a variety of asymmetrical and symmetrical problems. Otherwise, students' mental models of what constitutes multiplication and division may be seriously compromised. While it is not essential for students to identify a problem as asymmetrical or symmetrical, it may help them to be able to classify it as a multiplicative compare or an area problem. And it is important for students to consider the role of the quantities in these problems. Furthermore, in order to understand the relationships within these problems, students need to model situations and discuss the relationships between the quantities. They need to become comfortable determining different types of "unknowns." Traditional instruction rarely addresses the different features of problems and in some cases only includes examples from the equal grouping category. Instruction must include problems from all categories in order to challenge and expand students' existing mental models of multiplication and division.

2. Understanding Multiplication and Division

Multiplication and division are the visible part of an "enormous conceptual iceberg" (Vergnaud 1994, 46) that also includes ratio, rate, rational number, linear function, dimensional analysis, and vector space. A variety of phrases and words are used to describe multiplication and division situations. Knowledge that includes multiplication and division relationships is sometimes referred to as *multiplicative knowledge*. When we identify, understand, and use relationships between quantities that are based on multiplication or division, we are applying *multiplicative reasoning*.

Students' understanding of multiplication and division develops slowly—generally between grades 2 and 5. Understanding involves both conceptual and procedural knowledge—students must be able to identify multiplicative situations and be able to apply knowledge of multiplication and division facts and algorithms in finding a solution. How do children progress in their application of multiplicative reasoning?

In the early grades, students make sense of and solve simple multiplication and division problems without realizing that they are dealing with multiplicative situations. They tend to use additive solution strategies such as counting and repeated addition/subtraction. For example, to solve the problem *Karen bought four books at $10.00 apiece. How much did they cost altogether?*, a student might add four 10s and represent the problem symbolically as $10 + 10 + 10 + 10$ rather than as 4×10. Researchers such as Fischbein, Deri, Nello, and Marino (1985) suggest that additive reasoning, which is based on joining and separating, is intuitive—it develops naturally through encounters with many situations in one's environment (see Chapters 3 and 8). Schooling builds on students' intuitive understanding of addition and subtraction by focusing on additive situations in the early grades and then introducing situations that can be addressed through multiplicative reasoning in the later grades. In most cases, students require instruction to help them understand multiplicative relationships. Yet over time students develop an understanding of multiplicative situations and are able to determine whether to apply additive or multiplicative reasoning to solve specific problems (or to realize, as in the example above, that both can be used).

As students become better able to identify and make sense of multiplicative situations, they tend to start applying more sophisticated solution strategies. The progression of solution strategies from direct counting to repeated addition/subtraction to multiplicative operations is neither linear nor clear-cut. The strategies students employ depend on the size of the numbers in the problem, the semantic structure or subcategory of the problem, and the quantity that is unknown. Furthermore, the progression from additive strategies (counting and repeated addition/subtraction) to the use of multiplicative strategies requires several major cognitive shifts in students' thinking.

To think multiplicatively, students must be able to consider numbers as units in a different way from when they are simply adding or subtracting. They must consider units of one and they must also consider units of more than one—composite units. For example, the number 6 in an additive situation can represent 6 discrete objects that can be counted and operated on, yet in a multiplicative situation the 6 might represent a unit of 6 (or a group of 6). In our place value system, multiplicative reasoning is applied to counting groups of 100, 10, and 1. The number 346 is equivalent to the sum of 3 composite groups of 100, 4 composite groups of 10, and 6 ones.

Whether dealing with place value or operations, in order to reason multiplicatively, students must understand the idea that composite groups (groups of more than one) can be counted multiple times and operated on as an entity. They must also recognize that the quantitative relationship centers around equal-size groups. In order to help students make these cognitive shifts in reasoning, instruction in the early stages of learning multiplication and division should focus on helping students identify, create, and count composite, equal-size groups.

Another cognitive shift for students in progressing from additive to multiplicative reasoning is understanding the nature of the units of the quantities. In multiplication and division some of the quantities express relationships between two units (e.g., price per gallon, miles per hour, apples per bag). Students must make sense of these many-to-one relationships. Also, whereas in addition and subtraction students work with quantities of the same unit (e.g., eight dollars plus two dollars), in asymmetrical multiplication and division problems students work with quantities of different units (e.g., *Carla walked ten miles in two hours. What was her walking speed?*). Additive problems are "unit preserving" in that the solution quantity has the same label as the quantities in the problem. Multiplicative problems are "unit transforming" in that the units of the quantities in the problem are not the unit of the solution. For instance, considering the problem above, the units *miles* and *hours* are transformed into a third unit, *miles per hour*. This is also true of symmetrical problems such as rectangular array problems: *Find the area of a room that is 8 feet by 12 feet*. In this case the two factors have the same unit, feet, but the solution, 96, has a completely different unit, square feet.

Other factors that influence children's understanding of multiplication and division are related to the models we use to teach these operations. The most common model is repeated addition (e.g., 5×4 is presented as $4 + 4 + 4 + 4 + 4$) and usually involves problems categorized as equal grouping. This model is appropriate for introducing multiplication but is limiting if it is the only model used—repeated addition cannot be used to model multiplicative situations such as Cartesian products and rates. Furthermore, while repeated addition builds on students' understanding of addition, if this is the only model students know, it suggests a very narrow view of the meaning of multiplication and division. In addition, the model of repeated addition/subtraction carries with it the restraint that the multiplier must always be a whole number, since repeatedly adding or subtracting portions of a group is difficult to conceptualize (e.g., interpreting $\frac{1}{5} \times 23$ as taking $\frac{1}{5}$ groups of 23 and adding these groups together does not make a lot of sense and is counterintuitive). Compounding this difficulty, the emphasis on whole number multiplication and division problems leads elementary school students to generalize incorrectly that multiplication always results in products that are larger than the factors and division always results in quotients that are smaller than the dividend. Typically students will state, "Multiplication makes bigger, division makes smaller." Imagine how difficult it is for students to make sense of solutions in which both factors are fractions or decimals if they try to apply the repeated addition model to these problems.

This raises the question, what models should we use to help students learn about multiplicative situations? Repeated addition/subtraction definitely should be used in early instruction. However, it should not be the only model.

Rectangular arrays have proven to be useful because they can be linked to repeated addition. This array shows two rows of three columns: $3 + 3 = 6$:

Cartesian product problems can also be shown using arrays. Six shirt-and-tie combinations can be made with two ties and three shirts:

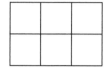

Furthermore, arrays can be used to illustrate the commutative and distributive properties of multiplication. The array below shows visually how 2×3 is equivalent to 3×2:

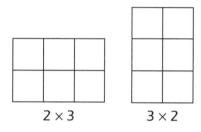

2×3 3×2

This array illustrates how $2 \times 3 = (2 \times 2) + (2 \times 1)$:

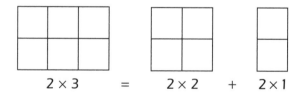

2×3 $=$ 2×2 $+$ 2×1

Finally, arrays can also be used to illustrate fraction and decimal multiplication. The one below can be used to help visualize $\frac{1}{2} \times \frac{1}{3}$ ($\frac{1}{3}$ of $\frac{1}{2}$ of a square unit is shaded):

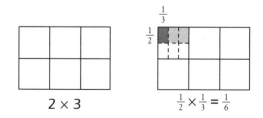

2×3 $\frac{1}{2} \times \frac{1}{3} = \frac{1}{6}$

Another model teachers should consider using to illustrate multiplicative situations involves making a group or set and then acting upon the set in one of three ways: (1) taking a part of the set, (2) making several copies of the set, or (3) making several copies of the set and also taking a part of it. For example, start with a group or set of six objects:

A part of the set (6×0.5) can be taken:

Several copies of the set can be made (6×3):

Finally, several copies can be made and a part taken (6×3.5):

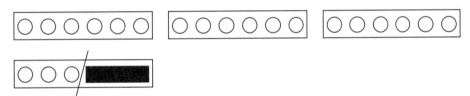

Multiplicative compare problems can be illustrated using this model where the number in the starting set is one of the factors and the action on the set is determined by the comparison factor.

Cartesian product or combination problems can be modeled in a variety of ways. First, as mentioned earlier, an array is a useful model. Matching strategies by listing the possible combinations is another model students often use. And tree diagrams help some students consider the number of combinations.

Ties	**Shirts**	**Combinations**
Tie 1	Shirt 1	Tie 1, Shirt 1
	Shirt 2	Tie 1, Shirt 2
	Shirt 3	Tie 1, Shirt 3
Tie 2	Shirt 1	Tie 2, Shirt 1
	Shirt 2	Tie 2, Shirt 2
	Shirt 3	Tie 2, Shirt 3

Instructional techniques other than models can help students learn to reason multiplicatively by focusing on the numerical relationships between quantities. For example, teachers can introduce tables that show the proportional relationships in a rate problem, since it appears that students are better able to identify and understand the relationships between pairs of quantities when the information is presented this way. For the problem *Gumdrops cost $3.89 per pound. How much will it cost to buy four pounds?*, the following table relates or links dollars and pounds:

POUND		DOLLARS
(× 4) ⌐ 1 ⌐ 4	× $3.89 ⇒ × $3.89 ⇒	$3.89 ⌐ ? ⌐ (× 4)

The multiplicative relationship between pounds and dollars (× 3.89) as well as the multiplicative relationships between pounds and pounds (× 4) and dollars and dollars (× 4) is highlighted.

3. Factors, Multiples, and Divisors

There are many relationships within and between multiplication and division that need to be considered when teaching elementary and middle school students. Important topics include prime factors (see page 20), multiples, and divisors. All of these topics are related: in order for a number to be divisible (i.e., with a remainder of zero) by another number, the divisor must be a factor of the dividend. Young students often talk informally of how a "number divides evenly with none left over" when expressing this idea of divisibility. The rules regarding divisibility are related to factors and divisors. (The most common divisibility rules are described in Activity 2.) Divisibility rules or tests usually are introduced to students in grade 4, 5, or 6. Asking students to figure out why certain divisibility rules or tests work and to justify their ideas contributes to students' ability to make sense of numbers. For example, divisibility rules can be applied when determining factors and checking to see whether a number is a multiple of another number. These rules are very handy when considering options in problem situations (for example, can 57 band members be grouped by threes?), especially since the calculations can be done mentally.

Activity

Divisibility Rules

Objective: review and apply the rules of divisibility.

Review the rules regarding divisibility by 2, 3, 4, 5, 6, 8, 9, and 10. (There is also a divisibility test for 7, but it is neither simple nor efficient and thus is not included; checking to see whether a number is divisible by 7 is best done with a calculator.)

Divisibility by 2: The number is even.

Divisibility by 3: The sum of the digits is divisible by 3.

Divisibility by 4: Either the last two digits are 00 or they form a number that is divisible by 4.

Divisibility by 5: The ones digit of the number is either 0 or 5.

Divisibility by 6: The number is even and the sum of the digits is divisible by 3.

Divisibility by 8: Either the last three digits are 000 or they form a number that is divisible by 8.

Divisibility by 9: The sum of the digits is divisible by 9.

Divisibility by 10: The ones digit of the number is 0.

Determine which of these numbers (2, 3, 4, 5, 6, 8, 9, and 10) divides evenly into 234,567,012. Then develop a divisibility rule for 15 and for 18.

Things to Think About

What is the number 234,567,012 divisible by? It is divisible by 2 because it is an even number. It is divisible by 3 because the sum of the digits is 30 (2 + 3 + 4 + 5 + 6 + 7 + 0 + 1 + 2 = 30) and 30 is divisible by 3. It is divisible by 4 because the last two digits form the number 12, and 12 is divisible by 4. It is divisible by 6 because it is both an even number and divisible by 3. It is not divisible by 5, 8, 9 or 10.

The fact that 234,567,012 is not divisible by 8 when it is divisible by 2 and 4 leads us to consider how the divisibility of a number relates to the factors of that number. In order for a number (n) to be divisible by another number (a), it must possess all of the prime factors of that number. The prime factorization of 8 is $2 \times 2 \times 2$ or 2^3; the number 8 has only one prime factor, 2, but it is multiplied by itself three times! For 234,567,012 to be divisible by 8 it must have 2^3 in its prime factorization; 234,567,012 has 2×2 in its prime factorization because it is divisible by 4, but it does not have the additional 2 as a prime factor to make it divisible by 8.

To determine whether a number is divisible by 15, consider the prime factors of 15—3 and 5. Applying divisibility rules for both 3 and 5 will determine whether a number is divisible by 15. The same method can be used for 18: apply the divisibility rules for 2 and for 9 to any number to determine whether it is divisible by 18. Why can't you use the divisibility rules for 3 and 6 to determine whether a number is divisible by 18? Again, it is related to factors. The prime factorization of 18 is $2 \times 3 \times 3$ or 2×3^2. Thus, for a number to be divisible by 18, it must possess *all* of those factors. When you use the divisibility rule for 6, you are checking to see whether a number contains the factors 2 and 3. When you use the divisibility rule for 3, you are again checking to see whether the number has 3 as a prime factor (it does—you determined that with the 6 rule), but you aren't checking to see whether the number has two 3s (3×3) as factors.

Another example may help clarify this idea: we know that 24 is divisible by 3 and 24 is divisible by 6, but 24 is not divisible by 18 even though it is divisible by 3 and 6; why not? The rule for divisibility by 3 and the rule for divisibility by 6 both check to see whether 3 is a factor of 24 (it is), but the rules do not check to see whether 9 (3×3) is a factor of 24 (it isn't).

What if you want to create a rule for divisibility by 12? Which divisibility rules should you use? Did you pick 2 and 6 or 3 and 4? Only if we use the rules for 3 and 4 can we be sure that a number is divisible by 12. If we use the rules for 2 and 6, we don't learn if the number has two 2s (2×2) as factors.

Think about the examples discussed: a rule for 15 uses rules for 3 and 5, a rule for 18 uses rules for 2 and 9, and a rule for 12 uses rules for 3 and 4. Why do these rules work, whereas the combination of rules for 3 and 6 (for 18) and for 2 and 6 (for 12) do not work? If divisibility rules in combination are to work, the numbers can't have any factors in common. Numbers that have no prime factors in common are said to be *relatively prime*. Thus, 3 and 4 are relatively prime; the only factor common to both is 1. ▲

What about division problems that have a remainder? What are the relationships between the remainder and the other numbers in a division problem? What patterns do remainders form? (Patterns when remainders are written as decimals are investigated in Chapter 6.)

Activity

Recurring Remainders

Objective: investigate patterns in division problems with remainders.

Divide each number on the chart below by 5. Circle all numbers that when divided by 5 have a remainder of 1. Draw a square around the numbers that when divided have a remainder of 2. Place a triangle around those numbers that when divided by 5 have a remainder of 3. Underline the numbers that have a remainder of 4. Describe the patterns. How do the patterns change if the divisor is 7 instead of 5?

1	2	3	4	5	6	7	8	9	10
11	12	13	14	15	16	17	18	19	20
21	22	23	24	25	26	27	28	29	30
31	32	33	34	35	36	37	38	39	40
41	42	43	44	45	46	47	48	49	50

Things to Think About

What patterns occurred? Numbers with a remainder of 1 when the divisor is 5 all end in 1 or 6 and are in the first and sixth columns. This is because numbers with a 0 or 5 in the ones place are divisible by 5, and if the number has a remainder of 1 it must be one more than a multiple of 5. The numbers that have remainders of 2, 3, or 4 fall into the subsequent columns because they are each 2, 3, or 4 more than a multiple of 5.

Why can't you have a remainder of 5 or greater when you divide by 5? If the remainder is 5 or more, another group of 5 can be removed from the dividend. Students often make the mistake of having too big a remainder when learning long division, especially when their understanding of the long division algorithm is limited:

$$\begin{array}{r} 7\text{ r }7 \\ 5\overline{)42} \\ 35 \\ \hline 7 \end{array} \qquad \begin{array}{r} 8\text{ r }2 \\ 5\overline{)42} \\ 40 \\ \hline 2 \end{array}$$

What do you notice about the remainders you get when you divide the numbers on the chart by a different divisor? How do the patterns change? How do they stay the same? The number of remainders is always one less than the divisor ($n - 1$ when n is the divisor). This is an important idea in division, one that we want students to discuss. Therefore, take a minute and use your own words to explain why the number of remainders is always $n - 1$.

While the patterns of remainders when the divisor is 5 fall into columns, other visual remainder patterns form diagonals. The patterns are all based on the multiples of the number. For example, since the multiples of 7 are 0, 7, 14, 21, 28, 35, 42, 49, . . . , the remainder patterns are 1, 2, 3, 4, 5, and 6 more than these multiples. Thus the numbers 1, 8, 15, 22, 29, 36, 43, and 50 all have remainders of 1 when divided by 7. These numbers fall along diagonals. ▲

How is the remainder interpreted in word problems? If we are dividing without a context, we tend to record the remainder as a fraction or decimal. But what happens to the remainder in real division situations? Is the remainder always used? Is the quotient ever rounded up or down? Can the remainder be the solution to a problem?

Activity

Interpreting Remainders

Objective: analyze word problems to determine how to interpret a remainder in context.

Examine each of the following problem situations and decide what happens to the remainder. What factors affected your decisions?

1. You have a rope that is 25 feet long. How many 8-foot jump ropes can you make?
2. You have 30 toys to share fairly with 7 children. How many will each child receive?
3. The ferry can hold 8 cars. How many trips will it have to make to carry 42 cars across the river?
4. Six children are planning to share a bag of 50 large cookies. About how many will each get?
5. You have a 10-foot wooden board that you want to cut into 4 pieces. How long will each piece be?
6. Kinne picked 14 quarts of blueberries to make jam. Each batch of jam uses 3 quarts of berries. How many quarts of blueberries will Kinne have left for muffins?
7. At the local supermarket, 3 cans of tomatoes are advertised for $3.89. Jasmine buys only one can. How much does the can of tomatoes cost?

Things to Think About

There are many different ways of interpreting the remainder in a division problem. It depends primarily on the context of the problem. The first problem illustrates a situation in which the remainder is not used. If the jump ropes are to be exactly eight feet long, then three jump ropes can be made and the extra one foot of rope will be tossed or saved for another project. The second problem is similar; each child will receive four toys. Perhaps the two extra toys will be given away or passed along between the seven children at periodic intervals. At any rate, cutting the extra toys into fractional parts makes no sense. These two problems illustrate that a remainder can occur whether the number of groups or the number within one group is being determined.

In Problem 3, the quotient, 5.25, must be rounded up. Five trips of the ferry will not get all of the cars across the river and a portion of a trip is impossible. Thus, six ferry trips are required. A great deal of research has been conducted on students' interpretation of problem situations in which the quotient must be rounded up to the next whole number because of the remainder. Do students really believe that an answer such as 5.25 trips is reasonable and possible? Investigation has revealed that students understand you cannot have a part of certain situations such as ferry crossings but that they are so accustomed to doing computations without a context they simply don't bother to check whether their answer makes sense. The implication for us as teachers is that we must focus more instruction on interpretation of answers (perhaps using estimation) so that students apply common sense in determining what to do with remainders. (For example, students might be asked to suggest the kind of answer that would make sense in the situation in Problem 3 rather than to find the solution.)

Sometimes a remainder is expressed as a fraction or as a decimal. Problems 4, 5, and 7 illustrate contexts in which this makes sense. Since the cookies in problem 4 are large, it might be possible to divide the last two cookies into thirds so that each child receives $8\frac{1}{3}$ cookies. However, if a bag of hard candies were being divided, the remainder would be dealt with differently. In Problem 5 the plank of wood is divided into four pieces, each $2\frac{1}{2}$ feet long. In the case of measurements such as lengths and weights, it usually makes sense to record the remainder as a fraction or as a decimal. In Problem 7, 3 cans of tomatoes cost $3.89, and 1 can costs 1.29\overline{6}$. Money is always recorded using decimals and if the decimal expansion is beyond the hundredths place, the amount is rounded to the nearest hundredth. Since Jasmine is only buying 1 can of tomatoes, it will cost her $1.30.

In Problem 6, division is used to find the solution but the remainder is the answer. Situations such as these take students by surprise simply because they don't expect the remainder to be the solution. This example again points to the need to provide students with experiences interpreting different types of remainders. As teachers we must help students understand how the context of a problem affects the interpretation of remainders and lead discussions about the various roles of the remainder based on the types of numbers and labels. ▲

Another topic related to multiplication and division involves multiples. Multiples are first introduced in school when children learn to skip count. Later they are used when multiplying and when finding least common denominators in order to work with fractions. Eventually students will generalize relationships with factors of numbers to find multiples of algebraic expressions.

Activity

Patterns with Multiples

Objective: identify patterns in the multiples of numbers.

List the first twenty-one multiples of 3. What patterns do you notice? Is 423 a multiple of 3?

Things to Think About

Multiplying 3 by consecutive whole numbers (e.g., 0, 1, 2, 3, . . .) gives the set of multiples of 3. (Zero is a multiple of all numbers since any number times zero equals zero.) The first twenty-one multiples of 3 are 0, 3, 6, 9, 12, 15, 18, 21, 24, 27, 30, 33, 36, 39, 42, 45, 48, 51, 54, 57, and 60. Some of the patterns you might have observed in the first twenty-one multiples are:

▲ The multiples alternate between even and odd numbers.

▲ There are groupings of three or four multiples for each tens digit (12, 15, 18 or 30, 33, 36, 39).

▲ The units digit repeats after a cycle of 10 (0, 3, 6, 9, 2, 5, 8, 1, 4, 7).

When students are asked to list the multiples of a number and are encouraged to look for patterns, they will find the ones mentioned and more! Looking for patterns builds familiarity with multiples of particular numbers, helps students link skip counting and multiplication, and highlights the orderliness of numerical relationships. It also may help some students remember some of the multiplication facts. Furthermore, the patterns can be used to explore relationships between operations such as repeated addition and multiplication.

Why do the multiples alternate between even and odd numbers? The odd number 3 is being added to obtain each subsequent multiple ($0 + 3 = 3, 3 + 3 = 6, 6 + 3 = 9, 9 + 3 = 12, \ldots$). An even number plus an odd number sums to an odd number, and an odd number plus an odd number sums to an even number (see page 10 in Chapter 1).

Why are the groupings of multiples of 3 in sets of three or four? The connection between divisors and multiples produces this pattern. If you consider the first set of ten numbers (0–9), three groups of 3 can be created. Consider the next two sets of ten (10–19 and 20–29). Three groups of 3 can be made from each set, each with a remainder of 1. With the fourth set of ten (30–39) not only can three groups of 3 be made, but the extra remainder can be matched with the earlier remainders to form another group of 3 (30, 33, 36, 39). Four groups of 3 will occur again in the 60s (60, 63, 66, 69) when the extra remainders from earlier tens are combined.

Why are multiples of 3 divisible by 3? It is related to why the divisibility rule for 3 works. Consider any three-digit number: *abc*. It can be expressed as ($a \times 100$) + ($b \times 10$) + ($c \times 1$) or $a(99 + 1) + b(9 + 1) + c$. This can be rewritten as $99a + a + 9b + b + c$ or ($99a + 9b$) + ($a + b + c$). The number ($99a + 9b$) is divisible by 3 because 99 and 9 are divisible by 3. Thus, if ($a + b + c$) is also divisible by 3 then the original three-digit number (*abc*) is divisible by 3 and so are all subsequent multiples of 3. Applying this to a number such as 423, we have:

$$
\begin{aligned}
423 \;&= (4 \times 100) + (2 \times 10) + (3 \times 1) \\
&= 4(99 + 1) + 2(9 + 1) + 3 \\
&= [99(4) + 4] + [9(2) + 2] + 3 \\
&= [99(4) + 9(2)] + (4 + 2 + 3)
\end{aligned}
$$

Examine $[99(4) + 9(2)] + (4 + 2 + 3)$. The first part of the expression—$[99(4) + 9(2)]$—is divisible by 3 because 99(4) is divisible by 3 and 9(2) is divisible by 3. Therefore, to check whether the original number, 423, is divisible by 3, add the digits—$(4 + 2 + 3)$. Since $4 + 2 + 3 = 9$ and 9 is divisible by 3, then 423 is also divisible by and a multiple of 3. ▲

Activity

Least Common Multiples

Objective: explore applications where the concept of least common multiples is used to solve problems.

As you solve the following somewhat more perplexing problems, consider how the concept of least common multiple is used in the solution process.

1. You may have noticed that hot dog rolls always come in packages of eight, whereas hot dogs are packaged in groups of ten. What are the fewest packages of buns and hot dogs you have to buy so that you have the same number of hot dogs and buns?
2. One lighthouse takes 45 seconds to make a complete revolution, and a second lighthouse revolves every 30 seconds. If the lighthouses are synchronized to begin a revolution at 9:00 A.M., how long will it take before they are again synchronized?
3. The life cycle of a species of cicadas is 17 years. The last time this particular species emerged during a presidential election year was 1996. (Presidential elections occur every four years.) When will this species next emerge during a presidential election year?

Things to Think About

In the first problem did you simply multiply 8 and 10 to get 80—a common multiple of both 8 and 10? Yet you don't need 80 buns and hot dogs. Here's why: 8 and 10 have a common factor of 2: $8 = 2 \times 4$ and $10 = 2 \times 5$. The least common multiple has to have all of the factors of 8 (2×4) and all of the factors of 10 (the 2 is already accounted for but the 5 is not), but no other factors (or you have common multiples). So the factors needed are $2 \times 4 \times 5$, for a product of 40. The least common multiple is 40; four packages of hot dogs (4×10) and five packages of hot dog rolls (5×8) will give the same number of hot dogs and buns.

Problem 2 is similar to the first one. A common multiple must be found in order to determine when the lighthouses again will be synchronized. Because 45 and 30 have some common factors ($45 = 15 \times 3$ and $30 = 15 \times 2$), common multiples less than 1,350 (45×30) exist. Yet the least common multiple must have all of the factors of both numbers. These factors are $15 \times 3 \times 2$. Thus, the least common multiple is 90—in 90 minutes, or at 10:30 A.M., the two lighthouses will again be synchronized.

In the final problem the two numbers, 17 and 4, have no common factors. In this case, the least common multiple is found by multiplying 17 and 4 to obtain a product of 68. This species of cicadas will again emerge during a presidential election year in 2064 (1996 + 68). ▲

We can use what we know about remainders, divisibility, and multiples to solve a wide range of number theory problems. For example, what number when divided by both 5 and 7 has a remainder of 2? If the number has a remainder of 2 when divided by 5 and by 7 it has to be two more than a multiple of 5 and 7. You can use the chart in Activity 5, mark the numbers with remainders of 2, and then look for the intersection, or you can list numbers that are two more than the multiples.

Numbers divided by 5 with remainder 2: 7, 12, 17, 22, 27, 32, 37, 42, 47 . . .

Numbers divided by 7 with remainder 2: 9, 16, 23, 30, 37, 44, 51, 58, 65 . . .

The least common multiple of 5 and 7 is 35. Two more than 35 is 37, so 37 is one solution to this problem. The next number that when divided by 5 and 7 has a remainder of 2 is 72 because the next multiple of 5 and 7 is 70 and two more is 72.

Another type of problem from number theory involves finding factors and multiples common to two numbers. Let's consider the numbers 36 and 24. One way to find common factors is to list the factors of each number (using divisibility rules we know that 36 is divisible by 1, 2, 3, 4, 6, 9, 12, 18, and 36 and 24 is divisible by 1, 2, 3, 4, 6, 8, 12, and 24). Common factors are 1, 2, 3, 4, 6, and 12 (1 is a common factor of all number pairs so often is not listed). Another way to find common factors is to use the prime factorizations of both numbers:

$$36 = 2 \times 2 \times 3 \times 3 \quad \text{or} \quad 2^2 \times 3^2 \qquad 24 = 2 \times 2 \times 2 \times 3 \quad \text{or} \quad 2^3 \times 3$$

and to display the prime factors in a Venn diagram. Common factors are placed in the intersection of the sets (circles).

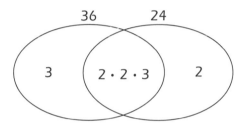

Notice that there are three prime factors common to both 36 and 24—$2 \times 2 \times 3$. Thus 2 and 3 are common factors of 36 and 24 as are 4 ($2 \times 2 = 4$) and 6 ($2 \times 3 = 6$). We get the greatest common factor (GCF) of the two numbers when we multiply all of the common prime factors together ($2 \times 2 \times 3 = 12$).

Can prime factors be used to determine the least common multiple of 36 and 24? The least common multiple (LCM) must be a multiple of both 36 and 24, which means that the LCM has all of the prime factors of 36 (and some additional ones) and all of the prime factors of 24 (and some additional ones). Examine the factors in the Venn diagram. Multiplying all of the prime factors together, $3 \times 3 \times 2 \times 2 \times 2$, gives us 72 which is the LCM of 36 and 24. Can you explain why this works?

4. Multiplying and Dividing Signed Numbers

In middle school, students learn about signed numbers and how to operate on them. Helping students understand these operations is considered a challenge. Why? First, there are not many applications of multiplication and division of negative numbers that are meaningful for students. Below are a two, but they are difficult to generalize:

During a five-hour period, a cold front moved into New England with an overall temperature change of ⁻40. What was the average hourly change in the temperature?

A scuba diver starts at an elevation of 0 feet and descends at a constant rate of ⁻3 feet per second. How long will it take her to reach an elevation of ⁻120 feet?

Second, the models for addition and subtraction of signed numbers we explored in Chapter 3 are not ideal when applied to all variations of multiplication and division problems (if we use the chip model to model a negative number times a negative number, we must first redefine what actions the factors represent). Third, this topic is one of the first in which students are introduced to mathematics as a formal system and properties are used to justify answers. Some students have difficulty understanding these concepts through the manipulation of symbols. That said, let's look at a number of ways, both informal and formal, to make sense of these operations.

The product resulting from multiplying a positive number by a negative number, such as $3 \times {}^-2$, can be shown using a red/black chips model and a number line model (see Chapter 3). Using the equal grouping interpretation of multiplication, 3 groups with $^-2$ in each group can be represented using groups of red chips or grouped movements on a number line. We can observe that a positive number times a negative number results in a negative product using either model.

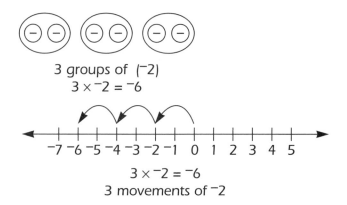

3 groups of $(^-2)$
$3 \times {}^-2 = {}^-6$

$3 \times {}^-2 = {}^-6$
3 movements of $^-2$

How do we justify that a negative number times a positive number also results in a negative product? (For most of us, it is difficult to conceive of a negative number of groups!) We can use the commutative property of multiplication to show that since a positive number times a negative number resulted in a negative product, the corresponding negative number times the corresponding positive number will also result in a negative product: since $3 \times {}^-2 = {}^-6$ and $^-2 \times 3 = 3 \times {}^-2$, then $^-2 \times 3 = {}^-6$. The use of a property is a more formal way of justifying the sign of the product.

Why does multiplying two negative numbers result in a positive product? This is not easy to explain informally, but patterns can be used to generalize relationships. Examine the multiplications below. What do you notice about the products?

$$4 \times {}^-8 = {}^-32$$
$$3 \times {}^-8 = {}^-24$$
$$2 \times {}^-8 = {}^-16$$
$$1 \times {}^-8 = {}^-8$$
$$0 \times {}^-8 = 0$$
$${}^-1 \times {}^-8 = 8$$

$$^-2 \times {}^-8 = 16$$
$$^-3 \times {}^-8 = \square$$
$$^-4 \times {}^-8 = \square$$

Did you notice that as the first factor gets smaller, the product becomes greater? The product is increasing by 8s. Based on the patterns established, we generalize to say that the product of two negative numbers is a positive number. Notice that this approach doesn't prove the fact that $(-a) \times (-b) = ab$, but it may help students better remember the sign of the product.

Students are sometimes taught nonmathematical "tricks" to help them remember whether products are negative or positive; it is believed that these tricks will somehow help them accurately compute with negative numbers. In general, tricks that are not based on mathematical relationships are easily forgotten or misapplied, since students cannot rely on their understanding of the situation to help them remember.

As division is the inverse operation of multiplication, we can use multiplication to help solve division problems. For example, to solve $36 \div {}^-4 = \square$, think $\square \times {}^-4 = 36$. Since we know that $4 \times 9 = 36$ and two negative numbers give a positive product, we can conclude that $\square = {}^-9$. Likewise, to solve $^-72 \div 6 = \square$, we can encourage students to think, $\square \times 6 = {}^-72$. Knowing that a negative number times a positive number gives a negative product, we can conclude that $\square = {}^-12$. However, in order for students to be able to use inverse operations to make sense of division of negative numbers, it is essential that they first have a firm grounding in whole number operations and relationships. Yet, many students start the study of multiplication and division of integers without fully grasping how they can use multiplication to solve a division problem (or vice versa) with whole numbers. As a result, teachers may need to help students first become flexible with rewriting and interpreting whole number multiplication and division sentences by providing activities that support the development of students' understanding of the inverse relationships between operations.

Teaching Multiplication and Division

Students need to develop a strong and complete conceptual knowledge of multiplication and division. If they don't, they will have difficulty with more advanced multiplicative situations such as proportions, measurement conversion, linear functions, and exponential growth. Therefore, they need to explore many different types of asymmetric and symmetric word problems. Instruction should build on students' intuitive understanding of additive situations by using the repeated addition models but must also include other models and strategies in order to extend students' understanding of these operations. Whole numbers, decimals, fractions, and integers should be used with all problem types in order to dispel the common misconception that "multiplication makes larger, division makes smaller." Instruction must also include opportunities for students to explore the role of factors, different types of units, and properties of multiplication and division.

Questions for Discussion

1. Briefly describe each type of multiplication and division problem. How might you use this information to teach these topics?
2. What is the difference between additive and multiplicative reasoning? Why is it important to help older elementary school and middle school students learn to reason about quantities multiplicatively?
3. Describe your solution method and any patterns you notice for this problem:

   A tennis club buys tennis balls either in 3-ball packs or 4-ball packs. Last week a water main broke at the club, ruining all the balls. When the staff went to repack the balls for insurance purposes, they noticed that when packed in 3-ball packs there was 1 ball left over but when packed in 4-ball packs there were 2 balls left over. If the staff repackaged over 200 balls, how many 3-ball or 4-ball containers were filled?

4. There are many components to learning multiplication and division that are challenging for students. Describe at least three components and explain why you think they might pose difficulties for learners.
5. How is multiplication and division of whole numbers similar and different to these operations with integers? with fractions? with decimals?
6. Use a Venn diagram and prime factorization to determine the GCF and LCM of 28 and 42.

5

Fractions

Fractions are a rich part of mathematics, but we tend to manipulate fractions by rote rather than try to make sense of the concepts and procedures. Researchers have concluded that this complex topic causes more trouble for elementary and middle school students than any other area of mathematics (Bezuk and Bieck 1993). Teaching fractions is therefore both important and challenging. The National Council of Teachers of Mathematics recommends that instruction in fractions emphasize equivalent forms, estimating and comparing, and the reasonableness of results, not just correct answers and the steps in performing fraction algorithms. This chapter will help you make sense of a number of concepts related to fractions.

1. What Are Fractions?

Fractions were first used thousands of years ago, by both the Babylonians and the Egyptians, to answer questions involving how much and how many. Whereas at that time many quantities could be expressed using "counting" numbers (28 cattle, 176 scoops of rice), other situations, like sharing seven apples between two people or dividing an acre of land among four children, could not be described using counting numbers. A different type of number was needed to express amounts that were less than one but greater than zero: fractions. It wasn't until the Renaissance, however, that the use of fractions, as we know them today, became commonplace. More formally, fractions belong to the set of numbers known as the rational numbers—numbers that can be written in the form $\frac{a}{b}$ where a and b are integers and $b \neq 0$. (Because it isn't possible to divide by zero, division by zero is "undefined" in mathematics; see page 35 for an explanation.) In the set of rational numbers, a is called the *numerator* (from the Latin word meaning *number*) and b is called the *denominator* (from the Latin word meaning *namer*) of the fraction. The terms *fraction* and *rational number* are often used interchangeably. But the word *fraction* can be used to indicate a variety of things: a symbol of the form $\frac{a}{b}$, a notational system (*write that value as a fraction*), as well as a quantity that is not a rational number ($\frac{\pi}{10}$). Thus, not all numbers written using fraction notation actually represent rational numbers.

Interestingly, fractions have multiple meanings and interpretations. Educators generally agree that there are five main interpretations: fractions as parts of wholes or parts of sets; fractions as the result of dividing two numbers; fractions as the ratio of two quantities; fractions as operators; and fractions as measures (Behr, Harel, Post, and Lesh 1992; Kieren 1988; Lamon 1999).

▲ *Fractions as parts of wholes or parts of sets*. One meaning of fraction is as a part of a whole. In this interpretation, a unit is partitioned into equivalent pieces or a set is partitioned equally into smaller amounts (e.g., eighths, sixths, or halves) and numbers of these pieces are used to represent fractional amounts (e.g., three eighths, five sixths, one half). A pizza divided into equal-size pieces illustrates the part-of-a-whole meaning; a bushel of peaches separated equally into smaller boxes of peaches illustrates the parts-of-a-set meaning. In the parts-of-a-whole interpretation, the fractional parts do not have to be identical in shape and size (i.e., congruent), but they must be equivalent in some attribute such as area, volume, or number.

▲ *Fractions as the result of dividing two numbers*. A fraction can also represent the result obtained when two numbers are divided. This interpretation of fraction is sometimes referred to as the *quotient meaning*, since the quotient is the answer to a division problem. For example, the number of gumdrops each child receives when 40 gumdrops are shared among 5 children can be expressed as $\frac{40}{5}$, $\frac{8}{1}$, or 8; when two steaks are shared equally among three people, each person receives $\frac{2}{3}$ of a steak for dinner. We often express the quotient as a mixed number rather than an improper fraction—15 feet of rope can be divided to make two jump ropes, each $7\frac{1}{2}$ ($\frac{15}{2}$) feet long.

▲ *Fractions as the ratio of two quantities*. A ratio is a comparison between two quantities (see Chapter 8). When a ratio compares a part to a whole, the part-to-whole interpretation of fraction is being used. For example, if there are 15 children at a family gathering compared with a total of 33 people, we can write this comparison using a ratio (15:33), but we are more likely to refer to this part-to-whole relationship as a fraction ($\frac{15}{33}$). All fractions are ratios, but all ratios are not fractions. Why? Some ratios compare parts of a set to other parts of a set. For example, we can compare the 15 children with the 18 adults at the family gathering and then express the ratio of number of children to number of adults as 15:18, or 5:6. These part-to-part ratios are not fractions, because the ratio does not name a rational number but instead presents a comparison of two numbers. Furthermore, the formal definition of rational number indicates that zero is not allowed as the number in the denominator; the ratio 2:0 can be used to compare two blue marbles with zero green marbles, but it is not a fraction. Interestingly, students sometimes use part-to-part ratios to make sense of part-to-whole fractions.

▲ *Fractions as operators*. Here a fraction is understood to be a number that acts on another number in the sense of stretching or shrinking the magnitude of the number. A model plane, for example, can be $\frac{1}{25}$ the size of the original plane, or an image of a red blood cell might be magnified under a microscope to 300 times its actual size. In these cases, a multiplicative relationship, or multiplication rule, exists between two quantities (e.g., if the length of the plane's wingspan is 50 feet and the length of the model's wingspan is $\frac{1}{25}$ times as long, then to find the wingspan of the model, we multiply $50 \times \frac{1}{25}$).

▲ *Fractions as measures.* The idea of a fraction as a length on the number line, created by partitioning units into subunits, is at the heart of this interpretation. A unit of measure can always be partitioned into smaller and smaller subunits. When we measure a distance using a ruler, we line up the object to be measured against hash marks. If the object doesn't line up precisely, however, this doesn't mean we can't measure its length! There is a dynamic aspect to the measurement interpretation of fraction—we name the fractional amount based on the number of subunits we are willing to create. Inherent to this interpretation of fraction is the understanding that there are an infinite number of rational numbers on the number line. We can always partition units and subunits into tinier and tinier subunits.

When a fraction is presented in symbolic form devoid of context, you cannot determine which interpretation of the fraction is intended. The various interpretations are needed, however, in order to make sense of fraction problems and situations. Furthermore, in many problem situations students are faced with results that must be interpreted using more than one meaning of fraction. For example, when two pizzas are shared among six children, the amount that each receives is $\frac{1}{3}$, which refers to the quotient meaning of fractions (the result of dividing two numbers), whereas the comparison of pizza to children (2 pizzas for 6 persons, or 1 for 3) is a ratio. If students are not familiar with meanings other than the part-whole interpretation, their understanding of situations like these is often incomplete.

When do students learn the different meanings of fractions? Research supports the idea that the part-whole interpretation, which involves partitioning wholes (or sets) into equal-size pieces and identifying different-size units, is the best way to approach learning about fractions in the early grades; students' experience with "fair shares" in everyday life is often the starting point for assisting students in understanding some important ideas about the size and number of units in a whole and how units can be divided up into smaller and smaller subunits. The other interpretations are best studied in more depth later in elementary and middle school, when connections between fractions and division and multiplication help students build on their initial understanding of part-whole relationships. However, this does not mean that students should not have experiences with all the other interpretations before fifth grade. On the contrary, students benefit from building a broad base of meaning and being able to move flexibly among meanings.

Fractions as Parts of Wholes or Parts of Sets

Since the interpretation of a fraction as a part of a whole is so fundamental to establishing a foundation for understanding fractions, let's examine three different relationships among parts and wholes.

One relationship involves being given the whole unit and the symbolic fraction and determining what the part looks like. We use this type of relationship every day. Suppose you want to put a portion of your earnings, say $\frac{1}{10}$, into a savings account. First you have to determine the "part" of the whole to save—in other words, what is $\frac{1}{10}$ of your weekly salary?

Let's take another example. If a whole set consists of twelve apples, how much is $\frac{1}{6}$ of the set? $\frac{3}{4}$ of the set? $\frac{5}{3}$ of the set?

The fraction $\frac{1}{6}$ is called a unit fraction because it has a numerator of one. Unit fractions are the easiest for students to understand, one reason being that you only have to consider one part in relationship to the whole unit. Therefore, instruction in the early grades emphasizes unit fractions. In this case, two apples are $\frac{1}{6}$ of the set. Fractions that are less than one and have a numerator that is less than the denominator are called *proper fractions*. In this case, for the proper fraction $\frac{3}{4}$, you must divide the set into four equal subsets (three apples) and then combine three of the subsets, thereby ending up with nine apples. Fractions that are greater than one are called *improper fractions*. The improper fraction in this example, $\frac{5}{3}$, is equivalent to twenty apples (four apples are $\frac{1}{3}$, and $5 \times 4 = 20$).

Another part-to-whole relationship involves being given the whole unit and the part and determining the fractional amount the part represents. For example, if six apples make up the whole set, what fraction of that whole is two apples?

To determine the fraction, you first have to partition the whole into equivalent parts. Two apples are equivalent to $\frac{1}{3}$ of a six-apple set, since the six apples can be divided into three equal groups of two apples each. Problems similar to this one, often using unit fractions only, can be used to introduce students to the concept of fractions. While this relationship is straightforward for adults, young children have difficulty partitioning sets into groups with more than one element in each (what fraction of six apples is five apples? $\frac{5}{6}$) and in understanding that $\frac{1}{3}$ and $\frac{2}{6}$ are equivalent. It is also important to explore relationships in which the part is greater than the whole: for example, the fractional relationship of ten apples to six apples is $\frac{10}{6}$, or $\frac{5}{3}$, or $1\frac{2}{3}$.

A third relationship in the part-to-whole interpretation involves determining the whole after being given the fraction and the part. This relationship can be especially difficult for students to grasp, because the size of the whole must be extrapolated from the part. For example, if $\frac{2}{5}$ of a whole is six apples, then how much is the whole set? Using the given information, it can be determined that $\frac{1}{5}$ is equivalent to three apples, and since there are five fifths in a whole set, multiplying five by three tells us how much. Thus, six is $\frac{2}{5}$ of fifteen. The relationship can be illustrated like this:

This type of part-to-whole relationship is common in many word problems. For example: *Eight puppies in a litter are all black. The remaining $\frac{1}{3}$ of the litter are spotted. How many puppies are in the litter?* (Answer: 12.) Many adults have difficulty with this type of problem because their understanding of fraction and fraction relationships is not robust. In order to help students develop numerical power with fractions, we need to include mathematical tasks in our instruction that require students to explore and make sense of these various relationships.

The examples above use the concept of sets to explore part-whole relationships. These part-whole relationships also can be investigated using regions divided into equal-size areas (such as rectangles or circles), or using linear models in which the lengths are divided, such as on a number line.

Activity

Exploring the Part-Whole Meaning of Fractions

Objective: investigate the relationships among part-whole fractions and the wholes using lengths as the wholes.

Materials: Cuisenaire rods.

Use Cuisenaire rods to answer these part-whole questions:

1. If we assign the blue rod a value of 1, what is the value of the light green rod?
2. If we assign the value of 1 to the light green rod, what is the value of the blue rod?
3. If the orange rod plus the red rod is one whole, which rods represent $\frac{1}{2}$, $\frac{2}{3}$, and $\frac{3}{4}$?
4. If the orange rod plus the red is one whole, which rods represent $\frac{3}{2}$, $\frac{4}{3}$, $\frac{5}{4}$, and $\frac{7}{6}$?
5. Which fraction in Question 4 is the greatest? Is there a pattern? Which is greater, $\frac{26}{25}$ or $\frac{17}{16}$? Explain how you determined the greater fractions.
6. If the red rod is $\frac{1}{3}$, what rod is the whole?
7. If the dark green rod is $\frac{2}{3}$, what rod is the whole?
8. If the yellow rod is $\frac{5}{4}$, what rod is one whole?

Things to Think About

When manipulatives are used to explore part-whole relationships, teachers can directly observe what students understand about the relationships. Watching students solve these problems can be quite revealing. For example, in solving Question 1 do students represent the blue rod using three light green rods and indicate that each light green rod is $\frac{1}{3}$ of the blue rod, or do they use a variety of rods in addition to or instead of green ones to make a rod the same length as the blue one?

This activity raises a number of questions. Can a whole number be expressed as a fractional relationship? Yes. Whole numbers can be represented as fractions with denominators of one (e.g., 4 is equivalent to $\frac{4}{1}$). Thus, since the light green rod in Question 2 has been designated 1, the blue rod is 3, or $\frac{3}{1}$. Did using different rods to represent one whole confuse you? One difficulty children encounter when studying fractions is that different amounts can be used as the whole, and therefore the same fractions may not be identical in size. For example, half of a medium-size pizza is smaller than half of a large pizza, though both can be represented numerically as $\frac{1}{2}$ and the relationship represented by $\frac{1}{2}$ is the same in each case. It is important for children to pay attention to the size of the "whole" when they are dealing with fractions in context. Likewise, in order to compare two fractions, the referent whole must be identical for both.

The length of the orange rod plus the red one is equivalent to twelve white rods. These rods can be used to demonstrate many fractional relationships. The various fractional relationships in Questions 3 and 4 are shown pictorially below.

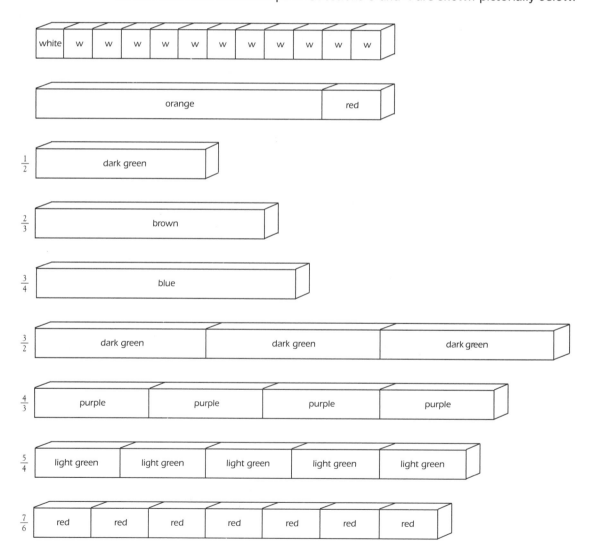

Notice that of the four fractions in Question 4, $\frac{3}{2}$ is the greatest. Each of these improper fractions is just one fractional part greater than one (e.g., $\frac{7}{6}$ is equivalent to $1\frac{1}{6}$: it is one sixth larger than one). Thus, $\frac{3}{2} > \frac{4}{3} > \frac{5}{4}$, since in terms of the extra fractional piece greater than one, $\frac{1}{2} > \frac{1}{3} > \frac{1}{4}$. Using this line of reasoning, $\frac{17}{16} > \frac{26}{25}$.

The last three questions require you to determine the whole or unit given the part and its fractional value. If the red rod is $\frac{1}{3}$, then the dark green rod is the whole, because three reds are the same length as a dark green. If the dark green rod is $\frac{2}{3}$, then the blue rod is the whole. The answer to Question 8 can be explained using a diagram:

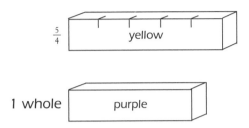

Since the yellow rod is five fourths of one, we need to find a rod equivalent to four fourths. It is the purple rod. ▲

In order for students to attach meaning to fractions and make sense of the various part-whole relationships, a variety of physical materials should be introduced and explored during instruction. The pictorial representations included in most textbooks are not sufficient. Consider how difficult it would have been to answer some of the questions in Activity 1 if you only had drawings of the rods. When investigating fractions as a part of a whole, the fractional parts can be represented using cardboard or paper circles cut into wedges, cardboard or paper rectangles cut into smaller rectangles, drawings on dot or graph paper, areas on geoboards, sections in a piece of folded paper, Cuisenaire rods, pattern blocks, distances on a ruler or number line, and other commercial materials. Working with a variety of discrete objects—counters, beans, marbles, Xs and Os—can help students see parts of a set. One important feature of fraction instruction is that mathematical tasks be meaning oriented rather than symbol oriented.

Fractions as the Result of Dividing Two Numbers

A fraction can be viewed as the result of a division. For example, $\frac{1}{3}$ can be interpreted as 1 whole unit or item (candy bar, pizza, money) divided into 3 equal parts. Partitioning, the process of dividing an object or set into parts, is the essential activity that underlies students' ability to make sense of this interpretation of fraction. Children progress through stages in partitioning; first, they become competent at cutting items in half. They then move to dividing units into fourths, eighths, and sixteenths by halving successively. Later students figure out the more complex process of how to divide items into an odd number of pieces. Interpreting a fraction as the result of division, or as a quotient, occurs in the elementary curriculum when we ask students to share small quantities with many others (2 cookies shared among 4 people) and when students represent quotients with fractions instead of whole-number remainders. For example, when dividing 7 by 5, we can represent the answer as $\frac{7}{5}$ or $1\frac{2}{5}$. When dividing 1 by 5, we can represent the answer as $\frac{1}{5}$.

Interpreting Fractions as the Result of a Division

Objective: demonstrate the quotient understanding of fraction through a linear model in which a point on a number line represents a fraction.

On a line segment drawn on a piece of paper, the start labeled 0 and the end labeled 12, locate the fraction $\frac{12}{5}$.

Things to Think About

How did you locate $\frac{12}{5}$ on the number line? Many people first change $\frac{12}{5}$ to $2\frac{2}{5}$ and then divide the segment into 12 ones. They locate $2\frac{2}{5}$ on the number line by placing a point two fifths beyond the number 2:

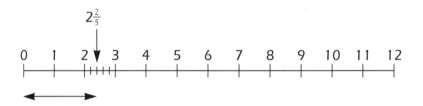

Other people divide the segment into 12 units and then further divide each unit into fifths. They locate the point representing $\frac{12}{5}$ at the twelfth fifth unit:

Each of the approaches above is based on the understanding of a fraction as part of a whole, since the line segment is first divided or partitioned into 12 units or "wholes."

If you used either of the above approaches, draw another segment and again label the endpoints 0 and 12. This time think of $\frac{12}{5}$ as the result of a division—that is, divide the length of the segment into 5 equal pieces ($12 \div 5$). Each piece or segment is $\frac{12}{5}$ of the total length:

You can also explore fractions as the result of division with discrete models. For example, $\frac{4}{2}$, or four divided by two, can be illustrated by separating four counters into two groups:

This is shown symbolically as $\frac{4}{2} = 2$. But what if you were asked to illustrate $\frac{4}{3}$ using counters? If you are thinking about the fraction $\frac{4}{3}$ in terms of division, you might divide the four counters into three equal groups. Each group consists of one whole counter plus $\frac{1}{3}$ of another counter:

However, if you think about the fraction $\frac{4}{3}$ as representing parts of a whole, you might first partition each counter into thirds (since three thirds is one whole) and then take four of these thirds (which is the same amount as $1\frac{1}{3}$):

Fractions as the Ratios of Two Quantities

The interpretation of fractions as ratios is usually introduced to students in fourth through sixth grade. Ratios can be written symbolically in a number of ways (e.g., 2:3, 2 to 3, $\frac{2}{3}$), and this can cause confusion in students who are unclear about whether to interpret the symbols as a ratio or as a fraction or both. However, we can help students differentiate by using fraction notation with part-whole ratios/fractions ($\frac{2}{5}$) and ratio notation with part-part ratios (2:3). A rate is a special type of ratio that compares quantities with different units, such as 130 miles in two hours, or 65 miles per hour. Since proportional reasoning, which includes ratios and rates, is such an important topic in mathematics, a more thorough description of this topic can be found in Chapter 8.

There are many similarities between fractions and ratios in terms of how we manipulate their symbolic forms. We form equivalent ratios and rates in the same way as fractions—whether dividing or multiplying them. However, there is an important difference between equivalent fractions and ratios in terms of interpretation of the final value. Equivalent fractions, such as $\frac{2}{5}$, $\frac{4}{10}$, and $\frac{12}{30}$, are part-to-whole comparisons and all represent the same number and position on the number line. Equivalent part-to-part ratios, 2:5, 4:10, and 12:30, all represent the same comparison relationship but not the same number. Two woodwind instruments compared with 5 brass instruments and 12 woodwinds with 30 brass instruments both have the same comparison relationship of 2 to 5 (woodwinds to brass instruments) but the different quantities within the ratios give us, for example, a small ensemble of 7 instruments compared with a large chamber group of 42 instruments.

Fractions and ratios are different when it comes to the operations of addition and subtraction. We cannot add and subtract ratios in the same way we add and subtract fractions. When adding or subtracting fractions, we are interpreting the quantities as parts of wholes and are joining parts to make wholes. Remember that some ratios are not comparisons of parts to whole but are comparisons between a part and another part. For example, if in a coed a cappella group there are always 3 boys for every 4 girls, we can express this relationship as a part-part ratio of 3 to 4. When part-part ratios are combined, the end result is another comparison. For example, when we combine two ratios that compare the number of boys to girls in these singing groups (3:4 + 3:4), we write the resulting ratio of boys to girls as 6:8, which means six boys compared with eight girls; when we combine two fractions ($\frac{3}{4} + \frac{3}{4}$), we are finding the total amount. The sum is $\frac{6}{4}$ or $1\frac{1}{2}$. To avoid confusion or the misinterpretation of a ratio as a fraction or vice versa, it is important to be aware of these differences and to ask students to determine whether comparisons are between parts and wholes or parts and parts. Furthermore, some teachers use the colon (:) to indicate part-part ratios and fraction notation to indicate part-whole relationships.

Fractions as Operators

A fraction as an operator is an algebraic interpretation. For example, an operator such as $\frac{3}{4}$ can be thought of as a "function" or rule that transforms one set of objects into another set with $\frac{3}{4}$ times as many elements. If there are eight apples in one bowl and you want to put $\frac{3}{4}$ times as many apples in another bowl, this can be determined by multiplying $\frac{3}{4}$ by 8: six apples go into the other bowl. An operator can also be viewed as a function that transforms geometric figures into either enlarged or reduced similar figures.

Activity

Fractions as Operators

Objective: demonstrate how the operator interpretation of fraction is used in "function machines."

Determine an input-output rule for each of these function machines:

A. Input (a)	Output (b)	B. Input (a)	Output (b)
2	1	1	$\frac{2}{3}$
3	1.5	2	$\frac{4}{3}$
6	3	3	$\frac{6}{3}$
8	4	4	$\frac{8}{3}$
a	?	a	?

Things to Think About

Function machines are often constructed using addition and subtraction rules
($+ 3$, $- 7$) or whole-number multiplication and division rules ($\times 3$, $\div 5$). While
function machines are now included in many curriculum materials, the multiplicative relationship between input and output values is rarely a fraction. However,
middle school students benefit from exploring relationships between inputs and
outputs that require them to use multiplicative reasoning and fractions.

What is the relationship between the inputs and outputs in example A? Did
you notice that the input divided by two equals the output? What is another way
to state this relationship using fractions? The outputs are one half of the inputs.
This can be expressed symbolically as $\frac{1}{2}$ times the quantity a equals the output
b ($\frac{1}{2}a = b$). When we express the relationship using multiplication and the fraction $\frac{1}{2}$, we are using that fraction to operate on the quantity, a.

What is the relationship in the function machine in example B? The outputs are
all fractions with denominators of 3. The outputs increase by $\frac{2}{3}$ with each input
and are $\frac{2}{3}$ of the input. Another way to state this is that the output is $\frac{2}{3}$ times as
much as the input—in other words, $\frac{2}{3}$ times the input equals the output ($\frac{2}{3}a = b$). ▲

Notice that situations in which a fraction is used as an operator are multiplicative
(i.e., multiplication is being performed). The operator meaning of fraction is not
used when adding or subtracting fractions, since in those operations one number
does not "operate" on another. For example, if we add one half of an apple and six
apples ($\frac{1}{2} + 6$), the sum is $6\frac{1}{2}$ apples. The $\frac{1}{2}$ represents one half of a whole apple. However, if we wish to find one half of six apples ($\frac{1}{2} \times 6$), the one half is not part of a
whole apple, it is a quantity that is operating on the six apples (taking a portion of
the set of six apples), and the result is three apples. Because this interpretation of
multiplication is confusing, it will be dealt with again in Section 3, Operations with
Fractions.

Fractions as Measures

In this interpretation, a rational number is the measure of some distance or region.
We can measure a linear distance and record this as an interval from zero or we can
measure the area of a region and use fractions to increase the precision of our
measurement. Fractions are used in situations in which we measure using liters, centimeters, degrees, ounces, or miles to name a few examples. We sometimes refer to
rational numbers as points on a number line, but it is important to realize that those
points actually are measures of distance. Many ideas from the other interpretations of
fraction are used when interpreting a fraction as a measure: part-to-whole comparisons, quotients, and operators. That we can take a length and partition it into whole
units and parts of units links this interpretation to the part-whole interpretation;
division is used in naming distances on the number line (see Activity 2 above) and
to partition units; and understanding how we can operate on, say, sixths to produce
twelfths uses what we know about operators and performing calculations on both
numerators and denominators ($\frac{5}{6} \times \frac{2}{2} = \frac{10}{12}$).

The size of the subunits within a unit is related to the number of subunits needed to
measure the distance. If the subunits are small, a greater number of subunits are
needed, but if the subunits are large, we need fewer subunits. When different subunits

are used to measure the same distance, different fraction names result. But since the distance from zero is the same, these fraction names represent the same rational number and are known as *equivalent fractions*.

When students understand this interpretation of fraction they can partition units on a number line into any number of equal-size parts (not just halves), are able to find fractions between any two given fractions, and can measure a distance from zero using any-size interval. A student's ability to read a ruler is related to these concepts and is as much a fraction topic as a measurement topic!

Activity

Fractions as Measures

Objective: partition a number line into parts in order to identify and name distances.

A. On the number line below, locate $\frac{31}{36}$.

0   1

B. On the following number line, locate $\frac{9}{24}$ and name the point directly to the right of $\frac{9}{24}$. Then find another fraction between these two points.

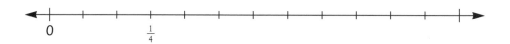

0         $\frac{1}{4}$

Things to Think About

How did you begin to find the location of $\frac{31}{36}$? Most people divide the line in half. You may have then divided each of the halves in half, producing fourths. The process of halving is one of the first strategies students use when partitioning. We can show these actions using symbols.

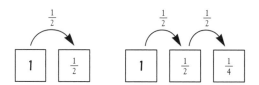

There are choices as to what to do next. You might divide the fourths into nine pieces, making thirty-sixths. Or you might partition the fourths into thirds, producing twelfths. You would then need to again find thirds of the twelfths. Notice how we "operate" on the subunit (taking $\frac{1}{9}$ of each $\frac{1}{4}$ for example) and how there is more than one way to partition the whole.

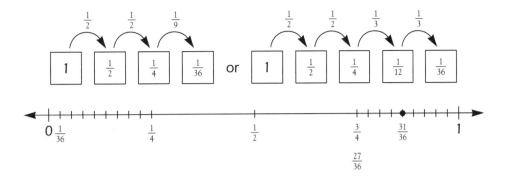

We can count $\frac{1}{36}$ths to find the location of $\frac{31}{36}$. Since $\frac{31}{36}$ is $\frac{1}{36}$ less than $\frac{32}{36}$, or $\frac{8}{9}$, we can also locate this distance using equivalent fractions.

There is no unit indicated on the second number line, but we can place 1 by using what we know about parts—they must all be the same length. So fourths can be shown on the line.

Notice that the hash marks above indicate $\frac{1}{12}$ths. To locate $\frac{9}{24}$, divide each of the smallest subunits in half, giving $\frac{1}{24}$ths.

How can we determine another fraction between $\frac{9}{24}$ and $\frac{10}{24}$? By further partitioning! If we choose to divide each $\frac{1}{24}$ in half, $\frac{19}{48}$ is between $\frac{9}{24}$ and $\frac{10}{24}$. But if we divide each $\frac{1}{24}$ into three pieces, we discover that $\frac{28}{72}$ and $\frac{29}{72}$ are also between $\frac{9}{24}$ and $\frac{10}{24}$. Exploring this interpretation of fraction enables students to investigate the property of density or how close together fractions are on the number line. When it is stated that rational numbers are "dense" it means that there are an infinite number of fractions between any two fractions. Successive partitioning helps us to name some of these fractions. ▲

Many problems can be solved using more than one interpretation of fraction. Students develop strategies that become more efficient as their understanding of the different meanings expands. The flexibility to use a variety of solution methods and interpretations is what makes these relationships so powerful but also so confusing for students.

Activity

Fair Shares

Objective: solve a problem using different interpretations of fractions.

Solve the following problem using three different interpretations of fraction.

> *After a morning of fishing, three boats of fishermen arrived back on shore to compare their catches. The fishermen in all three boats claimed they caught the most fish per person. How would you respond?*

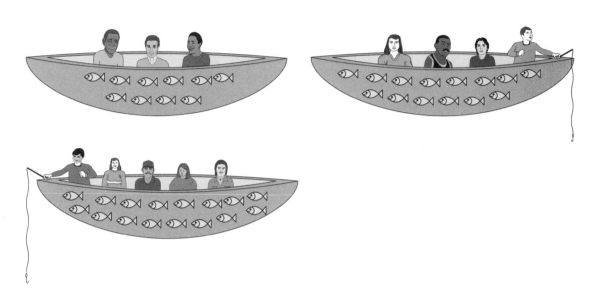

Things to Think About

Which interpretation did you first use to solve the problem? Many adults divide, finding the amount of fish per person. This approach employs the fraction-as-a-quotient interpretation. In this case, $10 \div 3 = 3\frac{1}{3}$, $14 \div 4 = 3\frac{1}{2}$, and $16 \div 5 = 3\frac{1}{5}$. The fishermen in the 4-person boat caught the most fish per person.

Another way to interpret this problem is to think of the relationship between fish and people as a part-to-part ratio and not as a fraction at all. Students often use part-to-part ratios to make sense of situations that could also be interpreted as part-to-whole fractions. By multiplying both the number of fish and the number of people by the same numbers, equivalent ratio tables can be constructed. This solution method is possible because we create equivalent fractions and ratios in the same way—using multiplication and division.

# OF FISH	10	20	30	40	50	200
# OF PEOPLE	3	6	9	12	15	60

# OF FISH	14	28	42	56	70	210
# OF PEOPLE	4	8	12	16	20	60

# OF FISH	16	32	48	64	80	192
# OF PEOPLE	5	10	15	20	25	60

Common multiples can be used to compare two boats. The 3-person boat and the 4-person boat have a common multiple of 12. When we form equivalent ratios with 12 people in each boat, we see that the 3-person boat would catch 40 fish and the 4-person boat would catch 42 fish—indicating that the people in the 4-person boat are the more prolific fishermen. If we want to compare all three boats, we need to find a multiple of 3, 4, and 5, which is 60. The equivalent fish-to-people ratios are 200 to 60, 210 to 60, and 192 to 60, again indicating that the fishermen in the 4-person boat caught the most fish.

Equivalent ratios can also be created where all three boats catch the same number of fish. In this case, a common multiple of 10, 14, and 16 fish is needed. The least common multiple is 560 fish and the corresponding equivalent fish-to-people ratios are 560:168, 560:160, and 560:175. Notice in this case the fish-to-people ratio must be interpreted in light of the original question—which boat caught the most fish per person? The fewer the number of people, the more fish per person so the middle boat of 14 fish compared to 4 people (560:160) caught the most.

Another way to answer this question is to use a part-whole interpretation. Many students think of this problem in terms of what *part* of the fish do the men in the boat get? They partition the fish into parts depending on the number of men in each boat. Thus, students draw pictures of fish, divide them into groups based on the number of fishermen, and then divide up any leftover fish into parts for sharing. As shown below, 10 fish are divided into three groups and one fish into thirds, 14 fish are divided into four groups and the leftover two fish into fourths, and 16 fish are divided into five groups and the leftover fish into fifths. We again see that the fishermen in the 3-person boat caught $3\frac{1}{3}$ fish each, the fishermen in the 4-person boat caught $3\frac{2}{4}$ fish each, and the fishermen in the 5-person boat caught $3\frac{1}{5}$ fish each. This method is similar to the division method because the underlying operation is partitioning.

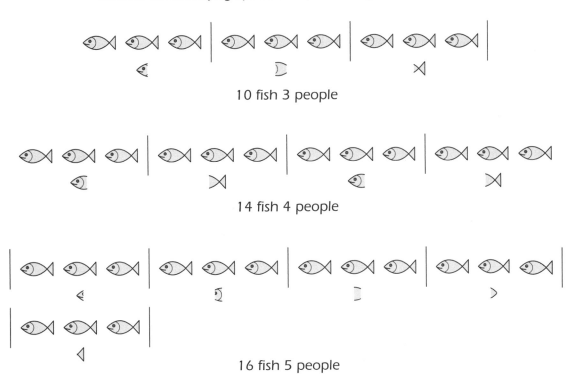

10 fish 3 people

14 fish 4 people

16 fish 5 people

The operator interpretation of fraction can also be used to solve this problem. If we divide all 10 fish into thirds, all 14 fish into fourths, and all 16 fish into fifths, each unit fraction can operate on the total number of fish. For example, multiplying $\frac{1}{3}$ by 10 gives a mixed number, $\frac{10}{3}$, or $3\frac{1}{3}$; multiplying $\frac{1}{4}$ by 14 gives $\frac{14}{4}$, or $3\frac{2}{4}$; and multiplying 16 by $\frac{1}{5}$ results in $\frac{16}{5}$, or $3\frac{1}{5}$ fish per person.

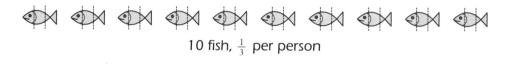

10 fish, $\frac{1}{3}$ per person

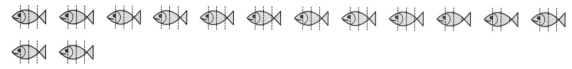

14 fish, $\frac{1}{4}$ per person

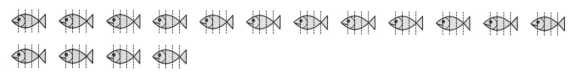

16 fish, $\frac{1}{5}$ per person

▲

2. Equivalence and Ordering

Equivalence is one of the most important mathematical ideas for students to understand, particularly with regard to fractions. Equivalence is used when comparing fractions, ordering fractions, and adding and subtracting fractions. Equivalent fractions are fractions that represent equal value; they are numerals that name the same fractional number. When represented using a number line, equivalent fractions represent the same distance. Equivalent fractions are obtained when both the numerator and the denominator of a fraction are either multiplied or divided by the same number:

$$\frac{a}{b} = \frac{a \times c}{b \times c} = \frac{ac}{bc} \quad \text{or} \quad \frac{ac}{bc} = \frac{ac \div c}{bc \div c} = \frac{a}{b}$$

These relationships are illustrated in the diagrams on page 115, using the parts-of-a-whole interpretation of fraction. The shaded portion of Figure 1 shows $\frac{3}{8}$. Figure 2 was created by dividing each of the eighths in half—we can also say that the number of shaded regions is doubled, as is the total number of regions:

$$\frac{3}{8} = \frac{3 \times 2}{8 \times 2} = \frac{6}{16}$$

If each eighth was instead cut into four pieces, another equivalent fraction would be obtained (see Figure 3):

$$\frac{3}{8} = \frac{3 \times 4}{8 \times 4} = \frac{12}{32}$$

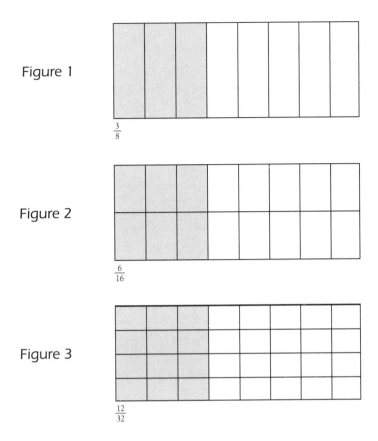

Figure 1

$\frac{3}{8}$

Figure 2

$\frac{6}{16}$

Figure 3

$\frac{12}{32}$

Children often use a doubling strategy to form equivalent fractions. This can be an effective strategy in some situations, as shown in Figures 1 through 3 ($\frac{3}{8} = \frac{6}{16} = \frac{12}{32}$), but notice that doubling does not produce all equivalent fractions ($\frac{9}{24}$ and $\frac{15}{40}$ to name a few).

One underlying assumption regarding equivalent fractions is that when we state that two fractions are equivalent, this implies the "wholes" are the same size. However, students do not always recognize this important fact. Furthermore, students sometimes do not focus on the areas covered by equivalent fractional amounts but instead count the number of pieces, incorrectly assuming that $\frac{3}{8}$ is not equivalent to $\frac{6}{16}$ because 3 ≠ 6. Instructional tasks that focus on equivalence need to direct students' attention to whether or not the "wholes" are the same size and whether the fractional amounts, distances on a number line, or areas in each of the wholes are the same.

Encountering a variety of instructional models and applications may help students generalize some of the key ideas about equivalent fractions. In particular, the idea that multiplication and division can be used to form equivalent fractions needs to be examined in different situations with the different interpretations of fractions. For example, number lines can be used to show that $\frac{3}{4}$ is equivalent to $\frac{15}{20}$; both fractions represent the same distance though on the second number line each fourth is divided into five sections in order to create twentieths.

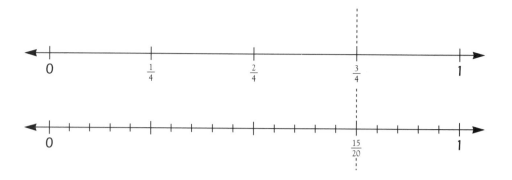

Dividing each fourth into five equal parts is equivalent to multiplying the numerator and denominator of $\frac{3}{4}$ by 5.

Using the operator interpretation, students might explore how $\frac{2}{3}$ of 9 is equivalent to $\frac{6}{9}$ of 9 using objects or pictures. One way to think of $\frac{2}{3}$ of 9 is to divide the 9 apples below into 3 groups, with 3 apples in each. Two groups of 3 is 6.

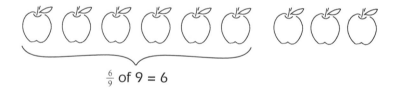

$\frac{2}{3}$ of 9 = 6

Likewise, $\frac{6}{9}$ of 9 also equals 6. Since $\frac{2}{3} = \frac{6}{9}$, operating (in fact, multiplying 9 by the fraction) with either of these fractions results in the same product, 6.

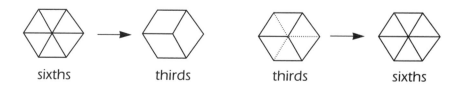

$\frac{6}{9}$ of 9 = 6

Pattern blocks can also be used to explore the multiplicative relationships in equivalence. If the yellow hexagon from a set of pattern blocks represents one "whole," then a blue rhombus represents one third and two green triangles represent two sixths. Students can construct models of these fractions and then use the models to describe how sixths can be grouped to form thirds or how thirds can be divided to form sixths.

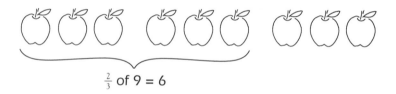

sixths   thirds   thirds   sixths

Children deal with equivalence informally when counting money, using measuring cups, telling time, folding paper, sharing snacks, and eating pizza. Thus, many children are familiar with the general idea of equivalency long before the concept is introduced in school. Why then do children have such difficulty with this important idea? In part it is because we sometimes forget to design instruction around children's prior knowledge—we jump into a topic as if they know nothing or know everything! In addition, some textbooks devote very little time to exploring the meaning of equivalent fractions and instead focus on symbolic manipulation (having students practice finding common denominators, for example). Instructional activities that use models and drawings and ask students to reflect on why two fractions are or are not equivalent are necessary. The activities in this section highlight important ideas related to equivalence and order.

Activity

Exploring Fourths on a Geoboard

Objective: explore the idea that equal fractions, using a part-whole model, do not have to have the same shape but must have equal area.

Materials: a geoboard or geoboard dot paper.

On a geoboard (or geoboard dot paper) make the largest square possible. Now divide the square to show fourths. Each fourth must be an area that if cut out of paper would remain in one piece. Make another square and show fourths that are irregularly shaped. Next make fourths that are not congruent but have equal area. Take each of your previous drawings of fourths and divide them further to show eighths.

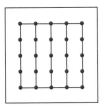 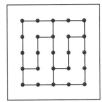 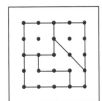

Things to Think About

What strategies did you use to make fourths? Since there are 16 square units in the square, each fourth must cover exactly 4 square units. Textbooks often unwittingly create misconceptions about fractions by presenting pictures of "wholes" partitioned into identical fractional parts. In this case, where there are 16 square units in total, any configuration that uses 4 square units is one fourth of the total area. The idea that equal fractional pieces don't have to be identical in shape but simply must cover the same area or space is an important one: it's part of the foundation on which other equivalence relationships are built. For example, a rectangular-shaped $\frac{1}{4}$ of the geoboard covers the same area as an irregularly shaped $\frac{1}{4}$ of the geoboard (4 square units), but the $\frac{1}{4}$s do not look identical. Students must overcome their tendency to rely on visualization for verification of equality and instead consider the relationships established by dividing a whole into *n* number of parts.

The geoboard also can be used to show why $\frac{1}{4} = \frac{2}{8}$. Although these fractions cover an equivalent area, $\frac{2}{8}$ consists of more but smaller fractional pieces. This can be demonstrated by cutting each fourth of the geoboard into two pieces. Notice that this is represented symbolically by multiplying by one ($\frac{2}{2}$):

$$\frac{1 \times 2}{4 \times 2} = \frac{2}{8} \qquad \blacktriangle$$

Activity

Tangram Fractions

Objective: use tangram puzzle pieces to find equal but noncongruent areas that have equivalent representations in terms of fourths, eighths, and sixteenths.

Materials: a tangram puzzle.

Use a tangram puzzle or the drawing below and determine the fractional values of each of the pieces. The complete tangram square is the unit, or whole. Which of the pieces have equal area? Think about how you can identify the fractional value of each piece. What role will equivalent fractions play in your decisions? Label each piece using denominators of fourths, eighths, and sixteenths.

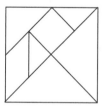

Things to Think About

There are a number of ways to determine the values of the tangram pieces. Since the two large triangles cover one half of the whole square, each large triangle represents $\frac{1}{4}$. Imagine covering the other half of the tangram square with small triangles. Eight small triangles cover one half of the whole, so sixteen of these small triangles cover the whole square. Thus, a small triangle is $\frac{1}{16}$ of the whole. The square, the medium triangle, and the parallelogram each cover the same area as two small triangles; each has a fractional value of $\frac{2}{16}$, or $\frac{1}{8}$. How might you demonstrate that $\frac{1}{4}$ is equivalent to $\frac{4}{16}$? Try covering the large triangle with the medium triangle and the two small triangles. Other equivalencies, such as $\frac{2}{8} = \frac{1}{4}$, can be illustrated using two medium triangles, which are the same size as one large triangle.

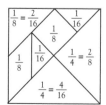

▲

When we compare two fractions or order three or more fractions, we apply ideas involving equivalence. For example, if you are given two fractions to compare, what steps do you take? Most adults first apply rules they have learned to form equivalent fractions with common denominators, and then they compare these equivalent fractions. They don't first think about the fractions in terms of their relative size—that is, they don't reason about how large or small these fractions are until after they have equivalent fractions with common denominators. However, informal methods that focus on understanding the size of a fraction can initially be used to compare and order fractions in conjunction with formal procedures such as finding common denominators. The next three activities ask you to explore some informal but efficient methods for comparing and ordering fractions.

Activity

Numerators and Denominators

Objective: use relationships among common numerators and common denominators to compare and order fractions.

How is the size of a fraction related to the numerator and denominator of the fraction? More specifically, how is the size of $\frac{2}{4}$ changed when you increase the numerator by one—to $\frac{3}{4}$? How is the size of $\frac{2}{4}$ changed when you increase the denominator by one—to $\frac{2}{5}$? Pick a common fraction. Increase the numerator by one and write the resulting fraction. Use the same initial fraction and increase the denominator by one and write the resulting fraction. Compare each resulting fraction with the original. Explain why the resulting fractions are greater or less than the initial fraction.

Things to Think About

What happens to the size of the fraction when the numerator is increased? Increasing the numerator increases the number of parts being considered within the same whole amount and thus results in a larger fraction (e.g., $\frac{3}{4} > \frac{2}{4}$). Note that while the numerators differ, both fractions have a denominator of four. The "common denominator" technique that is used to compare fractions is based on the fact that if two fractions are divided into the same number of fractional pieces, then the larger fraction is the one with the most pieces.

What happens to the size of a fraction when the denominator is increased? Increasing the denominator increases the number of parts needed to make a whole. The fraction $\frac{2}{5}$ is smaller than $\frac{2}{4}$, since $\frac{2}{5}$ requires five parts to make a whole and $\frac{2}{4}$ requires only four parts to make a whole. Consider this set of fractions with increasing denominators: $\frac{2}{4}$, $\frac{2}{5}$, $\frac{2}{6}$, $\frac{2}{7}$, $\frac{2}{8}$, and $\frac{2}{9}$. Each fraction has a numerator of two, which indicates that there are two parts of some whole amount. However, as the denominator increases, the size of each of the two parts decreases. That is, $\frac{2}{5}$ is greater than $\frac{2}{9}$, because the parts or pieces in $\frac{2}{5}$ are larger than the parts or pieces in $\frac{2}{9}$. When two fractions have the same numerator (e.g., $\frac{3}{5}$ and $\frac{3}{7}$), you can compare them by simply considering the size of the parts; you do not need to find a common denominator! The "common numerator" technique is an efficient, conceptually based method for comparing fractions with identical numerators. For example, which of these fractions is greater: $\frac{8}{10}$ or $\frac{8}{12}$? In both fractions there are eight fractional pieces, but twelfths are smaller than tenths so $\frac{8}{10} > \frac{8}{12}$. ▲

Activity

Benchmarks

Objective: use benchmarks to order fractions when neither the numerators nor the denominators are the same.

A benchmark is a standard value that is used for comparison purposes. In fractions, two important benchmarks are $\frac{1}{2}$ and 1. The fraction $\frac{1}{2}$ can be used as a benchmark for determining the relative size of other fractions. If you wish to compare two fractions, first determine whether each fraction is greater than, less than, or equal to $\frac{1}{2}$. Then use that information to compare the original quantities.

Which is larger? $\quad\quad \frac{5}{8}$ *or* $\frac{4}{10}$ $\quad \frac{6}{20}$ *or* $\frac{17}{19}$ $\quad \frac{2}{3}$ *or* $\frac{4}{9}$ $\quad \frac{2}{5}$ *or* $\frac{8}{16}$

Things to Think About

Is there a quick way to compare a fraction to the benchmark of $\frac{1}{2}$? Yes. Examine the denominator of the fraction (e.g., the 8 in $\frac{5}{8}$) and halve it to find the number of pieces equivalent to one half (4). Thus, $\frac{4}{8}$ is equivalent to $\frac{1}{2}$, the fractions $\frac{1}{8}$, $\frac{2}{8}$, and $\frac{3}{8}$ are less than $\frac{1}{2}$, and the fractions $\frac{5}{8}$, $\frac{6}{8}$, $\frac{7}{8}$, and $\frac{8}{8}$ are more than $\frac{1}{2}$. What if the denominator is an odd number, like 9? Use the same approach of halving the denominator:

$$\frac{4.5}{9}, \quad or \quad \frac{4\frac{1}{2}}{9}$$

is equivalent to $\frac{1}{2}$. While we rarely use decimals or fractions within fractions (it is possible), you can use this decimal amount to decide quickly how the size of other fractions compare to $\frac{1}{2}$. For example, $\frac{4}{9} < \frac{1}{2}$ but $\frac{5}{9} > \frac{1}{2}$.

When comparing two fractions, first determine whether each fraction is more than or less than one half (e.g., $\frac{5}{8} > \frac{1}{2}$ and $\frac{1}{2} > \frac{4}{10}$), then use this information to compare the two fractions—$\frac{5}{8} > \frac{4}{10}$. In order to use a benchmark effectively, you must understand the concept of equivalence and be aware of relative size compared to one half of the same whole. Students may use the location of $\frac{1}{2}$ on the number line to help make comparisons. Previous work with part-whole models and number lines contributes to our making sense of the benchmark concept. Other benchmarks such as 1 also can be used to compare fractions.

Another informal approach for comparing two fractions involves thinking about the fractional part that is needed to make one whole. Let's call it the "missing part" method. If we wish to compare $\frac{6}{7}$ and $\frac{8}{9}$, the benchmark approach does not work, since both fractions are greater than one half. Examine the sketches below:

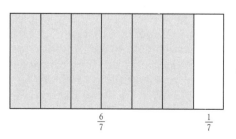

$\frac{6}{7}$ $\quad\quad\quad$ $\frac{1}{7}$

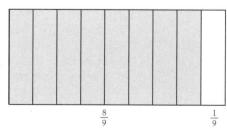

$\frac{8}{9}$ $\quad\quad\quad$ $\frac{1}{9}$

Both rectangles are "missing" one piece. The first rectangle is missing $\frac{1}{7}$ to make a whole. The second rectangle is missing $\frac{1}{9}$ to make a whole. Since $\frac{1}{7} > \frac{1}{9}$, the first rectangle is missing a larger piece to make a whole, and consequently the first rectangle is smaller. Thus $\frac{6}{7} < \frac{8}{9}$. This method works when both fractions are missing the same number of pieces to make a whole (it guarantees that you are comparing the size of the missing pieces). For example, $\frac{4}{6}$ and $\frac{11}{13}$ are both missing two pieces to make a whole. Use the missing-part method to compare $\frac{2}{3}$ with $\frac{3}{4}$ and $\frac{11}{14}$ with $\frac{5}{8}$. You may want to make a sketch of each fractional amount. ▲

Activity

Ordering a Set of Fractions

Objective: use all of the informal conceptually based methods we've discussed—common denominators, common numerators, equivalent fractions, benchmarks, and missing parts—to order a set of fractions.

Order the following fractions without using decimal representations or converting all of the fractions to a common denominator:

$$\frac{2}{5}, \frac{7}{8}, \frac{1}{4}, \frac{9}{10}, \frac{12}{7}, \frac{13}{11}, \frac{7}{9}, \frac{1}{3}, \frac{5}{8}$$

Things to Think About

What did you do first? Using the idea of benchmarks, many people sort the fractions into groups: fractions less than one half, fractions greater than one half, and fractions greater than one. The fractions less than one half are $\frac{2}{5}$, $\frac{1}{4}$, and $\frac{1}{3}$; the fractions greater than one half are $\frac{7}{8}$, $\frac{9}{10}$, $\frac{7}{9}$, and $\frac{5}{8}$; and the fractions greater than one are $\frac{12}{7}$ and $\frac{13}{11}$. The fractions less than one half can be ordered by using the common numerator method ($\frac{1}{4} < \frac{1}{3}$) and by changing $\frac{1}{3}$ to an equivalent fraction with a numerator of two ($\frac{2}{6}$) so it can easily be compared to $\frac{2}{5}$. Thus the order of these three fractions is $\frac{1}{4}$, $\frac{1}{3}$, $\frac{2}{5}$.

The fractions greater than one half can be compared using the common denominator, common numerator, and missing-parts methods. For example, $\frac{5}{8} < \frac{7}{8}$ using common denominators, $\frac{7}{9} < \frac{7}{8}$ using common numerators, and $\frac{7}{8} < \frac{9}{10}$ using the missing-parts method. However, none of the informal methods will help us compare $\frac{5}{8}$ and $\frac{7}{9}$. Thus we apply the common denominator algorithm to show that $\frac{7}{9} > \frac{5}{8}$. The order of these fractions is $\frac{5}{8}$, $\frac{7}{9}$, $\frac{7}{8}$, $\frac{9}{10}$.

Finally the two fractions greater than one can be compared using a benchmark of $1\frac{1}{2}$. The fraction $\frac{13}{11}$ is less than $\frac{12}{7}$, since $\frac{13}{11}$ is less than $1\frac{1}{2}$ and $\frac{12}{7}$ is greater than $1\frac{1}{2}$.

The order of the fractions from least to greatest is $\frac{1}{4}$, $\frac{1}{3}$, $\frac{2}{5}$, $\frac{5}{8}$, $\frac{7}{9}$, $\frac{7}{8}$, $\frac{9}{10}$, $\frac{13}{11}$, and $\frac{12}{7}$. While we could also have ordered these fractions by renaming them as decimals or changing them all to fractions with a common denominator, this activity demonstrates that it isn't always necessary to use either of these algorithms. ▲

3. Operations with Fractions

Operations with fractions are taught in elementary and middle school using well-defined algorithms for each operation. The difficulties that students experience with fraction operations are well documented in national assessments and research studies. Often students perform algorithms with fractions by applying rules without understanding what the operations or fractions mean. Without conceptual understanding, students become inflexible about applying rules and don't think about whether the answer makes sense. They are unable to monitor their own performance because they have no idea about the reasonableness of a solution; their only approach to checking an answer involves reexecuting a rule. Although algorithms are efficient computational methods and are important when working with fractions, instruction must emphasize both conceptual and procedural understanding so that students can develop meaningful mental models that are linked to the real world.

Of the five different interpretations of fraction, the one that is used most often when adding and subtracting fractions is the parts-of-a-whole or set. In these operations we are answering the question *how much?* and our referent usually is one whole. Fraction addition and subtraction arise naturally in the process of naming fractional parts of a particular manipulative model or when thinking about many real-life situations. For example, eating $\frac{1}{4}$ of a pizza and then eating another $\frac{2}{4}$ of the same pizza means $\frac{3}{4}$ of the pizza has been eaten. Also, because there were $\frac{4}{4}$ in the whole pizza, $\frac{1}{4}$ of a pizza remains. Although students may refer to these pieces as units (e.g., 1 piece plus 2 more pieces makes 3 pieces), in this familiar context students usually understand the "fourthness" of each piece as it relates to the whole pizza.

Early problem solving should be directly linked to students' actions on models they create or use and the related symbolic representations. Drawings, tables, and manipulative materials that highlight relationships can be used to model sums and differences of fractional amounts. Some common models include pictures showing parts of wholes, double number lines, clocks, or arrays. Ratio tables can also be used (see Chapter 8). However, it is important to remember that students must develop and use models that make sense to them within the context of problems and investigations. This does not mean that teachers can't introduce models, but that they should not expect all students to use them in the same way or at all! As described earlier, the yellow hexagon in a set of pattern blocks is a concrete model that can be used to represent one whole. Green triangles are $\frac{1}{6}$ of the whole, blue rhombi are $\frac{1}{3}$ of the whole, and red trapezoids are $\frac{1}{2}$ of the whole.

Activity

Adding and Subtracting Fractions with Models

Objective: link the operation of addition of fractions to the actions performed on fraction models.

Materials: pattern blocks.

Solve the following problems first by using models such as pictures of cakes, a clock, a number line, or pattern blocks and then by using symbols. Did you solve the problems in the same way each time? How did the models help you recognize and generalize relationships?

> *For breakfast, Vicki ate $\frac{1}{3}$ of a small coffee cake. Later in the morning she ate $\frac{1}{6}$ more of the coffee cake. How much of the coffee cake did Vicki eat altogether?*

Stephen baked 3 pies for a party. He ate $\frac{1}{6}$ of one pie when the pies came out of the oven (to test that his baking skills were still okay!). At the party $1\frac{1}{2}$ pies were consumed. How much pie is left over?

Things to Think About

The first problem can be modeled by combining the pattern blocks that represent $\frac{1}{3}$ and $\frac{1}{6}$—a blue rhombus and a green triangle. When you place these two blocks on the hexagon (the whole unit), they cover $\frac{1}{2}$ of the whole, which indicates that $\frac{1}{2}$ (of the coffee cake) is left:

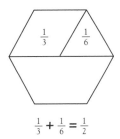

$$\tfrac{1}{3} + \tfrac{1}{6} = \tfrac{1}{2}$$

You also might use a clock to think about the relationships. One-third of an hour is 20 minutes, $\frac{1}{6}$ of an hour is 10 minutes, for a total of 30 minutes. Since 30 minutes is equivalent to $\frac{1}{2}$ hour, we can generalize that one half of the coffee cake was eaten. While with the symbolic algorithm you may have changed the $\frac{1}{3}$ to an equivalent fraction with a common denominator of 6, it is not necessary when using the concrete materials. However, this is not the case for all problems; the common denominator algorithm enables us to add all fractions, even ones we cannot model.

How can we connect the symbols and the models? In whole number and decimal addition, like units (e.g., ones, hundreds, tenths) are combined. We want students to generalize this idea to fractions as well—sixths and thirds are different-size pieces and in order to combine them we must find equivalent fractions that are divided into the same number of parts. When asked to explain, using the models and the symbols, why $\frac{1}{3} + \frac{1}{6} = \frac{1}{2}$, students can, by manipulating the pattern blocks or minutes on a clock and discussing what they observe, conclude that $\frac{1}{3}$ is equivalent to $\frac{2}{6}$ and that the total is therefore $\frac{3}{6}$, or $\frac{1}{2}$. By being asked leading questions about the need for equal-size pieces or parts when adding they can be helped to make sense of the rules for addition.

A typical student error that most often occurs when working with symbols is $\frac{1}{3} + \frac{1}{6} = \frac{2}{9}$. Does this answer make sense when looking at the models and answering the question *how much?* No; $\frac{2}{9}$ is quite a bit less than $\frac{1}{2}$, yet using either pattern blocks or a clock, we can see that the answer is equal to $\frac{1}{2}$. It is important for students to first make sense of the contextual situation and then coordinate what they discover using models with the more abstract representation of symbols.

Did you solve the second problem the same way? Probably not. Three hexagons can be used to represent the three pies. One hexagon can be divided into sixths using triangles, and one triangle (the one sixth Stephen ate) can be removed. Next you can remove one whole hexagon and then an additional half from the hexagon already divided into sixths. This leaves one and one third (or two sixths) hexagons (pies) left over.

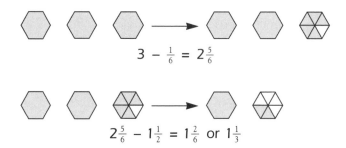

$$3 - \tfrac{1}{6} = 2\tfrac{5}{6}$$

$$2\tfrac{5}{6} - 1\tfrac{1}{2} = 1\tfrac{2}{6} \text{ or } 1\tfrac{1}{3}$$

Some algorithms would have you change the three to an improper fraction with a denominator of six ($\tfrac{18}{6}$). However, as working with the models has shown, you only have to represent one of the wholes as $\tfrac{6}{6}$. This can be expressed symbolically as $3 = 2\tfrac{6}{6}$. Expressing 3 as the mixed number $2\tfrac{6}{6}$ is one step in another algorithm that is taught to students. One sixth then is removed from the $\tfrac{6}{6}$. To take away the additional $1\tfrac{1}{2}$, the $\tfrac{1}{2}$ can also be changed to an equivalent fraction with a denominator of six:

$$
\begin{array}{cc}
3 & 2\tfrac{5}{6} = 2\tfrac{5}{6} \\
-\ \tfrac{1}{6} & -1\tfrac{1}{2} = 1\tfrac{3}{6} \\
\hline
2\tfrac{5}{6} & 1\tfrac{2}{6} = 1\tfrac{1}{3}
\end{array}
$$

In general, using models helps us make sense of the operation and the solution. Linking the models and the symbolic representations is crucial. Remember, however, that it is the students who must do this through problem solving and discussion. Simply telling students about these connections is like trying to teach them to ride a bicycle by telling them how you do it. Once students have made sense of the procedures, they can focus on generalizing them to all fraction sums and differences, including those they can model only in their mind's eye. ▲

Different types of problems tend to illicit different problem-solving approaches and eventual generalizations. One middle school student developed the following algorithm for subtraction based on an approach she had used to subtract whole numbers. For the problem $4\tfrac{1}{5} - 1\tfrac{3}{5}$, her reasoning was, *I have $\tfrac{1}{5}$ but I need to subtract $\tfrac{3}{5}$. I can only take away $\tfrac{1}{5}$ so I still need to remove an additional $\tfrac{2}{5}$* [represented symbolically as $^{-}(\tfrac{2}{5})$]. *Then 4 minus 1 is 3. Now $3 - \tfrac{2}{5}$ is easy to do, that's $2\tfrac{3}{5}$.*

$$
\begin{array}{cc}
4\tfrac{1}{5} & \text{Think:} \quad \tfrac{1}{5} - \tfrac{3}{5} = \tfrac{-2}{5} \\
-1\tfrac{3}{5} & 4 - 1 = 3 \\
\hline
3^{-\tfrac{2}{5}} & 3 - \tfrac{2}{5} = 2\tfrac{3}{5}
\end{array}
$$

Multiplying and dividing fractions are known to be difficult for students. It might appear on the surface that these are easier operations for students to master computationally, because they do not require common denominators or regrouping. However, the rules for multiplication and division operations are often confused or forgotten. More significant, students who only interpret these operations as "multiplication makes bigger" and "division makes smaller" may not be able to make sense of multiplication and division situations involving fractions or to monitor their work for reasonableness. (You may wish to refer to Chapter 6 for a related discussion of multiplying or dividing decimal fractions.)

One reason students find multiplication of fractions difficult is that their understanding of multiplication is linked to repeated addition or groupings using whole numbers. Multiplication by fractions requires an alternate understanding of multiplication based on the fraction as operator. In this case a fraction is operating on another number (whole number, mixed number, or fraction) and changes the other number. We often tell students that the word *of* means to multiply. This use of the word is based on the operator interpretation of fraction: when we multiply $\frac{1}{2}$ and 8, we are taking one half of eight.

Modeling Fraction Multiplication

Objective: model the operation of taking a part of a part.

Fold a piece of paper to model the following situation:

> *I planted half my garden with vegetables this summer. One third of the half that is vegetables is planted with green beans. What fraction of the whole garden is planted with green beans?*

Things to Think About

This activity demonstrates how the product of two fractions is a "part of a part" and helps explain what happens when one fraction is multiplied by another fraction. First fold the paper in half to represent half of the garden; then fold the half into thirds to show the part planted with green beans. Unfold the paper to inspect the number of parts.

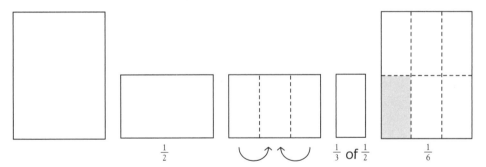

There are six sections in the original rectangle, and one of these sections represents the green beans. Hence $\frac{1}{3} \times \frac{1}{2} = \frac{1}{6}$. Does the order of folding make a difference in terms of the final product? Using the example $\frac{1}{3} \times \frac{1}{2}$, first fold a piece of paper into thirds and then fold the one third in half. The result is also $\frac{1}{6}$. This is an example of the commutative property of multiplication, which states that the order of the factors does not affect the product. You may want to experiment with paper folding to show $\frac{1}{4} \times \frac{1}{3}$ or $\frac{2}{3} \times \frac{1}{2}$. ▲

Function tables and area models can be used to help students make sense of fraction multiplication. Take a set of numbers and multiply them all by a fraction close to but less than 1, say $\frac{9}{10}$. Or multiply the numbers by $\frac{1}{2}$. Have students analyze the size of the products based on the size of the fraction multiplier and any patterns they notice regarding the calculations. This also provides an opportunity for students to explore the inverse relationship between multiplication and division: multiplying by $\frac{9}{10}$ is the same as dividing by $\frac{10}{9}$ and multiplying by $\frac{1}{2}$ is the same as dividing by 2. A calculator could be used to take the emphasis away from calculations and focus instruction more on number sense.

NUMBER	MULTIPLY BY $\frac{9}{10}$		NUMBER	MULTIPLY BY $\frac{1}{2}$	
10	$\times \frac{9}{10}$	9	10	$\times \frac{1}{2}$	5
30	$\times \frac{9}{10}$	27	30	$\times \frac{1}{2}$	15
50	$\times \frac{9}{10}$	45	50	$\times \frac{1}{2}$	25
120	$\times \frac{9}{10}$	108	120	$\times \frac{1}{2}$	60
65	$\times \frac{9}{10}$	$58\frac{1}{2}$	65	$\times \frac{1}{2}$	$32\frac{1}{2}$

An area model can be used to explain some fraction-times-fraction word problems. The number sentence $\frac{1}{4}$ of $\frac{2}{3}$ might represent the following situation: *You have two thirds of an enormous chocolate bar and decide to eat one fourth of the two thirds. How much of the chocolate bar are you eating?* This situation can be modeled by drawing a rectangle to represent the candy bar.

Next divide the chocolate bar into thirds and shade $\frac{2}{3}$ to show the starting amount. Then divide the $\frac{2}{3}$s section into fourths, to indicate that we are going to eat $\frac{1}{4}$ of $\frac{2}{3}$.

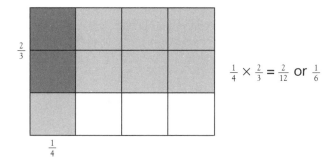

$$\frac{1}{4} \times \frac{2}{3} = \frac{2}{12} \text{ or } \frac{1}{6}$$

Notice that the chocolate bar is now divided into 12 equal pieces; each piece represents $\frac{1}{12}$ of the whole chocolate bar. Two of the 12 pieces are shaded, indicating that is the area of interest: $\frac{1}{4}$ of $\frac{2}{3}$ equals $\frac{2}{12}$, or $\frac{1}{6}$, of the total area of the chocolate bar.

Area models also can be used to model mixed-number-times-fraction and mixed-number-times-mixed-number situations, such as determining how much $\frac{1}{2}$ of $2\frac{3}{4}$ yards of fabric represents or calculating the size of a plot of land that is $1\frac{1}{2}$ acres by $1\frac{1}{2}$ acres.

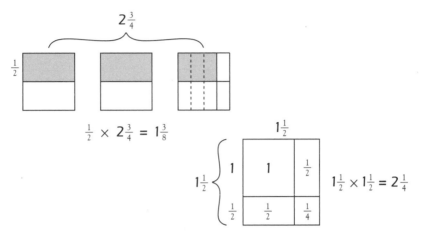

After students begin to understand the meaning of multiplication of fractions by using models, we want to help them generalize procedures and make sense of the algorithms most often used to perform this operation. How can we help students make sense of computations such as multiplying a mixed number and a proper fraction (e.g., $2\frac{1}{2} \times \frac{3}{4}$) and multiplying two mixed numbers (e.g., $1\frac{1}{3} \times 4\frac{5}{6}$)? First, it helps if students use estimation to find a general range for the product. For example, when you multiply a proper fraction and a mixed number, the product will be in between these two values. The product of $2\frac{1}{2}$ and $\frac{3}{4}$ is between $2\frac{1}{2}$ and $\frac{3}{4}$ ($\frac{5}{2} \times \frac{3}{4} = \frac{15}{8}$, or $1\frac{7}{8}$), because the fraction is operating on the mixed number and taking a portion of it. The product of a mixed number and a mixed number will be greater than both numbers. Rounding the mixed number to the nearest whole amount gives a reasonable estimate ($1\frac{1}{3} \times 4\frac{5}{6}$ is approximately 1×5, or 5).

A variety of other methods can be used to explain how we obtain solutions to these types of problems, depending on the values involved. Repeated addition can be used to illustrate a situation like $6 \times \frac{1}{3}$:

$$6 \times \tfrac{1}{3} = \tfrac{1}{3} + \tfrac{1}{3} + \tfrac{1}{3} + \tfrac{1}{3} + \tfrac{1}{3} + \tfrac{1}{3} = 2$$

The distributive property of multiplication over addition can be used to explore the solutions to problems like $\frac{3}{4} \times 2\frac{1}{2}$ and $1\frac{1}{3} \times 4\frac{5}{6}$:

$$\begin{aligned}
\tfrac{3}{4} \times 2\tfrac{1}{2} &= \tfrac{3}{4} \times (2 + \tfrac{1}{2}) \\
&= (\tfrac{3}{4} \times \tfrac{2}{1}) + (\tfrac{3}{4} \times \tfrac{1}{2}) \\
&= \tfrac{6}{4} + \tfrac{3}{8} \\
&= \tfrac{12}{8} + \tfrac{3}{8} \\
&= \tfrac{15}{8} \\
&= 1\tfrac{7}{8}
\end{aligned}$$

$$1\tfrac{1}{3} \times 4\tfrac{5}{6} = (1 + \tfrac{1}{3}) \times (4 + \tfrac{5}{6})$$
$$= (1 \times 4) + (1 \times \tfrac{5}{6}) + (\tfrac{1}{3} \times 4) + (\tfrac{1}{3} \times \tfrac{5}{6})$$
$$= 4 + \tfrac{5}{6} + \tfrac{4}{3} + \tfrac{5}{18}$$
$$= 4 + \tfrac{15}{18} + \tfrac{24}{18} + \tfrac{5}{18}$$
$$= 4 + \tfrac{44}{18}$$
$$= 4 + 2\tfrac{8}{18}$$
$$= 6\tfrac{8}{18}$$
$$= 6\tfrac{4}{9}$$

Because the procedures students use to multiply fractions are not always easy to illustrate with pictures or objects, it is important to help them make sense of the procedures by connecting them to previously learned mathematical concepts and properties.

There are a variety of mental strategies that can be used to multiply fractions (Dowker 1992; Fosnot and Dolk 2002). When solving a fraction computation in one's head, many problem solvers examined the numbers first and then chose approaches that made the computations easier and "friendlier." Some of the strategies discussed in Chapter 2 can be applied effectively to fraction multiplication problems like $3\tfrac{1}{2} \times 12$ and $\tfrac{3}{8} \times \tfrac{2}{9}$.

▲ Use a doubling and halving technique, since multiplying by 2 and dividing by 2 is equivalent to 1, the multiplicative identity.

$$3\tfrac{1}{2} \times 12 = 7 \times 6 \qquad (3\tfrac{1}{2} \text{ doubled and 12 halved})$$
$$= 42$$

▲ Use the commutative property of multiplication to switch the order of the numerators. Since order doesn't matter when multiplying, exchange the numerators to make fractions that can be simplified. Notice that the product is the same regardless of the order of the numerators or denominators or which number is linked with which.

$$\tfrac{3}{8} \times \tfrac{2}{9} = \tfrac{2}{8} \times \tfrac{3}{9} \qquad \text{(switch numerators)}$$
$$= \tfrac{1}{4} \times \tfrac{1}{3} \qquad \text{(simplify the fractions)}$$
$$= \tfrac{1}{12} \qquad \text{(multiply the simplified fractions)}$$

Number sense can play an important role in fraction computation, especially in making the mental work easier!

Fraction division is something that many of us learned to perform but were never asked to explain. For example, consider the following problem:

You have a 4-cup container of cottage cheese and are planning on making servings that are $\tfrac{2}{3}$ cup. How many servings of cottage cheese can you prepare?

This problem is a division problem and is represented symbolically by $4 \div \tfrac{2}{3}$. We can determine that the answer is 6 servings by using the "invert and multiply" algorithm. But let's try to explain this problem. Why is this a division situation rather than a subtraction problem? Why does the "invert and multiply" algorithm work? And why is the answer a whole number that is greater than the dividend and the divisor? Work through the next activity and discussion in order to gain insight into these questions.

Activity

Division of Fractions

Objective: use different interpretations of the meaning of division to make sense of fraction division problems.

Use a model (e.g., manipulative materials, pictures, number line) to find the answers to the problems below. Be sure to write a number sentence to illustrate each situation. Think about how the meaning of the operation is a bit different in the two problems.

> A. In preparing a project for students, an art teacher realizes she needs $\frac{2}{3}$ yard of ribbon for every group of students. She has 2 yards of ribbon. Does she have enough ribbon for four groups of students?
>
> B. In order to prepare for her next art class, a teacher divides up her supplies ahead of time. She has 2 yards of ribbon to be shared equally among 3 groups of students. How much ribbon does each group of students receive?

Things to Think About

Our understanding of division of fractions is related to our understanding of the different meanings of division in general, specifically how these meanings are interpreted in fraction situations. For example, the "repeated subtraction" interpretation of division can be used to make sense of Problem A, represented by the equation $2 \div \frac{2}{3} = 3$. Using this interpretation, $\frac{2}{3}$ is "subtracted" or measured out of the 2 whole yards. Thus, each group contains $\frac{2}{3}$, and there are three such groups in 2. In the repeated subtraction interpretation of division, the quotient represents the number of groups, or in this case, the number of groups of students that will get ribbon for the art project. The teacher does not have enough ribbon for four groups of students.

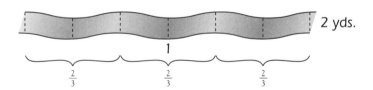

The second situation, represented by the equation $2 \div 3 = \frac{2}{3}$, can be interpreted as partitive division. The "partitive" interpretation of division involves dividing or partitioning quantities into a given number of equal-size groups. In the partitive interpretation of division, the quotient represents the amount that is in each group: in this situation the length of the ribbon to be given to each group of students. The diagram below shows 2 yards divided into 3 groups, with each group containing $\frac{2}{3}$ yard.

2 yds.

1

▲

The examples in Activity 13 were chosen because they clearly illustrate two interpretations of division and model the relationships among the dividend, divisor, and quotient. Many division equations include fractions that cannot easily be modeled using pictures or materials (e.g., $\frac{5}{8} \div \frac{2}{3}$). Furthermore, it is important to realize that not all division situations are represented by actions based on partitive division or repeated subtraction. For example, if the area of a rectangle is 10 square centimeters and the width is $\frac{1}{2}$ centimeter, the length of the rectangle can be found by calculating $10 \div \frac{1}{2}$. The use of either partitive division or repeated subtraction within this context makes no sense. Area is a multidimensional quantity that is the product of length and width. The "invert-and-multiply" algorithm, which relies on the inverse relationship between multiplication and division and between reciprocals, enables us not only to make sense of other situations but also to divide "messy" fractions.

Why does the "invert and multiply" algorithm work? How is it that we can convert a division expression into a multiplication expression by multiplying by the reciprocal of the divisor? There are a number of ways to explain this. One method is based on the *multiplicative identity property*: you can multiply any expression by one and not change the value of the expression. First, write the expression $\frac{5}{8} \div \frac{2}{3}$ as a fraction in which there is a fraction in the numerator and a fraction in the denominator. Next, multiply the numerator and the denominator by $\frac{3}{2}$. A fraction with $\frac{3}{2}$ as the numerator and also $\frac{3}{2}$ as the denominator is equivalent to 1. Thus, we are multiplying the entire expression by 1.

$$\frac{\frac{5}{8}}{\frac{2}{3}} \times \frac{\frac{3}{2}}{\frac{3}{2}}$$

Completing the multiplication in the denominator results in a product of 1 ($\frac{6}{6}$) and leads to dividing by 1; the numerator is equivalent to $\frac{5}{8} \times \frac{3}{2}$, or $\frac{15}{16}$.

$$\frac{\frac{5}{8}}{\frac{2}{3}} \left(\frac{\frac{3}{2}}{\frac{3}{2}} \right) = \frac{\frac{5}{8} \times \frac{3}{2}}{\frac{3}{2} \times \frac{3}{2}}$$

$$= \frac{\frac{15}{16}}{\frac{6}{6}} \quad \text{or} \quad \frac{\frac{15}{16}}{1} \quad \text{or} \quad \frac{15}{16}$$

Another method illustrating why multiplying by the reciprocal works involves the missing-factor interpretation of division. When considering $\frac{5}{8} \div \frac{2}{3}$, we can rewrite this expression as a multiplication operation in which a factor is missing: $\frac{2}{3} \times a = \frac{5}{8}$. To find the value of a we can multiply by the reciprocal of $\frac{2}{3}$:

$$\frac{2}{3} \times a = \frac{5}{8}$$
$$(\frac{3}{2} \times \frac{2}{3})a = \frac{5}{8} \times \frac{3}{2}$$
$$\frac{6}{6}a = \frac{15}{16}$$
$$a = \frac{15}{16}$$

One way teachers can help students understand multiplication and division with fractions is to connect whole number multiplication and division to multiplication and division with fractions and decimals. Teachers can expand the contexts of problem situations, expand the range of numbers from whole numbers to fractions, and expand the language that we use to describe situations. However, it is also important to extend students' understanding of these operations beyond whole numbers by using a range of problem situations and helping students note the similarities and differences between fractional and whole number relationships.

Teaching Fractions

Fractional numbers are a rich part of mathematics. However, many students find them difficult to understand. To help students learn about and use fractions, it is important to introduce the multiple meanings of fraction and to emphasize sense making in all mathematical activities. Instruction in the early grades should focus on the part-whole interpretation of fraction but include all other interpretations as well. Students most likely will solve problems involving divisions, ratios, operators, or measures informally at first. However, having experiences with these interpretations prior to more formal work in middle school will help students develop fractional sense. Students should be encouraged to use models of fractional quantities (including blocks, number lines, and ratio tables) and to model equivalencies and operations before they are introduced to procedures and rules. Too often instruction moves quickly to the symbolic, asking students to memorize algorithms. Ideally we want middle grades students to be flexible in their approach to problems, to be able to perform computations accurately and fluidly, and to be able to reason carefully about rational numbers and operations. The long-range goal is for students to understand this complex topic and to be fully prepared to deal with rational expressions in algebra and other upper-level courses.

Questions for Discussion

1. Describe the different meanings or interpretations of fractions. Examine a mathematics textbook (grades 4–7) and analyze how fractions are interpreted throughout the book.
2. What are some of the "big ideas" of fractions that students must understand? Why are these important ideas?
3. Teach someone else the strategies for comparing and ordering fractions. Reflect on your instruction and discuss how you helped them make sense of the strategies.

4. A model is any tool that can be used to help students think about mathematics. Models can include physical materials, graphs, charts, number lines, pictures, and calculators. Do you think models are necessary for understanding fraction operations? Give examples of how two different models can be used to solve fraction problems with each of the four operations.
5. What mental techniques can be used when computing with fractions? Describe how each mental technique is related to number sense and mathematical properties.

Decimals

Decimal numbers allow us to represent fractional quantities using our base ten number system. With the advent of the inexpensive calculator, decimals are used much more frequently than in the past. We use decimals whenever we deal with money, convert metric measures, rank our favorite baseball players by their hitting record, or record precise measurements.

Few teachers have difficulty performing computations with decimals. However, when asked to state important concepts related to decimals, many of us find it hard to articulate even the most fundamental ideas. As a result, instruction in many classrooms focuses on developing students' computational skills rather than on helping students develop a conceptual understanding of quantity, order, and equivalence related to decimal quantities. Looking at some of the "big ideas" related to decimals will help us come to a more focused understanding of some of the mathematical relationships decimals represent.

1. Decimal Concepts

Decimals in many ways appear simply to be an extension of whole numbers. The value of each place to the right of the decimal point is found by dividing the previous value by ten. This is similar to how values to the left of the decimal point are established—namely, grouping by powers of ten. However, the decimal number system is considerably more complex mathematically than the whole number system. The quantities represented by the decimal system are real numbers (of which whole numbers are a subset). Thus, some decimals (e.g., .85, $.\overline{3}$) can be written as fractions, but other decimals (e.g., 0.12112111211112 . . .) cannot. What can also be confusing is that the symbols that represent these fractional values look a lot like whole numbers—that is, 32.5 and 3.25 both have the digits 3, 2, and 5 and a decimal point and look similar to 325. Furthermore, the language of decimals does not always make it clear that the quantities are of a different nature—for example, *hundredths* sounds a lot like *hundreds* and sometimes is interpreted as such. And finally, since many of us lack mental models for decimal fractional quantities, interpreting the symbols is more complex.

Students often think a "decimal" is the decimal point rather than a number. When asked to write down a decimal numeral, they might put "." on their paper. In order to use and interpret decimal quantities, students must first understand that the decimal point is a symbol that indicates the location of the ones place and all other subsequent place values in the decimal system. The decimal point separates a whole number amount from a number that is less than one. Finding examples of decimals (5.2 on an odometer, say), explaining what the decimal numeral means in the context of its use (I traveled 5.2 miles to work), indicating the general value of the decimal numeral (I live a little more than five miles from work), and then stating what two whole numbers the decimal is between (5.2 miles is between 5 miles and 6 miles) helps students recognize that the decimal amount is the sum of a whole number and a number that is less than one. When reading decimal amounts, the word *and* is used to indicate the decimal point and to separate the whole number from the part of the number that is less than one. Thus, we don't use the word *and* when reading large whole numbers: thirty-nine million twelve thousand sixty-three.

The ideas behind whole number place value extend to decimals. Grouping into sets of ten is one of the main principles of our Hindu-Arabic (base ten) numeration system. In whole number numeration, ten "ones" are grouped together and replaced by one "ten," and ten "tens" are replaced by one "hundred." In decimal numeration, ten "hundredths" are grouped together and replaced by one "tenth" and ten "tenths" are replaced by one "one." The relationship between any two adjacent places is that the place on the left is worth ten times as much as the place on the right, and the place on the right is worth one tenth as much as the place on the left:

$$\times 10 \quad \times 10 \quad \times 10 \qquad \times 10 \qquad\qquad \times 10$$

hundreds tens ones tenths hundredths thousandths

$$\div 10 \quad \div 10 \quad \div 10 \qquad \div 10 \qquad\qquad \div 10$$

This place value relationship is based on multiplication by a common factor. Enter 0.00001 into a calculator and multiply the display repeatedly by 10. Each multiplication results in a number that is ten times greater, shown by the movement of the 1 to the left. Likewise, if we enter 10,000,000 into a calculator and multiply the display by 0.1 (which is the same as dividing by 10), we observe how the quantity decreases as the 1 moves to the right. Students often can name a specific place in the decimal system—tenths, millionths—but may not understand the value of that place (e.g., a tenth represents one tenth of a whole). If students don't understand the relationship between place values (that 0.6 is ten times larger than 0.06, for example) or realize that the value of a place can be represented using other place values (that 13 tenths is equal to 130 hundredths, for example), they will have great difficulty with decimal numbers.

Another important idea in our base ten system that extends to decimal numbers is that the quantity represented by a digit is the product of its face value and its place value. The face value is the value of the digit without regard to its position. In the number 73.6, the quantity represented by the 7, for example, is its face value (7) multiplied by its place value (10), which is 7×10, or 70. Similarly, the face value of the 6 is 6, but the quantity it represents (or its value) is 6×0.1; or 0.6, because the

6 is in the tenths position. Students who incorrectly indicate that 0.04 = 0.4 may only be considering the face value of the numerals (4 = 4). A related concept is that the value of a decimal numeral is the sum of the values of the individual digits. For example, the value of 25.86 is $(2 \times 10) + (5 \times 1) + (8 \times .1) + (6 \times .01)$. This concept can perplex students because of how we read decimal amounts—"twenty-five and eighty-six hundredths." Notice that "eighty-six hundredths" directs us to think of the quantity as hundredths rather than as 8 tenths + 6 hundredths.

Decimal concepts are often presented to students using symbols. However, physical models that represent the quantities and the multiplicative relationship between place values can help individuals make sense of these ideas.

Activity

Face Value and Place Value

Objective: use the same physical models to represent different quantities.

Materials: base ten blocks.

Take the following base ten blocks: two units (ones), three longs (tens), one flat (hundred), and one cube (thousand). The whole number value of these blocks is 1,132. Imagine assigning a value of "one" to the thousands block. What are the values of the other blocks relative to this new "one"? What number is represented by the blocks now? Assign other values to the blocks in order to represent the following numbers: 113.2, 11.32, 1.132, and 0.1132.

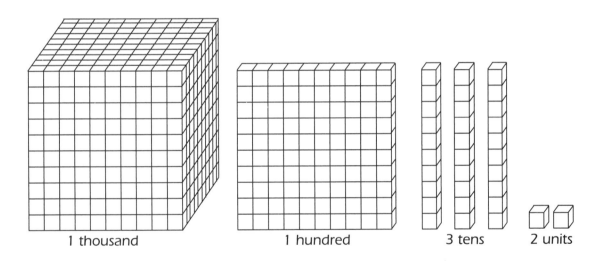

1 thousand   1 hundred   3 tens   2 units

Things to Think About

When the thousand block is assigned a value of "one," then a flat (hundred) block has a value of one tenth, a long (ten) block has a value of one hundredth, and a unit cube has a value of one thousandth. The decimal number represented by these blocks is now 1.132. Notice how the blocks support the idea that 1.132 is the sum of 1 + 0.1 + 0.03 + 0.002.

How do you read 1.132? As "one point one three two"? The way we read decimal amounts, especially when we just read digits, can either support or hinder students' understanding of decimal place values. Even when we read 1.132 as "one and one hundred thirty-two thousandths," students have difficulty interpreting the quantity, because the word *hundred* is used with a digit in the tenths position! The other words and position values are equally mismatched. There is an additional mismatch between the words used to represent face and place values. For example, the face value of the decimal amount in 0.132 is a number in the hundreds (one hundred thirty-two) while its decimal value is thousandths (one hundred thirty-two thousandths). All decimal amounts are "off by one" from the whole number used to identify the face value and the counting unit that indicates the place value.

Which block needs to be assigned the value of "one" in order for the blocks to show 113.2? Here, each of the long (ten) blocks represents "one," the flat (hundred) block represents "ten," and the thousand block has a value of "hundred." What about showing 11.32? Here, the flat (hundred) block is assigned the value of "one," the thousand block now has a value of "ten," the long (ten) blocks are equivalent to tenths, and the unit blocks represents hundredths.

Changing the block that represents one, sometimes referred to as a *referent*, means that the values of all the other blocks also change but the multiplicative relationship between adjacent place values remains the same. The drawing below illustrates how the blocks can be used to represent 0.1132:

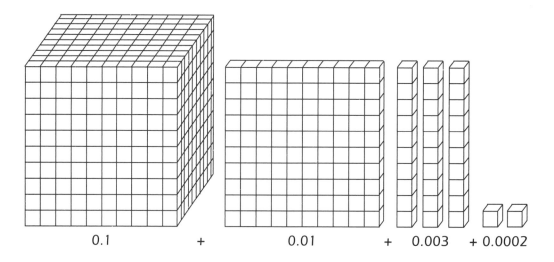

0.1   +   0.01   +   0.003   + 0.0002

In this example, none of the blocks we are using represent "one." The thousand block has a value of one tenth, and the units have a value of one ten-thousandth: 1,000 ten-thousandths are equivalent to one tenth. What block could you construct to represent "one"? Remember that it will be ten times larger than the one-tenth block. ▲

Models such as base ten blocks and decimal squares (a commercial product specifically for decimal numbers) can be used to support students' understanding of decimal place values. They can also be used to help students develop an understanding of the quantities that are represented by decimal notation. Another model that presents decimal numbers as measurements or lengths and that is available in most classrooms involves meter sticks and centimeter cubes. If the length of a meter represents one unit, then decimeters represent tenths, centimeters represent hundredths, and millimeters represent thousandths. Often the long blocks in base ten sets are one decimeter in length; these become a visual referent for tenths when a meter represents one unit. The units in these base ten sets, which are one centimeter in length, then physically represent hundredths. The number 2.45 can be represented concretely using two meter sticks (ones), four long blocks (tenths), and five unit blocks (hundredths):

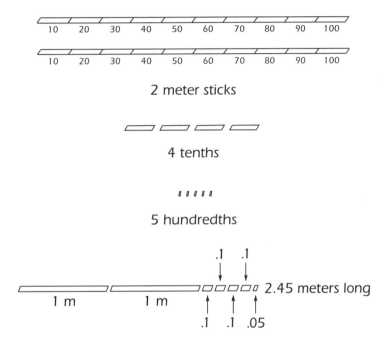

Similarly, the number line is another model that presents decimal fractions as measures or distances from zero.

Some educators believe that using a variety of models to represent decimals confuses students. However, recent cognitive research seems to indicate that using a variety of models and explicitly asking students to focus on the underlying similarities among models helps them generalize important ideas.

Models can also help students understand that some decimal numbers are equivalent. Affixing zeroes to the right of a decimal numeral does not change its value. Using the meter stick as the "one," we can compare 0.3 and 0.30 by examining the length of three tenths (long blocks) and the length of 30 hundredths (small cubes). Likewise, we can use number lines showing tenths and hundredths. Questions such as *Do 0.3 and 0.30 represent the same amount? How can you tell? What is the same about them? Are they the same length? How are they different? Why are they the same amount?* help focus our attention on the fact that each of the tenths in 0.3 has been divided into ten equal pieces. This returns us to the multiplicative relationship between adjacent place values. Think about the insights that are revealed as we compare models of 0.5, 0.50, and 0.500. How might we generalize the fact that an infinite number of zeroes can be added to the far right of any decimal numeral?

Students must not only understand that some decimal numbers are equivalent but also be able to compare and order decimals. This skill requires that students understand the meaning of decimal numerals. Otherwise, they may consider only the face value rather than the place value of the numeral. For example, some students incorrectly state that 0.14 is greater than 0.3 because 14 > 3. Asking students either to build models or to draw pictures to represent the decimals that are being compared will help them visualize quantity and focus on both the face values and the place values of the numerals. Another instructional technique is to confront the misconceptions directly. For example: *Some students think that 0.14 is greater than 0.3 because 14 is greater 3. What do you think?* Or: *Why aren't 0.6 and 0.06 equal?* Also, comparing decimal numerals in context (when examining scores or records of athletic events, for example) enables students to use other knowledge of that context to help make sense of the quantities.

We can use decimal numbers to indicate quantities that are less than one or between any two whole numbers. In fact, between any two decimal numbers there is always another decimal number. Students who say there aren't any numbers between 0.34 and 0.35, for example, may be interpreting these quantities as whole numbers.

Activity

Decimals Between Decimals

Objective: explore the concept of the density of decimal numbers and practice reading decimal numbers.

Materials: graph paper.

Draw a ten-by-ten square on graph paper; let this represent one. Divide the square vertically into ten strips to show tenths and lightly shade two tenths:

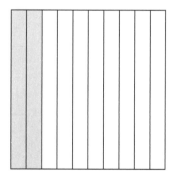

Notice that when only tenths are shaded it appears that there are no numbers between 0.1 and 0.2. Now divide the square horizontally into ten strips to show hundredths. What numerals show amounts that are more than ten hundredths but less than twenty hundredths? List them. Examine 0.15 and 0.16. What numbers are between 0.15 and 0.16? What can you do to your ten-by-ten square that will help you visualize the quantities? What can you do symbolically to 0.15 and 0.16 to help you think about the numbers that are in between? Continue finding numbers that are in between until you have a decimal amount in the millionths place. Each time read the decimal number.

Things to Think About

Some of the numbers that are between 0.1 and 0.2 are: 0.11, 0.12, 0.13, 0.14, 0.15, 0.16, 0.17, 0.18, and 0.19. Drawing hundredths on the ten-by-ten square may have helped you think about these smaller quantities. What happens if we divide each hundredth into ten equal-size pieces? The shaded quantity can be referred to using thousandths (0.100 and 0.200), and we can now list any number of decimal numerals between the original two. In order to find numbers between two decimal numbers we continually partition decimal amounts into smaller units, and this can be done an infinite number of times. For example, 0.15 is between 0.1 and 0.2; 0.153 is between 0.15 and 0.16; and 0.1537 is between 0.153 and 0.154. Examine each of these in-between decimal numbers. Notice that as each place value is partitioned to form the next place value to, the right, the in-between quantity is increasing but by smaller and smaller amounts—0.1537 is greater than 0.153 but only by 0.0007!

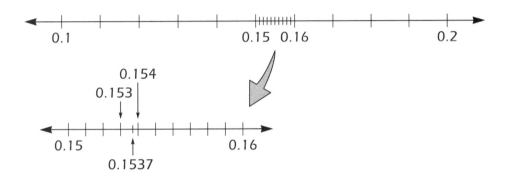

How do we read 0.1537? As one thousand five hundred thirty-seven ten-thousandths. Pick another number between 0.1537 and 0.1538 such as 0.15374 and read it—fifteen thousand three hundred seventy-four hundred-thousandths. Notice that we read the digits to the right of the decimal place as if the number were a whole number, but then we let others know it is a decimal number by stating the place value of the digit farthest to the right (in the numeral above, the 4 is farthest to the right and in the hundred-thousandths place). Try not to use the word *and* when reading the numeral.

The in-between feature of decimal numbers is known as the density property of rational numbers; it means that there is an infinite number of rational numbers between any two rational numbers. ▲

One fundamental concept that students need to make sense of with regard to decimal numbers is this: decimals are used to represent quantities that have values less than one. Students must have knowledge of these quantities (ideally based on models), be familiar with the notation system that is used to represent these quantities, understand fractions as parts of a whole and that decimals can be used to represent fractional values, and have investigated the relationships that both link the decimal system to the whole number system and also differentiate them.

2. Connecting Decimals and Fractions

Decimal fractions are often classified as either *terminating* decimals or *repeating* decimals. In fact, all rational numbers can be expressed in decimal form as either terminating or repeating. (Note, however, that irrational numbers such as π and $\sqrt{2}$ are neither terminating nor repeating.) Decimals such as $0.666\ldots$ and $1.723232323\ldots$, in which, from some specific digit on, a finite sequence of digits repeats again and again in the same order without interruption, are called repeating decimals. The block of digits forming the repeating part is called the *repetend*. The number of digits in the repetend is called the *period* of the decimal. A bar is placed over the repetend to indicate that the block of digits underneath is repeated infinitely.

$0.142857142857\ldots$ *is written as* $0.\overline{142857}$ $1.1666666\ldots$ *is written as* $1.1\overline{6}$

Decimals such as 0.25, 0.625, 3.0002, and 76.84 are called terminating decimals, because they can be represented using a finite number of nonzero digits to the right of the decimal point. Technically, terminating decimals are those repeating decimals whose repetend is zero.

All terminating decimals can be written as fractions with denominators of a power of ten. When converting a terminating decimal to an equivalent fraction, we write the face value of the decimal as the numerator and the place value of the decimal as the denominator. Thus, 0.6 is equivalent to $\frac{6}{10}$ (or $\frac{3}{5}$ when changed to simplest form), and 1.23 is equivalent to $1\frac{23}{100}$. Notice that when the decimal numeral includes whole numbers, the whole number does not have to be converted to a fraction (although it can be—1.23 is also equivalent to $\frac{123}{100}$).

Repeating decimals can also be expressed in fractional form. To convert a repeating decimal to a fraction we first write an equation in which we set the decimal equal to n, then multiply both sides of the equation by a power of 10 equal to the number of repeating digits, and finally subtract the first equation from the second. For example, let $n = 0.\overline{45}$. Because there are two digits in the repeating sequence, we multiply n by 100 and then subtract n:

$$
\begin{array}{rcl}
100n & = & 45.454545\ldots \\
-\quad n & = & 0.454545\ldots \\
\hline
99n & = & 45.000000 \\
n & = & \dfrac{45}{99} \text{ or } \dfrac{5}{11}
\end{array}
$$

By multiplying the repeating decimal by a power of 10 and then subtracting the decimal, we get a finite decimal that can be converted to a fraction. The number of repeating sequences in the decimal period indicates by which power of 10 we multiply: to convert $0.\overline{6}$ to a fraction, we multiply by 10; to convert $2.\overline{456}$ to a fraction, we multiply by 1000.

It is important to realize that the decimal notation recorded for some fractions is approximate, not exact. We often encounter this when using a calculator. For example, the fraction $\frac{1}{3}$ displayed on a calculator as a decimal is 0.333333333—a rounded approximation of $0.\overline{3}$. Since the decimal value was rounded, 0.333333333 does not convert back to $\frac{1}{3}$. In order to interpret results accurately and to decide which form of representation (decimal or fraction) to work with, we need to know which fractions have an exact decimal representation.

Activity

Does It Terminate?

Objective: find out whether there is a way to tell whether a fraction can be written using a terminating or repeating decimal.

Convert each of the fractions below to a decimal by dividing the numerator by the denominator. This will give you the decimal expansion of the fraction. Then sort the fractions into two groups: those that are equivalent to terminating decimals and those that are not.

$$\frac{1}{2}, \frac{1}{3}, \frac{1}{4}, \frac{1}{5}, \frac{2}{5}, \frac{3}{5}, \frac{4}{5}, \frac{1}{6}, \frac{2}{6}, \frac{4}{6}, \frac{5}{6}, \frac{1}{7}, \frac{1}{8}, \frac{1}{9}, \frac{1}{11}, \frac{1}{12}, \frac{1}{15}, \frac{1}{16}, \frac{1}{20}, \frac{1}{24}, \frac{1}{25}, \frac{1}{30}, \frac{1}{32}, \frac{1}{40}, \frac{1}{50}$$

Examine the two groups and answer the following questions:

1. If a unit fraction (a fraction with 1 as the numerator) is represented as a terminating decimal, do all fractions with that denominator terminate?
2. If a unit fraction is represented as a repeating decimal, do all fractions with that denominator repeat?
3. What patterns are observed in the denominators of fractions that represent terminating decimals? that represent repeating decimals?
4. Determine the prime factorization of the denominators of the fractions. Which prime numbers are factors of the denominators of terminating fractions?
5. Why can some fractions be written as terminating decimals while others cannot?

Things to Think About

The following fractions can be written as terminating decimals: $\frac{1}{2}, \frac{1}{4}, \frac{1}{5}, \frac{2}{5}, \frac{3}{5}, \frac{4}{5}, \frac{1}{8}, \frac{1}{10}, \frac{1}{16}, \frac{1}{20}, \frac{1}{25}, \frac{1}{32}, \frac{1}{40}, \frac{1}{50}$. If a unit fraction is represented as a terminating decimal, then all fractions with that denominator also terminate. For example, $\frac{1}{20}$ is a terminating decimal and $\frac{2}{20}, \frac{3}{20}, \frac{4}{20}, \ldots, \frac{19}{20}$ also terminate. Since $\frac{1}{20} = 0.05$, then all other fractions with a denominator of 20 are multiples of 0.05. This same pattern occurs with repeating decimals. If a unit fraction is represented as a repeating decimal, then all fractions with that denominator that are in simplest form also repeat: $\frac{1}{6}$ repeats, as does $\frac{5}{6}$, but $\frac{3}{6}$, which can be simplified to $\frac{1}{2}$, is a terminating decimal.

The prime factorizations of the denominators in fractions that terminate when written as decimals and in those that repeat when written as decimals are shown below. From this chart, we can generalize that the denominators of fractions that terminate contain only 2s and/or 5s in their prime factorization.

FRACTIONS THAT TERMINATE	PRIME FACTORIZATION OF DENOMINATOR	FRACTIONS THAT REPEAT	PRIME FACTORIZATION OF DENOMINATOR
$\frac{1}{2}$	2	$\frac{1}{3}$	3
$\frac{1}{4}$	2×2	$\frac{1}{6}$	2×3
$\frac{1}{5}$	5	$\frac{1}{7}$	7
$\frac{1}{8}$	$2 \times 2 \times 2$	$\frac{1}{9}$	3×3
$\frac{1}{10}$	2×5	$\frac{1}{12}$	$2 \times 2 \times 3$
$\frac{1}{16}$	$2 \times 2 \times 2 \times 2$	$\frac{1}{15}$	3×5
$\frac{1}{20}$	$2 \times 2 \times 5$	$\frac{1}{24}$	$2 \times 2 \times 2 \times 3$
$\frac{1}{25}$	5×5	$\frac{1}{30}$	$2 \times 3 \times 5$

Why do fractions that terminate have only 2s and/or 5s as prime factors of their denominators? First, consider the prime factors of various powers of 10. Notice that they all have 2s and 5s as prime factors:

$$10 = 2 \times 5$$
$$100 = 2 \times 2 \times 5 \times 5$$
$$1,000 = 2 \times 2 \times 2 \times 5 \times 5 \times 5$$

When a fraction has a decimal expansion that terminates, that fraction can also be expressed as an equivalent fraction with a denominator of 10, 100, 1000, or any other power of 10. Fractions with only 2s and 5s as prime factors in the denominators can always be multiplied by additional 2s and/or 5s to make any power of 10.

$$\frac{1}{8} = \frac{1}{2 \times 2 \times 2} \qquad \frac{1}{2 \times 2 \times 2} \times \frac{5 \times 5 \times 5}{5 \times 5 \times 5} = \frac{125}{1000} \qquad 0.125 = \frac{1}{8}$$

Fractions that are represented by repeating decimals have prime factors that do not divide evenly into 10, 100, 1,000, or other powers of 10. ▲

Activity

Repeating Decimals

Objective: classify decimal expansions of unit fractions based on whether they terminate, repeat without a delay, or repeat after a delay.

Some repeating decimal expansions repeat immediately: for example, the decimal expansion of $\frac{2}{3}$ is $0.\overline{6}$. Other repeating decimal expansions repeat after a delay: for example, the decimal expansion of $\frac{1}{6}$ is $0.1\overline{6}$ (the 1 does not repeat, but the 6 does). What patterns occur in the decimal expansions of repeating decimals? In particular:

▲ Which unit fractions produce decimal expansions that repeat without a delay?
▲ Which unit fractions produce decimal expansions that repeat after a delay?
▲ When converting a unit fraction to a decimal, what is the longest possible period?

Things to Think About

In the table below, unit fractions have been placed into groups based on whether their decimal expansions terminate, repeat, or repeat after a delay (e.g., $0.0\overline{6}$). All of these fractions and decimals are rational numbers—the quantities can be represented using both decimal and fraction notations.

FRACTIONS THAT TERMINATE	FRACTIONS THAT REPEAT	FRACTIONS THAT REPEAT AFTER A DELAY
$\frac{1}{2}$	$\frac{1}{3}$	$\frac{1}{6}$
$\frac{1}{4}$	$\frac{1}{7}$	$\frac{1}{12}$
$\frac{1}{5}$	$\frac{1}{9}$	$\frac{1}{14}$
$\frac{1}{8}$	$\frac{1}{11}$	$\frac{1}{15}$

FRACTIONS THAT TERMINATE	FRACTIONS THAT REPEAT	FRACTIONS THAT REPEAT AFTER A DELAY
$\frac{1}{10}$	$\frac{1}{13}$	$\frac{1}{18}$
$\frac{1}{16}$	$\frac{1}{17}$	$\frac{1}{22}$
$\frac{1}{20}$	$\frac{1}{19}$	$\frac{1}{24}$
$\frac{1}{25}$	$\frac{1}{21}$	

A fraction converted to a decimal will repeat without delay if the denominator of the fraction does not have the factors 2 or 5. For example, $\frac{1}{11}$, a unit fraction in which the factors of the denominator are 1 and 11 (no 2s or 5s), is equivalent to $0.\overline{09}$. If the denominator of the fraction has at least one 2 or one 5 as well as other prime factors, then the equivalent decimal will repeat after a delay (e.g., $\frac{1}{6}$, or $0.1\overline{6}$).

Some unit fractions have very long decimal periods: $\frac{1}{17}$ has a 16-digit period, $\frac{1}{19}$ has an 18-digit period, and $\frac{1}{23}$ has a 22-digit period. The period for the decimal representation of any fraction, $\frac{1}{n}$, is always less than n but can be at most $n - 1$. ▲

3. Operations with Decimals

Given the mathematical complexities of decimal numbers and the difficulty some students have understanding them, it isn't surprising that students learn and execute rules for performing decimal operations without knowing what the symbols mean. How can we design instructional sequences that support more meaningful learning about decimals?

First and foremost, in order to perform operations accurately and make sense of these operations, students must know about and understand decimal quantities, decimal symbols, and the connections that link the symbols to the quantities (see Section 1 of this chapter). Students who are familiar with quantity usually have internal referents for decimal amounts (e.g., they visualize tenths in relationship to the whole and to hundredths). They are able to order decimals and explain which number is the largest by comparing the sizes of the quantities represented by the written numerals, not by simply stating a rule. They can provide detailed explanations of why 1.4 and 1.40, for example, are equivalent.

The second condition that must be met in order for students to make sense of decimal operations is that they have attached the correct meaning to operational symbols ($+, -, \times, \div$). Usually by the time students reach the upper elementary grades, their understanding of addition and subtraction with whole numbers is robust enough that they can generalize these operations to decimal numbers. However, students' understanding of multiplication and division of whole numbers ("multiplication makes bigger and division makes smaller") may have an effect on their understanding of decimal multiplication and division. Students have to suppress certain whole number notions about these operations and extend the meaning of multiplication and division. As a result, multiplication and division of decimals are more problematic (in terms of meaning, not in terms of simply memorizing rules) than addition and subtraction. Operation sense regarding outcomes when multiplying and dividing small quantities must be developed simultaneously.

Assuming that a great deal of instructional time has previously been spent helping students understand decimal quantities and notation, one way to build meaning regarding the decimal operations of addition and subtraction is to have students first estimate problem solutions and then derive their own procedures or rules. For example, fourth graders given this problem—*Chris, who is on the track team, ran 5.3 km on Monday and 6.9 km on Wednesday. How far, in total, did Chris run on these two days?*—estimated that he ran more than 11 km. They then used base ten materials to help them think about the sum of 0.3 and 0.9 and concluded that this sum was 1.2 km; thus Chris ran a total of 12.2 km. After solving many similar problems using estimation and models, these students eventually came up with a generalized rule of grouping equivalent place values when adding, something they most likely would not have been able to do if the decimal quantities were meaningless for them.

Activity

Decimal Products and Quotients

Objective: highlight the effects of multiplying and dividing whole numbers by decimal numbers that are close to one, equal to one half, and close to zero.

Fill in the table below. Pick a number and multiply it by 0.9, then divide the same number by 0.9. Next, multiply your original number by 0.5, and divide it by 0.5. Finally, multiply the original number by 0.1, and divide it by 0.1. Pick other numbers and perform the same multiplications and divisions. What do you notice about the products and the quotients? Try generalizing your conclusions.

NUMBER	MULTIPLY BY 0.9	DIVIDE BY 0.9	MULTIPLY BY 0.5	DIVIDE BY 0.5	MULTIPLY BY 0.1	DIVIDE BY 0.1
18	16.2	20	9	36	1.8	180

Things to Think About

The product of a whole number and a number less than but close to one (e.g., 0.9) is less than the original whole number. In fact, the closer the decimal is to one, the closer the product is to the whole number. For example, $18 \times 0.9 = 16.2$ but $18 \times 0.99 = 17.82$. What happens when we multiply a whole number by one half (0.5)? The product is exactly half of the whole number. The operation of multiplying by 0.5 is equivalent to dividing the whole number by two (e.g., $18 \times 0.5 = 9$ and $18 \div 2 = 9$). Since multiplying any number by zero is equal to zero, it might seem reasonable to assume that multiplying any whole number by a decimal close to zero will give a product that is quite small relative to the whole number. The closer the decimal is to zero, the closer the product will be to zero. For example, $18 \times 0.1 = 1.8$ but $18 \times 0.0001 = 0.0018$.

Why does the multiplication of a whole number and a decimal number result in a small product? If we look at multiplication as grouping, 6×0.4 means six groups with four tenths in each group, or 24 tenths, or 2.4. If we look at multiplication as repeated addition, 6×0.4 means 0.4 plus 0.4 plus 0.4 plus 0.4 plus 0.4 plus 0.4, or 24 tenths, or 2.4.

Similar relationships hold for division. The quotient of a whole number and a number less than but close to one (e.g., 0.9) is a little more than the original whole number. In fact, the closer the decimal is to one, the closer the quotient is to the whole number. For example, 18 ÷ 0.9 = 20 but 18 ÷ 0.99 = 18.18. What happens when we divide a whole number by one half (0.5)? The quotient is exactly twice the whole number. The operation of dividing by 0.5 is equivalent to multiplying the whole number by two (e.g., 18 ÷ 0.5 = 36 and 18 × 2 = 36). Since dividing any number by zero is undefined, you might have been surprised by the results of dividing a whole number by a number close to zero. The closer the decimal is to zero, the greater the quotient. For example, 18 ÷ 0.1 = 180 but 18 ÷ 0.0001 = 180,000.

Why do these division problems result in such large quotients? The interpretation of division as repeated subtraction provides some insight: a small amount (the decimal amount) is repeatedly subtracted from the whole number. In 4 ÷ 0.5, for example, five tenths can be subtracted from four eight times. The quotient tells us the number of groups of 0.5 that were removed (subtracted) from 4, namely 8 groups. When a decimal divisor is very small, such as 0.0001, a large number of groups of this small amount can be removed. ▲

Understanding how multiplication and division with decimals affect the resulting products and quotients enables students to make sense of the rules that govern multiplication and division computations. Let's examine some of these rules in order to tease out the mathematical relationships used when computing.

First, when two numbers less than one are multiplied, why is the product smaller than either of the numbers? For example, why is 0.5 × 0.1 equal to 0.05? One way to interpret this equation is to find one tenth of 0.5. Imagine five tenths. To take one tenth of these five tenths, we need to divide each of the tenths into ten pieces, which would result in hundredths. One tenth of each tenth is one hundredth; since there were five tenths to start with, there would be five hundredths.

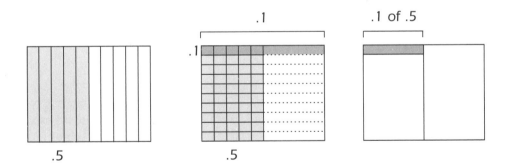

Notice how multiplying decimal numbers less than one is parallel to multiplying fractions. This is because the terminating decimals used in the example can be represented as fractions, $\frac{5}{10}$ and $\frac{1}{10}$. A similar explanation of fraction multiplication can be found in Chapter 5.

Second, how do we explain the fact that when dividing two decimals that are less than one (such as 0.5 ÷ 0.1), the quotient is greater than either decimal? Using the same interpretation of division as explained in Activity 5, think about subtracting out groups of 0.1 from 0.5. Five groups of one tenth can be subtracted out, so the quotient is 5.

Third, why when dividing by a decimal, do we teach the procedure to "move" the decimal point? In the division $0.2\overline{)3.64}$, we write the equivalent division expression, $2\overline{)36.4}$, and use it to find the quotient. Why can we do this? The answer involves equivalence and the multiplicative identity. Writing the division as a fraction, $\frac{3.64}{0.2}$, and multiplying the fraction by any form of 1 (multiplicative identity element), may help you see how to create equivalent division expressions. Examine the equations below:

$$\frac{3.64}{0.2} \times \frac{2}{2} = \frac{7.28}{0.4} = 18.2 \qquad\qquad \frac{3.64}{0.2} \times \frac{5}{5} = \frac{18.2}{1} = 18.2$$

$$\frac{3.64}{0.2} \times \frac{10}{10} = \frac{36.4}{2} = 18.2 \qquad\qquad \frac{3.64}{0.2} \times \frac{100}{100} = \frac{364}{20} = 18.2$$

Notice that the quotients are identical (18.2) since we multiplied the original division expression ($\frac{3.64}{0.2}$) by different forms of 1. Which form of 1 should we use since they all work to give us the correct quotient? It depends—multiplying by $\frac{5}{5}$ makes sense when we need to compute mentally (can you explain why?), but multiplying by either $\frac{10}{10}$ or $\frac{100}{100}$ is also easy since multiplication by powers of 10 can be accomplished by simply moving decimal points to the right. When we move the decimal point in the standard division algorithm, we are transforming the divisor into a whole number by multiplying the divisor and dividend by 1 ($\frac{3.64}{0.2} \times \frac{10}{10}$). Once the divisor is a whole number, division can proceed using the steps previously learned for whole numbers.

Finally, the multiplication algorithm tends to be performed mechanically without obvious understanding. Why do we sum the number of decimal places in the factors and make sure the product also has the same number of decimal places? Based on what you have explored in this chapter, see if you can make sense of this algorithm.

Activity

Meaningful Multiplication!

Objective: understand the steps in the standard decimal multiplication algorithm.

Explain the multiplication algorithm for decimals using 3.2 × 2.4. Why does the product have hundredths? Consider how you might explain the location of the decimal point using fractions, compensation strategies, an array model, or the distributive property.

Things to Think About

One way to explain this algorithm is to use fraction representations, $3\frac{2}{10} \times 2\frac{4}{10}$. To multiply mixed numbers, we change the mixed numbers to improper fractions and multiply the numerators and denominators: $\frac{32}{10} \times \frac{24}{10} = \frac{768}{100}$. Notice that multiplying the numerators of the improper fractions is equivalent to multiplying the factors as if they were whole numbers (32 × 24 = 768), and that dividing by 100 (the product of the denominators) is equivalent to placing the decimal point so there are two places in the product. Stated another way, multiplying tenths by tenths gives hundredths, so the product must involve hundredths.

The compensation strategy can also be used to form equivalent expressions. Take each factor, 3.2 and 2.4, and multiply each by 10. The corresponding multiplication, 32 × 24, will be equivalent when divided by 100 (10 × 10). Can you explain why? (Hint: consider what happens when you multiply and divide an expression by the same number.)

The distributive property as well as an array can be used to show that when we multiply the component parts of 3.2 and 2.4 we get partial products that involve tenths and hundreds. When we add tenths and hundredths together, the sum will be expressed with hundredths.

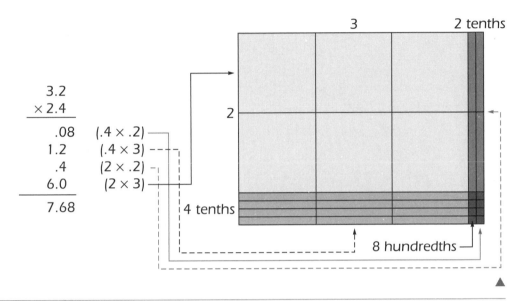

Teaching Decimals

The decimal system is introduced in the elementary grades and studied throughout middle school. The expectation is that after middle school students will be able to use decimal numbers in both science and mathematics. In the rush to build students' skills, teachers often stress decimal operations and teach them as isolated procedures. They spend little time on decimal concepts and relationships and helping students use what they know about fractions to make sense of terminating and repeating decimals. Thus, teachers of middle school students often discover that students lack a fundamental understanding of decimal numbers. This lack of understanding impacts students' abilities to use decimals to solve problems, make measurements, perform accurate computations, make sense of answers, understand scientific notation, interpret a variety of data displays, and graph data.

Instruction needs to focus on helping students connect notation and quantity, make generalizations about the results of operations on decimal numbers, and relate decimals and fractions. Since the language used to express decimal numerals often hides rather than highlights important similarities and differences between decimals and whole numbers and since textbooks mainly stress symbolic manipulation and computational proficiency, it is up to teachers to shift the instructional emphasis to helping students develop meaning for these symbols.

Questions for Discussion

1. What are the important decimal concepts that all students should understand?

2. Discuss how to help students make sense of the fact that affixing zeroes to the right of a decimal numeral does not change its value.

3. What do you do as a teacher when a student says there are no numbers between 5.3 and 5.4?

4. What are repeating decimals? terminating decimals? nonrepeating decimals? Which of these are rational numbers and which are irrationals? Why do some fractions have terminating decimal expansions and others do not?

5. A common error that students make is to set up the subtraction $25 - 9.863$ as

$$\begin{array}{r} 9.863 \\ -25 \\ \hline \end{array}$$

What does this tell you about the student's understanding? As a teacher, what might you do?

7

Percent

One of the most common applications of mathematics in everyday life is percent. Percentages are used to describe a wide range of situations: there is a 70% chance of rain, the interest on a credit card is 18.9%, the sales tax on a purchase is 5%, an item's price is marked down 20%, and 68% of all homes in the United Sates are connected to the Internet. As common as percent is, it can be a source of difficulty for students and adults in the way it relates to fractions and decimals and as it is used in problem solving.

1. What Is Percent?

The term percent is derived from a Latin expression meaning "per hundred." Percents were historically developed as another form for fractions and decimals, and today we represent percents as both fractions and decimals. Another valid interpretation is that a percent is a part-whole ratio comparing one number with 100. Thus, 44% is understood to represent the ratio 44:100 or the fraction $\frac{44}{100}$ or the decimal 0.44. In general, it is easier to compare percents than to compare fractions. For example, in a group of 19 students, 5 preferred movie A over movie B, but in another group of 29 students, 8 preferred movie A over movie B. In which group was movie A more popular? Because these fractions—$\frac{5}{19}$ and $\frac{8}{29}$—have neither the same denominator nor the same numerator, it is difficult to determine which fraction is larger without detailed calculations. However, if these data are instead presented as percentages—about 26% of the first group liked movie A and 28% of the second group liked movie A—it is simple to see that movie A was about equally popular in both groups. Similarly, discounts of 30% and 25% on the same item of clothing at competing stores are easily compared, as are credit card interest rates of 12%, 14%, and 18%.

While quantities can be represented using decimals, fractions, or percents, which form is used depends a lot on the situation: for example, baseball statistics are always presented in decimal form (a batting average of .345), measurements are expressed using fractions and decimals but never percents (the length of a string is one fourth of a foot or 0.25 of a foot but not 25% of a foot), and weather data are referred to only by percentages (a 30% chance of snow, not a three-tenths likelihood of snow).

Since a percent can represent a fraction or a decimal, we often focus on this aspect, referring to 3% as 3 out of 100 ($\frac{3}{100}$, or 0.03) and 65% as 65 out of 100 ($\frac{65}{100}$, or 0.65) or presenting diagrams in which 3 squares and 65 squares respectively out of 100 squares are shaded. This emphasis on a percent's being a part of 100 rather than a comparison with 100 leads students to think that percents over 100%—175%, for example—are absurd, because 100% is the whole and you can't have more than all there is! To avoid this incomplete generalization, we need to broaden students' interpretation to include the idea of a percent as a ratio and use phrases like "per 100," "compared with 100," and "for every hundred" when introducing the concept. Likewise, models that show percent as a comparison as well as a part of a whole should also be included in instruction. Sometimes linking fractions and decimals that are greater than one and percents that are greater than 100% helps students generalize these ideas. In any case, percents over one hundred should be used right from the start—not reserved for study in subsequent years.

There is more to percent than representing fractional quantities or comparing magnitudes. The study of percent is usually linked to the study of proportionality, since percent problems are solved using multiplicative reasoning. However, prior to solving problems involving percents, it is critical to build a concept of percent that connects to what students already know about percents and makes a strong connection to previously gained knowledge about fractions and decimals. Students have informal knowledge of percents from encountering them in newspaper articles, in advertising, and on television. In particular, many students know that 50% is the same as one half and are familiar with 25%, 75%, and 100%. Many students receive grades on quizzes and tests that are represented as percentages. However, most students' overall understanding of percent is limited in depth and scope. The activities in this first section can help you develop and strengthen your own understanding of percent as part of a whole (fraction/decimal) and as a ratio compared with 100.

Activity

Percent as a Part of a Whole, Part 1

Objective: estimate percents using part-to-whole reasoning.

The pie chart below is divided up into percentages, with the whole circle representing 100%.

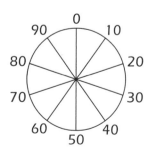

Use the pie chart to help estimate what percent of each circle below is shaded:

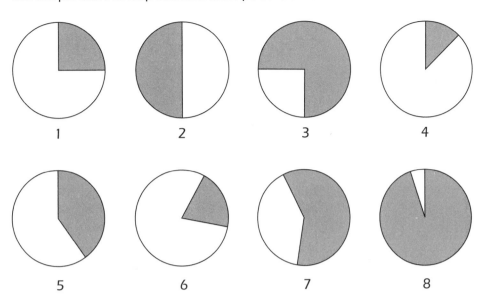

1   2   3   4

5   6   7   8

Things to Think About

The shaded areas in the first three circles can be linked to what we know about fractions: one fourth of circle 1, one half of circle 2, and three fourths of circle 3 are shaded. These fractions are equivalent to 25%, 50%, and 75%, respectively. The right angles at the centers of circles 1 and 3 help us estimate the shaded areas. Since in circle 1 the angle is 25% of 360°, or 90°, the shaded area is also 25% of the entire circle. Likewise, in circle 3 the unshaded area is 25% of the circle, so the shaded area is 75% of the circle. This reasoning illustrates an important idea related to percent as a fraction of a whole: if the whole circle represents 100%, then the percents that represent the various parts must sum to 100% (75% + 25% = 100%).

What about the shaded areas of the remaining circles? Did you first decide whether the shaded area was more or less than 50%? We often use 50%, or half, as a benchmark for making other estimates. You might also have used benchmarks of 25% and 75%—the shaded area in circle 4 appears to be about half the size of the shaded area in circle 1, or somewhere between 12% or 13%. Making use of these additional benchmarks narrows the range of possibilities, which in turn contributes to estimating more accurately. You may also have estimated the central angle of the shaded region and then compared that angle with 360°, since this is another way of representing the fraction of the circle that is shaded. The remaining percentages for circles 4 through 8 are 12.5%, 40%, 20%, 60%, and 95%. ▲

Activity

Percent as a Part of a Whole, Part 2

Objective: estimate percents using part-to-whole reasoning.

Estimate what percent of each noncircular figure below is shaded:

How did you approach this task? One fifth plus another one tenth of the pentagon is shaded: 30% (20% + 10%). It might be easier to focus on the unshaded sections of the square: half plus an additional one eighth. Five eighths as a decimal is 0.625, so the percent that is unshaded is 62.5%. This leaves 37.5% shaded. For the hexagon, you can first determine either the shaded or the unshaded portion. The shaded part of the hexagon is one half (50%) plus an extra one twelfth (about 8%), or about 58%. The upper unshaded section is 25%, and the lower triangular unshaded section is one sixth, or about 17%—together, approximately 42%. One hundred percent minus 42% is 58%. The final figure, the triangle, is divided into thirds, with two thirds, or $0.\overline{6}$, shaded—about 67%.

Determining the amount of area that is shaded in each figure requires that we think of the figure as a whole. We then divide the shaded areas into parts and determine the value of each part using fractions, decimals, or percents. Combining the different parts enables us to find the percentages of the shaded figures: 30%, 37.5%, 58%, and 67%. ▲

The examples above use an area model to show percents of a whole. Students often have difficulty estimating percents of figures similar to those in Activities 1 and 2 because the whole is not divided into 100 pieces. Before asking your students to determine percents, you may want to give them opportunities to connect fractions with equivalent fractions that have denominators of 100 and then with percents (e.g., $\frac{1}{2}$ and $\frac{50}{100}$ both need to be linked to 50%).

The connection between decimals and percents is more direct for many students, especially when dealing with tenths and hundredths. If students are asked to record shaded amounts as percents, as decimals, as fractions with denominators of 100, and as other equivalent fractions and then to discuss the relationships among these forms, they are more likely to make sense of the multiple representations of the same quantity:

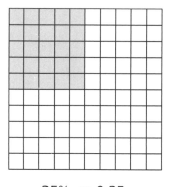

25%, or 0.25,

or $\frac{25}{100}$, or $\frac{1}{4}$

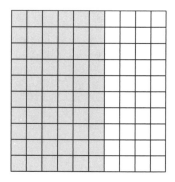

60%, or 0.6, or 0.60,

or $\frac{60}{100}$, or $\frac{6}{10}$, or $\frac{3}{5}$

Since percentages can be interpreted as ratios that compare a number with 100, it is most straightforward to show students a visual of a comparison set obviously representing 100 units. One such comparison set is a square made up of 100 smaller squares. Figures can then be compared with the 100 smaller squares, and their size represented as a percentage of these 100 squares. Percents greater than 100% are easily understood when looked at in this way.

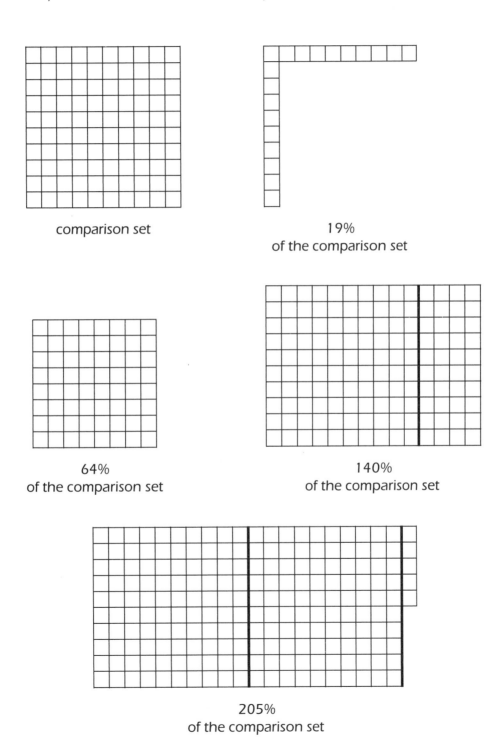

comparison set

19%
of the comparison set

64%
of the comparison set

140%
of the comparison set

205%
of the comparison set

Of course, it's not necessary to represent the comparison set of 100 as a square grid. A meter (which is 100 centimeters) can serve as a linear model, a dollar bill (which is 100 pennies) is another representation, and other models can also be used.

A more complex challenge, however, is to find out what percent one number is of another when the comparison set is not 100. Again, visual representations can help, but thinking about fractional relationships is also necessary.

Activity

Percent as a Comparison

Objective: determine percents based on the relationship between two sets.

In each item below there are two reference sets, X and Y. Fill in the following statements for each pair of sets: X is __% of Y, and Y is __% of X.

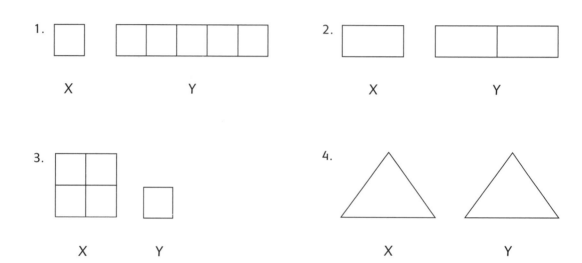

Things to Think About

There are a number of approaches for estimating the percent of the figures. One way uses fractions. In number 1, if Y is 100% and has five equal sections, then X is $\frac{1}{5}$, or 20%, of Y (100% ÷ 5). We can make sense of the reverse statement, *Y is what percent of X?*, by thinking of the relationship as a comparison. If X is now 100%, then Y is five times as large as X, or 500% of X (100% × 5). Apply both approaches to number 2: X is 50% of Y, and Y is 200% of X. Number 3 has the larger figure as X and the smaller figure as Y: X is 400% of Y, and Y is 25% of X. In number 4, in which X and Y are identical, X is 100% of Y, and Y is 100% of X.

Try making up some of these "forward and backward" percent problems. For example, if X is 5% of Y, what percent of X is Y? If X is 300% of Y, determine a possible value for both X and Y. ▲

In this book we have separated the discussion of fractions, decimals, ratios, and percents into separate chapters in order to present large quantities of material in smaller chunks. However, the connections among these topics are what make them powerful and complex, and it is these connections that we want to highlight continually in instruction. In particular, we want to assist students in grades 4 through 7 in realizing that the term *percent* is simply another name for hundredths (because of the comparison with, or the number out of, 100) and can be expressed as a fraction or a decimal. Students can apply what they understand about fractions and decimals to making sense of percents and solving percent problems.

Activity

Linking Fractions, Decimals, and Percents

Objective: connect our understanding of percents to our knowledge of fractions and decimals.

Materials: Cuisenaire rods, graph paper.

Solve the following problems. How are you using the models? How are you using your knowledge of fractions or decimals to make sense of each situation?

1. What percent of the orange plus red rod is the light green rod? the blue rod? three orange rods in a row?
2. If the dark green rod is 100%, what rod is 50%? what rod is about 67%? what rod is about 116%?
3. If the yellow rod is 20%, what rod is 40%? what is the length of the rod that is 100%?

Things to Think About

These problems are similar to ones in Chapter 5 where we examined different relationships between parts and wholes. In this activity we want to link what we know about fractions to percents. In the first problem, the orange and red rods combined form the length against which we are making our comparisons: 12 cm. The light green rod is 25% of the orange + red length, since four of the light green rods are equivalent in length to the orange + red rod. Also, the light green is 3 cm long, and $\frac{3}{12}$, or $\frac{1}{4}$, equals 25%. The blue rod is more than half as long. In fact, it is $\frac{3}{4}$ the length of the orange + red rod. As a percent, $\frac{3}{4}$ is 75%. Three orange rods are 30 centimeters long. Thirty is 250% of 12. Can you use the rods to explain why?

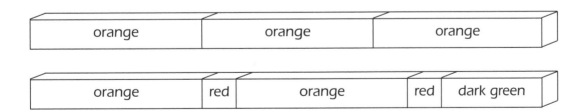

If the dark green rod is 100%, what rod is 50%? Understanding that 50% is another name for $\frac{1}{2}$ makes is easier to see that it is light green. The purple rod is about 67% of the dark green since 67% is another name for $\frac{2}{3}$. Finally the rod that is 116% of dark green must be longer than dark green because dark green is

100% of itself. Sixteen percent is not a great deal, about $\frac{1}{6}$. The black rod is 116% of the dark green rod (namely it is $\frac{1}{6}$ longer than the dark green rod).

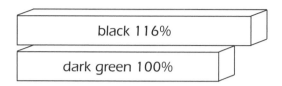

In the last question, the part and the percent are given and you must determine the whole. If yellow is 20%, then a 40% rod must be twice as long—this is an orange rod. To create 100% you have to lay five yellow rods in a row, since $5 \times 20\% = 100\%$, for a length that is 25 cm. ▲

While diagrams and models are extremely useful in making sense of percent relationships in terms of fractions and decimals, we also want students to be able to connect percents to ratios. By using equivalent ratios we are able to deal with percents in a more abstract way.

Activity

Percent as a Ratio

Objective: use equivalent ratios to solve percent problems.

Use equivalent ratios to fill in the blanks in the following statements.

1. 30% means
   - __ for every 100
   - __ for every 10
   - __ for every 1000
   - __ for every 700
   - __ for every 20
   - __ for every 2
2. 50% means
   - __ per 100
   - __ per 10
   - __ per 1000
   - __ per 700
   - __ per 20
   - __ per 2
3. 175% means
   - __ compared with 100
   - __ compared with 10
   - __ compared with 1000
   - __ compared with 700
   - __ compared with 20
   - __ compared with 2
4. If a sale guarantees a saving of 24%, you will save __ on every $100, __ on every $25, __ on every $50, and __ on every $250.

Things to Think About

Equivalent ratios are found either by dividing both numbers in a ratio by the same factor or by multiplying both numbers in a ratio by the same factor. We can express 30% as 30 for every 100 and write it as 30:100 or $\frac{30}{100}$. Dividing each of these numbers (30 and 100) by 10 gives us an equivalent ratio of 3:10 or $\frac{3}{10}$. Multiplying both 30 and 100 by 7 gives an equivalent ratio of 210 to 700; $\frac{210}{700}$ is equivalent to 30%. The equivalent ratio of 0.6 for every 2 is found by dividing both 30 and 100 by 50. Any ratio that is equivalent to 30% can be used to find additional equivalent ratios.

In the second series of statements, we can say that 50% means 50 per 100, 5 per 10, 500 per 1000, 350 per 700, 10 per 20, and 1 per 2. Notice that all of the ratios are equivalent to one half.

In the third series of statements, the percentage is greater than 100. This means that all the numbers that are filled in will be greater than the comparison number: 175 compared with 100, 17.5 compared with 10, 1750 compared with 1000, 1225 compared with 700, 35 compared with 20, and 3.5 compared with 2.

Percents are used extensively in the commercial world of buying and selling. In statement 4, we will save $24 on every $100, $6 on every $25 (divide 24 and 100 by 4), $12 on every $50 (divide 24 and 100 by 2), and $60 on every $250 (multiply 24 and 100 by 2.5). You can also find the final equivalent ratio using addition. If you save $24 per $100, you will save $24 + $24 on $200. Half of $24, or $12, is what you'll save on $50. Adding $24 + $24 + $12 gives you the total of $60 you will save on $250. ▲

---

2. Solving Percent Problems

We solve problems involving percents all the time. Whenever we compute monthly payments under different mortgage rates, determine the discounted price of a new car, calculate sales tax, or figure out how much tip to leave after an excellent meal, we are applying concepts related to percent. Percent problems are commonly approached in a number of ways: thinking of the percent as a fraction and applying multiplicative reasoning, using ratio tables, using equivalent ratios, writing a proportion, or writing an equation to name just a few. The proportion approach is based on the ratio interpretation of percent: two equivalent ratios are set equal to each other, and the unknown value is computed:

$$\frac{\text{percent}}{100} = \frac{\text{part}}{\text{whole}}$$

The first ratio in a proportion involving percents is often referred to as the *percent ratio*. It compares a specific number (the percent) with 100. (Remember, percents can be less than 1 and greater than 100.) The second ratio compares the part/whole data. While we tend to think of a part as being less than the whole, a part can also be greater than the whole. This would correspond to a percentage greater than 100.

Let's examine the proportion related to the problem *If a $30 shirt is on sale for 20% off, what is the savings?* The percent is 20%, which is the equivalent of comparing 20 with 100, so the first ratio is $\frac{20}{100}$. Next we have to determine whether the $30 in the problem represents the whole amount of the shirt or the part corresponding to 20%.

In this case, $30 represents the whole, or total, and the savings, or discount, is un-known. Thus the second ratio is $\frac{x}{30}$. The proportion solution is based on the fact that we can have the same multiplicative relationship within each ratio (percent to 100 and discount to $30) and that there is a relationship between these two ratios. When the relationships are equivalent, we can set up the following proportion and think about ways to find the value of *x*:

$$\frac{20}{100} = \frac{x}{30}$$

The general equation used to solve percent problems follows the form *part = percent × whole*, with the percent being written as a decimal or fraction. For example, the shirt problem can be solved using the equation *x* = .20 × 30, where *x* represents the discount or savings. Notice that 20% is recorded as a decimal, 0.20, though a fraction could also have been used. Equivalent equations can be constructed depend-ing on the missing value in a problem. For example, the general equation *part = percent × whole*, can be rewritten as:

part ÷ whole = percent (divide each side of the general equation by the whole value)

part ÷ percent = whole (divide each side of general equation by the percent)

You may recollect learning specific equations for solving three types of percent problems. While there is nothing wrong with using equations or proportions to solve percent problems, mechanically applying either approach based on key words and phrases can undermine students' ability to understand the mathematics inherent in a problem.

Students need time to develop their reasoning of percent and other proportional situations before being taught the more formal solution methods. Having an oppor-tunity to discuss their reasoning helps students become flexible in how they solve future percent problems—the goal being that they choose methods (formal and in-formal) based on their understanding of situations and ease of computations. Solve the following problems, which illustrate informal and formal methods that students have used, using at least two different methods. What are the advantages of being able to think about and solve these problems in multiple ways? Is one approach better than another?

> *Eileen left a $3.00 tip for her lunch at Chez Stadium Restaurant. This tip was 15% of her entire bill. What did her meal cost?*

> *Students agreed to sell 40 candy bars each to raise money for a class project. Over the weekend, Sally sold 11 candy bars. What percent of her quota did she reach?*

The restaurant problem can be approached using reasoning about equivalent ra-tios. Students might build a ratio table and compare $3.00 to 15%. Notice that if the ratio $3 to 15% is multiplied by 6, we get an equivalent ratio of $18 to 90%.

COST	$3.00	$6.00	$9.00	$12.00	$15.00	$18.00
PERCENT	15%	30%	45%	60%	75%	90%

How do we get to 100% to find the total cost of the meal? One student suggested dividing the equivalent ratio $6.00 to 30% by 3 to form another equivalent ratio, $2.00 to 10%. She then added the $2.00 and the $18.00 (10% + 90%)—the meal cost $20.00 (100%). Another student used a similar strategy based on the idea of equivalent ratios. He compared $3.00 with 15% and divided the ratio by 3 to form the equivalent ratio $1.00 to 5%. Knowing that there are 20 groups of 5% in 100%, he multiplied $1 by 20 to find the cost of the meal.

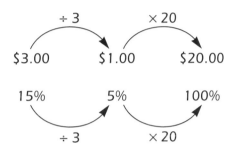

Did you also solve the restaurant problem using an equation or a proportion? In order to use either of these methods we need to analyze the components of the problem in terms of parts and wholes: the percent is known, the part of the whole amount that was left as a tip is known, but the whole, or total cost of the meal, is unknown. The equation is not so straightforward. When students are presented with a problem like this one, they realize they need to represent the percent as a fraction or decimal but are not sure what to do with the part ($3.00)—do they multiply or divide? There are not many clues in the problem to help with this translation. Students might use the idea that 15% can act as an operator on a whole, write the equation $3.00 = .15 \times$ whole, and conclude that they need to divide: $3 \div .15 = 20$. However, they might not come to that conclusion and instead incorrectly multiply 3.00 and 0.15. An advanced level of understanding of both the problem and the relationships among quantities is needed to use an equation meaningfully.

We can also construct a proportion using a percent ratio and a part-to-whole ratio. Once the proportion is constructed, students solve for the missing term using any of a number of methods, such as equivalent ratios or the cross product algorithm. For example, $\frac{15}{100} = \frac{3}{x}$ might be solved by noticing that the ratio $\frac{15}{100}$ can be divided by $\frac{5}{5}$ to form an equivalent ratio with a numerator of 3 and a denominator of 20. On the other hand, the proportion $\frac{15}{100} = \frac{3}{x}$ might be solved using cross products: $100 \times 3 = 15x$, so $x = 20$. Thus the meal cost Eileen $20.

The candy bar problem asks us to find the percent of candy bars Sally sold. One method is to use the ratio 11:40 and the concept of equivalent ratios to find the percent ratio (a ratio compared with 100). In the ratio table on page 160, notice that 11:40 is multiplied by 2 to form 22:80, and 11:40 is also divided by 2 to form the ratio 5.5:20. Combining ratios, 22:80 and 5.5:20, we get a comparison to 100—27.5:100. Sally sold 27.5% of her candy bars.

	÷ 2 × 2		
Candy bars sold	5.5 11 22		5.5 + 22 = 27.5
Total of candy bars	20 40 80		20 + 80 = 100
	÷ 2 × 2		

Number sense can be used verify that an answer of about 28% makes sense: 11 is a little more than $\frac{1}{4}$ of 40, so the answer should be a bit more than 25%, which it is.

In the restaurant problem, the cross product algorithm was used to solve for the missing term. The cross product method is usually taught in grades 5 through 7, sometimes as the only way to solve proportions. Researchers have found that while the cross product algorithm is easy for students to memorize, it is difficult for them to understand and therefore best left to the latter stages of the study of proportional relationships (Cramer, Post, and Currier 1993). Although the cross product algorithm is efficient and results in the correct solution whether or not the values in the problem are whole numbers, integers, or fractions, its use often hides the fact that students don't understand proportionality. Students develop a better conceptual grasp of proportions when they use other methods first, including ratio tables, fractions, and equivalent ratios. However, not all ratios simplify to useful equivalent ratios, so students must also be able to apply the cross product algorithm. In these cases, students should use estimation to check the reasonableness of their cross product answer.

Having a variety of methods to use when solving percent problems lets students evaluate the situation and the numerical values to determine which method will be most efficient and reliable. At times they will want to change the percent to a fraction and operate on the quantity; or they may make a ratio table and use multiplication and division to find equivalent ratios; or they may use proportions and the cross product algorithm; or they will convert a percent to a decimal or a fraction and use an equation.

Activity

Percent Word Problems

Objective: explore a variety of solution methods for percent problems.

Solve the following problems using a variety of methods. Choose the method based on the quantities involved.

Gold is a very soft metal and is easily bent and dented. As a consequence, gold jewelry is rarely made from pure gold. Instead it is mixed with another metal to make an alloy. Twenty-four-karat gold is pure gold, or 100% gold.

Some gold jewelry from Italy is 75% gold. How many karats are in the alloy that is 75% pure gold?

Gold from China can be as much as 92% gold. How many karats are in the alloy that is 92% pure gold?

What percent gold is 14-karat gold?

Things to Think About

An important consideration when solving percent problems is whether or not the numbers are "friendly," namely easy to use.

In the first problem we know that 75% of the alloy used in this particular kind of Italian jewelry is gold. Seventy-five percent is equivalent to the proper fraction $\frac{3}{4}$. Since 24-karat gold is pure gold, we can find $\frac{3}{4}$ of 24 by first finding $\frac{1}{4}$ of 24 ($\frac{1}{4} \times 24 = 6$) and multiplying 6 by 3. A simple drawing can be used to help with reasoning.

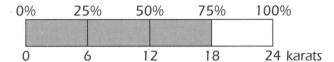

Another method students use is a ratio table in which both numbers in the ratio of 75 to 100 are divided and multiplied to find the number of karats.

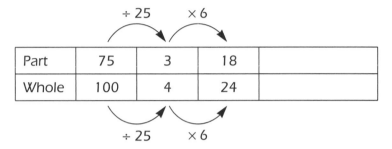

There are 18 karats in this Italian gold jewelry.

The second problem is similar to the first in that the number of karats compared with 24-karat pure gold are not known. However, compared with 75%, 92% is not as easy to use when computing mentally. We can express 92% as a fraction—$\frac{92}{100}$ or $\frac{23}{25}$—and this helps us estimate, since we are interested in a comparison with 24 (karats). Because $\frac{92}{100}$ is equivalent to 23 out of 25, a reasonable estimate would be 22 out of 24. However, when actually calculating the answer, the numbers in this problem lend themselves to representing the percent as a decimal and thinking of the percent as an operator. We can write an equation and multiply:

$$0.92 \times 24 = x$$

There are about 22 karats (22.08) in Chinese gold that is 92% pure.

In the final problem we are asked to determine the percent of gold in 14-karat gold jewelry. Since $\frac{14}{24}$ is a part-to-whole fraction, let's use fractions to solve this problem. The fraction $\frac{14}{24}$ is $\frac{2}{24}$, or $\frac{1}{12}$, more than $\frac{1}{2}$ ($\frac{12}{24} + \frac{2}{24} = \frac{14}{24}$). Since $\frac{12}{24}$ is equivalent to 50% and $\frac{1}{12}$ is equivalent to about 8.3%, the percent of gold in 14-karat jewelry is approximately 58.3%. Since the numbers are not as friendly in this problem as in others, we might want to set up a proportion in which we compare the percent ratio to the part-whole ratio represented by 14 karats compared with 24 karats of gold. In the ratio, the part and whole are known and the percent is unknown:

$$\frac{x}{100} = \frac{14}{24}$$
$$24x = 1400$$
$$x = 58.\overline{3}$$

Fourteen-karat gold jewelry is about 58% pure gold. ▲

One final common misconception about percent is that many adults and students assume there are no real applications of percentages greater than 100. After all, how can you have more than 100% of some real thing? If you have more than 100% of a group or an item, you must have more than one group or more than one item. Let's investigate some contexts that produce percentages that exceed 100. One such context is the percent of increase: A *single pencil once cost 5¢, but the price has risen to 25¢. What is the percent of increase in the price of pencils?*

Reasoning this out—the price increase is 20¢, which is 4 times the original price—can be done mentally. Thus, the percent of increase is 400%, since 4 times 100% equals 400%. In percent-of-increase (or percent-of-decrease) problems, the difference between the increased or decreased quantity and the original quantity is the focus of investigation. We could also have solved this problem using a proportion, but it requires a bit more computation: $\frac{x}{100} = \frac{20}{5}$. In the first ratio, the percent is unknown and is represented by x. The second ratio compares the amount of increase (25¢ − 5¢ = 20¢) to the whole, or original, amount (5¢).

Contrast this problem to one that is almost identical: A *single pencil once cost 5¢, but the price has risen to 25¢. What percent is the new price compared with the old price?* Here the comparison is between the new price (25¢) and the original price (5¢), not between the increase and the original price. This problem is a lot like the ones in Activity 3 using comparison sets. You can sketch a diagram like the one below to help you understand why the new price is 500% of the original price.

5¢	25¢
100%	? %

Try this problem: *If the cost of a soda doubles from $1.00 to $2.00, what is the percent of increase?* The increase is only 100%, even though the price has doubled. It is easy to confuse the arithmetic relationship of doubling with the percent of increase and expect the percent increase to be 200%.

Activity

Percents Greater Than 100%

Objective: analyze and solve problems that involve percents greater than 100%.
Solve the following percent problems.

> *House prices have risen dramatically over the past 20 years. A house that was purchased in 1980 for $60,000 recently sold for $280,000. What is the percent of increase?*

> *Many school systems are experiencing record increases in the number of students each year. One superintendent stated: "Our enrollments are 125% compared with last year." If there were 2,400 students in the school system last year, how many students are enrolled this year?*

Things to Think About

The percent of change—either the percent of increase or the percent of decrease—involves comparing the amount of change with the original, or starting, value. Since the first problem asks us to determine the percent of increase, we have to find the difference between the price of the house in 1980 and today: $280,000 – $60,000 = $220,000. We then want to compare the change in price ($220,000) with the original price ($60,000). It helps to remember that the $60,000 represents 100% of the original value and we want to find out the percent of change from this starting value. The ratio 220,000:60,000 is equivalent to 22:6, or 11:3. Notice that 11 is greater than 3. How many times greater? We can divide (11 ÷ 3), which results in $3\frac{2}{3}$ (or 3.67 rounded as a decimal)—the increase, 11, is $3\frac{2}{3}$ times 3. To determine the percent of increase, multiply 3.67 times 100: the value of the house increased by about 367%.

The second problem does not involve percent of change. It is simply a comparison of one year's enrollment with the next year's. Since the percent is greater than 100%, we know that the enrollment this year is greater than 2,400 students (if the number of students this year is 2,400, the two enrollments are 100% of each other). This problem also is similar to the comparison problems in Activity 3 except that here numbers are used. Since 125% is equivalent to $1\frac{1}{4}$, finding $\frac{1}{4}$ of 2,400 will tell us the amount of increase to add to 2,400. One fourth of 2,400 is 600, so the new enrollment figure is 3,000 (2,400 + 600) students. A proportion or an equation could also be used to show this comparison relationship (when using an equation we represent the percent, 125%, as a decimal, 1.25):

$$\frac{125}{100} = \frac{x}{2,400} \qquad 2,400 \times 1.25 = x$$
$$x = 3,000 \qquad\qquad 3,000 = x$$

The number of students enrolled in the school system this year is 3,000. ▲

Teaching Percent

Since percents are used in so many applications, this is a very practical mathematics topic. Students must understand the meaning of percent in terms of fractions, decimals, and ratios and be able to solve a wide variety of problems that use percents. Students are first introduced to percents in upper elementary school and then study them in more depth in middle school. Students benefit from using models, diagrams, and algorithms to explore the meaning of percent. Instruction should first emphasize using reasoning and making sense and ask students to solve problems informally using fractions, decimals, and ratio tables. Later in middle school students should explore using proportions and equations to solve percent problems. As adults, students will use percents in many everyday contexts, ranging from paying taxes and interest on loans to receiving discounts. They should therefore be able to use percents flexibly and accurately.

Questions for Discussion

1. How are percents similar to fractions and decimals? How are they different?
2. Some textbooks teach percents, fractions, and decimals together, whereas other textbooks have separate chapters or units on each. What are the benefits of each approach? What are the problems of each approach?

3. How did you learn to solve problems that involve percents? How do your methods compare with the ones described in this chapter?
4. Examine percent word problems in a sixth- or seventh-grade textbook. Try to solve some of these problems using reasoning rather than formal algorithms (proportions or equations). What are the benefits of reasoning about percent situations before learning more formal solution methods?

Ratios

Ratios are part of a large web of mathematical concepts and skills known as *proportional reasoning* that make use of ideas from multiplication, division, fractions, and measurement. Proportional reasoning is the ability to make and use multiplicative comparisons among quantities. These comparisons are expressed as ratios and rates. We use ratios and rates every day to convey information: the car is traveling at 25 mph, place 2 roses and 3 pieces of greenery in every bouquet, ground beef costs $1.89 per pound, 3 out of every 8 doctors majored in biochemistry, and there is a 30% chance of thunderstorms.

Proportionality is a complex topic; it is estimated that over half the adult population do not reason proportionally (Lamon 1999). Furthermore, students' understanding of this topic takes years to develop—a two-week unit on ratios in sixth grade is not enough for most students to acquire anything but a superficial ability to apply an algorithm. Instead, it is necessary for students informally to explore ideas related to thinking multiplicatively throughout the elementary grades and spend significant time developing these concepts in middle school.

1. What Are Ratios?

A *ratio* is a comparison between two or more quantities. The quantities can be either numbers or measurements. Comparisons such as 5 pencils for $1.09, 12 degrees per hour, 4 girls for every 5 boys, $\frac{1}{2}$ cup lemonade concentrate to 4 cups of water, and 3 red marbles compared with 8 marbles altogether are all ratios. Sometimes ratios are used to compare more than two quantities; 1 part vinegar, 1 part linseed oil, and 1 part turpentine is a ratio for an old-fashion solution used to refinish antique furniture.

Ratios are further classified based on the type of comparison. If we are comparing measures of the same type, such as people, inches, and marbles, we can either make part-to-whole comparisons or part-to-part comparisons. Part-to-whole ratios can be interpreted as fractions because they compare a part with a whole (e.g., the ratio 7 to 20, when comparing 7 girls with a total of 20 students in a classroom, is a fraction that tells us what part of the set—$\frac{7}{20}$—are girls). Other ratios compare parts of a set to other parts of a set. For example, we can compare 2 blue marbles with 6 red marbles in a set of marbles and then express the ratio of blue marbles to red marbles as 2:6, or 1:3. Starting with either a part-to-whole ratio or a part-to-part ratio, we are able to construct other ratios that apply. For example, if we use the 2 blue marbles to 6 red marbles ratio, the ratios of blue marbles to total number of marbles (2:8, part-whole ratio); red marbles to total number of marbles (6:8, part-whole ratio); and red marbles to blue marbles (6:2, part-part ratio) all provide information about the relationship between the two colors of marbles.

When two different types of measures are being compared, the ratio is usually called a *rate*. Comparisons involving number of miles and number of hours, number of dollars and bags of sugar, and number of minutes and number of feet are all rates. Rates sometimes involve a comparison with 1 (60 miles per 1 hour, 2 bags for 1 dollar, 0.25 feet in 1 minute); these "unit" rates are easier for us to generalize and extend (if I can drive 60 miles in 1 hour, my trip of 180 miles will take about 3 hours). Everyday usage of the terms *ratio* and *rate* is not always precise or correct. For example, rates are often simply referred to as ratios (which is correct but not very precise). On the other hand, some relationships are incorrectly called rates—they are not actually rates—since the measures are the same: birth rates compare number of people born with a designated number of people (usually 1000) and while this comparison is a ratio, it technically isn't a rate. A diagram may help you make sense of the different types of ratios.

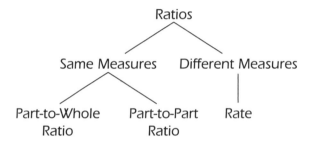

There are two common notations used to identify ratios: the colon notation and the fraction notation. While interchangeable, the choice of notation helps focus our attention on different aspects of interpretation. The colon notation is most often used with part-to-part comparisons (3 adults compared with 8 children, 3:8), while the fraction notation is favored with part-to-whole comparisons (3 adults compared with 11 people total, $\frac{3}{11}$). When fraction notation is used to compare two parts, it helps if the parts are labeled: $\frac{3\ adults}{8\ children}$. Otherwise, devoid of context, the conceptual differences between ratios and fractions can be lost and symbols can be interpreted in unexpected ways (you might think $\frac{3}{8}$ represents 3 out of a total of 8). Finally, fraction notation is commonly used when computing with ratios (e.g., finding equivalent ratios or finding the value of an unknown in a proportion) regardless of the type of relationship between the numbers.

Types of Comparisons

The concept of comparison or change between quantities is both simple and quite complex. Children start comparing quantities at a very young age—they notice a friend has more matchbox cars, they want a smaller helping of mashed potatoes at dinner, they wonder why there are fewer girls playing basketball than playing soccer. As teachers we regularly ask comparison questions: *If there are 8 boys in grade 1 and 7 boys in grade 2, are there more boys in the first or the second grade? How many more students have brown eyes than blue eyes? The temperature dropped how many degrees yesterday?* To answer these comparison questions, in which we are considering quantities with only one variable (e.g., number of boys, number of students, and number of degrees), we use additive thinking, relying on addition and subtraction to answer questions of how many, how much more, and how many fewer. Students start analyzing change between quantities using additive thinking before they start school and with time are able to apply this reasoning to a range of number types and sizes.

However, sometimes we compare the change between quantities in a more complex way, by looking at the multiplicative relationships between quantities. The question *If there are 8 boys in grade 1 and 7 boys in grade 2, are there more boys in the first or the second grade?* calls for comparing the two quantities, 8 and 7. However, if the question instead asked which class has a larger fraction, or percentage, or proportion, of boys, then we'd need to analyze the problem differently and would need to know the total number of children in each class. We might reason: *There are 8 boys out of 20 children in grade 1 ($\frac{8}{20}$, which is less than half) and 7 boys out of 14 children in grade 2 ($\frac{7}{14}$, which is exactly half).* So the grade 1 class has a smaller fraction of boys. Or we might think: *Let's compare 8 to 20, or $\frac{8}{20}$, with 7 to 14, or $\frac{7}{14}$. These ratios are equivalent to 2 to 5 ($\frac{2}{5}$) and 1 to 2 ($\frac{1}{2}$). So in the first grade there are 2 boys out of every 5 students whereas in the second grade there is 1 boy for every 2 students.* Or we could use percents: *40% of the children in grade 1 are boys and 50% of the children in grade 2 are boys.* Using multiplicative thinking, we state that there are more boys in grade 2 because the proportion of boys is greater, but thinking additively there are more boys in grade 1 ($8 - 7 = 1$).

Let's look at another example of how the relationship between two quantities in a ratio conveys different multiplicative information (Lamon 1999):

> 20 students in a classroom
>
> 20 students in the auditorium
>
> 20 students in a 10-seat minivan

In each of the examples above, the same quantity (20 students) is used. If we just compare the number of students in each situation, we might note that they are the same or that there is no difference between them; we have used additive thinking to compare the quantities. But when 20 students are compared with the other (implied) quantities, each of the comparisons, or ratios, imparts a different meaning that calls for multiplicative reasoning. Twenty students in one classroom is seen by many educators as ideal; an auditorium with 20 students is quite empty compared with the number of seats available; and a 10-seat minivan with 20 students in it is very crowded if not downright unsafe! When we ask which situation is the most crowded, we think multiplicatively and consider both quantities at the same time. Namely, we use multiplication and division in our solution.

Activity

More Than One Way to Compare

Objective: compare situations using both additive and multiplicative reasoning.

Every July 1st, the children in the Hollinger family are measured and the height recorded on the inside sill of their kitchen door. And every July 1st there is a family debate over who grew the most during the past year. Explore this problem in two ways: using additive and multiplicative thinking.

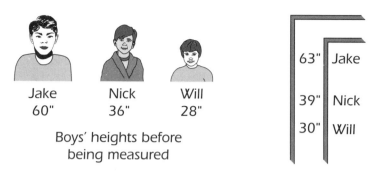

Jake
60"

Nick
36"

Will
28"

Boys' heights before
being measured

63" Jake

39" Nick

30" Will

Boys' heights after
being measured

Things to Think About

Both Jake and Nick grew 3 inches, while Will only grew 2 inches. Using additive reasoning, we can state that two of the boys grew the same amount (and the most that year) and they both grew 1 more inch than Will. But we can consider growth in another way—in relation to their starting heights. When we compare the amount of growth to each boy's starting height, we are using multiplicative thinking. Jake grew $\frac{3}{60}$, or $\frac{1}{20}$, of his starting height; Nick grew $\frac{3}{36}$, or $\frac{1}{12}$, of his starting height; and Will grew $\frac{2}{28}$, or $\frac{1}{14}$, of his starting height. Even though Jake and Nick each grew 3 inches, we can now see that compared with where they started, Nick shot up more relative to his original height. One way to think about this is to compare the simplified ratios: $\frac{1}{20} < \frac{1}{12}$. Using this type of *multiplicative* reasoning, we find that Will also grew relatively more than Jake since he increased his height by $\frac{1}{14}$ compared with $\frac{1}{20}$. Notice that just as we use the operations of addition and subtraction for additive reasoning, we use the operations of multiplication and division for multiplicative reasoning when we compare relative amounts.

Another way to compare the boys' growths multiplicatively is to record them as a percent: $\frac{3}{60} = 5\%$, $\frac{3}{36} = 8\%$, and $\frac{2}{28} = 7\%$. Nick's height increased by 8%, Will's height by 7%, and Jake's height by 5%. If we calculate percents by comparing the new heights with the old heights, we get similar results: $\frac{63}{60} = 105\%$, $\frac{39}{36} = 108\%$, and $\frac{30}{28} = 107\%$. The 107%, for example, indicates that Will exceeded his earlier height (100%) by an additional 7%. Thus, this year the Hollingers agreed that Nick grew the most, followed by Will, followed by Jake—relatively speaking! ▲

Ratios as Rational Numbers

Many ratios belong to the rational number set. Some ratios, however, do not. Rational numbers cannot have zero in the denominator (see Chapter 5, page 100, for more information), but it is possible to have a ratio with zero as the second number; the ratio 11:0 can be used to compare 11 male Boston Red Sox players with 0 female Boston Red Sox players, but it is neither a fraction nor a rational number. Other ratios may involve irrational numbers such as π and $\sqrt{2}$ and also are not part of the rational numbers (see Chapter 1, page 5).

Some interpretations of ratio are closely connected to the meanings of fractions described in Chapter 5 but others are not. For example, we have seen how part-to-whole ratios and fractions are related. Another fraction interpretation, the interpretation of fractions as the result of dividing two numbers, can be connected to ratios. In these instances, ratios are reported as a single number (instead of a comparison) that is created by performing a division. For example, the ratio of circumference to diameter is reported as π and approximated at 3.14. The average number of people per household in the United States was recently reported as 2.57. Batting averages are found by dividing the number of hits by the total number of times at bat (in 1923 Babe Ruth had a batting average of .393). The interpretation of these divided ratios must be considered carefully. Sometimes the divided ratio conveys information as an average (while there aren't 2.57 people in any household, we get a sense of the size of many American households). Other times it describes special relationships about particular geometric figures or about an ability to hit baseballs. Notice that unlike a unit rate where a comparison with 1 is made but not always explicitly stated, some ratios created by performing a division do not convey a comparison of two quantities. Depending on the quantities in the division, some of these divided ratios are rational numbers and some are not.

One aspect of understanding ratios that is related to rational number knowledge involves understanding equivalence. Students benefit from comparing and reasoning about equivalent ratios and rates. The rules for finding equivalent ratios (regardless of the type of ratio) are exactly the same as the rules for finding equivalent fractions. However, equivalent ratios are different in one important way from equivalent fractions. Equivalent fractions, such as $\frac{1}{2}$, $\frac{3}{6}$, and $\frac{40}{80}$, are different symbols that refer to the same quantity or rational number—one half—a number that you can locate on a number line. On the other hand, equivalent part-part ratios do not name the same quantity but rather represent the same comparison between two quantities. The following equivalent ratios—1 girl to 2 boys (1:2), 3 girls to 6 boys (3:6), and 40 girls to 80 boys (40:80)—name a comparison between two quantities, and each also names the same comparison of quantities—there are half as many girls as boys. Likewise, rates such as 125 miles in 5 hours and 50 miles in 2 hours are equivalent because they represent the same hourly speed of 25 mph, but they do not refer to the same distance traveled (125 versus 50 miles). Since some ratios are part-to-whole fractions, we can see how confusing this must be for students. Thus, when discussing the meaning of number sentences, we need to consider the context or situation in which the symbols arise in order to interpret them correctly and consider the type of comparison used (part-whole versus part-part versus rate).

Activity

Exploring Equivalent Ratios

Objective: examine equivalence of ratios.

Materials: pattern blocks.

Using pattern blocks, we can build a polygon "chain" that consists of 2 equilateral triangles and 3 trapezoids, in the ratio of 2:3:

If we have 4 triangles and 6 trapezoids, we can build two chains:

Using the ratio of 2 triangles for every 3 trapezoids, complete the table below and answer the questions that follow.

NUMBER OF CHAINS	NUMBER OF TRIANGLES	NUMBER OF TRAPEZOIDS	RATIO OF TRIANGLES TO TRAPEZOIDS
1	2	3	2:3
2			
3			
4			
		18	
	135		
			32:48

1. If the number of trapezoids used to make chains is 18, how many triangles are needed? What is the ratio of triangles to trapezoids? Is this ratio equivalent to 2:3? Why or why not? Is this ratio a part-whole or part-part ratio?
2. If you want to use 135 triangles, how many trapezoids will you need so the relationship between triangles and trapezoids is maintained?
3. If the total number of blocks is 65, how many triangles and trapezoids are there?

Things to Think About

Did you notice any patterns in the table? The numbers of triangles are multiples of two, and the numbers of trapezoids are multiples of three. Two chains have a triangle/trapezoid ratio of 4:6, and three chains have a ratio of 6:9. In addition, all the ratios of triangles to trapezoids (2:3, 4:6, 6:9, etc.) are equivalent. Why? Because each subsequent ratio compares a different number of triangles and trapezoids, but all the comparisons are multiples of the original comparison, the ratio 2:3. Put differently, we can take 6 triangles and 9 trapezoids and arrange them to show the same comparison of quantities—3 chains of 2 triangles and 3 trapezoids.

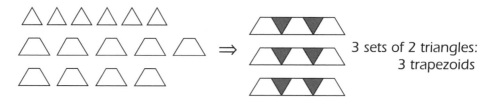

3 sets of 2 triangles: 3 trapezoids

If 18 trapezoids are used to make polygon chains, there are six 2-triangle-3-trapezoid chains. Thus, six sets of 2 triangles, or 12 triangles, are needed, and the ratio can be written as 12:18. Tables like the one above are helpful tools for organizing one's work, but may not lead to developing students' understanding of the multiplicative relationships inherent in proportional situations. This is especially true if students successively add 2 in the triangle column and 3 in the trapezoid column, building up the values in each column until they reach 12 triangles and 18 trapezoids: there is some question whether students see multiplicative relationships in situations that they solved using addition strategies. One way to promote multiplicative reasoning is to introduce students to ratio tables that display equivalent ratios, with the guideline that predominately multiplication and division should be used to find equivalent values. The focus is on the relationship between the two quantities in the ratio and on operating on both of these quantities in order to form equivalent relationships that have the same comparison of quantities. Two different ratio tables that might be used to solve this problem are shown below.

RATIO TABLE A	RATIO TABLE B

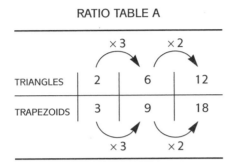
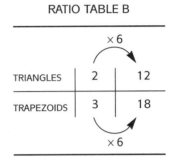

How many trapezoids are needed if there are 135 triangles? Did you divide 135 by 2 (67.5) and then multiply that quantity by 3? If we take 67.5 sets of the 2:3 ratio, we end up with an equivalent ratio of 135:202.5. If 135 triangles are used to make chains, we can make 67 complete chains and half of another chain! One way students might approach this problem is to analyze the quantities and then use a ratio table. There are many correct ways to build a ratio table, and as can be seen, to combine operations to solve problems. In Table A, a student first multiplied 2:3 by 135 to get an equivalent ratio of 270:405, then subsequently divided each part of the ratio by 2 to end up with 135 compared with 202.5. The student using Table B multiplied the 2:3 ratio twice and then combined the parts. First, she multiplied 2:3 by 60 to get the equivalent ratio 120:180. Then, instead of continuing from 120:180, she again multiplied the ratio 2:3 by $7\frac{1}{2}$ to produce the equivalent ratio $15:22\frac{1}{2}$. By combining the ratios, 120:180 and $15:22\frac{1}{2}$, she ended up with 135 to $202\frac{1}{2}$.

RATIO TABLE A	RATIO TABLE B

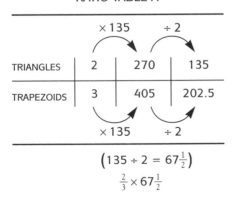
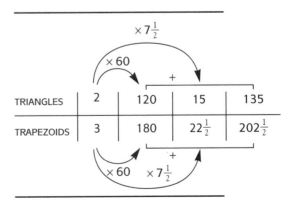

If the total number of blocks is 65, how many triangles and trapezoids are there? One way to answer this question is to extend the table and record the number of triangles and trapezoids until a total of 65 blocks are used. Another way involves noting that 5 blocks are needed for the ratio 2:3 and there are 13 sets of 5 in 65. Since in the original ratio there are two triangles to three trapezoids and there are 13 sets of this ratio, you can multiply each of these parts by 13 (2 × 13 and 3 × 13) to find the equivalent ratio, 26:39. Another approach is to use a ratio table with three rows (triangles, trapezoids, total blocks). Try using the ratio table as a tool for solving this problem.

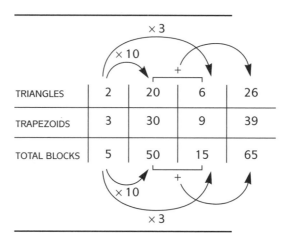

If there are 65 blocks, 26 are triangles and 39 are trapezoids. ▲

We do not add and subtract part-part ratios in the same way we add and subtract fractions. When adding or subtracting fractions, we are interpreting the quantities as parts of wholes and are joining parts to make wholes. The triangle/trapezoid ratio in Activity 2 is not a comparison of parts with a whole but a comparison between a part and another part. When these part-part ratios are combined, the end result is another equivalent comparison, not a total. When we combine two polygon chains (2:3 + 2:3), we write the resulting ratio of triangles to trapezoids as 4:6, which means four triangles compared with six trapezoids; when we combine two fractions $(\frac{2}{3} + \frac{2}{3})$, we are finding the total amount. The sum is $\frac{4}{3}$, or $1\frac{1}{3}$, which means one whole unit and one third of a second unit. Therefore, contextual information is very important and aids in helping students focus on the type of relationship they are considering— a comparison between parts and parts rather than between parts and a whole.

Proportions

Lessons about proportions are often included in instructional materials about ratios and rates in the middle grades. A *proportion* is a mathematical statement of equality between two ratios. Stated another way, proportions tell us about the equivalence of ratios. For example, $\frac{6}{9} = \frac{8}{12}$ is a proportion. Both ratios can be simplified, indicating they represent the same comparison: $\frac{2}{3} = \frac{2}{3}$. The fractional form of writing proportions is generally preferred since it is more suitable for solving equations. However, proportions can also be presented using ratio notation: 6:9 = 8:12 or 6:9 :: 8:12. The double colon indicates the ratios are equivalent. When proportions are presented devoid of context, the symbols can be interpreted as equivalent fractions or as equivalent ratios (which includes rates).

A proportion includes multiplicative relationships "within" the individual ratios and multiplicative relationships "between" the two ratios. For example, to make an apple pie we need 2 cups of sugar for every 6 cups of apples, or 3 cups of sugar for every 9 cups of apples. The proportion $\frac{2}{6} = \frac{3}{9}$ represents this relationship. The "within" ratios are 2:6 and 3:9 and both simplify to 1:3, or $0.\overline{3}$. The "between" ratios are 2:3 and 6:9 and both simplify to 2:3, or $0.\overline{6}$. The diagram below illustrates that in a proportion, the two "within" ratios are the same and the two "between" ratios are the same.

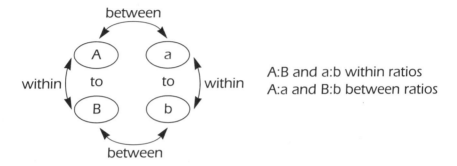

A:B and a:b within ratios
A:a and B:b between ratios

There is another "within" ratio relationship: if we multiply the first number in the 2:6 ratio by 3 we will obtain the second number in the ratio ($2 \times 3 = 6$). If we examine the multiplicative relationship "between" the ratios, we discover that multiplying both numbers in the first ratio by 1.5 ($2 \times 1.5 = 3$; $6 \times 1.5 = 9$) gives us the second ratio. Likewise, dividing both numbers in the second ratio by 1.5 returns us to the first ratio.

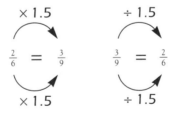

This quantity (1.5) is known as a *scale factor* and is discussed in detail on page 178. Choose a different scale factor, such as 2, and make another proportion ($\frac{2}{6} = \frac{4}{12}$). Can you figure out why these two ratios are equivalent?

A characteristic of proportions is that the "cross products" are equal. Using the proportion $\frac{2}{6} = \frac{3}{9}$, this means that 2×9 should equal 6×3, which is true: $18 = 18$. Let's explore why this occurs. One way to think of it is that since the ratios are equivalent, they simplify to an identical ratio—the "within" ratio—an identical comparison of quantities—in this case 1 to 3—and $\frac{1}{3} = \frac{1}{3}$. Likewise, both of the ratios can be rewritten as a comparison of 6 to 18 ($\frac{6}{18}$). This equivalent ratio is found by taking three sets of the ratio 2:6 and two sets of the ratio 3:9. The first number of one ratio indicates how many sets of the other ratio are needed to make them equivalent. As with $\frac{1}{3} = \frac{1}{3}$, the cross products for $\frac{6}{18} = \frac{6}{18}$ are the same.

Unfortunately, students are taught how to use cross products to find missing values ($\frac{4}{12} = \frac{x}{6}$, $12x = 24$, $x = 2$) before they have developed an understanding of proportional situations. As a result they apply the cross product algorithm to any and all situations even though cross products are only equal when the ratios are equivalent—the relationship doesn't hold for all pairs of ratios! Students instead should first have extensive opportunities to solve problems that involve proportions and multiplicative thinking using their own ideas and methods before being introduced to the cross product algorithm. For example, the value of x can be found in the proportion above by using multiplicative relationships in the "within" ratios or the "between" ratios.

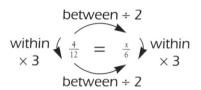

The phrase *proportional reasoning* is used when describing the thinking that has been applied to the solution of problems that involve multiplicative relationships. Topics studied in upper elementary and middle school such as fractions, percents, ratios, similarity, scale indirect measurement, and probability involve some aspects of proportional thinking. That said, proportional reasoning involves more than simply using a proportion or cross products as part of a solution. An important step in understanding proportions occurs when students think of a ratio as an entity unto itself—they don't just consider the two quantities that make up the ratio separately but are focused on the relationship between the quantities. In addition, when students start to recognize proportional situations in everyday settings and to reason multiplicatively about them, they are developing insight into this topic. Teachers should provide students with a variety of problems to solve in these areas starting in about fourth grade, because it is now known that it takes a number of years for students to develop the ability to use and thus be able to reason proportionally. One major recommendation from many researchers is that we should hold off teaching the standard algorithms for operating on fractions and solving proportions until students have made sense of some of the fundamental concepts.

2. Applications of Ratios and Rates

Proportional reasoning is an essential component of many courses in mathematics and science, including algebra, geometry, chemistry, and physics. Ratios and rates are used to answer questions about unit pricing, population density, percents (see Chapter 7), speed, slopes, conversion of money, map reading, reductions and enlargements of figures, fractions (see Chapter 5), and drug concentrations.

Similarity

In everyday life we talk about things being "similar" or "a little bit alike," but the mathematical meaning of this term refers to a particular geometric concept. What does it mean for two shapes to be similar? Students in grade 5 or 6 are often introduced informally to the concept of similarity by examining figures that have the same shape but not the same size. Are the figures below similar? They all are rectangles (same shape).

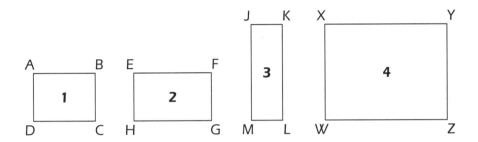

Even though all of the rectangles have the same rectangular shape, using the mathematical meaning of similarity only Figures 1 and 4 have the "same shape"; Figures 2 and 3 do not. However, the phrase "same shape" is unclear. When we use it, either we are being very general and talking about classification (they are all rectangles) or we are referring to geometry concepts—congruency and similarity. So what characteristics must shapes have if they are considered the same shape mathematically (that is, similar)?

First, for two shapes to be similar, it is necessary for the corresponding angles to be congruent; put in another way, the angle measures must be exactly the same size. The term *corresponding* is used to connect related parts of two figures. Corresponding parts (whether angles or sides) occur in the same relative position in figures. Sides $\overline{AB}$ and $\overline{XY}$ above are corresponding sides and ∠A and ∠X are corresponding angles. But for two shapes to have congruent angles is not sufficient for the rectangles to be mathematically similar. Notice that all four rectangles have right angles; we can even say that ∠E and ∠K are corresponding angles since they are in the same relative position in Figures 2 and 3 respectively. But Figures 2 and 3 are not similar, whereas Figures 1 and 4 are. So what other feature is important to similarity?

The second property found in similar shapes or figures is that the corresponding dimensions are proportional. This means that for rectangles to be similar, the ratios of length to width (or width to length) within each shape are equivalent. Examine Figures 1 and 4 below. Notice that the ratio of 4:3 in rectangle 1 and the ratio of 8:6 in rectangle 4 are both equivalent and can be written as $1\frac{1}{3}$:1. However the length-to-width ratios in rectangles 2 and 3 (5:3 or $1\frac{2}{3}$:1, and 6:2 or 3:1, respectively) are not equivalent, and thus the shapes are not similar.

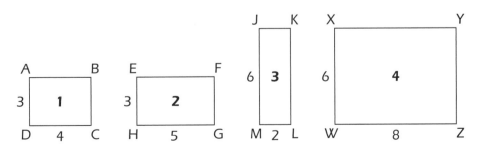

Exploring Similar Figures on a Coordinate Grid

Objective: explore how equivalent ratios can be expressed arithmetically, geometrically, and algebraically.

Materials: graph paper.

Draw a graph of the first quadrant and label the *x*-axis "length" and the *y*-axis "width." Draw the rectangles with the following dimensions (width to length) on the coordinate grid: 3 × 4, 6 × 8, 8 × 10, 9 × 12, and 12 × 16. Each rectangle should start at the origin (0,0) and its shorter side should align with the *y*-axis and its longer side should align with the *x*-axis. Next draw a line from the origin through the upper right corner of the 12-by-16 rectangle. Which rectangles are similar to one another? Which width-to-length ratios are equivalent? How are the width-to-length ratios shown on the coordinate grid? Draw another line from the origin through the upper right vertex (corner) of the 8 × 10 rectangle and use it to determine the dimensions of four rectangles similar to it.

Things to Think About

Did your line go through the upper right corner of the 3 × 4, 6 × 8, 9 × 12, and 12 × 16 rectangles? This is because the width-to-length ratios of these rectangles are equivalent—they name the same comparison between quantities, since each of these ratios can be simplified to the "within" ratio of .75:1. In addition, we can say that these four rectangles are all similar because they have corresponding angles that are congruent and corresponding dimensions that are proportional. Using this line we can find other rectangles that are similar to these four. Take a point on the line such as (6, 4.5) and draw vertical and horizontal lines to the axes. The resulting rectangle, 4.5 × 6, is similar to the other rectangles. These multiplicative relationships can be expressed arithmetically using width-to-length equivalent ratios but also geometrically using similar rectangles nested within each other.

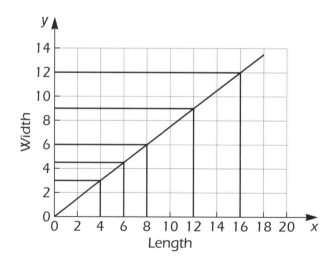

The slope of this line is $\frac{3}{4}$, or .75. The slope, which is a comparison of vertical change with horizontal change, algebraically connects these equivalent ratios.

Ratios that are equivalent, such as 3:4, 4.5:6, 6:8, 9:12, 12:16, and many more, all fall on the same line on the grid.

The width-to-length ratio of the other rectangle, 8 × 10, does not name the same comparison. Let's find other ratios (and thus rectangles) that are equivalent (or similar) to 8:10. One way is to use a ratio table to list equivalent ratios such as 4:5 or 12:15. Another is to draw a line from the origin (0,0) through the point (10,8) and extend it. The coordinates of points on the line represent width-to-length ratios equivalent to 8:10. If you draw vertical and horizontal lines from points along the line, you create similar rectangles, such as 2 × 2.5, 4 × 5, 6 × 7.5, and 12 × 15. The slope of this new line is $\frac{4}{5}$—the simplified "within" ratio for this set of equivalent ratios.

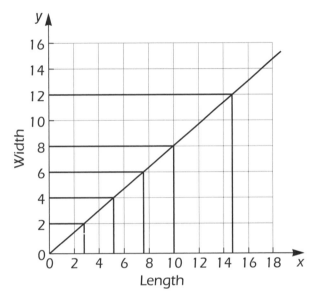

Rectangles similar to 8:10
(width:length)

Draw a line from the origin with slope $\frac{3}{4}$ on this second graph. How do the different lines compare? Notice that the line with slope $\frac{4}{5}$ is steeper. Can you estimate where a line representing all equivalent ratios to 9:10 would go on the graph? ▲

A common application of the principles of similarity involves making scale drawings and models. Scale drawings are drawings of similar figures that have either been enlarged or reduced. Drawings of microscopic organisms are enlarged in biology books, while pictures of our solar system are reduced. Three-dimensional scale models are used in automobile and aircraft design and in architectural plans. Students may have read about both enlargements and reductions in children's literature (*Gulliver's Travels*, *The Littles*) and may have firsthand experience with models in the form of miniature cars and train sets. Some of your students may have tried to make sense of a set of blueprints or to enlarge a drawing in art class.

How do we make enlargements and reductions? To create a scale drawing, we need a *scale factor*. The scale factor is a number by which all of the dimensions of an original figure are multiplied to produce the dimensions of the enlargement or reduction. When the scale factor is greater than 1, the new figure, sometimes referred to as an *image*, is an enlargement. When the scale factor is a number between 0 and 1, the resulting figure will be reduced in size, and is often referred to as a *reduction*. Scale factors use the operator interpretation of rational number in which the fraction acts either to stretch (enlarge) or to shrink (reduce) all dimensions of a drawing or three-dimensional model (see Chapter 5, page 108, for additional information about this interpretation). Mathematicians often use the letter k to stand for the scale factor.

How do the perimeters and areas of similar figures compare? What relationship exists between the volumes of enlarged or reduced figures? These questions are explored in the following activities.

Activity

Perimeters and Areas of Squares

Objective: look for patterns in the perimeters and areas of similar squares.

Materials: graph paper.

What happens to the perimeter of a square when the dimensions (sides) of that square are doubled? tripled? quadrupled? What happens to the area of a square when its dimensions (sides) also are doubled? tripled? quadrupled? Investigate doubling dimensions by drawing a square of any size and calculating its perimeter and area. Next double the length of the sides of that square and calculate its "doubled" perimeter and area. Do this for several squares, keeping track of your measurements and looking for patterns in the "doubled" data. Then investigate what happens to the perimeter and area of squares if you triple or quadruple the side lengths.

Things to Think About

Did you notice that by doubling and tripling dimensions, you were making enlargements? What is the scale factor, k, in each case? When the sides are doubled, $k = 2$; tripling dimensions means that $k = 3$; and quadrupling gives us $k = 4$. Did you notice that when the side lengths were doubled, the perimeter was 2 times longer? When the side lengths were tripled the perimeter was 3 times longer, and when the sides were quadrupled, the perimeter was 4 times longer than the original perimeter. We can generalize that the perimeter of an enlarged square with scale factor k is equal to k times the original perimeter. Take a minute and explain why.

When the dimensions or sides of a square are doubled, the new area is 4 times as large; when the side lengths are tripled, the new area is 9 times as large; and when the side lengths are quadrupled, the new area is 16 times as large. Why? Let's use a 1-by-1 square to explain. Doubling each dimension means that the new dimensions are 2 by 2, or (1×2) by (1×2). The area of this "doubled" square can be found through this series of calculations:

Original Area $= 1 \times 1$

Doubled Area $= 2 \times 2$

$\qquad = (1 \times 2) \times (1 \times 2)$ double each side of the original square

$\qquad = (1 \times 1) \times (2 \times 2)$ rearrange the order and grouping of the factors

$\qquad = 1 \times 4$ original area times 4

$\qquad = 4$ the new area is 4 times greater than the original area

This can also be shown by analyzing the following diagram:

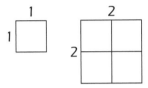

Notice that four 1-by-1 squares fit in the "doubled" square. Since each dimension is doubled ($k = 2$), the resulting area is quadrupled (2×2 or $k = 4$). The diagrams below show why the area of a square is 9 times greater when each side is tripled and 16 times greater when each side is quadrupled.

tripling dimensions   quadrupling dimensions

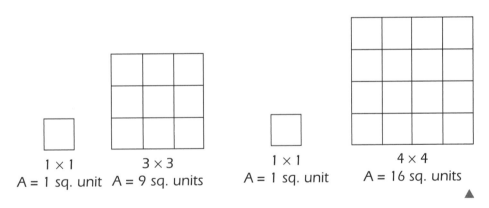

1×1 3×3 1×1 4×4

A = 1 sq. unit   A = 9 sq. units   A = 1 sq. unit   A = 16 sq. units

Activity

Areas of Similar Figures

Objective: generalize how the scale factor affects the area of similar figures.

Do the relationships between areas that result when the dimensions of squares are doubled, tripled, and quadrupled hold true for rectangles, triangles, and circles? That is, do the areas of other similar figures using scale factors of 2, 3, and 4 follow what we observed with squares? Using a calculator to find areas (area of rectangle = lw; area of triangle = $\frac{1}{2}bh$; area of circle = πr^2), complete the "doubling" table on page 180. Each time you double, triple, or quadruple all of the dimensions, the angles in the enlarged figures should be congruent (have exactly the same measure) with the angles in the original shapes, as you are creating similar figures. Examine the data for patterns. Construct your own tables for "tripling" and "quadrupling" dimensions. Explain the patterns you observe.

SHAPE	DIMENSIONS (IN CM)	AREA (IN CM²)	DIMENSIONS DOUBLED (IN CM)	DIMENSIONS DOUBLED AREA (IN CM²)	RATIO OF DIMENSIONS DOUBLED AREA TO AREA
Rectangle	$l = 4, w = 3$		$l = 8, w = 6$		
Rectangle					
Triangle	$b = 5, h = 4$		$b = 10, h = 8$		
Triangle					
Circle	$r = 3$		$r = 6$		
Circle					

Things to Think About

The relationships you observed with squares does hold true for rectangles, triangles, and circles. Doubling the dimensions of these shapes results in areas that are 4 times as large as the original areas. Likewise, tripling and quadrupling dimensions leads to areas of the enlarged shapes being 9 and 16 times larger, respectively. Stated in another way, if the scale factor is k, the area of the enlarged figure is k^2 times the original area. Does this relationship hold for scale factors that are less than 1? Yes. Let's say the scale factor is $\frac{1}{2}$. This means we multiply both dimensions by $\frac{1}{2}$ for a combined reduction of $(\frac{1}{2})^2$, or $\frac{1}{4}$. In summary, the area of a scaled figure is k^2 times the original area, where k is the scale factor, regardless of the size of k or the original area of the figure. A diagram might help you visualize these relationships.

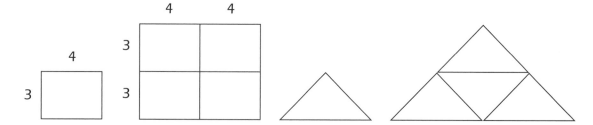

A circle doesn't have two dimensions like those of length and width. Why then is the area of the circle four times greater when the radius is doubled? In the formula for finding the area of a circle ($A = \pi r^2$), notice that the radius is squared. This means that you multiply the radius by itself, rather than having two different dimensions such as length and width. When you double and then square the radius, the new area is $(2r)^2$, or $4r^2$. The relationship holds: the area of the scaled circle, using scale factor k, is k^2 times the original area. ▲

The relationship between the dimensions of a figure and the area of that figure is very similar to the relationship that occurs when one square unit of measurement is converted to another. One square meter is equivalent in size to a square that is

100 centimeters per side. Since a smaller unit of measurement is used to determine the length of each side, the numerical value of the area based on these smaller square units will be greater—10,000 (100 × 100) times greater! The area of the original square meter doesn't change, but the size of the unit used to measure the area does.

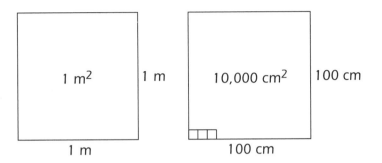

Activity

Doubling Dimensions of a Solid

Objective: explore the relationship between volumes and scale factors of similar figures.

Materials: multilink or unit cubes.

What happens to the volume of a rectangular prism if one, two, or all dimensions are doubled?

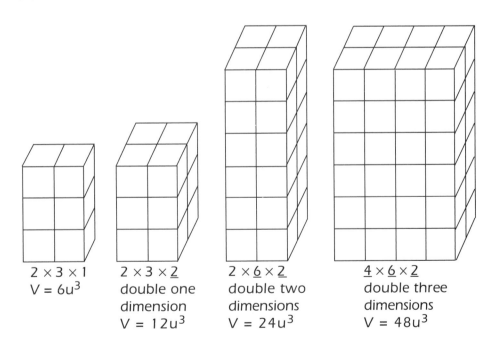

$2 \times 3 \times 1$
$V = 6u^3$

$2 \times 3 \times \underline{2}$
double one
dimension
$V = 12u^3$

$2 \times \underline{6} \times \underline{2}$
double two
dimensions
$V = 24u^3$

$\underline{4} \times \underline{6} \times \underline{2}$
double three
dimensions
$V = 48u^3$

You can use unit cubes, drawings and sketches, or numerical data to explore the changes as you double one dimension at a time. You may find it easier to recognize relationships and patterns if you organize your data in a table like the one on page 182. In the example given, each doubled dimension is underlined. You may also wish to use unit cubes or multilink cubes to build one prism and the subsequent "doubled" prisms in order to "see" the results of doubling dimensions.

DIMENSIONS OF PRISM	ORIGINAL VOLUME (CUBIC UNITS: u^3)	VOLUME AFTER ONE DIMENSION DOUBLED (CUBIC UNITS: u^3)	VOLUME AFTER TWO DIMENSIONS DOUBLED (CUBIC UNITS: u^3)	VOLUME AFTER THREE DIMENSIONS DOUBLED (CUBIC UNITS: u^3)
$1 \times 2 \times 5$	10	$\mathbf{2} \times 2 \times 5 = 20$	$\mathbf{2} \times \mathbf{4} \times 5 = 40$	$\mathbf{2} \times \mathbf{4} \times \mathbf{10} = 80$

If you triple all the dimensions of the prism, how many times greater is the volume of the prism? How are the volumes of similar figures related?

Things to Think About

What happens to the volume when one dimension is doubled? two dimensions are doubled? all three dimensions are doubled? The volume changes by powers of two. Doubling one dimension doubles the volume ($\times$ 2); doubling two dimensions quadruples the volume ($\times$ 2 $\times$ 2); doubling all three dimensions results in an eightfold increase in volume ($\times$ 2 $\times$ 2 $\times$ 2). This final volume ($\times$ 8) is the result of each dimension (length, width, and height) being multiplied by two (doubled), and then multiplied together.

When all three dimensions are tripled, the volume becomes 3 $\times$ 3 $\times$ 3, or 27 times greater, since each dimension is multiplied by 3. The volumes of similar figures are related by the scale factor. If the scale factor is 2, the new volume is 2^3, or 8 times greater. If the scale factor is 3, the new volume is 3^3, or 27 times greater. We can say that when the scale factor is k, the volume of the similar figure is k^3 times the original volume. The relationship holds for reductions as well. If a scale factor is $\frac{1}{4}$ then the volume of a reduced figure is $(\frac{1}{4})^3$—or $\frac{1}{64}$—times the original volume.

The relationship between increasing dimensions and volume can be used to explain why the existence of giants is mathematically questionable. Imagine a six-foot, 200-pound man and consider how he is similar to a rectangular prism. He might measure two feet across the chest, one foot front to back, and we know he is six feet tall. If we double all three of those dimensions, the resulting giant is four feet across at the chest, two feet front to back, and twelve feet tall. The volume of the giant, however, is eight times greater. Because of the relationship between volume and mass we can state that the mass of the giant is 1600 pounds. This weight is too heavy for human bones (even big ones) to support! Using this same line of reasoning, it also is unlikely that a giant-sized grasshopper would be possible. In this case, the large size and weight of a giant grasshopper couldn't be sustained by its delicate structure and lack of an internal skeleton. ▲

Unit Rates

When a rate is simplified so that a quantity is compared with 1, it is called a *unit rate*. Unit rates answer the question *how many (or how much) for 1?* Some unit rates are constant. This means that the simplified rate does not change (e.g., there are 2.54 centimeters for every 1 inch). Conversions between measurements (inches to feet, ounces to pounds, kilograms to pounds) are examples of constant unit rates. Other unit rates vary. The most common example of a varying rate is the monetary exchange rate. The rate of 1.20 Euros for 1 U.S. dollar is not fixed. Six months from now the rate may be 1.34 Euros for 1 U.S. dollar or it may be 1.05 Euros for 1 U.S. dollar! Whether or not a rate is constant or varies is rarely addressed in instructional materials, but it is an important topic for students to discuss.

Sometimes a rate is expressed as a single number. As seen earlier, single number rates are created by dividing one quantity by another. Some of these single number rates are actually unit rates, where the unit is implied but not explicitly stated. In other cases the comparison is not so clear. For example, in the paper we might learn about the death rate in a particular country being 6.8. Death rates are comparisons to 1000 people so this is not a unit rate (nor is it actually a rate, since people are being compared to people!). On the other hand, a heart rate of 130 is a unit rate, because the comparison is the number of heart beats with 1 minute of elapsed time. In general, it is difficult to establish whether or not a single number is a unit rate without investigating how the rate was derived. Unemployment rates, postal rates, mortgage rates, and inflation rates are interesting to research and discuss.

One of the interesting things about unit rates is that there are two ways to express the relationship. For example, at a local farm stand, tomatoes are $1.49 per pound. Most of us are very familiar with this type of unit rate from grocery shopping, where the unit refers to the number of pounds (1 pound of tomatoes for $1.49). But what if the unit refers to the number of dollars? How many pounds of tomatoes can you buy for $1.00? We can buy about 0.67 pound of tomatoes for $1.00. Usually, students find one form of a unit rate easier to interpret, but the context of when and how the rate is being used makes a difference. In this next activity, think about which unit rates make the most sense to you and why.

Activity

Unit Rates

Objective: understand the dual nature of unit rates.

Express the following ratios as two different unit rates. Try using a variety of tools to help you determine the unit rate, such as ratio tables, pictures, or graphs. Which form of each ratio makes the most sense? Why?

120 miles in 2 hours
5 pizzas for 3 teenagers
$42 for 7 watermelons
50 GBP (British pounds) being equivalent to $88.48 USD (U.S. dollars)
20 candies for $2.50

Things to Think About

Two different unit rates are possible for each of the above ratios:

60 miles in 1 hour	or	1 mile in $\frac{1}{60}$ hour (1 minute)
$1\frac{2}{3}$ pizzas for 1 teenager	or	1 pizza for $\frac{3}{5}$ teenager
$6 for 1 watermelon	or	$1 buys $\frac{1}{6}$ watermelon
1 GBP is equivalent to $1.7696 USD	or	$1 USD is equivalent to 0.5651 GBP
1 candy for $12\frac{1}{2}$¢	or	$1 buys 8 candies

Some unit rates make no sense, such as 1 pizza for $\frac{3}{5}$ teenager. And some unit rates are more practical in one form than in another, such as miles traveled in 1 hour. However, often both unit rates provide useful information. In a candy store, we sometimes may want to spend $1.00; at other times, when we only want a few pieces, it is useful to know the cost of 1 candy. When visiting another country we need to be able to convert currencies depending on the circumstance (*I just arrived in London. How many GBP will I get for $25?* or *I am about to get on the plane for home and I didn't spend 6 GBP. How many U.S. dollars have I tied up in GBPs?*).

How did you find the unit rates? Constructing a ratio table and then dividing is one approach. Labels are essential in order to keep track of the relationships. For example:

		÷ 7		÷ 6	
DOLLARS	$42		$6		1
WATERMELONS	7		1		$\frac{1}{6}$
		÷ 7		÷ 6	

It helps if you decide ahead of time which variable you wish to be 1 and then think about the operation that will produce that result.

Students often use pictures to make sense of these relationships, especially when the numbers are small and easy to manipulate.

5 pizzas for 3 children

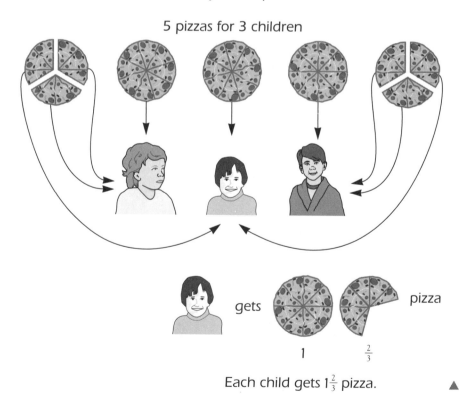

Each child gets $1\frac{2}{3}$ pizza. ▲

Sometimes finding a unit rate is an especially efficient method for solving a proportion problem. For example, if 4 gallons of gasoline cost $10 and we need to calculate the cost to fill up a 17-gallon tank, one method is to find the unit cost ($2.50 per gallon) and multiply that amount by 17 ($2.50 × 17 = $42.50). However, unit rates should not be used to the exclusion of other methods. A similar problem—if 4 gallons of gasoline cost $10, how much will 16 gallons cost?—can be solved quite differently and more easily. Notice that 4 groups of the rate 4 to 10 is equivalent to 16 gallons for $40. By multiplying the initial rate by a factor of 4 ($\frac{4\ gallons}{\$10} \times \frac{4}{4} = \frac{16\ gallons}{\$40}$), we have saved time and mental energy and perhaps avoided error since 10×4 is so straightforward! The second method is sometimes referred to as a *factor-of-change method*. The factor-of-change method could have been used to solve the first problem ($\frac{4\ gallons}{\$10} \times \frac{4.25}{4.25} = \frac{17\ gallons}{\$42.50}$), but the numbers in that problem don't lend themselves to that method; we are not likely to recognize that 4.25 is the correct factor of change, nor multiply by that factor mentally. Try to give students problems with numbers that lend themselves to the use of both approaches (not in the same problem) and encourage discussions about how we should choose a solution method based on the numbers in a problem.

Distance, Rate, and Time

The relationships among distance, rate, and time are known by the formula $D = rt$. Students learn about distance from personal experience getting to different locations on foot, by bicycle, or in a car. They realize that it takes different amounts of time, depending on the mode of transportation, to cover the same distance. Many students do not understand that *speed* is the common term for rate and is actually the comparison of distance with time. Since speedometers give us speed as one number, we tend not to think of it as miles per hour. In terms of instruction, researchers suggest that students in grades 6 through 8 would benefit from thinking about and discussing ways of comparing speeds, the difference between constant speed and average speed, and how rates are used to measure speed. Lamon (1999, 215) states: "Knowing the rule [$D = rt$] does not provide the level of comprehension needed to solve problems. We want students to develop an understanding of the structure of this set of relationships that comes from, but goes beyond, the investigation of specific situations. . . . [T]hey should be able to make generalizations such as this: if distance doubles, time will have to double if speed remains the same, or speed has to double if time remains the same."

One way to expand students' interpretation of the distance-rate-time relationship is to use graphs to compare different speeds. Two bicyclists, who live 10 miles apart on the same road, follow the exact same route every Sunday morning. Roberta's average speed on this route is 11 mph and Jeff's average speed is 15 mph. They both leave at 8:00 A.M. They meet at the same location every Sunday for a cup of coffee. How far have they biked and what time is it when they meet for coffee?

There are a lot of things to consider in this problem. First, what does it mean that their average speeds are 11 and 15 miles per hour, respectively? Average speed implies that if we could have maintained a constant speed for the whole distance, this would be it! When biking we slow down, speed up, stop, and sometimes maintain a constant speed. Average speed is the total distance traveled compared with the total time it takes us to travel that distance (rather than the average of all of the individual segments of a trip). Since Roberta and Jeff bike this route regularly, they know their average speeds. When we graph average speed, we treat it as if the speed were constant but it is important to realize that it really is not.

Second, when graphing distance-rate-time relationships, which variable goes on each axis? Usually time is on the x-axis as it is the independent variable (see Chapter 9). Distance traveled depends on the time and is on the y-axis. To graph these speeds we plot (time, distance) points such as (1, 15), which represents that after 1 hour, Jeff has traveled a total of 15 miles. Did you notice that Roberta and Jeff live 10 miles apart? Who lives farther away from their coffee spot? It is not explicitly defined in the problem, although we are told that they always meet there. Since Jeff's speed is faster, if Roberta lives farther away, they could never arrive at the same time.

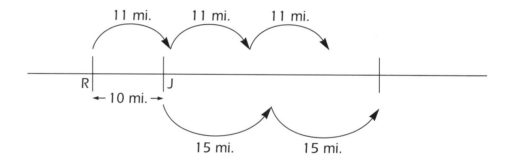

However, if Jeff lives farther away, then he might be able to catch up to her since he bicycles at a faster speed.

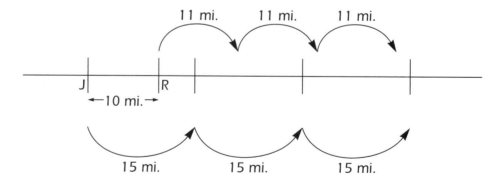

How is this difference in starting location shown on a coordinate graph? The graph of Jeff's trip starts at (0,0), meaning he has traveled 0 minutes and gone 0 distance at the beginning of the bike ride. We start the graph of Roberta's trip at (0,10); she has traveled 0 minutes but is already 10 miles closer to the coffee shop since they are starting at different locations along the route. The line representing Jeff's trip increases by 15 miles for every hour while the line representing Roberta's trip increases by 11 miles per hour. Why are these trips shown as straight lines? Remember we are interpreting average speed as constant speed even though we know in reality that this isn't the case. The graph of the two trips is shown below.

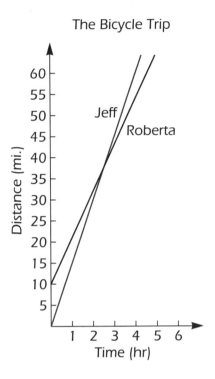

The Bicycle Trip

Notice that the line representing Jeff's speed is steeper than the line representing Roberta's speed. What does this mean in reality? Does Jeff go farther? Does he ride faster? Is he riding uphill? Students sometimes interpret graphs as pictures rather than as relationships between variables (students think that the steepness of the line representing Jeff's speed indicates he is going up a steep hill). Answering these questions, examining the relationship between distance and time, and linking the responses to the slopes of the lines ($\frac{distance}{time}$, or $\frac{15}{1}$ and $\frac{11}{1}$) aids in developing students' understanding of speed as a comparison of distance with time. When do Roberta and Jeff meet for coffee? Two and one-half hours after starting, when Jeff will have ridden 37.5 miles and Roberta will have ridden 27.5 miles.

Activity

Distance-Rate-Time

Objective: interpret speed as a comparison of distance to time with circular motion.

Not all distance-rate-time problems involve average speed or forward motion. Sometimes we travel in circles—on a track or on a designated loop that brings us back to the starting position. Jeff and Roberta also bicycle on a short track. Jeff can make it around the track in 3 minutes; it takes Roberta 4 minutes. They start at the same place and decide to race around the track 5 times. How long does the race take? Who wins? Are they ever at the same spot along the track at the same moment? If so, at what time and where?

Things to Think About

In this problem we are not given any information about the speed or rate of the riders but we can draw some conclusions. First, they are traveling the same distance, as they are going around the same track 5 times. Second, Jeff must be traveling at a faster speed, since it only takes him 3 minutes to bike around the track versus Roberta's 4 minutes. A picture can help us visualize the relationships. Every time Jeff does a complete lap (in 3 minutes), Roberta has completed $\frac{3}{4}$ lap since in 3 minutes she has gone $\frac{3}{4}$ of 4 minutes.

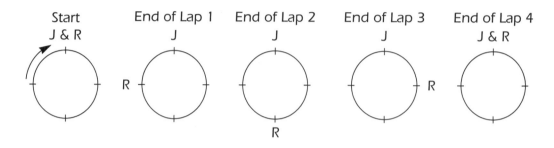

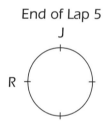

A ratio table can also be used to keep track of the information.

MINUTES	3	6	9	12	15
LAPS: JEFF	1	2	3	4	5
LAPS: ROBERTA	$\frac{3}{4}$	$1\frac{1}{2}$	$2\frac{1}{4}$	3	$3\frac{3}{4}$

It takes 15 minutes for Jeff to complete the 5 laps. The two riders meet at the starting point after 12 minutes when Jeff has completed 4 complete laps and Roberta has completed 3 complete laps, but Jeff than passes Roberta to win the race in 15 minutes. How long does it take Roberta to finish? It takes her 20 minutes (can you explain why?). Since Roberta bikes at a slower speed than Jeff, it will take her a longer time to cover the same distance. Jeff, biking at a faster speed, takes less time to cover the same distance.

Distance-rate-time situations are proportional situations, since the comparison of distance to time is a rate. Did you notice that when distance is a constant amount (5 times around the track), rate and time vary inversely? This means that when a biker's rate goes up or increases, the time needed to complete the race goes down or decreases; but if a biker's speed or rate is slower (like Roberta's) than the time needed to complete the same course has to increase.

Opportunities to explore relationships such as these informally help prepare students for the more formal study of proportionality in middle and high school algebra. ▲

Teaching Ratio Concepts

Ratios and rates are just two of the interconnected topics that contribute to students' ability to reason proportionally. Many researchers suggest that students should be introduced to these topics earlier, perhaps in fourth grade, with the focus on reasoning (developing ratio sense) rather than on formal procedures. At the very least, we should try to blend instruction of fractions, decimals, percents, and ratios together in middle school; if we regularly facilitate discussions about the similarities, differences, meanings within contexts, and strategies and solutions when solving problems involving ratios, we will help students build understanding over time. It is important to realize that much time and many experiences are needed for students to build up a web of knowledge, since these ideas are mathematically complex. Introducing students to ways of thinking multiplicatively that use part-to-part reasoning as well as part-to-whole comparisons and using models such as ratio tables that facilitate the use of multiplicative comparisons are essential. While as teachers we want to strive for precision in language and classification, our more important job is to help students make sense of this complex topic.

Questions for Discussion

1. What is the difference between additive and multiplicative thinking? When do you think students start to reason multiplicatively? What might we do to facilitate this type of thinking?

2. Generate concepts about ratios, and situations and examples where ratios and rates are used. Check the newspaper, Internet, and other resources for ideas. Draw a concept map that connects the topics you listed.

3. How are perimeters, areas, and volumes of similar figures related to the perimeter, area, and volume of the original figure? Describe the important features of a lesson you would use to introduce the idea of scale factor to sixth graders.

4. One method for solving proportion problems is the cross product method. Why does this method work? What are the disadvantages of showing this method to students prior to their developing understanding of proportional situations?

Algebra

Algebra is the fundamental language of mathematics. It enables us to create a mathematical model of a situation, provides the mathematical structure necessary to use the model to solve problems, and links numerical and graphical representations of data. Algebra is the vehicle for condensing large amounts of data into efficient mathematical statements.

As we move into the twenty-first century, there is a great deal of concern about how much algebra today's students need to know to be successful in the workplace. While experts differ about the specifics, they agree that instruction that includes algebra and algebraic thinking is necessary for everyone: "It is essential for students to learn algebra as a style of thinking involving the formalization of patterns, functions, and generalizations, and as a set of competencies involving the representation of quantitative relationships" (Silver 1997, 206).

While the formal study of algebra usually occurs in grades 8 through 10, research has shown that elementary students can think about arithmetic in ways that provide a foundation for learning algebra. In fact, introducing basic forms of algebraic thinking into instruction in the elementary grades has been shown to enhance students' learning of arithmetic (Carpenter et al. 2003). Researchers suggest that there are three processes that when applied to a mathematical task support the development of students' algebraic reasoning: generalizing, formalizing, and justifying.

Generalizing is the process of developing a general mathematical statement about the structure, properties, or relationships that underlie a mathematical idea.

Formalizing is the process of representing the mathematical generalizations in some sort of formal way. Students progress in their ability to represent ideas formally—from talking about them in everyday language; to increasingly using mathematical terms; to representing generalizations using pictures, drawings, and graphs; to recording their insights using symbols. For example, students might notice that when you multiply zero and any number, the product is zero. They generalize their observation to all numbers and talk and write about what they notice. Eventually students progress to formally representing this property using variables: $a \times 0 = 0$ where a is any number. Likewise, young students first notice that the number pattern 3, 8, 13, 18, 23, 28, 33, . . . , is growing by 5s. They represent the increase in the pattern in more and more sophisticated ways, perhaps noting that the pattern in the ones place alternates between 3s and 8s or by using the operation + 5.

The third process, *justifying*, goes hand in hand with conjecturing. When students conjecture, they propose a mathematical statement that they think might be true but has not yet been proven true. Justifying is the "process of developing mathematical arguments to explore and critique the validity of mathematical claims" (NCISLA 2003, 5). For many teachers and students, the first step is realizing that claims should and can be justified. Justification of generalizations or conjectures requires more than providing many examples. Students need to be able to explain why they know something will be true for all numbers.

A teacher's ability to help all students learn algebra depends in part on his or her awareness of the most important concepts and ideas: variables, symbols, structure, representation, patterns, graphing, expressions and equations, and rules and functions. Many of these concepts are introduced in the elementary grades, in particular the study of variables, patterns, rules and relationships, equality, and graphing. In the middle grades instruction is expanded and also focuses on representation, expressions, equations, and functions. Teachers who ask questions that assist students in generalizing, formalizing, and justifying their statements about problems and situations are laying the foundation for understanding more complex mathematics, including algebra.

1. The Concept of Variable

Historically, algebra has progressed through three major stages, each defined by the concept of variable prevalent during that period. Algebra in its earliest stage did not include symbols but rather used ordinary language to describe solution processes for certain types of problems. The second stage (circa A.D. 250–1600) included using symbols to represent unknown specific quantities, the goal being to solve problems for these unknowns. In the third stage (1600–present), symbols have been used to express general relationships, to prove rules, and to describe functions.

Francoise Viète (1540–1603) was the first to use letters in formal mathematics notation. Shortly thereafter, René Descartes used letters in a more systematic way: a, b, c for constants and x, y, z for unknowns. When Descartes went to have his manuscript *La Geometrie* published in 1637, the printer, Jan Maire, of Leyden, Holland, began running out of some of the letters in the type set. He asked Descartes whether it mattered which letters represented the unknowns. Descartes replied that the specific letter was unimportant, as long as the unknown was represented by x, y, or z. Having plenty of the letter x on hand, the printer used it to represent the unknowns, thus contributing to the formulation of the algebraic dictum, "Solve for x."

As the concept of variable developed historically, the ways in which letters were used expanded. Experts categorize variables in different ways, but any particular use of a variable is determined by the mathematical context. In elementary and middle school, variables are primarily used to represent specific unknown values in equations, sets of numbers in inequalities (e.g., $x < 10$), property and pattern generalizers ($a + b = b + a$), formulas ($A = l \times w$), and varying quantities in functions ($y = 2x + 1$). The most common uses of variables are as specific unknowns, as generalizers, and as varying quantities.

Considering Variables

Objective: identify examples of the different uses of variables.

In the following equations and inequalities, variables are used in different ways. How is the variable being used in the examples below? What is the value of the variable in each example?

1. $2 \times \square = 15 - \square$
2. $y \leq 32$
3. $2x + 3 = y$
4. $(a \bullet b) \bullet c = a \bullet (b \bullet c)$
5. $49 = s^2$
6. $A = lw$

Things to Think About

One important use of a variable is as a particular but unknown number. For example, in $x + 6 = 10$ and $3m = 18$, the value of x is 4 and the value of m is 6. There is a specific number in each case that makes the equation true. This is the most common use of variable in the elementary grades. In the early grades, the unknown value is often represented using a shape such as a square or triangle: $\square - 8 = 10$. Algebraic equations that include one or more variables are sometimes referred to as *open sentences*. Open sentences are neither true nor false until values are substituted for the variables. For example, if we replace $\square$ with 18, the open sentence $\square - 8 = 10$ is true but if we replace $\square$ with any other number, the equation is false. Our goal when solving for unknowns is to find values that make equations or open sentences true!

Examples 1 and 5 use variables as unknowns: in 1, $\square = 5$; in 5, $s = 7$ and $^-7$. Were you surprised that example 5 has two solutions? In the equation $49 = s^2$, both $s = 7$ and $s = ^-7$ make the equation true. Even though there is more than one solution, the variable still represents specific unknowns—just two in this case.

How is the variable used in example 2? In this inequality, y is equal to a set of numbers that starts at 32 and decreases infinitely. The idea that a set of numbers is the solution to a mathematical statement can be difficult for students if they have only had experiences with variables as specific unknowns.

The equation in example 3 represents a function in which the value of one variable depends on the value of the other variable. One letter takes on a set of values and has a systematic relationship with the other letter ($y = 2x + 3$)—the value of y depends on the value of x. When the value of one variable changes in relation to the value of another variable, we refer to this as joint variation. In the chart below are values for x and y. The y values were calculated by replacing the x in the equation $y = 2x + 3$ with different x values. Notice how as the value of x increases, the value of y increases.

x	y
$^-4$	$^-5$
0	3
2	7
9	21

The set of values for x is called the *domain* and the set of values for y is called the *range*. This interpretation of variable as a varying quantity is essential to understanding the relationship of patterns to functions.

In example 4, variables are used to illustrate a general property, in this case the associative property of multiplication. The variables do not represent an unknown or a varying quantity that is related to another variable. This is a generalization in which the letters convey a relationship that is always true about the multiplication of real numbers.

In the last example, the formula $A = lw$ provides information on the area of a rectangle and describes the relationship between three quantities: the *area* of the rectangle, the *length* of the rectangle, and the *width* of the rectangle. Letters in a formula always represent varying numbers and delineate a real-world relationship. For example, the equation $F = ma$ represents the relationship between force, mass, and acceleration in physics. Thus, we could classify example 6 with example 3: variables as quantities in joint variation.

It is important for students to realize that there are a number of interpretations of the term *variable*. If they understand variables only as representations of specific unknowns, it is not surprising that they have difficulty interpreting inequalities in which variables represent sets of numbers. On the other hand, sometimes students take the term *variable* literally and assume that a variable is something that differs or varies. We compound the problem by not referring to a variable as an unknown when it is appropriate to do so. Other difficulties arise when students overgeneralize; students first come to realize that the symbol or letter in a problem (e.g., □ above) represents the same number throughout an equation no matter how many times it appears. Yet this leads them to mistakenly assume that when there are different variables in an equation (e.g., $a + b = 12$), they cannot be replaced by the same value (in this case, 6). Furthermore, they mistakenly conclude that in the equations $m + 3 = 7$ and $y + 3 = 7$, the m and y must be different quantities because different letters are used. ▲

A common misconception involving variables is that students interpret them as labels. If g represents the number of girls in a dorm room, $3g$ is interpreted by students as 3 girls instead of 3 times the number of girls in the dorm room. In addition, the use of particular letters in conversions ($3f = 1yd$) and formulas (l is used for length) sometimes contributes to students' mistakenly thinking of a variable as a label. For example, in the expression, $2t + 4$ where t represents the number of tiles, students often interpret $2t$ to mean 2 tiles rather than 2 times the number of tiles.

Teachers should consider how to transform problem situations to support students' understanding of variable, especially as a generalizer of patterns and properties. One way is to vary the numerical values of givens in problems—and to examine the patterns that emerge. For example, if a problem states that CDs cost $12 and a student only has $5, teachers can ask how the amount needed will change if CDs cost $13, $14, $15, or $16. Students can be asked to write number sentences for the amount needed to buy a CD for each CD value and observe what changes and what stays the same each time. Eventually they can be asked to generalize the situation ($N - 5$ where N equals the original cost of the CD).

Young children are capable of making conjectures about basic properties of number operations. For example, students might recognize that multiplying any number by zero results in a product of zero. They can be asked to express their conjecture using words, numerical examples, and eventually with an open sentence that includes a variable (e.g., $a \times 0 = 0$). After students are comfortable with their conjecture and generalization, they can be challenged to justify it. Students often suggest many more specific examples; if this occurs, teachers must encourage students to show that their generalizations are true for all numbers, not just some (Carpenter et al. 2003).

2. Symbols

Mathematical symbols provide us with an efficient way to convey information without using words. When people talk about the language of mathematics, they are often referring to the symbols and shorthand notations that we use to do mathematics. These symbols must be learned and then repeatedly interpreted within problems and procedures. There are many different kinds of mathematical symbols: numerals and variables (often called literal symbols) such as $^{-}5$, 36, x, $\square$, and V; operational symbols such as $+$ and $\div$; relational symbols such as $=$ and $>$; and geometric symbols such as $\angle$ and $\perp$, to name just a few. Shorthand notations such as LCM (least common multiple) and P(A) (probability of A) are also common. In Section 1 we discussed variables; in this section we describe operational and relational symbols.

What complicates the interpretation of symbols is that some symbols have more than one meaning. Parentheses are used to differentiate the operation of multiplication from a numerical value—2(3) versus 23—and to indicate a grouping that is to be performed first following the order of operations—$(3 + 9)^2$. In addition, some situations can be expressed using more than one symbol. For example, multiplication is indicated using the "times" sign—2×3—by a raised dot—$2 \cdot 3$—and by placing two symbols next to each other without spaces—2(3), lw, and $2x$. Take a minute and think of an operation that can be shown using a variety of symbols. Division can be expressed using $\div$, $/$, and $\overline{)}$. As adults we forget to explore explicitly with students the fact that there are multiple ways to represent an operation symbolically. Can you think of any symbols that are interpreted differently depending on their use? The fraction bar sign ($\frac{3}{5}$) can indicate a division, a fraction, or a ratio. Certain letters represent types of quantities in specific formulas but can represent any number in other equations. For example, the C in $C = 2r$ stands for the length of the circumference, the C in $F = 32 + (\frac{9}{5})C$ represents degrees in Centigrade, but the c in $6c = 18$ is an unknown value (3) and is unrelated to a particular context. While adults have internalized these subtle and not so subtle differences, students often are unaware of multiple meanings. Thus, it is extremely important that we engage students in discussions about the meaning of symbols.

It is important for students to think carefully about operational symbols. Operation symbols describe an action on one or two numbers or symbols. When we see these operation symbols, we are keyed to "do something." Students encounter operational symbols for addition and subtraction ($+$ and $-$) in their first year or two of schooling. These operations are *binary operations*: the operation is performed on two numbers. Multiplication and division ($\times$ and $\div$) are also binary operations—we can multiply or divide only two numbers at a time. Other operations, such as roots, absolute values, and powers ($\sqrt{25}$, $|^{-}4|$, and 8^3), are unitary operations. Unitary operations are conducted on one number at a time. What kind of operations are $(2 \div 6)^2$ or $|9 + ^{-}7|$? These expressions combine operations—the division ($2 \div 6$)

is a binary operation that equals $\frac{1}{3}$ and the exponent (power of 2) is a unitary operation: $(\frac{1}{3})^2 = \frac{1}{9}$. The parenthesis, a grouping symbol, lets us know which operation to perform first. Likewise, the addition $9 + {}^-7$ is a binary operation which is completed first. The absolute value is then taken on the result, 2.

Another important group of symbols are classified as *relational symbols*. Relational or relation symbols establish a relationship between two numbers, two number sentences, or two variable expressions. Some common relational symbols are $=$, $\neq$, $\leq$, $\geq$, $<$, and $>$. The relationship is either true ($10 = 10$) or false ($5 > 8$), though in the case of open sentences ($9 + 3 = \square + 4$) we always try to find a value to make the sentence true. What can be confusing is that on either side of the relational sign there may be operations that must be completed in order to evaluate whether or not the relationship is true or false. Examine the following and consider whether the relationships that are being established are true or false.

$6 \neq 14 \div 2$	True, 6 does not equal $14 \div 2$, or 7
$18 \geq 19$	False, 18 is not greater than or equal to 19
$5 + 7 = 2 \times 6$	True, $5 + 7$ equals 12 and 2×6 equals 12, $12 = 12$
$\square < \square + 3$	True, any number is less than that same number plus 3

Students need to examine many different number sentences such as the first three examples above and evaluate whether they are true or false. Teachers can then ask students to change the sentences, making true ones false and false ones true. Or students might be asked to group number sentences and explain why they placed different sentences together. Asking students to discuss the relationship between the quantities on each side of a relational symbol will help them interpret these symbols correctly. Open sentences in which one or more variables are represented are especially problematic for students. Research has shown that in open sentences like $8 + 4 = \square + 5$, students in grades 1 through 6 overwhelmingly think $\square$ equals either 12 or 17 (Falkner, Levi, and Carpenter 1999). They add the first two or all three numbers and do not interpret the equal sign as a symbol that establishes a relationship between the quantities on either side of it. This important idea is explored in more detail in the next section.

3. Equality

Another fundamental idea of algebra is *equality*. Equality is indicated by the equal sign and can be modeled by thinking of a level balance scale. Why is equality important for students to understand? First, the idea that two mathematical expressions can have the same value is at the heart of developing number sense. For example, we want students to realize that there are many ways to represent the same product ($9 \times 4 = 2 \times 3 \times 6$). We want students to use what they know about the composition of numbers to help them remember number facts and form equivalent statements ($7 + 6 = 6 + 6 + 1$ and $7 + 6 = 7 + 7 - 1$). Understanding these number sentences and the relationships expressed by them is linked to the correct interpretation of the equal symbol.

The second reason for understanding the concept of equality is that research has shown that lack of this understanding is one of the major stumbling blocks for students when solving algebraic equations. To solve $3x + 2 = 14$, we add $^-2$ to both sides of the equal sign, thus maintaining balance or equality ($3x + 2 + {}^-2 = 14 + {}^-2$, or $3x = 12$). The next step in the solution process involves multiplying both $3x$ and 12 by $\frac{1}{3}$, again because performing the same operation on equivalent expressions means they will remain equivalent (($\frac{1}{3}$)$3x = 12(\frac{1}{3})$, or $x = 4$). If students do not understand the idea of equality of expressions, they may perform computations on one rather than on both sides of an equal sign.

Yet the concept of equality is not easy for students and many do not correctly interpret the equal symbol. For example, often students think that the equal sign is a symbol that tells them to do something (such as subtract or multiply) rather than a symbol that represents equal values or balance. Students see an equation such as $6 + 4 = \square + 6$ and assume 10 is the answer because they have completed the addition on the left: to them the equal sign means "fill in the answer." Other children cannot make sense of $7 = 9 - 2$ because the operation symbol is to the right of the equal sign rather than the left. When students make these types of mistakes, we need to ask them to explain their thinking and to share with us what the equal sign means to them. However, telling students that the equal sign is, by convention, the symbol that lets us know that quantities are equal is not sufficient to clear up their misconceptions. We need to include activities and discussions in our instruction that focus on understanding equivalent values. Exploring whether number sentences are true or false is one activity that helps build understanding with number sense.

Another activity that supports understanding equality is to use balance scales. The balance scale is a visual model for the equality relationship. Most students intuitively understand that a balanced scale remains balanced if equal amounts are added to or subtracted from both sides of the scale. Balance scale problems can be used to investigate equivalence and to prepare students informally for symbolic representation and more abstract solution techniques.

Activity

Balance Scales

Objective: explore the concept of equality using a balance scale.

Solve the balance scale problems on page 197. On each of the balance scales, assume that the same shapes represent the same weights. In each problem, use the information from the balanced scales A and B to figure out what's needed to balance scale C.

Things to Think About

If you have never examined problems like these, there are a number of general principles you have to consider. First, a level scale implies that the quantities on one pan are equivalent in weight to the quantities on the other pan. Second, we can modify both sides of the balance scale and maintain equality using either additive reasoning—removing (or adding) the same amount from (to) both sides of the scale—or multiplicative reasoning—multiplying or dividing both sides by the same factor. (If two cylinders balance six spheres, then one cylinder is equivalent in weight to three spheres). Third, we can replace objects of equal weight. These

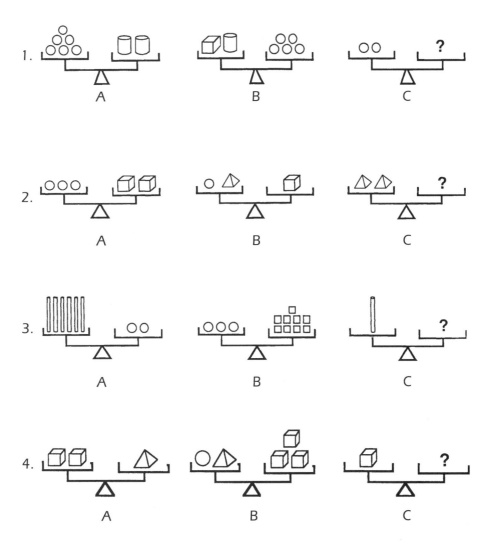

1.   A   B   C

2.   A   B   C

3.   A   B   C

4.   A   B   C

principles are not easy for students to understand, especially when presented in the form of equations and inequalities. However, they are more accessible and engaging when students encounter them in the form of balance scales.

Let's examine balance problem 1 in detail. Scale A shows that six spheres are equivalent to two cylinders. Dividing the number of spheres and the number of cylinders in half results in three spheres balancing one cylinder. We can use this equivalence relationship to adjust scale B. Let's remove the cylinder from the left side and three spheres from the right side of the balance (since they are equivalent). The remaining cube balances two spheres: two spheres are equivalent in weight to one cube. So a cube added to the right side of scale C will balance it.

Do we always need to start with scale A? Absolutely not! In problem 2, let's focus first on the relationship shown on scale B. Using this relationship to substitute specific shapes on scale A, we find that the two triangular pyramids on scale C equal one sphere. In problem 3, we can also start with scale B, establishing that one sphere weighs the same as three cubes. Using substitution on scale A, we can replace the two spheres with six cubes. Six sticks are equivalent to six cubes, so the single stick on scale C is equal to one cube.

We solve balance scale problems by reasoning about equal relationships. Another way to do this is to link these actions and relationships to algebraic symbols. The relationship depicted in scale A of balance problem 4, in which two cubes weigh the same as one pyramid, can be indicated as $c + c = p$. Scale B shows this same relationship, but in addition a cube has been placed on the left pan and a sphere on the right pan and the scale still balances. This implies that a cube weighs the same amount as a sphere. The weights on scale B can be indicated symbolically as $s + p = c + c + c$. When comparing the two equations, we can reverse the order of the second equation and then substitute information from the first equation into the second equation:

$$\text{scale A} \qquad\qquad c + c = p$$
$$\text{scale B} \qquad\qquad c + c + c = s + p$$
$$\text{so} \qquad\qquad c + p = s + p$$
$$c = s$$

This tells us that a cube weighs the same as a sphere. ▲

4. Patterns and Rules

Mathematicians repeatedly make the point that one of the primary activities in mathematics is to describe patterns: patterns in nature, patterns we invent, even patterns within other patterns. By examining a wide range of patterns, we notice regularity, variety, and the ways topics interconnect. We also see that certain patterns occur again and again. There are many types of patterns: repeating patterns, sequence patterns, and special patterns like Fibonacci numbers. Some patterns can be represented using rules or functions. Other patterns can be represented both numerically and geometrically and help us link arithmetic and geometry.

One type of pattern that is introduced in the early grades is a repeating pattern. Repeating patterns have a part, sometimes called the *core*, that repeats over and over. For example, in the pattern ♥♣♥♣♥♣♥♣ . . . , the core of ♥♣ repeats. Students must identify the core of a pattern in order to continue it. Repeating patterns can be presented orally (e.g., the refrains of many songs repeat) or by using motions such as clapping and turning. Repeating patterns can also be represented using numbers, pictures, and objects. Young children need to identify, describe, extend, and create a wide variety of repeating patterns.

Activity

Investigating Repeating Patterns

Objective: learn about the structure of repeating patterns.

Examine the pattern 1-2-3-4-1-2-3-4- . . . and make a list of three questions you might ask students regarding the pattern. Imagine extending this pattern indefinitely. What will the 19th number be? the 81st number? If you examine the first 42 numbers in the pattern, how many of the numbers will be 2s?

Things to Think About

What questions did you think of to pose to students? *Identify the core of the pattern?* *Continue the pattern?* *Fill in a missing value?* Questions like these are very appropriate for young children who are still learning to make sense of patterns. However, students also benefit from questions that force them to generalize relationships and use repeating patterns in more complex ways.

Determining the 19th number in the pattern takes two steps. First you have to notice that the core of the pattern involves four numbers, 1-2-3-4. Then you have to replicate the core a number of times to come close to 19 numbers. Did you make four copies of the core, using 16 numbers, and then count on 3 more numbers to reach the 19th number? Or did you make five replicas of the core, giving you the 20th number, and then count back 1 number? Either way a 3 is the 19th number in this pattern. Using this same form of reasoning, the 81st number is a 1.

How many 2s will be needed to write the first 42 numbers in this pattern? You will need ten sets of the core, which means you will use ten 2s. But since you also need an additional 1-2 to have a total of 42 numbers, the total number of 2s needed is eleven. ▲

Nonrepeating patterns are more difficult to understand. Students must not only determine what comes next in the pattern but also begin to generalize. Numerical relationships become more and more important. A particular type of pattern in which numbers, objects, letters, or geometric figures are in an ordered arrangement is called a *sequence* or, informally, a *growing pattern*. Growing patterns are found in instructional materials in grades 3, 4, and 5 and in middle school. The numbers, objects, letters, or geometric figures that make up the sequence are called the *terms*, *steps*, or *stages* of the sequence. Sequences are classified according to the methods used to determine subsequent terms. There are *arithmetic* sequences and *geometric* sequences.

In an arithmetic sequence, the same number, called the *common difference*, is added to each previous number to obtain the next number. Some numerical examples are:

$$5, 6, 7, 8, 9, 10, \ldots \qquad 2, 4, 6, 8, 10, \ldots \qquad 7, 10, 13, 16, 19, 22, \ldots$$

In the first sequence the common difference is 1: the first term is 5, the second term is 6, the third term is 7, and so on. The second sequence has a common difference of 2, since the number 2 is added to each previous term. In the third sequence, the common difference is 3: term number one is 7, term number two is 10, and term number three is 13.

Sometimes arithmetic sequences decrease rather than increase, because the number that is added each time is a negative number. In the examples below a ($^-5$) and a ($^-\frac{1}{2}$) are being added to the previous term. Extend each pattern.

$$15, 10, 5, 0, {}^-5, {}^-10, \ldots \qquad 10, 9\tfrac{1}{2}, 9, 8\tfrac{1}{2}, 8, 7\tfrac{1}{2}, \ldots$$

Sequences can also be represented using geometric designs or figures. How many squares will be in the 15th figure of the following pattern?

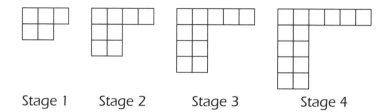

Stage 1   Stage 2   Stage 3   Stage 4

Students sometimes find it easier to notice the numeric pattern, or common difference, from one term to the next term when they record the steps in a table.

STEP	1	2	3	4	5	6	. . .	15
NO. OF SQUARES	5	8	11	14	?	?	. . .	?

Did the geometric design or the table help you notice that the pattern is successively increasing by 3? When a procedure is applied over and over again to a number or geometric figure to produce a sequence of numbers or figures, we say that the procedure is *recursive*. Each stage of a recursive procedure builds on the previous stage. Recursive procedures are sometimes referred to as *iterative* procedures because the same rule is repeated again and again. In the geometric pattern above we repeatedly add 3 squares to create each successive design. Students often identify recursive rules (the instructions for producing each term or step of a recursive sequence from the previous term) and then use the rule to find each subsequent term (in this case, we can determine each successive term by adding 3 to the previous term). This recursive strategy works to find the number of squares in a small number of terms like the 15th step (5, 8, 11, 14, 17, 20, 23, 26, 29, 32, 35, 38, 41, 44, 47) but is not efficient or reasonable if we have to find the number of squares in the 100th term. We would have to list the first 99 terms in order to find the 100th term!

The form of an arithmetic sequence can be expressed using variables. This enables us to generalize patterns and relationships. Many teachers prefer to use symbols such as triangles and squares before introducing letters as variables. Students can be first challenged to articulate the recursive rule (e.g., *this sequence is increasing by adding 6 to each term*) and then asked to represent the pattern more explicitly using words, symbols, and a variable. The mathematical purpose is to help students formalize the similarities and regularities they have observed.

How might we generalize the arithmetic sequences 2, 4, 6, 8, 10, . . . and 7, 14, 21, 28, 35, . . . ? In each of these sequences the common difference also happens to be the first term. Using a symbol ($\triangle$, for example) or a letter (x, for example) to represent both the difference and first term, we can express the sequence like this:

$$\triangle, \triangle + \triangle, \triangle + \triangle + \triangle, \triangle + \triangle + \triangle + \triangle, \ldots$$
$$x, x + x, x + x + x, x + x + x + x, \ldots$$

In the sequence above, the variables—$\triangle$s or xs—are repeatedly added to form the terms of the sequence. Another way to represent this is by using multiplication; first we have one $\triangle$, then two $\triangle$s, then three $\triangle$s, and so on, or $1x$, $2x$, $3x$, $4x$, and so on.

Variables can represent different things depending on how they are used. In this case, the variable ($\triangle$ or x) represents a set of numbers. Substituting different numbers for the common difference creates different sequences:

$1x, 2x, 3x, 4x, \ldots$ $1x, 2x, 3x, 4x, \ldots$

$1(2), 2(2), 3(2), 4(2), \ldots$ $1(7), 2(7), 3(7), 4(7), \ldots$

$2, 4, 6, 8, \ldots$ $7, 14, 21, 28, \ldots$

How might we determine the 32nd number in the first sequence ($2, 4, 6, 8, \ldots$) other than using the recursive rule of $+\ 2$ and listing the first 31 terms? Is there another pattern that can be used to link the term of the sequence to the actual number in the sequence? Yes, an explicit rule where we multiply the term number and the common difference can be used. The 32nd number in the sequence will be 32×2, or 64, since 2 is the common difference. The 32nd term in the sequence starting with 7 above is 32×7, or 224.

Not all arithmetic sequences begin with the common difference; most, such as 1, 3, 5, 7, 9, $\ldots$, start with a different first number (in this case, 1) and repeatedly add the common difference (in this case, $+\ 2$). We can represent this sequence using symbols by letting $\square$ represent the starting term and letting $\triangle$ represent the common difference (the number added to each term). We can also use letters. Let a equal the starting term and let x equal the common difference. In this case, there are two variables (shapes or letters) in our generalized statement.

$\square, \quad \triangle + \square, \quad (\triangle + \square) + \triangle, \quad (\triangle + \triangle + \square) + \triangle, \quad (\triangle + \triangle + \triangle + \square) + \triangle, \ldots$

$\square, \quad \triangle + \square, \quad 2\triangle + \square, \quad\quad 3\triangle + \square, \quad\quad\quad 4\triangle + \square, \ldots$

$a, \quad x + a, \quad 2x + a, \quad\quad 3x + a, \quad\quad\quad 4x + a, \ldots$

Let's substitute numbers into this generalized pattern. If $a = 1$ and $x = 2$ then:

$$a, x + a, 2x + a, 3x + a, 4x + a, \ldots$$
$$1, 2 + 1, 2(2) + 1, 3(2) + 1, 4(2) + 1, \ldots$$
$$1, 3, 5, 7, 9, \ldots$$

The generalization above works for all situations, whether the $\square$ represents zero, the common difference, or any other number. The use of variables to show the extension of an arithmetic sequences lays the foundation for students to be able to describe sequences using algebraic expressions or rules.

Activity

Exploring Arithmetic Sequences

Objective: practice using both recursive and explicit rules and generalized patterns to solve problems involving arithmetic sequences.

1. Make up an arithmetic sequence with a common difference of $^-6$. What would the 125th term be?
2. Make up an arithmetic sequence that starts with 3 and has a common difference of 5. Use the generalized pattern to find the 2,345th term in the sequence.

3. How many numbers (or terms) are there in the arithmetic sequence 4, 8, 12, 16, . . . , 124? What if you wanted to extend this sequence? Write a rule that you could use.

4. Examine the sequence 1, 5, 9, 13, 17, . . . , 65. What do you notice? How is this sequence similar to the one in Question 3? different?

Things to Think About

If a sequence has a common difference of ⁻6, each subsequent term of the sequence is smaller than the previous term (since we are adding a ⁻6 each time). Using our recursive rule and starting with ⁻6, some terms in this sequence would be: ⁻6, ⁻12, ⁻18, ⁻24, ⁻30, ... To find the 125th term, we need an explicit rule linking the term number and the sequence number—namely 125 × (⁻6). The 125th term in this sequence is ⁻750.

The arithmetic sequence for Question 2 is 3, 8, 13, 18, 23, 28, 33, 38, and so on. In each case, a common difference of 5 is being added. Did you notice the pattern in the ones digits of the numbers in this sequence? The ones digit is either a 3 or an 8. The 2,345th term can be found by multiplying 2,344 by 5 and then adding 3, because 3 was the starting point of the sequence ($2,344(5) + 3 = 11,723$); the 2,345th term is 11,723 (which ends in a 3!).

Did you notice that the sequence in Question 3 has a common difference of 4? Each value in the sequence is 4 more, or 4 times the number of the term ($4 = 4 \cdot 1, 8 = 4 \cdot 2, 12 = 4 \cdot 3, . . .$). To find how many numbers or terms are in the sequence, divide 124 by 4. There are 31 numbers in the sequence.

So far we have written rules in which the variable, x, represents the common difference. But what if, as in Question 3, you know the common difference? Then you might want to let the variable represent the position of the term in the sequence. Since the common difference in Question 3 is 4, we can represent any term as $4x$. Put another way, our explicit rule for any number in the sequence is $4x$ where x represents the term number. The idea that variables can represent anything (the common difference or the term or both) is what makes algebra so useful and also so confusing.

The sequence in Question 4 is very similar to the sequence in Question 3. It also has a common difference of 4, but the sequence begins with 1 rather than 4. All of the terms are 3 less than the corresponding terms in the Question 3 sequence:

$$1, 5, 9, 13, 17, . . .$$
$$4, 8, 12, 16, 20, . . .$$

Can we use the rule above in which x represents the position of the term in the sequence as the basis for a similar rule for the sequence in Question 4? Since the numbers in this sequence are each 3 less than the numbers in the $4x$ sequence, we can show this algebraically as $4x - 3$. Substitute various term numbers for x to show that this rule will generate the sequence. ▲

Exploring arithmetic sequences forms the basis for later work with functions, in which two variables are related in such a way that one depends on or is affected by the other. In arithmetic sequences, many things can be represented as a variable: the common difference, the starting number, the position in the sequence, and the actual value of each term. Some of these variables depend on one or more of the other variables. Investigating these relationships informally helps prepare students to explore these dependent relationships formally in middle and high school.

The other type of sequence is the geometric sequence. In a geometric sequence, instead of the same number being *added* to each term to obtain the subsequent term, the same number is *multiplied* by each term to obtain the subsequent term. Rather than having a common difference, as arithmetic sequences do, geometric sequences have what is known as a *constant multiplier*—a number that when multiplied by the previous term produces the next number in the sequence. The sequences below highlight how a common difference and a constant multiplier affect the numbers in a sequence. In the arithmetic sequence 1, 3, 5, 7, 9, . . . the common difference is 2. Now let's start a geometric sequence with 1 and let the constant multiplier be 2. Since we are multiplying each number by 2, the outcome is quite different: 1, 2, 4, 8, 16, ... Determine the common difference and the constant multiplier in the following sequences.

Arithmetic Sequences	*Geometric Sequences*
1, 3, 5, 7, 9, . . .	1, 2, 4, 8, 16, . . .
5, 6, 7, 8, 9, . . .	5, 5, 5, 5, 5, . . .
2, 4, 6, 8, 10, . . .	2, 4, 8, 16, 32, . . .
7, 10, 13, 16, 19, . . .	7, 21, 63, 189, 567, . . .
7, 14, 21, 28, 35, . . .	7, 49, 343, 2401, 16807, . . .

The form of a geometric sequence also can be expressed using variables—symbols or letters. Let the $\square$ or the letter a represent the starting term and $\triangle$ or the letter x represent the constant multiplier, the number that is multiplied by the previous term.

$$\square, \square \bullet \triangle, (\square \bullet \triangle) \bullet \triangle, (\square \bullet \triangle \bullet \triangle) \bullet \triangle, \ldots$$
$$a, a \bullet x, (a \bullet x) \bullet x, (a \bullet x \bullet x) \bullet x, \ldots$$

Since we are multiplying by the same number each time, we can represent the pattern using exponents. Exponents are a shortcut for repeated multiplication. In 8^3, the number 8 is called the *base* and the number 3 is called the *exponent*, or power. Furthermore, the symbols 8^3 together are referred to as an *exponent* or an *exponential*. Exponents represent a product (in the case of 8^3, 256). An important exponent definition is that any number, a (where $a \neq 0$), to the zero power is equivalent to 1 (e.g., $a^0 = 1$, $5^0 = 1$, $35^0 = 1$, $0.2^0 = 1$). Below are the two generalized statements for the sequences using exponents:

$$(\square \bullet \triangle^0), (\square \bullet \triangle^1), (\square \bullet \triangle^2), (\square \bullet \triangle^3), (\square \bullet \triangle^4), \ldots$$
$$(a \bullet x^0), (a \bullet x^1), (a \bullet x^2), (a \bullet x^3), (a \bullet x^4), \ldots$$

Some numerical examples are:

3, 6, 12, 24, 48, . . .	$(3 \bullet 2^0), (3 \bullet 2^1), (3 \bullet 2^2), (3 \bullet 2^3), (3 \bullet 2^4), \ldots$
1, 5, 25, 125, 625, . . .	$(1 \bullet 5^0), (1 \bullet 5^1), (1 \bullet 5^2), (1 \bullet 5^3), (1 \bullet 5^4), \ldots$
40, 10, 2.5, 0.625, . . .	$(40 \bullet 0.25^0), (40 \bullet 0.25^1), (40 \bullet 0.25^2), (40 \bullet 0.25^3), \ldots$

In descending geometric sequences it can appear that the terms are being repeatedly divided. In fact, the terms are being multiplied by a fraction ($\frac{1}{4}$). This has the same effect as dividing by the reciprocal of the fraction (in the example above, the reciprocal of $\frac{1}{4}$ is 4).

The terms in a geometric sequence increase or decrease much more quickly than the terms in an arithmetic sequence. This type of growth is known as *exponential growth*—and the decrease is known as *exponential decay*. Exponential growth and decay occur when the change between terms is the result of multiplication, not addition. Students informally learn about exponential growth and decay when solving problems or when working with geometric sequences. They study these concepts formally in middle and high school.

Activity

Choosing Between Salary Options

Objective: compare the growth of an arithmetic sequence and a geometric sequence.

Tom agrees to care for his neighbors' cat while they go on a two-week vacation and has to choose one of two pay options. Payment plan A consists of $2 on the first day, $4 on the second day, $6 on the third day, $8 on the fourth day, and so on for 14 days. Payment plan B is also by the day: 2¢ on the first day, 4¢ on the second day, 8¢ on the third day, 16¢ on the fourth day, 32¢ on the fifth day, and so on. Calculate how much money would be made each day according to the different plans. Which plan would you choose? Why?

Things to Think About

Were you surprised by the difference in the sizes of the salaries on the 14th day? Plan A increased slowly and steadily while plan B increased very slowly at first but then grew rapidly. The salary according to plan A is based on an arithmetic sequence in which the common difference is 2. Each day the salary increases by two more dollars; therefore, on day 14 you make $28 dollars. Generalizing using plan A, on day x you receive $2x$ dollars. The total amount of money for the 14 days is found by adding the amounts earned on day 1 through day 14—$210.00!

Plan B is based on a geometric sequence in which the constant multiplier is 2. Each day the salary from the day before is multiplied by 2. This salary plan pays less per day until day 12. However, the last three days pay so well that the total amount of money earned for the 14 days is $327.66! A comparison of the salary plans is shown below:

DAY	1	2	3	4	5	6	7
Plan A	$2	$4	$6	$8	$10	$12	$14
Plan B	$0.02	$0.04	$0.08	$0.16	$0.32	$0.64	$1.28

DAY	8	9	10	11	12	13	14
Plan A	$16	$18	$20	$22	$24	$26	$28
Plan B	$2.56	$5.12	$10.24	$20.48	$40.96	$81.92	$163.84

The doubling pattern in plan B may be easier to recognize when the dollar and cent signs are removed: 2, 4, 8, 16, 32, 64, 128, ... This sequence could be represented using exponents: 2^1, 2^2, 2^3, 2^4, and so on. In fact, the powers of 2, as this sequence is often called, is one that we want older students to recognize and link to exponents automatically. The salary on the 14th day is equivalent to

2^{14}, or 16,384¢. The exponent, 14, is the same number as the day (or term). The explicit rule can be generalized as 2^n where n is the day or term.

There are a number of children's stories that deal with exponential growth. *Anno's Magic Seeds*, by Mitsumasa Anno, *The King's Chessboard*, by David Birch, *A Grain of Rice*, by Helena Clare Pittman, and *The Rajah's Rice*, by David Barry, are just a few. These stories provide a context in which elementary and middle school students can explore geometric growth and work with patterns that involve exponents. Students' understanding of different types of growth is expanded when comparing arithmetic and geometric sequences. In addition, students enjoy learning how to represent products using exponents. ▲

When students explore patterns and generalize relationships among numbers, they are developing informal understanding of one of the most important topics in high school and college algebra—functions. A *function* is a relationship in which two sets are linked by a rule that pairs each element of the first set with exactly one element of the second set. We use functions every day without realizing it. The relationship between the cost of an item and the amount of sales tax is a function, the automatic calculations performed by computer spreadsheets are based on defined relationships between and/or among data fields, and our car's gasoline mileage is a function that depends on the speed of the car and the efficiency of the engine. When we were talking earlier about rules for arithmetic and geometric sequences, we were generating function rules, also referred to as explicit rules. The first set of numbers are the term or stage numbers (e.g., 1st, 2nd, 3rd, 4th, . . .) and the second set of numbers are the values of each term or, in other words, the numbers in the sequence (e.g., 10, 20, 30, 40, . . .). How do we assist students in the elementary and middle grades in generalizing explicit rules? One method is to start with patterns that are created using concrete objects such as pattern blocks, toothpicks, or square tiles. Students can be encourage to extend the pattern using objects or drawings and talk and write about what they notice. For example, examine the pattern and draw the next two terms:

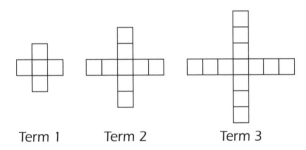

Term 1   Term 2   Term 3

How would you describe the change from one term to the next (the recursive pattern)? Some adults notice that the center five squares form a cross and the number of squares at the four ends of the cross increase by one starting at term 2. Other people notice a center square in each cross and that the lengths of the four legs of each cross increase by one as the term increases. Different ways of seeing the pattern are highlighted on the following page.

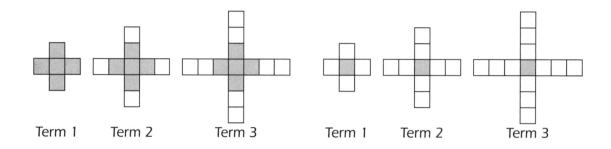

Term 1   Term 2   Term 3   Term 1   Term 2   Term 3

Asking students to describe in words what they observe and to look for parts of the design that stay the same and parts that change often assists students in generalizing.

However, in order to have students generalize the explicit or function rule, we must move beyond simply extending the pattern and instead help them to make sense of a rule between the term number and the pattern or sequence number. An expanded t-chart is especially useful. In an expanded t-chart the columns indicate both the constant amount and the change from term to term. Students can fill in their t-charts with the observed data and then predict the pattern for several larger terms or stages. We also want them to use these data to derive a rule for the pattern.

TERM NUMBER	CONSTANT + CHANGE IN SQUARES	PATTERN IN CHANGE	TOTAL NUMBER OF SQUARES
1	1 + 4	4 × 1	5
2	1 + 8	4 × 2	9
3	1 + 12	4 × 3	13
4	1 + 16	4 × 4	17
5			
15			
25	1 + 100	4 × 25	101
n		4 × n	1 + 4n

From the t-chart, we can see that for term number n, the number of squares can be represented with the explicit rule of $1 + 4n$. Students need many opportunities to extend patterns and to analyze constant and changing values in order to generalize and write explicit rules.

Another way for students to learn about functions and to practice generating explicit rules is by using function machines. A function machine is an imaginary device that links sets of numbers: an element (the input) is put into the machine and acted on according to a rule, and another, related element (the output) is produced:

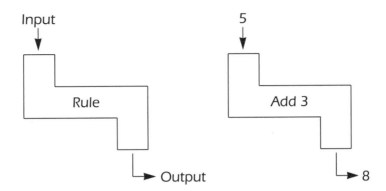

When any two of these three components (input, rule, output) are known, the third component can be analyzed (and often determined). In the examples that follow, finding the output in the first function machine (21) is very straightforward. Finding the missing input, as in the second function machine (it's 9), can be more complex, because we have to apply the inverse operation of the rule to the output. In the third example, however, since we are given only one input/output pair, we can't be certain what the rule is. That's because more than one rule can be applied (e.g., add 2, multiply by 2, or, perhaps, multiply by 3 and subtract 2).

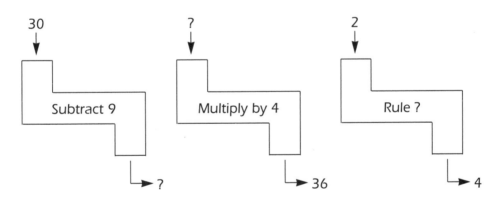

Function machines are useful both for applying rules (forward and backward) and for generating rules for data sets. However, we also want older students to generalize these function rules using variables. One way to present these functional relationships is by using input/output tables and asking students to examine the input and output data, look for patterns and relationships, and write a rule for the nth input value.

Activity

Finding Function Rules

Objective: determine the explicit rule for each function machine.

Examine the following tables. Determine the relationship between the two sets of numbers, represent that relationship using a rule, and fill in the blanks. Consider whether the numbers are increasing or decreasing because of a common difference or a constant multiplier.

TABLE A	
INPUT	OUTPUT
1	$^-2$
2	1
3	4
4	7
5	10
6	
. . .	. . .
9	
10	
	40
n	

TABLE B	
INPUT	OUTPUT
1	3
2	9
3	27
4	81
5	243
6	
. . .	. . .
9	
10	
	531,441
n	

TABLE C	
INPUT	OUTPUT
1	100
2	96
3	92
4	88
5	84
6	
. . .	. . .
9	
10	
	52
n	

Things to Think About

Numerous patterns jump out at us when we look at an input/output table. Looking at the two vertical columns in Table A, we see that the inputs are increasing by 1 each time and the outputs are increasing by 3. The repeated adding of 3 suggests that the relationship can be modeled by multiplying the input by 3. In order to determine a rule, however, we have to examine both the vertical and the horizontal patterns. What is consistent about how the input of 3 and the output of 4, the input of 4 and the output of 7, and the input of 5 and the output of 10 are related? The outputs are always greater than the inputs, but not by a constant amount. It sometimes helps to test a temporary rule suggested by the vertical outputs (multiplying by 3, in this case). Notice this is similar to what we did with the t-charts: identifying patterns in the change from term to term.

TABLE A	
INPUT	OUTPUT
1	$^-2$
2	1
3	4
4	7
5	10
n	?

TEMPORARY RULE ($3n$)	
INPUT	OUTPUT
1	$1 \times 3 = 3$
2	$2 \times 3 = 6$
3	$3 \times 3 = 9$
4	$4 \times 3 = 12$
5	$5 \times 3 = 15$
n	$3n$

Comparing the outputs in our temporary table to the corresponding outputs in Table A, we discover that they all differ by 5: $3 - (^-2) = 5$, $6 - 1 = 5$, $9 - 4 = 5$. Thus we can revise our temporary rule of $3n$ to $3n - 5$. Checking this rule against the inputs and outputs in Table A verifies that the rule holds. We then use it to fill in the blanks in Table A: 13, 22, 25, 15, $3n - 5$.

Did you notice that the outputs in Table B increase rapidly? This suggests that the rule might involve a constant multiplier. Looking at the vertical column of outputs we observe that each successive output is 3 times greater than the previous output, which suggests that the constant multiplier is 3. Writing each output as an exponent to the power of 3 (3^1, 3^2, 3^3, . . .), we can derive the function rule for Table B to be 3^n. The missing values in the table are 729, 19,683, 59,049, 12, and 3^n.

In Table C the inputs are increasing by 1 but the outputs are decreasing by 4. We can say we are either subtracting 4 each time or adding a ($^-4$) to each subsequent output. Since the common difference is ($^-4$), we can try out a temporary rule in which we multiply the input by $^-4$:

<table>
<tr><td colspan="2" align="center">TABLE C</td><td colspan="2" align="center">TEMPORARY RULE (^-4n)</td></tr>
<tr><td>INPUT</td><td>OUTPUT</td><td>INPUT</td><td>OUTPUT</td></tr>
<tr><td>1</td><td>100</td><td>1</td><td>$1 \times (^-4) = ^-4$</td></tr>
<tr><td>2</td><td>96</td><td>2</td><td>$2 \times (^-4) = ^-8$</td></tr>
<tr><td>3</td><td>92</td><td>3</td><td>$3 \times (^-4) = ^-12$</td></tr>
<tr><td>4</td><td>88</td><td>4</td><td>$4 \times (^-4) = ^-16$</td></tr>
<tr><td>5</td><td>84</td><td>5</td><td>$5 \times (^-4) = ^-20$</td></tr>
<tr><td>n</td><td>?</td><td>n</td><td>^-4n</td></tr>
</table>

Looking at the vertical column, we see that we need to subtract $4n$ from a larger number. Try 100: $100 - 4n$. This is close, but doesn't work exactly: if $n = 1$, then $100 - 4 = 96$. Aha, but what if we change the starting number to 104: $104 - 4n$. Now the function rule works for all inputs. The missing values in Table C are 80, 68, 64, 13, and $104 - 4n$.

Another way to determine these function rules is to find the value at the 0 stage or term—namely to work backward through the tables to figure out the output when the input is 0. In Table C we saw that the common difference was ($^-4$). To move back up through the table, we perform the opposite operation or add 4 to each output. For example, term 5's output is 84, term 4's output is 88 ($84 + 4$), and term 3's output is 92 ($88 + 4$). Using this approach, term 0's output is 104. Why is the 0 term important? Recursive sequences are defined by a starting value and a rule regarding common differences or constant multipliers. We generate the sequence by applying the rule to the starting value, then applying it to the resulting value, and repeating this process. In order to write a function rule for a sequence we have to know both the rule (the common difference or the constant multiplier) and the starting value. Earlier in the chapter we explored sequences that began with the common difference or constant multiplier; the starting value of those sequences actually is zero but we don't bother to record it. The sequence 2, 4, 6, 8, 10, . . . , could be written as 0, 2, 4, 6, 8, and so forth. In sequences that do not begin with zero, the 0 term gives us this starting number. Table C starts at 104 and the rule is $104 + (^-4)n$, (or $104 - 4n$). Use this strategy to find the starting value of Table A. Did you work backward through the table subtracting 3 to get a value of $^-5$? The rule for Table A is $^-5 + 3n$, or $3n - 5$. By convention we usually write rules by listing the variable first, but sometimes beginning the rule with the starting value makes more sense.

In any function machine, the value of the output varies depending on the value of the input. For example, when we substitute different values for *n* (the input) we get different outputs for 104 − 4*n* (the output). Sometimes the input/output relationship is represented using the letters *x* and *y*. In the case of Table C, the functional relationship is *y* = 104 − 4*x*. The variables, *x* and *y*, take on another interpretation of the word *variable,* perhaps the most familiar one—variables as varying quantities. ▲

Patterns, variables, and functions are linked in a number of ways. Some patterns can be generalized using variables, and some patterns can also be represented as functional relationships. A variety of repeating, arithmetic, and geometric patterns can be used to explore these ideas. The ancient Greeks noticed that many numbers could be used to make interesting dot patterns. For example, nine dots can be arranged in rows and columns to make a square array, but eight dots cannot be arranged into the shape of a square, only into a rectangular array. Numbers of dots that can be arranged in geometric patterns are known as *polygonal numbers* or *figurate numbers*. Number patterns based on these geometric patterns are very common. Two patterns occur so frequently that they are known by the shapes they represent—square numbers and triangular numbers.

Activity

Exploring Square and Triangular Numbers

Objective: learn about the square and triangular number patterns.

The dot arrays below represent the first four square numbers and the first four triangular numbers. Complete the fifth and sixth sequences in each pattern and then answer the following questions.

1. Describe the 10th square number.
2. How many dots are in each of the square arrays that represent the square numbers? List the number of dots in a t-chart. What patterns do you see?
3. Describe the 10th triangular number.
4. How many dots are in each of the triangular arrays that represent the triangular numbers? List the number of dots in a t-chart. What patterns do you see?

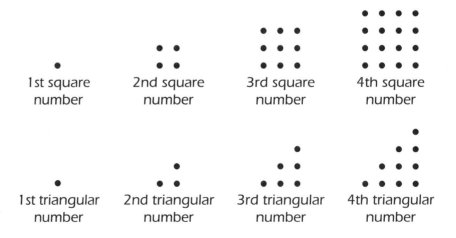

Things to Think About

Did you find that the 5th square number used 25 dots to make a 5-by-5 square and that the 6th square number used 36 dots to make a 6-by-6 square? Thus, the 10th square number is 100; 100 dots would be needed to make a 10-by-10 square. The square number pattern can be shown with dots in the form of square arrays but is more commonly represented by the number of dots: 1, 4, 9, 16, 25, 36, 49, and so on. These numbers are sometimes presented in exponent form: 1^2, 2^2, 3^2, 4^2, 5^2, 6^2, 7^2, etc. The explicit rule for generalizing the square number pattern is n^2, where n stands for the term (e.g., the 8th square number is 8^2, or 64). The second power (e.g., 6^2) of a number is often referred to as the number "squared" (6 squared equals 36), because that number of dots can be represented as a square.

Other interesting patterns are found in moving from one square number to the next. Notice that two consecutive square numbers differ by an odd number of dots.

1   (+ 3)   4   (+ 5)   9   (+ 7)   16   (+ 9)   25   (+ 11)   36

This can be shown visually in the construction of squares.

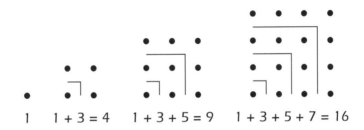

1   1 + 3 = 4   1 + 3 + 5 = 9   1 + 3 + 5 + 7 = 16

In order to answer Question 3 it helps to examine the fifth and sixth figures in the triangular numbers pattern. The fifth triangular number uses 15 dots to make a right triangle, with 5 dots on the bottom row, 4 dots on the next row, 3 dots above that, and then 2 dots and 1 dot respectively in the last two rows. The sixth triangular number uses 21 dots.

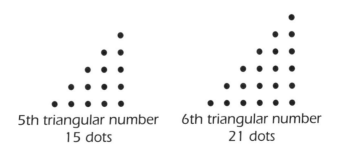

5th triangular number
15 dots

6th triangular number
21 dots

One way to make the 6th triangle in the triangular number pattern is to take the fifth triangle and simply add a bottom row of 6 more dots. This approach can be used to find the 10th triangular number. It is 55: 55 dots would be needed to make the 10th triangle. The triangular numbers are 1, 3, 6, 10, 15, 21, 28, 36, 45, 55, 66, 78, and so on.

What patterns did you notice in how these triangular numbers grow? The second triangle has 2 more dots than the first; the third triangle has 3 more dots than the second; the fourth triangle has 4 more dots than the third. These same patterns can be observed when looking at the numbers in the pattern.

TERM NUMBER	NUMBER OF DOTS	CHANGE
1	1	+2
2	3	+3
3	6	+4
4	10	+5
5	15	
⋮	⋮	

There is a rule for determining any triangular number:

$$\frac{n(n + 1)}{2}$$

where n represents the term in the triangular number pattern (e.g., to find the third triangular number, substitute 3 into the rule

$$\frac{3(3 + 1)}{2} = \frac{12}{2}$$

or 6; the third triangular number is 6). ▲

While many patterns can be categorized as repeating, arithmetic, geometric, or figurate, there are also special patterns that do not fit into these classification schemes. One of the most famous patterns is the Fibonacci sequence, which is made up of Fibonacci numbers. Fibonacci was the nickname of Leonardo de Pisa, an Italian mathematician (1175–1245); he is best known for the sequence of numbers that bears his name. The Fibonacci sequence of numbers begins with two numbers: 1, 1. Each new number is then found by adding the two preceding numbers:

$$1, 1, 2, 3, 5, 8, 13, 21, 34, 55, 89, 144, \ldots$$

Mathematicians have identified many interesting relationships among the Fibonacci numbers. For example, the sum of the first three Fibonacci numbers (1 + 1 + 2 = 4) is one less than the fifth number (5). The sum of the first four Fibonacci numbers (1 + 1 + 2 + 3 = 7) is one less than the sixth number (8). Find the sum of the first five Fibonacci numbers. Did the relationship hold? Yes, the sum of the first five Fibonacci numbers is 12, which is one less than the seventh Fibonacci number.

The Fibonacci numbers describe a variety of phenomena in art, music, and nature. The numbers of spirals on most pinecones and pineapples are Fibonacci numbers. The arrangement of leaves or branches on the stems of many plants are Fibonacci numbers. On a piano, the number of white (8) keys and black (5) keys in each octave (13) are all Fibonacci numbers. The center of a sunflower has clockwise and counterclockwise spirals, and these spirals tend to be consecutive Fibonacci numbers. The lengths and widths of many rectangular objects such as index cards, windows, playing cards, and light-switch plates are consecutive Fibonacci numbers.

natural occurrences of Fibonacci numbers

Fibonacci ratios are comparisons of two Fibonacci numbers, usually adjacent numbers in the sequence. These ratios are often expressed as decimals by dividing one number in the ratio by the other. As the numbers in the Fibonacci sequence increase, the ratios tend to approximate 1.618 (8/5 = 1.6, 55/34 = 1.6176, 233/144 = 1.61805). This special ratio (1.618034 . . .) is an irrational number (see Chapter 1, page 5) that occurs in many other shapes and objects. It is known as ϕ (phi) by mathematicians, and was labeled the *golden ratio* by the ancient Greeks. (People also call it the *golden proportion*.) It has been known and used for thousands of years—it is believed that it was a factor in the construction of some of the pyramids in Egypt. Rectangles whose length-to-width ratios approximate the golden ratio are called golden rectangles. Psychologists have found that people prefer golden rectangles to other rectangles; thus common objects such as cereal boxes and picture frames tend to have dimensions with a ratio of around 1.6. Which of the rectangles below do you find to be most aesthetically pleasing? Two are golden rectangles; you can check by measuring the lengths and widths and calculating the ratios.

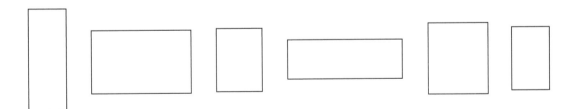

Activity

Fibonacci Numbers and You

Objective: investigate the occurrence of the golden ratio in the human body.

The human body is characterized by golden proportions, and these ratios have been used to draw figures accurately for centuries. Make the following measurements (use either inches or centimeters) and calculate the designated ratios. Can you find other golden ratios besides the ones mentioned?

▲ Your height compared with the distance from the floor to your navel.
▲ The distance from the floor to your navel compared with the distance from the floor to your kneecap.

▲ The length of your arm from the shoulder compared with the distance from your fingertips to your elbow.

▲ The distance from your chin to the center of your eyes compared with the distance from your chin to the tip of your nose.

▲ The length of your index finger compared with the distance from your index fingertip to the big knuckle.

Things to Think About

One way to represent these ratios is as decimals. If your height is 68 inches and the distance from the floor to your navel is 42 inches, the ratio is 68 to 42 or 1.619 to 1 (68 ÷ 42). This is very close to the golden ratio! You may instead have calculated a ratio of 1.7 or 1.5—not all individual proportions are exactly golden ratios. Some of us have long legs or arms compared with our overall heights. However, on average, the ratios will be close. Did you find other occurrences of the golden ratio? There are many other comparisons that produce the golden ratio, especially within the face and hands.

The golden ratio is more precisely defined as the cut in a line segment such that the ratio of the whole segment to the longer part is the same as the ratio of the longer part to the shorter part.

$$\frac{AC}{AB} = \frac{AB}{BC}$$

Thus, when we take body measurements, we are comparing a long section of the body to a shorter part. ▲

The relationship between Fibonacci ratios and the golden ratio is a curious phenomenon and has been the subject of study for generations. As a pattern, the Fibonacci sequence is an important one to know. Students benefit not only from identifying occurrences of the numbers in the pattern in nature but also from understanding the connection to the golden ratio. The golden ratio has been used in the design of many buildings (the Parthenon in Greece) and in the art of Leonardo da Vinci and Piet Mondrian.

5. Representation

Another important concept in algebra (and in mathematics in general) is *representation*—the display of mathematical relationships graphically, symbolically, pictorially, or verbally. Graphical representations include a variety of graphs—bar graphs, line graphs, histograms, line plots, and circle graphs (see Chapter 13 for additional information). Symbolic representations involve the use of symbols and include equations, formulas, and rules. Pictorial representations such as two- and three-dimensional drawings, maps, balance scales, and scale drawings are used in almost all areas of mathematics but especially geometry (see Chapters 10 and 11). Finally, relationships can also be expressed in words, either written or spoken. The situations you have been reasoning about in this chapter have been represented pictorially, symbolically, and verbally. Likewise, students need to create and match different representations in order to extend and deepen their understanding of relationships.

Activity

Representing Relationships in Problems

Objective: represent an algebraic relationship using a graph, table, and equation.

Generate the data needed to solve the following problem and organize the information into a table. Graph the data for each plan on a coordinate grid. Write equations to represent the relationships in each plan.

> *The Relax and Listen CD Club offers new members two plans from which to choose. Plan 1: Each CD costs $10.00. Plan 2: The first two CDs are free, and each additional CD costs $12.00. You are a big music fan and want to become a member of the Relax and Listen CD Club. Which plan would you choose? Explain.*

Things to Think About

Tables are a way of showing sets of data. In this problem you can set up a table that compares number of CDs and total cost for each plan. By listing the number of CDs in a systematic way, along with the corresponding cost, you can solve the problem and answer the question.

How many CDs should you include in the table? five? ten? twenty? In order to decide which plan is better for you, you have to find which quantity of CDs will cost the same under either plan. The table below shows that if you buy 12 CDs, you will spend the same amount under plan 1 and plan 2. This is often referred to as the "break even" point. If you plan to buy more than 12 CDs, plan 1 is the better choice. If you plan to buy fewer than 12 CDs, plan 2 is more economical.

NUMBER OF CDS	TOTAL COST FOR PLAN 1	TOTAL COST FOR PLAN 2
1	$10	0
2	$20	0
3	$30	$12
4	$40	$24
. . .	. . .	. . .
11	$110	$108
12	$120	$120
13	$130	$132

What are the benefits of using tables of data to solve problems? Working with numbers in an organized way often helps students note patterns. Having calculated numerous costs for plans 1 and 2, students will be able to cite specific examples. You can then help them link the specific examples to general statements about the relationships in the plans. For example:

Student: Plan 1 went from $10, to $20, to $30, up to over $100.

Teacher: Can you describe what's happening in more general terms?

Student: Well, the cost increases $10 every time you buy another CD.

How can we generalize the relationship in each plan with a rule? Plan 1 increases steadily by $10 with each CD; therefore, if n equals the number of CDs, the cost of plan 1 is $10n$ dollars. Plan 2 increases steadily by $12; but two CDs are free; therefore, if n equals the number of CDs, the cost of plan 2 is $12(n-2)$ dollars. To find the break-even point symbolically, we create a mathematical expression in which the two rules are set equal to each other: $10n = 12(n-2)$.

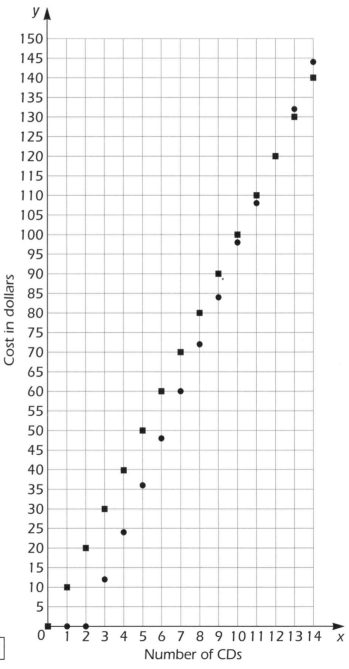

Comparison of Two Music Club Plans

■ Plan 1 ● Plan 2

The solution to this equation is the number of CDs you can buy and spend the same amount under either plan:

$$10n = 12(n - 2)$$
$$10n = 12n - 24$$
$$^-2n = ^-24$$
$$n = 12$$

Often rules or equations use x and y to represent the variables so that the equations can be more easily graphed. The equation for plan 1 is $10x = y$ and for plan 2 is $12(x - 2) = y$, where x is the number of CDs and y is the cost in dollars.

A graph will also show the relationship between the two plans. The title of the graph provides us with important information, as do the labels on each set of axes. (See page 216.)

The set of square points (plan 1) starts at the origin, or the (0,0) coordinate, and is plotted next at (1,10). This means that the cost of zero CDs is zero dollars and the cost of one CD is $10. The set of round points (plan 2) starts at the co-ordinate (2,0) and is plotted next at (3,12). This means that the cost of two CDs is zero dollars and the cost of 3 CDs is $12.

Why are the points on the graph not connected into lines? The data in this problem are discrete or countable data (see page 277 in Chapter 12 for more information): whole number values for CDs make sense, fractional numbers of CDs (e.g., three and a half) do not make sense. We cannot connect the points, because the values between whole numbers of CDs have no meaning. However, we can plot these points on a line graph because we are examing two different variables—number of CDs and cost.

The intersection point on the graph represents the break-even point, the point at which the two plans are equal. Notice that the points for plan 2 form a steeper incline than those for plan 1. However, because the points don't start at the same coordinate, it appears that plan 1 is steeper at the start. The steepness, or the slope, of incline provides us with information about the rate of change (in this case, the changing cost) between points. The steeper the incline, the greater the amount of change (dollars here) between values. ▲

Even though the information and relationships in a math problem can be expressed using prose, tables, equations, and graphs, one representation is sometimes easier to use than another or provides us with different insights into a problem. How would you represent the information in the following problem in order to solve it?

> *For their checking accounts, the Thrifty Bank charges $4.50 per month and $0.25 per check. The Fast Bank charges a flat rate of $0.50 per check for their checking accounts, with no additional monthly fee. How many checks must a person write to make the Fast Bank checking account the more economical plan?*

The specific context of a problem can either contribute to or distract from an individual's ability to make sense of it. If we don't know how a checking account works, for example, we would need some background information before being able to proceed with this problem. Whenever we are unfamiliar with a context, it often helps to organize the data in a table. As we determine the data that belong in the table, we become more familiar with the specifics of the problem. Then we may represent the numerical information for each bank's plan as points on a graph.

The place at which the two points overlap (18 checks) is the break-even point—for this number of checks, each account costs the same amount. If a person writes fewer than 18 checks a month, Fast Bank's plan is more economical. If he or she writes more than 18 checks a month, Thrifty Bank's is.

NUMBER OF CHECKS	THRIFTY BANK COSTS	FAST BANK COSTS
0	4.50	0
2	5.00	1.00
4	5.50	2.00
6	6.00	3.00
8	6.50	4.00
10	7.00	5.00
12	7.50	6.00
14	8.00	7.00
16	8.50	8.00
18	9.00	9.00
20	9.50	10.00

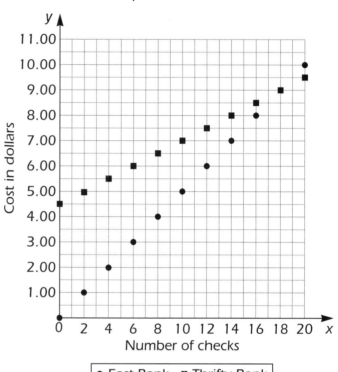

Comparison of Bank Fees

• Fast Bank   ■ Thrifty Bank

We could also represent the problem with equations: Thrifty Bank, $y = .25x + 4.50$; Fast Bank, $y = .50x$, where x represents the number of checks and y represents the cost of the account in dollars. Setting the two equations equal to each other, we can then solve for x algebraically:

$$.50x = .25x + 4.50$$
$$.25x = 4.50$$
$$x = 18$$

Teaching Algebra

While algebra used to be a subject reserved only for students going to college or those interested in advanced study, today we realize that algebraic reasoning is central to many other subjects and vocations. School systems throughout the country are requiring that all students take algebra. The National Council of Teachers of Mathematics has recommended that algebra be a curricular strand in kindergarten through grade 12 mathematics (NCTM 2000). If students have had algebraic experiences before they encounter algebra as a course in middle or high school, they will more easily make the transition from reasoning about number to reasoning about symbols and relationships. In the early elementary grades, studying patterns is the most prominent algebraic experience; patterns are the basis for reasoning about regularity and consistency. As students move into the upper elementary and middle grades, they need to generalize these patterns and express the relationships in a variety of ways. Students learn to use language, tables, and graphs to represent relationships and to formalize them using function rules and equations. At all levels, it is important to ask students to justify their statements using pictures, examples, and reasoning.

Questions for Discussion

1. Examine a textbook and find examples of where students are asked to reason algebraically. Explain the mathematical purpose of the activities.
2. Compare and contrast how variables are used.
3. Some people think that algebra is too complex a topic to teach to young children. What do you think? Support your statements.
4. Patterns are a major topic in mathematics. Describe the different types of patterns and describe one instructional activity that you could use to have students explore each pattern type.

10

Geometry

Although geometry is an important topic in the elementary and middle grades curriculum, it is generally given less attention than topics such as whole numbers, fractions, and decimals. Rather than providing students with activities that require them to describe, draw, model, build, and classify shapes or that help them develop spatial sense, textbook instruction often emphasizes procedures and definitions. The activities in this chapter will expand your knowledge and understanding of fundamental ideas (primarily point, line, angle, polygon, and polyhedron) in geometry.

1. Levels of Geometric Thought

Pierre and Dina van Hiele introduced their developmental model of geometric thinking in the late 1950s. The model describes students' geometric thinking from the initial identification of figures to the comprehension of different systems of geometry. Being aware of the van Hiele levels will help you make instructional choices for your students.

Based on their experiences as teachers in the Dutch public schools, the van Hieles posited that as students gain more experience with the properties and relationships of figures through hands-on activities and discussion of the geometric concepts involved, they progress through five levels of development. They also found that students' progress through the levels is directly related to the pertinent activities they experience; students who have experienced activities that enhance their understanding of geometric properties and relationships tend to function at higher levels. Each level describes a particular depth of understanding of geometric concepts and a principal focus of students' geometric thinking. Although the van Hiele hierarchy suggests that students will reach each level in order, students' thinking about particular concepts will likely be at different levels at any one time—that is, students might be at level 1 with regard to certain concepts but at level 2 or 3 on other geometric topics.

In contrast to some types of learning mastery, the van Hiele levels are not age-related: there is no correlation between age and level. Consequently, instructional activities and topics appropriate for students depend on the level of geometric thought they have achieved, not on their age or grade in school.

The first van Hiele level (level 1) is *recognition*. At this level, students identify shapes and figures only on the basis of appearance. They will identify a shape that is "almost" square as a square and may identify only the regularly shaped equilateral triangle as a triangle. They neither understand nor recognize properties of figures, and orientation affects how they view a figure. For example, they might not consider the shapes below triangles, the first because it is "upside down" and the second because it is a scalene triangle (the angles and the sides are different sizes).

Therefore, classroom instruction, especially in the early grades, needs to include examples of a variety of each type of shape (in the case of triangles, for example, isosceles, scalene, right), shown in various orientations. By encountering several different examples of any figure, students are able to generalize the common features and learn not to focus on irrelevant properties such as side length, angle measure, or orientation.

Level 2 is *analysis*. Students begin to analyze shapes and figures based on properties and attributes such as right angles and parallel sides. They are able to make generalizations about specific shapes. However, they cannot make generalizations about how different types of shapes relate to one another. For example, students may indicate that all squares have four equal sides, but they may not understand that because squares also have four right angles, all squares are rectangles. Instruction and activities, therefore, should focus on comparing and classifying properties of shapes and figures.

Level 3 is *informal deduction*. At this level, students can generalize relationships between various shapes. They are able to justify a generalization using minimal facts. For example, students generalize that all squares are rectangles because a square has the same attributes as a rectangle (opposite sides parallel and congruent, four right angles). Students can understand some proofs but aren't yet capable of creating a formal proof of their own. Instruction should encourage finding counterexamples and making generalizations, as well as exploring the converse of given statements.

Level 4 involves *formal deduction*. At this level, geometry is studied as formal mathematics. This level of analysis is achieved by some students at the successful completion of a high school geometry course. Students create their own proofs using deductive reasoning. They understand why a particular theorem may be proved in more than one way and learn to focus on the logic of an argument as well as the result. However, many students struggle with understanding certain topics in high school geometry courses because they have not reached level 4.

The final van Hiele level (level 5) is *rigor*. This level of study is encountered most often in college-level geometry courses. Students work on their understanding of different types or systems of geometry and different axiomatic systems, not just the deductions within the Euclidean system. In their work with other types of geometry, students begin to comprehend the distinctions and relationships between all the axiomatic systems they are studying.

Generally, students enter elementary school functioning at level 1 or level 2. No matter what the level, you may find inconsistencies in students' understanding of various topics. It is likely, for example, that students in grades 1 through 3 will be at more advanced levels with plane geometry topics than with topics involving three dimensions, in part because instruction in the early grades focuses on plane geometry. In addition, while students may have experiences with three-dimensional objects such as blocks in nursery school and kindergarten, they rarely are asked to consider the blocks as geometric objects—they don't learn their mathematical names (e.g., cubes, prisms) or examine their properties and attributes (e.g., shape of faces, number of edges).

For students to move through the various van Hiele levels, they need a variety of experiences involving geometry. Yet in many cases, textbook instruction provides mostly simple (level 1) identification tasks. Therefore, students must instead be exposed to activities that focus on properties of shapes and relationships among shapes. Mathematical tasks that require students to explore attributes, categorize findings, and make conjectures based on their findings are essential. This higher-level emphasis is also important in preparing students for the continued study of geometry in middle and high school.

2. Points and Lines

Points, lines, segments, rays, and angles are the "building blocks" of geometry. Understanding these concepts is essential, since they are used in a wide variety of applications. For example, students must understand points in order to identify the corners of a cube, must understand lines in order to explore parallel and intersecting lines, must understand segments in order to examine properties of shapes, and must understand rays in order to construct and interpret angles.

Point and *line* are basic ideas (also known as *abstractions*) in geometry that do not have definitions—they are undefined terms. Point and line are not things; they cannot be seen or touched. However, our understanding of these ideas evolves out of our experience with physical objects and situations that can be seen and manipulated. For example, the notion of a point can be suggested by the tip of a pencil or the smallest dot you can draw; it has position but no dimension. The notion of a line can be suggested by railroad tracks, a string held taut, or the path of a light beam. These physical models help cultivate in students' minds the notion of these ideas and provide the foundation for later abstraction.

Ancient Greek mathematician Euclid described a line by using two criteria or postulates: (1) through any two points there is always a line, and (2) every line contains at least two points. These postulates, which detail facts that Euclid believed were self-evident, appear in every geometry book that has since been written.

We can verify the first postulate by drawing a pair of points on a piece of paper. No matter how we draw the two points, a line can always be drawn through them. The second postulate uses the phrase "at least two" to describe the number of points on a line. Euclid knew that a line contains an infinite number of points. Why not simply state that in the postulate? One reason is that these postulates present facts that are the foundation for further geometry facts. Euclid wanted his postulates to be as brief and simple as possible. "At least two points" allows for but does not stipulate an infinite number of points. We can imagine that a line has an infinite number of points by first visualizing a set of three points, then a set of nine points, then a set of more points, and finally a set of many more points, as shown below:

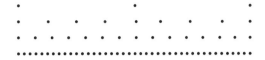

A *segment* is a part of a line that contains two points (called *endpoints*) and all the points between them. A *ray* is a subset of a line that contains a point (called the *endpoint*) and all the points of the line on one side of the point. To help think about segments and rays, imagine a piece of string extended across your classroom in either direction so that the ends cannot be seen. In your mind label a few points. This model of a line, in conjunction with a line drawn on paper or the blackboard, can be used to help students identify points, segments, and rays. Take line *l*, below:

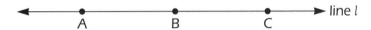

How many segments are there? Is ray $\overrightarrow{BC}$ part of ray $\overrightarrow{AB}$? Are there only three points on line *l*? Questions that probe students' conceptions of these ideas prepare them for a more abstract treatment of this topic.

As shown here, there are three segments on line *l*, $\overline{AB}$, $\overline{BC}$, and $\overline{AC}$. However, there are other points on line *l* that are not labeled in the diagram. If these points were labeled, then there would be many additional segments on line *l*. Because there are an infinite number of points on any line, there must be an infinite number of segments on line *l*, even though they are not labeled in this diagram. A ray is named by first listing the point where the ray begins and then a second point through which the ray passes. In the diagram, ray $\overrightarrow{AB}$ begins at point A and extends through point B. Ray $\overrightarrow{BC}$ begins at point B and extends through point C. Because ray $\overrightarrow{AB}$ will also pass through point C, it is correct to say that ray $\overrightarrow{BC}$ is part of ray $\overrightarrow{AB}$.

Depending on the age of our students, we may also need to identify objects that suggest segments (rungs on a ladder, gradations on a ruler) and rays (a flashlight beam, a sunbeam) in order to extend students' understanding.

The language we use to identify points, lines, and segments can cause confusion for students. We ask students to draw a point or a line on a piece of paper; we refer to a point as big or a line as thick; we talk about lines when we really mean line segments. By discussing the inaccuracies of language with students and by reinforcing that marks on paper are physical representations of ideas, we can help students interpret the language correctly.

Drawings raise some interesting questions about how to interpret lines, and properties of lines may be examined by exploring possible configurations. If one line is drawn exactly on top of another line so that they coincide, the two lines are considered to be a single line because a line has no thickness. Likewise, two lines drawn like this

are also considered one line because a line extends infinitely in both directions. Finally, two lines drawn like this

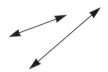

are considered to be intersecting lines. Since lines are infinite, these two lines may be extended to any length. When they are extended, they will eventually intersect at a single point.

Activity

Points of Intersection

Objective: help clarify the difference between parallel and intersecting lines.

Materials: flat toothpicks.

Using flat toothpicks to suggest lines, find ways to configure them so you get the maximum and minimum number of intersections for 2, 3, and 4 lines. Record your data in the table below. (Since the toothpicks are being used as models of lines, you will have to imagine that they extend infinitely in both directions, as do lines.)

NUMBER OF LINES	NUMBER OF POINTS OF INTERSECTION						
	0	1	2	3	4	5	6
2							
3							
4							

Things to Think About

Why do you think that two lines can have only zero or one point of intersection? The definition of parallel lines gives us some information: parallel lines consist of two lines in the same plane (or in this case on a flat surface such as a table) that do not have any points in common. As soon as one of the two lines is moved so that they are not parallel, the lines will eventually intersect (remember that the lines extend infinitely in both directions).

Why can't four lines be arranged so that there are two points of intersection? Start by placing the four lines so they are parallel to each other (zero points of intersection). If you move one of the four lines so that it is no longer parallel, it will eventually intersect with each of the other three lines (in your mind, extend the lines), resulting in three points of intersection. The fourth line can only be parallel to the other three or intersecting with the other three; thus there is no way to have just two points of intersection.

Placing all four lines so they intersect at one point also shows why having two points of intersection with four lines is impossible. Let's move one of the four lines so that it no longer intersects at that point. Anywhere we place the fourth line will result in two additional intersections, because the fourth line can be parallel to at most one of the other lines.

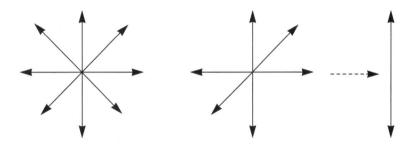

The maximum number of points of intersection of two lines is one point, of three lines is three points, and of four lines is six points. The numbers 1, 3, 6, are the first three terms in a sequence called *triangular numbers*. This pattern starts at 1 and is extended by adding 2 (1 + 2 = 3), then by adding 3 to the resulting term (3 + 3 = 6). Continuing this pattern of increase, we add 4 to find the next term in the sequence (6 + 4 = 10). Imagine doing Activity 1 with five and then six lines. Extending the pattern, you can determine that the maximum number of points of intersection of five lines is ten (6 + 4 = 10) and of six lines is fifteen (10 + 5 = 15).

Why does this pattern occur? Think about two lines intersecting at one point.

Now add a third line. Place it so it intersects with each of the two lines. There will be three points of intersection (1 + 2 = 3):

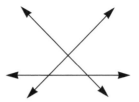

Now take the three lines that are intersecting in three points. Place a fourth line so that it intersects with each of the three lines. There are now 3 + 3, or 6, points of intersection:

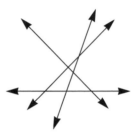

▲

Not only can lines be intersecting or parallel, they can also be skew. Skew lines neither are parallel nor intersect. Thinking about the edges of a cube can help you understand this idea. The edges are line segments. Some intersect, like these:

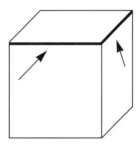

Some edges are parallel line segments. They lie on the same plane or flat surface and don't intersect (and wouldn't even if extended):

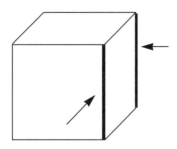

Other edges do not lie on the same plane or flat surface and therefore cannot be parallel, nor will they ever intersect:

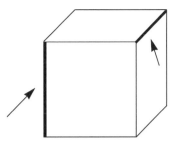

These edges are skew line segments. Notice that these skew line segments will never intersect, no matter how far they are extended, just like parallel line segments. Thus, one difference between parallel lines and skew lines is that parallel lines lie in the same plane and skew lines do not.

3. Angles

An angle is the union of two rays with a common endpoint. The common endpoint is called the *vertex*. Understanding the concept of angle is a prerequisite for understanding some of the properties of polygons. Students often consider angle measurement to be a static relationship rather than a dynamic one: they think angle size is fixed and is determined by the length of the rays rather than by the size of the turn. One way to help students better understand the dynamic nature of angle measurement is to have them use a protractor to construct various angles and then compare them.

You can make a simple protractor using two bendable straws (don't try to substitute regular straws; they won't work!). Take one bendable straw and cut a slit in the shorter section of it so the section will compress. Take the second straw and cut the short section off, including the bendable part. Insert the short compressed section of the first straw into the second straw. Voila! A protractor.

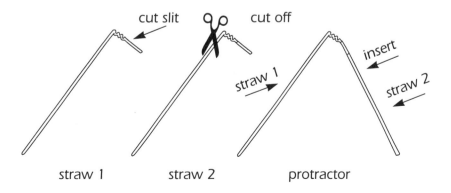

Using the straw protractor, students can make different angles and compare them with right angles. The right angle is used as a benchmark because it is easily described and modeled as a square corner. If the two straws are lying on top of each other so that the angle is closed, a right angle can be made by opening one straw a quarter ($\frac{1}{4}$) turn.

Angles equivalent to a half turn, three quarter turn, and less than a half turn but more than a quarter turn can easily be shown using this protractor and then classified according to their size—right (90°, or a square corner), acute (smaller than a right angle) and obtuse (larger than a right angle but less than 180°). This informal approach to angle measurement can serve as a foundation for students' understanding of angle and can contribute to their correct interpretation of angle measurement using a standard protractor.

When students explore angle relationships in various geometric settings they will expand their understanding of angles. For example, consider two lines that are intersected by a third line, commonly called a *transversal*. In the activity below, you will examine the angle relationships on the two lines.

Activity

Angles Formed by a Transversal

Objective: examine angle relationships that are formed when two lines are intersected by a transversal.

Materials: coffee stirrers, protractor, tracing paper.

When the two lines are oriented as shown here (they are not parallel) and are intersected by another line called the transversal, none of the letter angles are equal to any of the number angles. What happens as the orientation of one or both of the lines changes? Use coffee stirrers to represent the two lines and the transversal. Experiment to find an orientation that produces letter angles equal to number angles. The relationships can also be explored using geometry software if available.

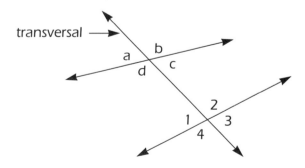

Things to Think About

In the previous diagram, which has no parallel lines, there are a number of angle relationships that you might observe. For example, there are several pairs of vertical angles. Vertical angles are two angles that share the same vertex but are not adjacent. The vertical angle pairs are ∠a and ∠c, ∠b and ∠d, ∠1 and ∠3, and ∠2 and ∠4. What seems to be true about each pair of vertical angles? Use tracing paper to form one of the vertical angles and then use it to verify that the vertical angle pairs are congruent. Repeat for the other vertical angle pairs.

Angles that share a common side and a common vertex, as for example ∠a and ∠b and ∠3 and ∠4, are known as adjacent angles. These adjacent angles form a straight line. This means that the sum of the angle measures of ∠a and ∠b is 180°. Similarly, the sum of the measures of ∠3 and ∠4 is 180°. What other pairs of adjacent angles in the diagram have measures that sum to 180°?

If the two lines are oriented so that they are parallel

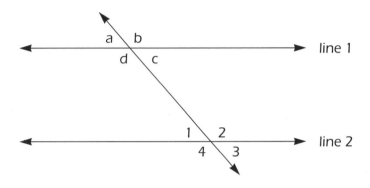

then there are two groups of angles with the same measure: ∠a = ∠c = ∠1 = ∠3 and ∠b = ∠d = ∠2 = ∠4. Draw two parallel lines and a transversal, then check to verify that the angles have equal measures. When two parallel lines are cut by a transversal, the corresponding angles formed by the transveral and each of the parallel lines will have the same measure. For example, ∠a and ∠1 are each to the left of the transversal and above one of the parallel lines and have the same measure. Can you explain why? Because the lines are parallel, the angles formed by the transversal and each parallel line will be identical. As long as you compare angles that are in corresponding locations relative to the parallel lines and the transversal, the measures will be the same. ▲

Activity

Angle Sums

Objective: discover the angle sum of interior angles in a triangle.

Exploring the angles within shapes provides insights into the relationships within and between shapes. What is the sum of the interior angle measurements in a triangle? Draw three different kinds of triangles—perhaps an equilateral triangle (all sides and all angles congruent), an isosceles triangle (two sides and two angles congruent), and a scalene triangle (all sides and all angles different). Mark the vertices on each triangle with a point, and label the angles 1, 2, and 3. Cut out the triangles. Tear off the corners of each triangle. Draw straight lines, label a point, and place the angles from the torn corners of one triangle adjacent and touching so that all three marked vertices meet at the point. What do you notice?

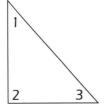 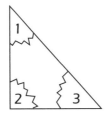 

Things to Think About

What conclusions can you draw about the sum of the interior angles in triangles? The three angles form a straight angle, which by definition measures 180°. Another way to consider the sum is to think of the three angles forming a half turn, which also measures 180°. You may have been surprised to note that the size of the triangle did not affect the sum of the angles. Because angle size is not affected by the length of the rays, the angles in both small and large triangles will sum to 180°. Likewise, the type of triangle does not affect the sum of the angles.

Can a triangle ever have two right angles? First imagine that a triangle has one right angle. This means that the sum of the other two angles in the triangle must also be 90° (180 − 90 = 90). If there is a second right angle in the triangle, then the third angle would measure 0°, which is impossible if we are considering triangles, which by definition have three angles. Thus, a triangle cannot have two right angles (though it could have three angles that measured 90°, 89°, and 1°!). ▲

Activity

Angle Measures in Other Shapes

Objective: determine the sum of interior angle measures in polygons.

Materials: pattern blocks.

What does each interior angle on the different pattern blocks measure? An interior angle is an angle on the inside of a polygon formed by the sides of the polygon. What information can you use to help you determine the individual angle measures? What is the sum of the angle measures in each block? Fill in the information on the drawings that follow.

Things to Think About

There are a number of ways to determine the measure of each of the interior angles. One approach is to use the measure of a known angle (for example, a right angle, which occurs in the square, is 90°). Placing three tan rhombi on top of the right angle reveals that one of the smaller angles in the tan rhombus measures 30°. Combining angle measures provides new information: one angle in the hexagon is congruent (the same measure) to the sum of one angle from the square and the small angle from the tan rhombus (120°).

The fact that there are 360° in a full turn around a point can also be used to determine the measure of some of the angles. For example, the angles in the green triangle are all 60°, since six of these triangles fit together around one vertex point to make a full turn (and sum to 360°). Likewise, the larger angle on the

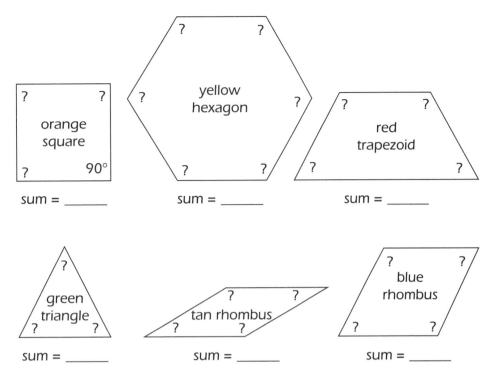

sum = _____   sum = _____   sum = _____

sum = _____   sum = _____   sum = _____

blue rhombus is 120°, since three blue rhombi also surround one vertex point to make a full turn.

Examine all of the four-sided pattern blocks (square, trapezoid, two rhombi). What is the sum of the angles in each of these shapes? Just as the measures of all of the angles in a triangle sum to 180°, the measures of all angles in a quadrilateral (a four-sided shape) sum to 360°. We can use the same technique to justify this as we used in Activity 3. Arranging all four of the angles from one shape around a point results in a full turn (360°). Another way to think about the sum of the angles in a quadrilateral is to draw a diagonal from one corner to the opposite corner, forming two triangles. Since the sum of the angles in a triangle is 180°, 2 × 180° = 360°. The same process can be used to find the total angle measures in polygons with more than four sides.

The chart below shows the sum of the angle measures in several many-sided shapes. Each of the shapes is divided into triangles. Do you see a pattern in the amount of the increase?

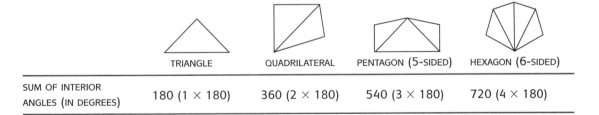

	TRIANGLE	QUADRILATERAL	PENTAGON (5-SIDED)	HEXAGON (6-SIDED)
SUM OF INTERIOR ANGLES (IN DEGREES)	180 (1 × 180)	360 (2 × 180)	540 (3 × 180)	720 (4 × 180)

Can you find a pattern in these data that will help you find the sum of the angles in a 20-sided figure, a 30-sided figure, or an n-sided figure? Notice that every time a side is added to a polygon, the angle sum increases by 180°. Each of the polygons above are divided into triangles. How many triangles are formed and how is the number of triangles related to the number of sides of the original figure? A triangle cannot be divided further, so there is one triangle formed with a 3-sided figure. For a quadrilateral (4 sides), there are two triangles. For a pentagon (5 sides), there are three triangles, and for a hexagon (6 sides), there are four triangles. The number of triangles is always two less than the number of sides of the figure. If we use n to represent the number of sides of a figure, $(n - 2)$ represents the number of triangles in any polygon. Since each triangle has an angle sum of 180°, the formula for the sum of the angle measures in a polygon is $(n - 2) \times 180$, were n represents the number of sides.

Another way to think about the angle sum in polygons is to take a figure, say a pentagon, and from the center point of the shape draw five triangles (one for each side). Since we divided the pentagon into five triangles, the sum of the angles in all five triangles is 900° (180° × 5).

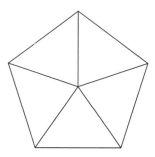

However, the angles that all meet at the center of the pentagon are not considered interior angles and thus do not contribute to the angle sum of the polygon. In order to find the sum of the interior angles of this pentagon we must subtract the measures of the center angles.

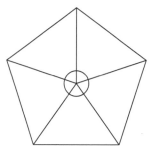

Because the center angles form a circle and sum to 360°, we can determine the sum of the interior angles in a pentagon is 540° (900 − 360 = 540). Try this method to find the sum of the interior angles in a dodecagon. Can you determine the measure of one angle in a dodecagon? What about if it was a regular dodecagon? Explain. ▲

4. Polygons

Exploring and investigating properties of polygons is one way to help students move to higher levels of the van Hiele hierarchy. What properties do all polygons have in common? Does every polygon have a distinctive name? How do we help students learn the definition of the word *polygon*? One way to help students with geometric ideas is to use examples and counterexamples. We might present the following table to students and challenge them to add examples to each column and think about how to define what makes a figure a polygon.

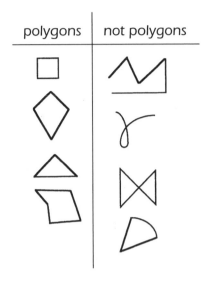

Students usually include "all sides are segments" and "figure must be closed (no openings)" in their definitions. You may have to suggest "no more than two segments can meet at a vertex point." Investigating examples of shapes that are and are not polygons is an effective way to encourage students to look at properties and distinguish the characteristics that define a polygon from those that don't. This approach integrates reasoning into instruction, in contrast with simply telling students definitions.

Polygons are classified in many ways. Some common names for specific polygons are *triangle* (three sides), *quadrilateral* (four sides), *pentagon* (five sides), *hexagon* (six sides), *heptagon* (seven sides), *octagon* (eight sides), *decagon* (ten sides) and *dodecagon* (twelve sides). (Greek prefixes are used to name polygons with more than eight sides.) *Regular* polygons have congruent sides and congruent angles, *nonregular* polygons do not. Polygons are also classified as *convex* or *concave* (nonconvex). There are two methods for testing convexity. The first is to locate two points inside a figure. Draw a segment to connect the two points. If all possible segments can be drawn so that they are entirely inside the figure, then the figure is convex. However, if a segment can be drawn so that a part of the segment is outside the figure, then the figure is concave.

convex

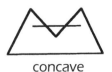

concave

The second method of testing convexity is to imagine tying a piece of string around the perimeter of a figure and pulling the string tight. If the string touches all the vertices of the figure, then it is convex; otherwise it is concave. This can be clearly demonstrated using a geoboard and rubber bands. The figure below shows a rubber band placed around a concave polygon like the one on page 233. Notice that the rubber band does not touch one of the five vertex points, indicating the polygon is concave.

Many polygons can be classified as quadrilaterals: *parallelograms*, *squares*, *trapezoids*, *kites*, *rhombi*, and *rectangles*. The kite shape is just like the classic kite flown in a meadow or on the beach: it has two pairs of adjacent sides that are the same length.

Activity

Properties of Quadrilaterals

Objective: identify properties of various quadrilaterals.

Materials: either use models or make drawings of each of the quadrilaterals before you begin.

Determine which of the listed quadrilaterals have the indicated characteristics. Fill in the chart. As you do, think about how distinctions can be made between these figures on the basis of their properties.

CHARACTERISTICS	PARALLELOGRAM	RHOMBUS	RECTANGLE	SQUARE	KITE	ISOSCELES TRAPEZOID
All sides congruent						
Both pairs of opposite sides congruent						
Adjacent sides congruent						
All angles congruent						

CHARACTERISTICS	PARALLELOGRAM	RHOMBUS	RECTANGLE	SQUARE	KITE	ISOSCELES TRAPEZOID
Opposite angles congruent						
Both pairs of opposite sides parallel						
Congruent diagonals						
Diagonals perpendicular						
Has reflective symmetry						
Has rotational symmetry						

Things to Think About

Since a rhombus, rectangle, and square can each be classified most generally as a parallelogram, these four shapes have much in common: both pairs of opposite sides are congruent, opposite angles are congruent, and both pairs of opposite sides are parallel. However, only in a rhombus and a square are all sides congruent, and only in a rectangle and a square are all angles congruent.

This activity uses an isosceles trapezoid, which is a special type of trapezoid. Trapezoids do not have to be isosceles; they just have to have only one pair of parallel sides. So a trapezoid might look like this:

How will your answers change if this more general trapezoid is used? With this trapezoid there are no pairs of congruent sides and the diagonals are not congruent.

A *diagonal* is a line segment formed by connecting nonadjacent vertices (corners). Quadrilaterals have two diagonals. Examine the diagonals of different quadrilaterals. What do you notice? Diagonals in some quadrilaterals (except for the rectangle, square, and isosceles trapezoid) are not congruent. Try to explain why. The diagonals in a square, kite, and rhombus are perpendicular (form right angles) when they cross. What do these three quadrilaterals have in common that results in perpendicular diagonals? (Hint: Examine the sides.)

Other important properties to consider are whether the shapes have *reflective symmetry* and/or *rotational symmetry*. If a figure possesses reflective symmetry, it will pass the "fold test." Sketch the figure and bisect it with a line such that one half of the figure fits exactly on the other half of the figure. In a parallelogram the diagonal divides the figure into two congruent halves, but the fold test shows that the diagonal is not a line of symmetry. No other line can be drawn in a parallelogram that passes the fold test. The fold test confirms that the diagonal of a square *is* a line of symmetry. There are two other lines of symmetry of a square. Make sure to find them. All of the shapes except the parallelogram have reflective symmetry. (For more information on symmetry, see Chapter 11.)

If a figure possesses rotational symmetry, it will pass the "trace-and-turn test." First trace the shape on acetate or paper and cut it out. Next place the cut-out shape onto the original so that all the points align. Holding the center point fixed, rotate the top figure until all the points of the two figures are again aligned. The number of times the points become aligned in a single 360° rotation will determine the rotational symmetry. All shapes can be turned a full 360° back onto themselves. However, some shapes also align with a turn that is less than 360°, such as 90°. These shapes are said to have rotational symmetry. The parallelogram, rhombus, rectangle, and square all have rotational symmetry.

Many polygons share some of the same properties, and their classifications are therefore not distinct. For example, a square is also a rectangle. Many students find this especially confounding. In order for them to make sense of these relationships, they need to compare and contrast figures. One way to help students classify polygons that belong to two or more groups is to play classification games that focus on properties of polygons and to use Venn diagrams to show relationships among polygons. ▲

Activity

Categorizing Quadrilaterals

Objective: categorize quadrilaterals according to their properties.

Which quadrilaterals fit each of the following clues? (A clue may apply to more than one figure, depending on its degree of specificity.)

1. Figure A has 4 congruent sides and 4 congruent angles.
2. Figure B has 4 sides that are congruent, but the 4 angle measures are not equal.
3. Figure C has 2 pairs of congruent sides and 4 congruent angles.
4. Figure D has only 1 pair of parallel sides.
5. Figure E has exactly 2 pairs of congruent sides.

Things to Think About

Consider which quadrilateral the figure has to be and how else it might be classified. Many polygons can be classified in more than one way. For example, a parallelogram is a quadrilateral the opposite sides of which are parallel and the same length. A square is defined as a quadrilateral with *four* congruent sides and *four* congruent angles. Yet a square can also be classified as a parallelogram because it satisfies the definition of parallelogram. A rhombus has all sides the same length and opposite sides parallel, so a rhombus is also a parallelogram. Can a rhombus be classified as a square? Can a square be classified as a rhombus? A rhombus is not a square, because a square must have four congruent angles (90°). However, a square is a rhombus, because it satisfies the criteria of four congruent sides and the definition of a rhombus does not mention angles.

Some of these relationships can be shown using Venn diagrams. For example:

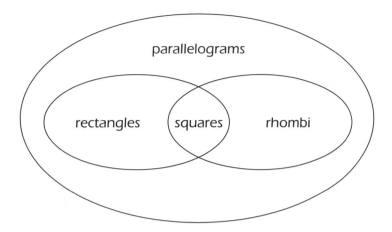

Rectangles, rhombi, and squares are all parallelograms. Squares can be classified both as rectangles and as rhombi.

Why can't trapezoids and kites be classified as parallelograms? The word *parallel* in *parallelogram* gives us a clue. In order to be classified as a parallelogram, the polygon needs to have two pairs of parallel and congruent sides. A trapezoid only has one pair of parallel sides. The kite has two sets of congruent sides but they are not parallel.

Figure A must be a square. A square can also be classified as a parallelogram, rhombus, and rectangle. Figure 2 must be a rhombus. A rhombus is a type of parallelogram. Figure C must be a rectangle, but it might also be a square, because the description mentions that it has two pairs of congruent sides; they could all be congruent. Figure D has to be a trapezoid; it could also be an isosceles trapezoid, but it doesn't have to be. Figure E could be almost any quadrilateral: a kite, rectangle, parallelogram, square, or rhombus. (Could it be a trapezoid?) ▲

---

5. The Pythagorean Theorem

The Pythagorean Theorem is one of the most famous theorems in all of mathematics. Most people can recall learning "a squared plus b squared equals c squared" ($a^2 + b^2 = c^2$) in their mathematics class. The theorem is named for Greek mathematician Pythagoras (c. 500 B.C.), who is credited with discovering it. Egyptian mathematicians had developed an early version of the theorem and Chinese mathematicians likely discovered the theorem independently. As with other geometry concepts, it is essential to have a deeper understanding of the relationship expressed in the theorem beyond memorizing a formula to solve for a side length of a triangle.

The Pythagorean Theorem refers to the relationship between the lengths of the sides of right triangles, which are identified by the letters a, b, and c. (The letters could as easily have been p, q, and r or some other set of three letters, but a, b, and c have been customarily used for centuries and are now the popularly accepted form of the theorem.) In the following diagram the letters of the theorem are paired with sides of the right triangle.

Notice that the side opposite the right angle is labeled c. This, the longest side of the right triangle, is known as the *hypotenuse* and in the customary formula of the Pythagorean Theorem is always labeled c. The other two sides of the triangle, the sides that form the right angle, are called *legs*. The lengths of these two legs are labeled a and b and can be interchanged. It is only the length of hypotenuse, c, that cannot be interchanged with another side length.

In the centuries since Pythagoras there have been literally hundreds of proofs of the Pythagorean Theorem, by people as diverse as Leonardo da Vinci, Greek philosopher Plato, British essayist Thomas Carlyle, and American president John Garfield. Some proofs involve simple observation, while others require complex reasoning and detailed diagrams. All of these proofs establish the validity of the theorem for all right triangles and not for just a few exemplary cases. Being able to provide a rationale for the Pythagorean Theorem can solidify understanding of the theorem.

Activity

Proving the Pythagorean Theorem

Objective: develop a proof of the Pythagorean Theorem.

Materials: scissors.

Below is a large square with a side length of c. We will call this square a c-square. The square has an area of $c \times c = c^2$. Some mathematics historians believe that Pythagoras used a similar diagram to prove his theorem.

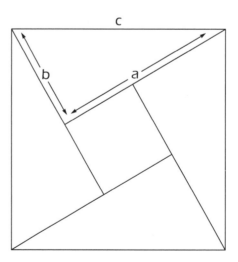

Trace the c-square onto a piece of paper and then cut out the five pieces. The challenge is to rearrange these five pieces into two new squares, one with a side length a, and the other with a side length b. (Hint: the two resulting squares are adjacent along one side.)

Things to Think About

Before rearranging the pieces, take a minute to notice some of the features of the c-square. Each of the triangles in the c-square is a right triangle with a and b for legs and a hypotenuse of length c. We want to make two new squares, one with side length a and the other with side length b, so experiment with orienting the shapes so that sides a and b are on the outside, not the inside. The four triangles and small square from the composite c-square can be rearranged as shown below.

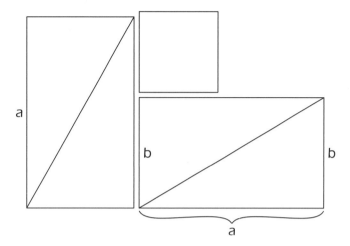

The diagram below shows more clearly how this rearrangement forms two smaller squares, one with a side length of a and the other with a side length of b.

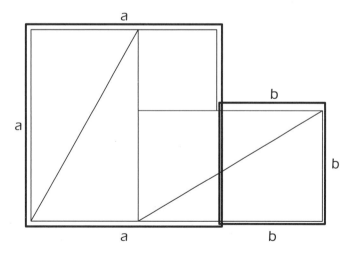

The area of one square is a^2 ($a \times a$) and the area of the other square is b^2 ($b \times b$). Because the pieces of the c-square can be rearranged to form the a-square and the b-square, then it follows that $a^2 + b^2 = c^2$. This type of proof is called *proof*

without words, because the conclusion, $a^2 + b^2 = c^2$, is established by rearranging the pieces and observing the result. This is often referred to as a *visual proof.* (See page 343 for Web sites with interactive visual proofs of the Pythagorean Theorem.)

Over 1500 years after Pythagoras, Indian mathematician Bhaskara used the same diagram, above the exhortation "Behold!" However, Bhaskara suggested an algebraic proof. In this diagram the area of the large square is c^2 ($c \times c$). It also is composed of four right triangles and a smaller square. The area of each of the right triangles is $A = \frac{1}{2}bh$, which can be expressed as $A = \frac{1}{2}ab$. The side of the smaller square is equal to $a - b$. Can you figure out why?

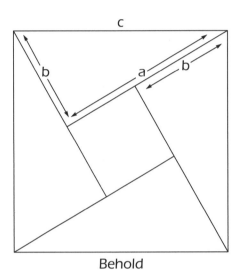

Behold

Bhaskara used the equations below to prove the Pythagorean Theorem:

Area of large square = area of the 4 right triangles + area of the small square

$$c^2 = 4(\tfrac{1}{2})ab + (a - b)^2$$
$$c^2 = 2ab + (a - b)(a - b)$$
$$c^2 = 2ab + a^2 - 2ab + b^2$$
$$c^2 = a^2 + b^2 \ \blacktriangle$$

The Pythagorean Theorem can be used to compute the third side of a right triangle when the two other side lengths are known. For example, in this right triangle

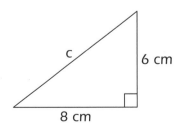

$a = 6$ and $b = 8$. To solve for side c, use the formula of the theorem as follows:

$$a^2 + b^2 = c^2$$
$$6^2 + 8^2 = c^2$$
$$36 + 64 = c^2$$
$$100 = c^2$$
$$\sqrt{100} = c$$
$$10 = c$$

The length of side c is 10 centimeters. Suppose the known lengths are $a = 12$ and $c = 25$:

$$a^2 + b^2 = c^2$$
$$12^2 + b^2 = 25^2$$
$$144 + b^2 = 625$$
$$b^2 = 481$$
$$b = \sqrt{481}$$

In this case the three side lengths are not all whole numbers. One of them is a radical number—or irrational number—that cannot be represented as a whole number or a fraction. All, two, one, or none of the side lengths of a right triangle may be whole numbers. When the three side lengths of a right triangle are all whole numbers, such as 9, 12, and 15 ($9^2 + 12^2 = 15^2$), the set of three side lengths is known as a *Pythagorean Triple*. There are an infinite number of Pythagorean Triples. Greek philosopher Plato discovered a way to generate some of them. For any number, n, the legs of a right triangle are $2n$ and $n^2 - 1$, and the hypotenuse is $n^2 + 1$. For example, for $n = 5$, the Pythagorean Triple is 10 (2×5), 24 ($5^2 - 1$), and 26 ($5^2 + 1$).

Activity

Using the Pythagorean Theorem to Identify Triangles

Objective: identify triangles by using the Pythagorean Theorem.

Materials: coffee stirrers, straws, thin strips of paper, brass fasteners.

The Pythagorean Theorem can also be used to tell if a triangle is acute, right, or obtuse. You will need straws, coffee stirrers, or thin strips of paper in the following centimeter lengths: 6, 6, 7, 8, 8, 9, 10, 11, 12, 13, 14. Use a 6 cm and an 8 cm segment to form the legs of a right angle as pictured here:

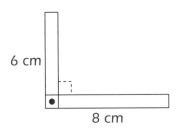

6 cm

8 cm

Use each of the remaining segment lengths in conjunction with the 6 cm and 8 cm segments to form triangles. Not all of the segments will fit together to make a triangle unless you change the angle between the 6 cm and 8 cm legs. You may need to either enlarge (form an obtuse angle) or shrink (form an acute angle) the right angle formed by the 6 cm and 8 cm lengths. Substitute values into the Pythagorean Theorem and record your results in the table.

| SIDE LENGTHS | | | RESULTING | |
a	b	c	TYPE OF TRIANGLE	PYTHAGOREAN THEOREM
8	6	6	acute	$8^2 + 6^2 > 6^2$
8	6	7		
8	6	8		
8	6	9		
8	6	10		
8	6	11		
8	6	12		
8	6	13		
8	6	14		

Things to Think About

Did you notice that some of the segments in combination formed right triangles but other segments formed acute or obtuse triangles? Why? When the third side length is 10 centimeters, the triangle is a right triangle and the equation for the Pythagorean Theorem ($6^2 + 8^2 = 10^2$) is true. In fact, if any three side lengths of a triangle satisfy the Pythagorean Theorem, then the triangle must be a right triangle! What if the three side lengths do not satisfy the Pythagorean Theorem? When the third segment is less than 10 cm in length (6, 7, 8, or 9) then the triangle is acute. Namely, you have to reduce the size of the angle between the 6 cm and 8 cm legs in order to make the three legs form a triangle. When the third side is longer than 10 cm (11, 12, 13), the triangle is obtuse. In this case, the right angle between the two legs (6 cm and 8 cm) has to be opened up to form a wider angle (an obtuse angle) so that the three segments fit together to form a triangle. Stated another way, when the square of the hypotenuse is *less than* the sum of the squares of the two legs, the triangle is acute. When the square of the hypotenuse is *greater than* the sum of the squares of the two legs, the triangle is obtuse.

In order to construct triangles you were able to adjust the size of the original right angle opposite the hypotenuse. Does this always work? Can you always adjust the angles and form three lengths into a triangle? Cut a 2 cm segment and make a new triangle with side lengths of 2 cm, 6 cm, and 8 cm. Were you able to construct a triangle that closed using these lengths?

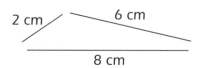

2 cm 6 cm

8 cm

Not all side lengths form triangles. If any two of the side lengths are less than or equal to the third side length (2 + 6 = 8), then the two smaller sides collapse onto the third length but do not form a triangle. No matter how you try to adjust the angles, the lengths cannot be formed into a triangle. Interestingly, if a triangle is possible, there is only one triangle that can be built using the three lengths. Thus triangles are very rigid and consequently are used in many buildings and designs where stability is required.

There is another relationship between the lengths of the sides in a triangle and the measures of the angles opposite each of those sides. In any triangle the largest angle is opposite the longest side, the middle size angle is opposite the middle length side, and the smallest angle is opposite the shortest side. The converse of this relationship is also true: the longest side is opposite the largest angle, the middle length side is opposite the middle size angle, and the shortest side is opposite the smallest angle. In the triangle here the angle sizes are as follows (*m* indicates the measure of the angle in degrees):

$$m \angle A = 80, \, m \angle B = 60, \, m \angle C = 40$$

Or $m \angle A > m \angle B > m \angle C$

Thus: BC > AC > AB

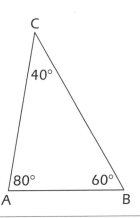

6. Geometry in Three Dimensions

Most of this chapter has focused on two-dimensional geometry, geometry in the plane. Three-dimensional geometry, the geometry of solids, is also an integral part of the study of geometry in the elementary and middle grades. Solids are classified by the types of surfaces they have: flat, curved, or both. One group of three-dimensional figures, *polyhedrons*, have polygon faces. There are no curved segments or curved surfaces in a polyhedron. Thus, cubes and pyramids are polyhedrons, but spheres, cones, and cylinders are not.

All polyhedrons have component parts called *faces*, *edges*, and *vertices*. Each flat surface or region on a polyhedron is known as a *face* and the faces of polyhedrons are all *polygons* (hence the name). An edge is a line segment formed by the intersection of two faces. Vertices name the point where three or more edges intersect. Examine the following cube. Check to see that the faces are polygons (squares), that the edges occur when two square faces intersect, and that there are eight different vertices where three edges meet at a point.

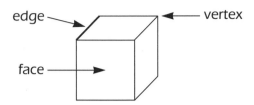

Students commonly use the term *side* to refer to a face and border or *ledge* to refer to an edge. Informally many people refer to vertices as *corners*. Since concepts are linked to one's use of language, it is important for students to use the proper terms *face*, *edge*, and *vertex* to avoid confusion.

Examine the solids shown below. Do they remind you of boxes? They are a common type of polyhedron called *prisms*. A prism is a polyhedron that has two congruent and parallel faces joined by faces that are parallelograms. In the cube, all of the faces are squares. In the rectangular solid, or rectangular prism, next to the cube, all of the faces are rectangles (remember that squares can be classified as rectangles). The third prism is called a *hexagonal prism*—two of its faces are hexagons and the rest are rectangles. The fourth prism is a *triangular prism*. The two congruent and parallel faces of a prism are often referred to as *bases*.

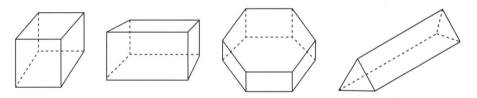

Prisms are classified by the shape of their bases, hence the names *rectangular*, *hexagonal*, and *triangular* prisms. Thus a cube could be called a square prism but rarely is! Whereas we often think that the bases of a prism are the top and bottom of the figure, this is not required. The triangular prism is not resting on its triangular base.

Another type of polyhedron is a *pyramid*. The simplicity and beauty of pyramids—whether the ancient Egyptian pyramids or that at the Louvre in Paris—have interested builders of all ages. A pyramid has at least three triangular faces that meet at a vertex point at the top (the *apex*) and one other face (the *base*), which can be any type of polygon. The shape of the base is used to differentiate and name pyramids. On the triangular, square, and pentagonal pyramids below, note the shape of the base and the number of edges, faces, and vertices.

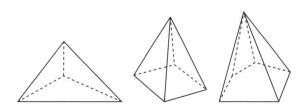

Finding Euler's Formula

Objective: discover Euler's Formula using data gathered from polyhedrons.

Materials: toothpicks, gum drops or mini-marshmallows.

Build the polyhedrons displayed on the previous page and two or three new poly-hedrons. You might use toothpicks, straws, or stirrers for edges and gumdrops or mini-marshmallows for vertex points. Count the number of edges, faces, and vertex points in each polyhedron and record your results in a table such as the one given here. There is a relationship between the number of faces, edges, and vertex points in any polyhedron. What is the relationship?

POLYHEDRON	NUMBER OF FACES	NUMBER OF VERTICES	NUMBER OF EDGES
Cube			
Triangular prism			
Triangular pyramid			
Square pyramid			

Things to Think About

The relationship between the number of edges, faces, and vertex points for any polyhedron was discovered by Swiss mathematician Leonhard Euler and is called *Euler's Formula* in his honor. Here's the completed table:

POLYHEDRON	NUMBER OF FACES	NUMBER OF VERTICES	NUMBER OF EDGES
Cube	6	8	12
Triangular prism	5	6	9
Triangular pyramid	4	4	6
Square pyramid	5	5	8

Euler discovered that in every polyhedron the sum of the number of faces and the number of vertices exceeds the number of edges by 2. In the following for-mula F represents the number of faces, V represents the number of vertices, and E represents the number of edges. Euler's Formula is $F + V - E = 2$, or $F + V = E + 2$. This relationship is true for every polyhedron, no matter how complex. Check the formula with each of the polyhedrons above. Or, you can manipulate several polyhedrons on line to count their composite parts to verify Euler's Theo-rem. (See the Web sites list at the back of the book.) ▲

Platonic Solids

The *Platonic solids* are a special type of polyhedron named after Plato, who used them to model his cosmology of the universe. The following diagram displays all five Platonic solids. What is it that distinguishes Platonic solids from other polyhedrons?

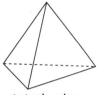
tetrahedron

hexahedron

octahedron

dodecahedron

icosahedron

Activity

Exploring Platonic Solids

Objective: determine the common attributes of the Platonic solids.

Materials: gum drops, toothpicks, Geofix shapes.

The five Platonic solids have two specific attributes in common. What are these two distinguishing attributes? Observe the Platonic solids in the diagram above or build some of them using either toothpicks and gumdrops or a commercial manipulative such as Geofix shapes. What attributes do they each share? Pay careful attention to the faces of each Platonic solid.

Things to Think About

Each Platonic solid has regular polygons for faces. Three of them have equilateral triangles for faces (tetrahedron, octahedron, and icosahedron), one has squares (cube), and one has regular pentagons (dodecahedron).

In addition, each Platonic solid has the same number of faces meeting at each vertex. In the tetrahedron three equilateral triangles meet at each vertex, in the octahedron four equilateral triangles meet at each vertex, in the icosahedron five equilateral triangles meet at each vertex, in the cube three squares meet at each vertex, and in the dodecahedron three regular pentagons meet at each vertex. The table below summarizes their common attributes.

PLATONIC SOLID	SHAPE OF FACES	NUMBER OF FACES MEETING AT EACH VERTEX
Tetrahedron	equilateral triangle	3
Octahedron	equilateral triangle	4
Icosahedron	equilateral triangle	5
Cube	square	3
Dodecahedron	regular pentagon	3

To sum up: a Platonic solid is a polyhedron with regular polygons as faces and with the same number of faces meeting at each vertex. ▲

Teaching Geometry

The entire system of Euclidean geometry is derived from a few postulates and definitions. Students' understanding of geometry flows from their foundational understanding of basic concepts such as lines and properties of figures. As students explore and collect data about geometric relationships, they learn to record their data, organize it, and then make conjectures based on observations and patterns. Generalizing and eventually justifying are key processes that eventually lead to the study of proof in formal geometry courses.

Understanding points, lines, segments, rays, and angles is essential to understanding more complex figures and relationships. Students who have a good foundation in the properties of figures are better prepared to analyze these figures on the basis of these properties and then develop a hierarchy for those figures based on their similarities and differences. Thus, the more experiences students have in elementary and middle school with visualization, classification, and explorations with models, the better. It is these kinds of experiences that the van Hieles found helped to move students to the higher levels of geometric understanding.

Questions for Discussion

1. Summarize the van Hiele levels of geometric thought. How might you use your knowledge of these developmental levels when planning instruction?

2. Certain shapes are classified in more than one way. For example, squares are a type of rectangle. Are equilateral triangles isosceles? Are isosceles triangles equilateral? Are rhombi squares? Are squares rhombi? Explain your reasoning.

3. Read the "Reasoning and Proof" standard in *The Principles and Standards for School Mathematics* (NCTM 2000). What is the role of justification in elementary and middle school classrooms?

4. Which are most important ideas about angles for students in grades K through 8 to understand? Describe the concepts and skills involving angles and polygons that upper elementary and middle school students should make sense of.

5. What are the roles of visualization and construction of models when learning about solid geometry?

II

Spatial Sense

Much of what we do in life requires knowing where we are or in what direction we're facing. Reading a map or following directions to a destination involves orientation on a plane. Careers in such areas as graphic arts, construction, architecture, engineering, and drafting require adults to translate images of three-dimensional objects into two-dimensional drawings and also to analyze two-dimensional images in terms of the images' three-dimensional counterparts.

Spatial sense is necessary in all areas of mathematics and at all levels. Every mathematics textbook portrays three-dimensional figures as two-dimensional drawings. Students are expected to interpret these two-dimensional images as the figures they actually represent: a cube, a pyramid, whatever. In addition, students must be able to recognize figures in different orientations by visualizing reflections and rotations. Research suggests that students who are able to make sense of visual images are better problem solvers. Students who use spatial as well as analytic means when problem solving think more flexibly and don't get stuck on just one type of approach. Some students have a natural spatial sense; others are easily confused by spatial information. Nevertheless, with proper experiences, all students' spatial sense can be improved (Ben-Chaim, Lappan, and Houang 1988).

1. What Is Spatial Sense?

Spatial sense is the recognition and interpretation of two-dimensional figures on a plane and three-dimensional figures in space. Spatial sense may be divided into two general areas: *spatial visualization* and *spatial orientation*. In spatial visualization the figure changes position on the plane and in space but an individual's point of view remains stationary. In spatial orientation, the figure remains in a fixed position and the individual's point of view varies (Yakimanskaya 1991).

Why is it important that we consider spatial sense when teaching mathematics? First, topics like reflections and rotations are important in many related fields, such as art and science. Second, these and similar topics are formal aspects of geometry, statistics, and algebra. Students must be able to identify, analyze, and transform shapes and figures in order to make sense of data and solve problems. Third, students are constantly presented with visual images—diagrams, pictures, and patterns that are based on the use of transformed shapes and relationships among shapes—and they must be able to interpret these images. Finally, many researchers believe that when data and relationships are presented spatially, students are better able to generalize and remember the underlying mathematical concepts. Yet despite the many reasons we should include instructional activities that focus on spatial sense, some teachers avoid the topic, usually because they have had only limited experiences with spatial topics themselves. Rest assured you can improve your spatial sense by completing the activities in this chapter and exploring some of Web sites listed at the end of this book.

2. Spatial Visualization

A key aspect of spatial visualization is the ability to slide, flip, turn, and otherwise move figures on a plane or in space. There are three different types of movement on a plane, also known as *transformations*: translation, reflection, and rotation. These movements are applied to shapes and figures in geometry and to functions and graphs in algebra.

Translations

When a pattern or figure is translated, it is shifted on the plane to a new position without changing its orientation. In the diagram below, triangle ABC is translated to a new position represented by triangle A′B′C′. Triangle A′B′C′ is called the image of the original triangle. Notice that image triangle A′B′C′ has the same size and shape as the original triangle and that the lengths of the sides and angle measures of the original triangle and its image are the same.

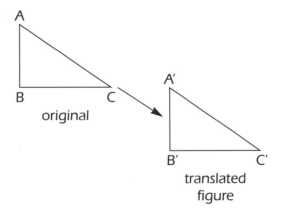

Translations, or slides, have a variety of applications, two of them being in fabric design and packaging. For example, a translation describes the relationship between a single postage stamp and the rest of the stamps on a sheet of stamps. Many fabric and wallpaper patterns are formed by translating a single geometric pattern. Can you identify the pattern that is translated in each of the following examples?

Dutch artist M. C. Escher is well known for using some types of translations (often referred to as *tessellations*) in his art work. A tessellation is made by repeating a single shape or pattern to cover a plane without any gaps or overlaps. If you place a transparency on the diagram of the Escher tessellation below and trace any one of the birds, you will find that the image of the bird can be translated up, down, left, or right onto another bird. You can continue to translate the bird's image onto every other bird in the diagram.

Reflections

A reflection, or flip, describes the orientation between an object and its image in a mirror. A figure in this type of transformation is flipped or reflected across a specific reflection line, as shown below.

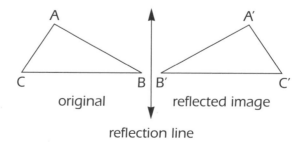

In a reflection, the reflected image has a different orientation from that of the original figure; it is its mirror image. Although the orientation of the reflected image and the original figure are different, the shape, lengths of the sides, and angle measures of both figures are the same.

Activity

Investigating Reflections

Objective: explore the properties of reflections.

Materials: pattern blocks.

Make the following design using pattern blocks. Reflect the diagram across the horizontal and vertical lines. Use pattern blocks to build the reflected images.

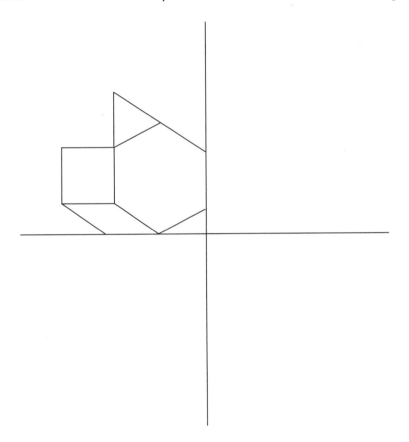

Things to Think About

What about the figure helped you form the reflection? Perhaps you noticed that in the original figure the triangle, square, and rhombus share a side with the hexagon. In reflections the relationships among shapes in the original figure and its reflected image are the same; thus, the reflected triangle, square, and rhombus still share a side with the hexagon. Sometimes it helps to analyze a figure shape by shape in order to figure out what the reflected image will look like. For example, compare the distance from the reflection line to one of the original pattern blocks and to its reflection. The distances should be the same. An important characteristic of reflections is that segments, angles, and shapes in a figure and its reflected image are congruent.

One method for checking whether the reflected image is accurate is to draw the original figure and its reflection on a piece of paper, and then fold the paper on the reflection line, checking that the figure and its reflection match up exactly. The reflected image should fold exactly on top of the original figure. Such a tactile verification of a reflection can be especially beneficial for younger students. Another method for verifying a reflected image is to place a mirror on the reflection line, next to the original figure. The reflection of the figure will be shown in the mirror. One way to help students create reflected images is first to let them use a mirror to "see" what the image looks like, then ask them to create the image on their own. They can use the mirror again later to check whether they created the reflected image accurately. It is important for students to discuss how they created the reflected image in order for them to articulate some of the relationships inherent in this transformation.

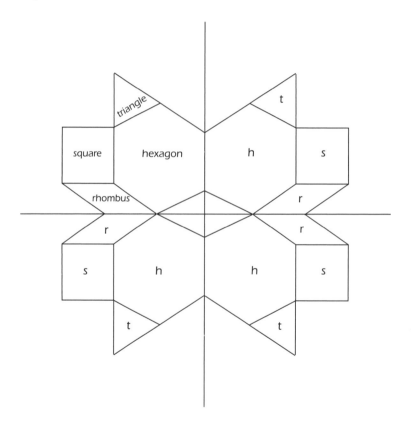

What happens to the image of a figure if it is reflected twice? Examine the image of the design after it is reflected across the horizontal grid line and then across the vertical grid line. Now reverse the process. Reflect the original design across the vertical grid line first, then reflect the image across the horizontal grid line. The two final images are the same. As in addition (and multiplication), where the order of the addends (or factors) does not affect the sum (product), the order of individual reflections does not affect the final image; the process of reflection is commutative. This connection between number properties and geometric properties demonstrates how some mathematics topics are interrelated. ▲

Related to reflecting images across reflection lines is finding a reflection line or symmetry line within a single figure. A figure has line symmetry when a line can be drawn through the figure that divides it into two parts that are reflected images of each other. The figures below are divided into two reflection images by a line of symmetry:

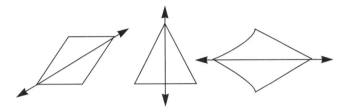

The line of symmetry divides each figure into two congruent parts. Each of these parts may be reflected across the line of symmetry onto the matching part of the figure. Commercial advertisements make use of the natural appeal of symmetric figures. Many logos have a line of symmetry, as do wallpaper and clothing patterns. Identify where the line(s) of symmetry are in the following logos.

Did you notice any lines of symmetry in the fabric patterns presented earlier in this chapter? You may want to return to those patterns and identify their symmetry lines.

Activity

Alphabet Symmetry

Objective: determine the line of symmetry in alphabet letters.

Some of the letters of our alphabet are symmetrical—that is, they have one or more lines of symmetry. Examine the capital letters below. Which of these letters have one or more lines of symmetry?

A B C D E F G H I J

K L M N O P Q R S T

U V W X Y Z

When we consider whether a figure or shape has one or more lines of symmetry, we are examining a characteristic or attribute of the shape. Mathematics educators suggest that more time be spent on comparing and classifying shapes in order to move students through the van Hiele hierarchy (see Chapter 10 for a detailed discussion). Line symmetry is one attribute that is often overlooked when analyzing shapes. However, relationships between congruent angles and sides may become more obvious when students answer questions like *why do regular shapes have a greater number of lines of symmetry than irregular shapes?* or *are the diagonals in this square [rectangle, kite, etc.] lines of symmetry? why or why not?* By asking students to sort and classify shapes using symmetry, we are having them focus on an important characteristic of shape versus a superficial feature like orientation on the page.

Rotations

The third type of transformation is a rotation. Rotations, like reflections, must be considered from two perspectives. First, a rotation can transform a figure by changing its orientation. For example, a Ferris wheel rotates around an axis or central point as it unloads and loads passengers. Or a dancer facing her partner may make a 360° spin on the dance floor and again face her partner. In addition, rotational symmetry is also an attribute of figures and shapes. As with reflectional symmetry, we can use this characteristic to analyze shapes and make conjectures about other related features.

In a rotation a figure is rotated any number of degrees about a given rotation point. In figure 1 a rotation of the flower around point A would mean spinning it around point A, which in this case is the center of the figure. Triangle ABC in figure 2 is rotated counterclockwise about point B, which is a point on the triangle. In figure 3 the triangle is rotated clockwise about point C, which is outside the figure.

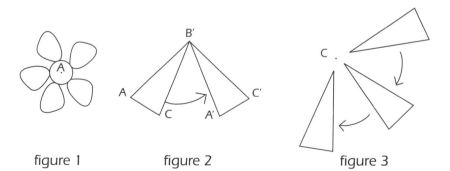

figure 1   figure 2   figure 3

Figures may be rotated about any specific point both within and outside the figure. However, most elementary school textbooks only use rotation points that are located at the center of the figure. When any figure is rotated one complete revolution about its center, a rotation of 360°, it rotates back onto itself. A figure that can be rotated onto itself by making less than a 360° rotation is said to have rotational symmetry. The capital letters H, I, N, O, S, X, and Z, for example, can be rotated onto themselves with only half a revolution, and are said to have 180° rotational symmetry. Squares have 90° rotational symmetry, since each turn of 90° brings the square's image back onto itself.

Activity

Rotational Symmetry on a Plane

Objective: explore the properties of rotations using pattern blocks.

Materials: tracing paper, pattern blocks.

1. Take a yellow hexagon from a set of pattern blocks and trace it onto a piece of paper. Place the hexagon block on top of the tracing, make a tiny mark on one angle, and rotate the pattern block until the block again coincides with the traced image underneath. What degree of rotational symmetry does a regular hexagon have?

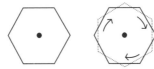

2. Examine the other pattern blocks. Do they all have rotational symmetry? If so, determine the degree of rotation necessary to rotate a block back onto itself.

Things to Think About

How many degrees of rotation were necessary to rotate the regular hexagon onto itself? One way to determine the degree of rotation is to mark one of the sides of the hexagon in order to keep track of the changing positions and to use a protractor to determine the number of degrees of rotation. If the hexagon is rotated 60°, then the sides and angles will coincide. If the hexagon is rotated another 60°, for a total of 120°, the shapes will again coincide. Thus, a 60° rotation describes the rotation for this figure. This is also known as a sixfold rotation because it requires six equal-size rotations for the turn image to be identical to the original. Will a 240° rotation rotate the hexagon onto itself? Yes, because it is a multiple of 60°.

Five of the six types of pattern blocks have rotational symmetry. Why? Examine the measure of the angles and lengths of the sides of the blocks. Notice that the regular polygons, whose sides and angles are all congruent, have rotational symmetry based on the number of angles in the shape. That is, the triangle has 120° rotational symmetry (360° ÷ 3), the square has 90° rotational symmetry (360° ÷ 4), and the hexagon has 60° rotational symmetry (360° ÷ 6). Suppose a five-sided regular pentagon is rotated onto itself. What is the degree of rotation for this shape? In this case the degree of rotation is 360° ÷ 5, or a 72° rotation. This is also known as fivefold symmetry. What can be said about the rotational symmetry of a regular polygon with *n* number of sides about its center? The symmetry is equal to *n*, the number of sides. Thus a regular octagon has eightfold symmetry and a regular decagon has tenfold symmetry. What about a circle? A circle has infinite rotational symmetry because every rotation, regardless of degree, will rotate a circle onto itself.

Both the blue and tan rhombi have twofold, or 180°, rotational symmetry. Why? Since opposite angles and sides are congruent in each rhombus, they can be turned onto themselves using a half turn. What about the trapezoid? Any figure that requires a full 360° revolution to be returned to the original does not have rotational symmetry. Two pairs of angles and two sides are congruent in the trapezoid, but since none of the congruent angles and sides are adjacent, the figure lacks rotational symmetry. ▲

As with translations and reflections, rotated figures are identical to or congruent with the original figure, with segment lengths and angle measures unchanged. Thus for all three types of transformations discussed so far the properties of shape—side length and measure of angle—are invariant (unchanged). The ability to understand and perform various transformations on a plane can help students with other aspects of geometry. For example, two figures with different orientations may be recognized as identical by using a combination of transformations to move one figure on top of the other. In the diagram below the figure on the left can be transformed into the other by a reflection followed by a translation (or slide) upward.

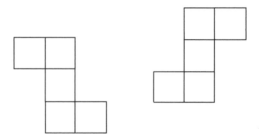

A complex figure may be simplified by using one or more of the three transformations to recognize congruent figures imbedded within it. Furthermore, these three transformations may be used to describe motion in everyday life. When a skateboarder goes down a hill, flips from facing left to facing right, then makes a 90° turn onto a side street, a comparison between his ending point and his starting point could be described by the combination of a translation, a reflection, and a rotation. Transformations are a constant source of fascination for mathematicians, artists, and engineers. They are used in kaleidoscopes, tessellations, tiles, and wallpaper and fabric patterns. (See pages 344–45 for Web sites where you can perform these transformations.)

Dilations

There is a fourth transformation in geometry called a *dilation*. It is different from the other three transformations because any transformation of a figure under a dilation will change the size of the figure. The other three transformations, translation, reflection, and rotation, are called *rigid transformations* because the resulting figure is congruent with the original figure. In a dilation the resulting figure is either larger or smaller than the original figure. When the resulting figure is larger than the original figure, the dilation is called an *enlargement*. When the resulting figure is smaller, the dilation is called a *reduction*. In the diagram below, △ABC is dilated to produce an enlargement (△QRS) and a reduction (△XYZ)

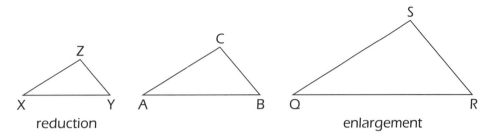

reduction   enlargement

How are all three triangles related to one another? Clearly they are not the same size, but they are the same shape. The corresponding sides of the three triangles are different, but their corresponding angles are congruent. All three triangles are similar to one another. Similar figures have congruent corresponding angles, and pairs of corresponding sides are in the same ratio. Notice that the orientations of the original figure and the dilated figures are also the same. Any dilation will produce a figure that is similar to the original figure and have the same orientation.

3. Transformations on the Coordinate Plane

All four transformations may be displayed on the coordinate plane. We will use △QRS, below, to demonstrate how to represent transformations on the coordinate plane.

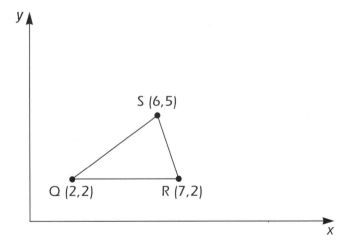

Translation

A translation involves sliding a point to another location. For example, if point Q were moved from (2,2) to Q′ (7,3) that would be a translation. In order for the same translation to hold for △QRS, every point of △QRS must be moved exactly the same way point Q was moved. In the case of point Q, the x coordinate increased by 5 and the y coordinate increased by 1. This same change must be made for every other point of △QRS. This change can be represented as $x + 5$ and $y + 1$, where x and y represent coordinates of any points in the original triangle. The new coordinates for point

R' and point S' may now be computed: R' $(7 + 5, 2 + 1)$ or $(12, 3)$; S' $(6 + 5, 5 + 1)$ or $(11,6)$. $\triangle QRS$ and $\triangle Q'R'S'$ are shown below on the coordinate plane.

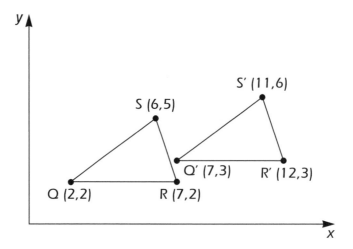

Reflection

Any reflection in the coordinate plane requires a specified reflection line. In this example we will use the y-axis as the reflection line. To reflect point Q across the reflection line to point Q' it is necessary to find a point that is the same distance from line y as point Q. Since point Q is two units to the *right* of line y, point Q' must be two units to the *left* of line y. The coordinates of point Q' are $(-2,2)$. Similarly, because point R is 7 units to the right of line y, then R' must be 7 units to the left of line y. The coordinates of point R' are $(-7,2)$. Finally, point S is 6 units to the right of line y, so point S' is 6 units to the left of line y. The coordinates of point S' are $(-6,5)$.

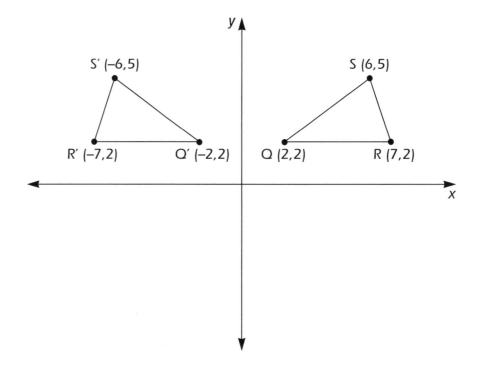

Exploring Reflections on the Coordinate Plane

Objective: examine the properties of reflections on the coordinate plane.

Materials: graph paper.

1. Determine the coordinates of △QRS when it is reflected across the x-axis. Verify your answers by drawing △QRS and △Q′R′S′ and folding the paper along the line of reflection (x-axis).
2. Suppose △QRS is reflected across the x-axis and the resulting triangle is then reflected across the y-axis. Will the final figure be the same as when △QRS is reflected across the y-axis first, and then reflected across the x-axis? Determine the coordinates and make a sketch to find out.

Things to Think About

When △QRS was reflected across the y-axis the y coordinate of point Q was not changed, but the x coordinate was changed, from 2 to −2. For point R and point S the y coordinate was not changed, but each x coordinate was changed to its opposite. For point R the x coordinate changed from 7 to −7, and for point S the x coordinate changed from 6 to −6. Similarly, when points are reflected across the x-axis the x coordinates do not change, but the y coordinates do. They will all be changed to the opposite value. Thus, when △QRS is reflected across the x-axis, point Q (2,2) becomes point Q′ (2,−2), point R (7,2) becomes R′ (7,−2) and Point S (6,5) becomes S′ (6,−5).

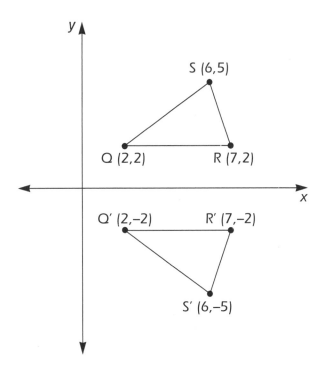

Reflections on the coordinate plane are commutative: that is, the order of reflections does not matter because the resulting figure is identical regardless of which reflection is performed first. Thus, the resulting triangle for reflecting

△QRS across the x-axis and then across the y-axis is the same as reflecting △QRS across the y-axis first and then across the x-axis.

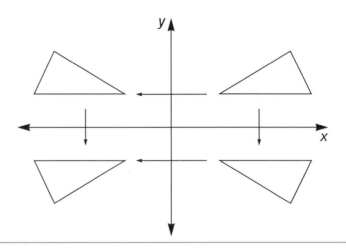

Rotation

Rotations are a bit more difficult to draw on the coordinate plane. In order to rotate a given figure in the coordinate plane you must have three given pieces of information: the rotation point, the angle of rotation, and the direction of rotation (clockwise or counterclockwise). In the diagram below △QRS is rotated 90° in a counterclockwise direction with point Q as the rotation point. A different rotation point or a different rotation angle will produce a different result, but the resulting figure will still be congruent to △QRS.

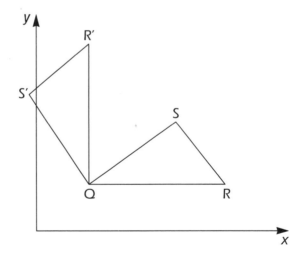

Dilation

A dilation involves enlarging or reducing the size of the original figure. In order to represent a dilation on the coordinate plane, the size of the enlargement or reduction must be stipulated by a *scale factor*. For example, suppose △QRS were to be dilated to

$\triangle Q'R'S'$ with a scale factor of 2. That means each coordinate of $\triangle QRS$ would be multiplied by a factor of 2 (point Q (2,2) dilates to Q' (4,4); point R (2,7) dilates to point R' (4,14) and point S (6,5) dilates to S' (12,10)). The resulting coordinates would then be the coordinates of the figure produced by enlarging $\triangle QRS$ by a scale factor of 2. $\triangle QRS$ and $\triangle Q'R'S'$ are shown below. Because the scale factor of the dilation was 2, the sides of $\triangle Q'R'S'$ are twice as long as the side lengths of $\triangle QRS$.

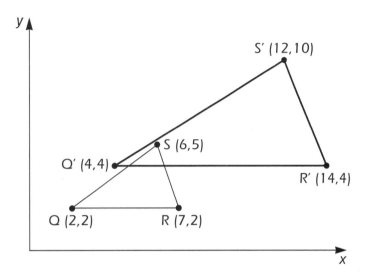

Other enlargements of $\triangle QRS$ may be computed and drawn by simply using a different scale factor. What about a reduction? What scale factor will produce a reduction? In order to reduce a figure, the coordinates must be decreased. This is accomplished by using a scale factor between 0 and 1. For example, to reduce $\triangle QRS$ to a triangle with sides that are half as long, use a scale factor of $\frac{1}{2}$ and multiply each point in the coordinate pair by $\frac{1}{2}$. For a triangle that has side lengths that are $\frac{1}{3}$ as long, use a scale factor of $\frac{1}{3}$, and so forth.

Activity

Building Pentominoes

Objective: show how knowing about translations, reflections, and rotations can be applied to making pentominoes.

Materials: graph paper or square tiles.

Using graph paper or square tiles, sketch or make pentominoes, figures in which five squares are combined so that each square shares an entire side with at least one other square. There are twelve different pentominoes.

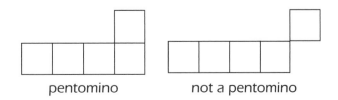

pentomino   not a pentomino

Things to Think About

Translation, reflection, and rotation are all used when making pentominoes. For example, squares are translated across the plane into positions that form different pentominoes. Completed pentominoes are flipped and rotated in order to identify identical pentominoes. Are the three pentominoes shown below the same or different pentominoes?

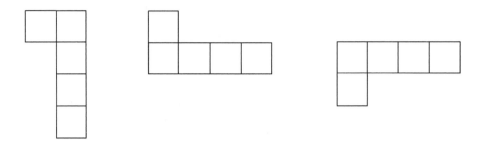

When the first pentomino is rotated 90° counterclockwise, its orientation is the same as the last pentomino. When the middle pentomino is reflected across a horizontal line it also has the same orientation as the last pentomino. Thus, these three pentominoes are identical.

Did you find all twelve pentominoes? You can systematically translate squares to form all twelve. Form the first pentomino by placing five squares in a row. Next place four squares in a row and translate one to different locations. Remember to check to see whether you already have a specific pentomino.

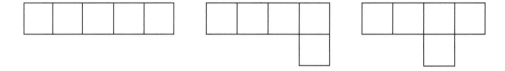

Now place three squares in a row and move the other two squares to form eight more pentominoes:

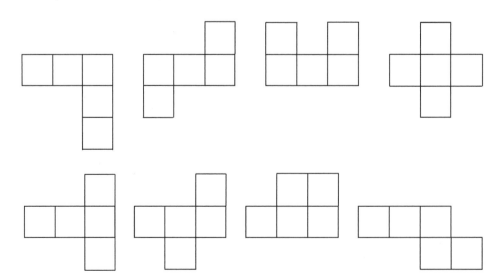

The last pentomino has only two squares in any given row:

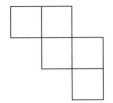

▲

4. Spatial Orientation

Spatial orientation has to do with the ability to view a specific figure or object from different viewpoints and to integrate the images to form a coherent mental model of the figure or object. When you examine a car by walking around it or look at yourself in a three-way mirror, you are using spatial orientation. Another way to think of it is in terms of a classroom seating chart, which is typically designed to be read from the front of the room. If you designed a new seating chart with a viewpoint from the rear of the room instead, students who were in the front of the old seating chart would now be in the back, and vice versa.

Our point of view affects how we read a seating chart, a floor plan, or a map. In order to standardize readings, maps and charts are oriented along the four compass points. Many students have difficulty making sense of maps, charts, floor plans, and diagrams because they are not sure how to orient themselves in terms of a viewpoint. Instructional activities that involve using a coordinate grid, reading a map, or using a compass require students to orient themselves in terms of space.

In one type of spatial-orientation task, you are given a series of directions and must determine your final orientation. For example: Begin by facing north. Do an about-face, and then make a 90° turn to the right. Next make another about-face, and then turn 90° to the left. In which direction are you now facing? One way to solve this type of problem is with a diagram. Another method is to use an object like a pencil to mimic the movements. A third method is to act out the directions with body movements. The diagram below replicates the directions.

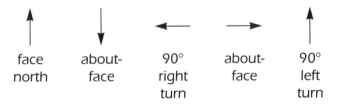

Experiences with tasks like this can improve students' ability to orient themselves spatially and reduce their need to act out the problem or use diagrams. Nevertheless, such methods are generally not unreasonable and should not be discouraged.

Translating Between Dimensions

Another aspect of spatial orientation is the ability to coordinate and integrate two-dimensional sketches to form a three-dimensional structure. In mathematics, we have to coordinate views of structures when calculating volume and surface area. An ability to move flexibly between two and three dimensions is also needed in such diverse fields as architecture, biochemistry, art, and graphic design. Furthermore, since powerful computer programs readily translate between dimensions, it is now even more important for individuals to be able to make sense of this type of material. The following activity asks you to translate between two-dimensional images of pentominoes and three-dimensional open boxes!

Activity

The Nets of an Open Cube

Objective: use spatial visualization to connect two-dimensional drawings and three-dimensional objects.

Some pentominoes will fold up to form a box without a top—an open cube. Pentominoes that fold up to form an open cube are also called *nets*. A net is a two-dimensional figure that folds up to form a three-dimensional structure. Cut out each pentomino from Activity 5 and, without folding, identify those pentominoes that are nets of an open cube.

Things to Think About

Activities with nets enable students to transform two-dimensional figures into three-dimensional objects and back again. When students move objects between two and three dimensions they begin to build a foundation for understanding solid geometry figures that will help them in subsequent mathematics courses.

There are eight pentominoes that can be folded to form an open cube. How can you verify that a pentomino when folded forms an open cube? One method is to fold each cut-out pentomino. The physical activity of folding and unfolding pentominoes can help you visualize the relationship between the two-dimensional pentomino and its corresponding three-dimensional figure. Did you find any common features of nets that fold into open boxes? If a pentomino has three squares in a row and single squares on each side of the row, as shown below, then it folds into an open cube:

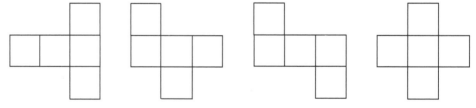

Will a pentomino with four squares in row fold into an open cube? Yes! The four squares in a row fold to form the sides of the cube. The single remaining square then folds up to form the bottom of the open cube:

Examine the last two pentominoes that fold into an open cube:

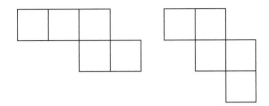

Describe how these pentominoes can be folded into an open cube. ▲

When we represent a three-dimensional structure, such as that in figure 1, below, in two dimensions, we need three different views, called *orthogonal* views: a top view (figure 2), a front view (figure 3), and a right view (figure 4).

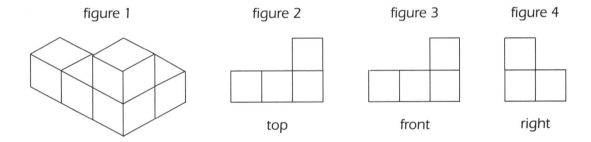

figure 1   figure 2   figure 3   figure 4

top   front   right

The four drawings above demonstrate two different ways to represent three-dimensional figures. Figure 1 shows the entire figure in a single sketch that indicates depth. It is drawn in perspective: that is, the depth of the structure is represented by drawing the portions at the back in a smaller scale. Three-dimensional buildings are often drawn on isometric paper (triangular dot or grid paper):

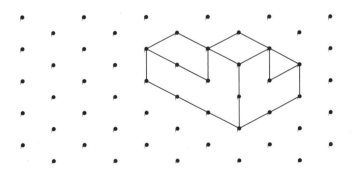

Figures 2, 3, and 4 show three different "head-on" views of the structure. There is no sense of depth in any of these head-on drawings, and it is impossible to picture the three-dimensional structure based on only one of the views—all three are necessary. Students will be asked to interpret sketches, compute surface areas and volumes, and draw cross sections of three-dimensional objects as part of their problem solving in middle and high school mathematics courses. (See page 345 for a Web site that can be used to draw isometric figures.)

Activity

Analyzing Block Structures

Objective: sketch orthogonal views of three-dimensional block structures.

Materials: cubes.

Build the following structures with cubes. Draw a top view, a front view, and a side view of each structure.

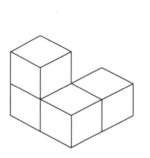 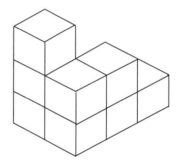

Things to Think About

How did you begin? Did you try to visualize the view from the front of the structure and then from the side, or did you physically move around the structure in order to see each view? Does it matter what face you used for the front? No. You can select any face of the structure as the front of your sketch, and then make related drawings for the top and the side. Although which face you select as the front affects your subsequent drawings, the three sketches beginning with any front view should provide enough information to build the original structure. Look at the three views you just drew. Can you see how they must be coordinated to make each building? ▲

Activity

Building Block Structures from Two-Dimensional Views

Objective: build three-dimensional block structures using two-dimensional orthogonal drawings.

Materials: cubes.

Study the three views of the two structures on the next page and use cubes to build each structure.

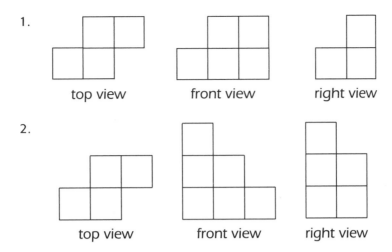

1.

top view   front view   right view

2.

top view   front view   right view

Things to Think About

Instead of trying to incorporate all three views into the structure simultaneously, you may find that it is easier to make a model using only two of the views, top and front for example, and then adjust your structure for the side view. The top view of the first figure shows that the base of the structure, or "footprint," consists of four cubes in the configuration shown. The front view shows that there are at least two columns in the footprint that are each two blocks tall. Finally, the right view shows that any two-block column is in the back row, not the front row. The solution to example 1 is shown below. Figure 1 shows the footprint of the structure; the numbers in the squares indicate the height of each column on that square. Figure 2 is a three-dimensional sketch of the figure.

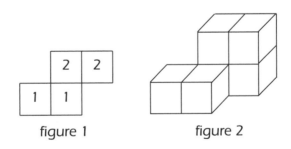

figure 1   figure 2

How are the front and back views of a structure related? the left and right side views? In both cases, one view is the mirror image or a reflection of the other.

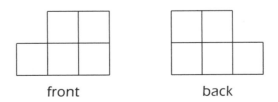

front   back

More than one structure can be constructed for example 2:

	figure 1			figure 2	
	2	1		2	1
3	1*		3	2*	

The square marked with an asterisk may contain either a one-block column or a two-block column. You may want to build both possible structures and then examine the front, top, and right views to verify that the head-on views for both structures are the same. (There is a Web site listed on page 345 where you can build and examine block structures such as these.) ▲

Cross Sections

The relationship between two and three dimensions may also be explored with cross sections. A cross section is the figure formed by the intersection of a plane and a solid figure. For example, if you cut a sphere with a plane, you will get a circle as a cross section, much like cutting an orange with a knife. What cross section shapes can you get from cutting a cylinder? There are a number of possibilities. Several of them are shown below. In the case of a cylinder it depends on the angle of the plane in relationship to the orientation of the cylinder.

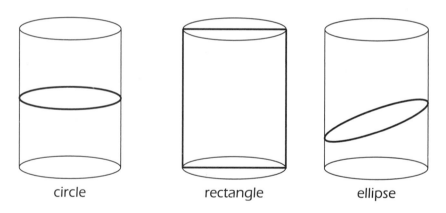

circle   rectangle   ellipse

Activity

Cross Sections of a Cube

Objective: discover and draw the cross sections of a cube.

Materials: plasticine, clay, and string (or plastic knife), or hollow plastic cube and colored water.

How many different cross sections of a cube can you find? You might build a cube out of clay and cut the clay cube using a taut string or knife to form the cross sections. Or you can fill a hollow plastic cube about one third full with colored water and tilt the cube to discover cross sections. The cross section is represented by the surface of the water.

Things to Think About

A number of different cross sections are possible. Some are displayed below, but there are many more. For example, there are many other triangles and rectangles possible in addition to the ones shown here. When a plane produces a cross section such as a triangle, changing the angle of the plane will produce additional triangles that are different from the first triangle cross section.

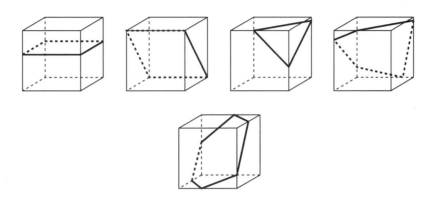

See page 345 for a Web site that will draw cross sections. ▲

Teaching Spatial Sense

Spatial perception is a crucial skill for work in geometry and other advanced mathematics courses. Activities in elementary school that focus on analyzing symmetry and other characteristics of figures help students move through the lower van Hiele levels of geometric understanding. In later grades students will be expected to interpret two-dimensional figures that represent three-dimensional figures. As students progress through their mathematics courses in middle school, they will examine additional aspects of reflections, using coordinate points to describe reflections across the x-axis (horizontal grid line) and the y-axis (vertical grid line). They will also interpret, sketch, and analyze three-dimensional figures. In high school, study of formal geometry will extend students' understanding of two-dimensional drawings and the three-dimensional figures they represent. Subsequent mathematics courses explore two-dimensional figures on the coordinate plane and three-dimensional figures in coordinate space. Students who have developed their spatial perception skills are better able to understand, interpret, and use visual data. The tie-in to geometry is obvious, but general problem-solving skills also are likely to be enhanced.

Questions for Discussion

1. How would you respond to someone who says, "Spatial sense comes naturally."
2. What is the difference between spatial visualization and spatial orientation? Why are both important?

3. Make a list of questions to ask students about translations, reflections, rotations, and dilations that will focus their attention on the mathematical relationships inherent to these transformations. Answer your questions.
4. Examine a students' mathematics textbook at a grade level of interest. Look through the book and find all instructional activities that involve spatial sense. Classify the activities. What is included in this text series? What is missing? Describe an activity you might want to include in instruction based on your analysis of the text.

12

Measurement

We measure things every day. This morning you may have weighed yourself; poured two cups of water into the coffeemaker; checked the temperature in order to decide what to wear; cut enough gift wrap off the roll to wrap a present; noted the distance to school on your car's odometer; monitored both your car's traveling speed and gas gauge; kept an eye on the time so you weren't late for a staff meeting; and asked your students to cover a bulletin board with colored paper as background for a display. It's clear that as a practical matter students need to learn about weight, capacity, length, mass, time, temperature, area, and volume.

In spite of how regularly we use measurement, results of national and international assessments indicate that U.S. students of all ages are significantly deficient in their knowledge of measurement concepts and skills. In order to design instructional sequences that will improve students' abilities to understand and use measurement, it is important to reflect on the components of learning to measure as well as on the many relationships within measurement systems.

1. Learning to Measure

The process of measuring consists of three main steps. First, you need to select an attribute of something that you wish to measure (the area of a playground, for example). Second, you need to choose an appropriate unit of measurement (in this case, square yards). Finally, you need to determine the number of units. This last step is usually accomplished by using some sort of measuring tool.

What concepts must students know and what skills must they possess in order to measure attributes following the above steps? Most researchers agree that there are four components of measuring: *conservation* (objects maintain their same size and shape when measured), *transitivity* (two objects can be compared in terms of a measurable quality using a third object), *units* (the type of units used to measure an object depends on the attribute being measured), and *unit iteration* (the units must be repeated, or *iterated*, in order to determine the measure of an object). Estimation, precision, and accuracy are other important ideas (described later) that contribute to students' understanding of measurement. For students to learn how to measure accurately and be able to use measurement concepts effectively, instructional sequences must focus on these components and must ask students to perform real measurements. Measurement should definitely be taught "hands on."

Early measurement experiences usually involve direct comparisons—two students decide who is taller by standing next to each other. However, direct comparisons are not always possible; therefore we require some sort of unit with which to compare attributes. In developing the concept of a measuring unit, we often first emphasize naturally occurring nonstandard units: the length of an unsharpened pencil, the weight of a paper clip, or the capacity of a paper cup. Historically, nonstandard units have been based on parts of the human body—a *cubit* (length from elbow to end of longest finger), a *pace* (walking step), and a *span* (distance from tip of thumb to tip of little finger with fingers spread out). The problem with nonstandard units like these is that the dimensions vary from person to person. Measuring with nonstandard units usually leads students to conclude that standard units are necessary.

Once students make sense of the concepts of conservation, transitivity, units, and unit iteration, they start to use standard units in meaningful ways. Measuring with standard units provides additional contexts for students to clarify measurement ideas and procedures. Because there are many standard units and many relationships among them, it takes a number of years for students to gain the necessary skills to use measurement tools carefully and accurately and to apply measurement concepts meaningfully.

Conservation

Conservation is the principle that an object maintains the same size and shape if it is rearranged, transformed, or divided in various ways. Students who understand this principle realize that a pencil's length remains constant when it is placed in different orientations. They understand that two pencils that are the same length remain equal in length when one pencil is placed ahead of the other:

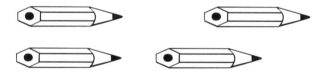

They realize that two differently shaped figures have the same area if they have the same component pieces. They agree that a jigsaw puzzle covers the same amount of space whether the puzzle is completed or in separate pieces. Piaget established ages when most children grasp the conservation of length, area, and volume. Today these benchmarks are questioned, since children's experiences with materials seem to play heavily into whether or not children understand conservation in a particular area. It is generally believed that the principle of conservation cannot be taught and is part of a child's natural cognitive development. However, children do not develop the ability to recognize this principle in a vacuum. Many experiences are needed to give a child the background from which the idea of conservation can develop. For example, covering areas with pattern blocks is a common instructional task. By having students discuss whether the blocks change size when they are rotated or flipped and whether the space covered by a completed design is the same as that covered by the component parts, we can help them grapple with the idea of conservation. Students benefit from participating in measurement activities, since components of these tasks support the development of the idea of conservation.

Transitivity

When two objects cannot be compared directly, it is necessary to compare them by means of a third object. To do this an individual must understand intuitively the mathematical notion of transitivity (if A = B and B = C then A = C; if A < B and B < C then A < C; or if A > B and B > C then A > C). For example, to compare the length of a bookshelf in one room with the length of a desk in another room, cut a string that is the same length as the bookshelf. The piece of string can then be compared with the desk. If the string is the same length as the desk then we know that the desk is the same length as the bookshelf. Conservation precedes the understanding of transitivity because a child must be sure a tool's length (or area, or volume, etc.) will stay the same when moved in the process of measuring. Students in the early elementary grades need experiences in which they must compare measures indirectly. For example, one first-grade teacher asked his students to compare the length of their classroom, the length of the corridor, and how high the windowsills of their second-floor classroom were above the ground. Students used string to measure the length of the classroom and then compared the string with the corridor (the corridor was longer). They then used string to measure how high the windowsills were above the ground and compared this string with the length of the classroom (the classroom length was longer). Thus, they concluded that the length of the corridor was longer than the height of the windowsills from the ground.

Units and Unit Iteration

In order to determine the measurement unit, students must understand what attribute is being measured. They must realize that when measuring distance a linear measure is appropriate. If measuring area, two-dimensional units such as squares are needed to cover the surface. A three-dimensional unit is needed if measuring volume.

Another key point for students to grasp is that the chosen unit influences the number of units. The relationship between size of unit and number of units is often referred to as the *compensatory principle*. It states that the smaller the unit used to measure a distance (area, volume, etc.), the more of those units will be needed. Likewise, the larger the unit, the fewer that will be needed to cover the distance (or area, volume, etc.). For example, a package weighed in grams results in a greater number of units (2,000 g) than if the package was weighed in kilograms (2 kg). This inverse relationship—a greater number of smaller units—is a conceptually difficult idea that we need to have young students explore and discuss.

Unit iteration is the repetition of a single unit. It is an abstract concept for young children. If they are measuring the length of a desk with straws, it is easy enough for them to lay straws out across the desk and then count them. However, if only one straw is available, then the unit (straw) must be iterated (repeated). Students first have to visualize the total length in terms of the single unit and then reposition the unit repeatedly. Students have difficulty keeping track of where the unit was last placed and the total number of units used. In addition, when first learning to measure, they are not concerned with placing units right next to each other with no holes or gaps.

Estimation, Precision, and Accuracy

Estimation is an important part of measurement. Often students are first asked to estimate a measure and then to check by measuring. Estimating helps students internalize measurement concepts, and your students' estimates will let you know how familiar they are with the size of a particular unit.

Estimation skills improve if students have many opportunities to use the same units again and again and to establish referent measures with those units. Students often make poor estimates as to size. This is usually because they aren't familiar enough with the various units of measurement and confuse one with another. It's beneficial to give children repeated experience using the same unit and also to give them a chance to sort out which units are appropriate for particular measurements. For example, the length of a room is best measured in feet or meters, while it's more appropriate to measure the dimensions of a picture frame in inches or centimeters.

Benchmarks can help students develop a working familiarity with various measurement units. For example, students might determine that a meter is about the height of a doorknob, the average third grader weighs between 60 and 80 pounds, an inch is the length of a finger between two of the knuckles, a dollar bill is about 6 inches long, a basketball rim is about 3 meters off the ground, or the weight of a full lunch box is about 1 kilogram. Such referent benchmarks enable students to estimate measures more accurately using these units (*if 1 meter is about the height of a doorknob, how many meters high do you estimate the classroom's walls to be?* or *if a third grader weighs approximately 30 kilograms, how much do you estimate an adult woman will weigh?*).

Benchmarks are also important for giving students some sense of how the customary and metric measurements relate to one another. Certainly students can convert inches into centimeters using the appropriate conversion factor, but multiplication or division by two-place decimal conversion factors is unlikely to help students create any real understanding of how inches and centimeters are related. Here are a few benchmarks that relate customary and metric measurement units:

> A liter is slightly larger than a quart.
>
> An inch is a bit longer than 2 centimeters.
>
> A meter is a hand-width longer than a yard.
>
> A kilogram is a little more than 2 pounds.
>
> A kilometer is about $\frac{2}{3}$ of a mile.

When conversion benchmarks such as these are combined with earlier referent benchmarks, then students will be able to make more accurate measurement estimations using either measurement system. (See page 345 for Web sites where students can estimate various measurements in an interactive setting.)

Measurements are different from "counts." By counting we can state exactly how many of some object is being considered: 10 apples, 8,750 people, 913 books, or 52 states. But measurements cannot be made exactly. Why not? Measuring devices such as rulers, thermometers, graduated cylinders, and scales have hash marks that indicate units and subunits. When we measure we compare a measurable attribute to the closest hash mark. But each of these units can be subdivided repeatedly even further allowing us (if possible) to use these new finer subunits to measure. Because a unit of measure can always be divided into smaller subunits, measurement is said to be by its very nature approximate.

The precision of a measurement depends upon the size of the smallest measuring unit. For example, whether a measurement is to the nearest meter, the nearest decimeter, the nearest centimeter, or the nearest millimeter determines its precision. The smaller the interval, the more we have "narrowed it down," and thus the more precise the measurement. Measurements made using small units (e.g., square inches) are more precise than measurements made using larger units (e.g., square yards).

The accuracy of a measure is how correctly a measurement has been made. Accuracy can be affected either by the person doing the measuring or by the measurement tool. Young children often do not measure accurately for a number of reasons. Sometimes they do not know how to interpret the subunits on a measuring device. Other times they may iterate units inaccurately, leaving holes and gaps by not paying attention to the continuous nature of the attribute. Sometimes a measurement tool produces inaccurate measurements (a scale improperly balanced, a broken timer). In addition, two measurements can both be accurate (e.g., a pumpkin weighs 7 pounds on one scale and 6 pounds 15 ounces on another scale), but one is more precise than another. Can you figure out why?

Accuracy and precision are often confused because they mean the same thing to many people. Older students need to discuss precision and accuracy as well as become comfortable with using language that features the approximate nature of measurement—*the stick is about two meters long; to be more precise, using this measuring tape, the stick is 197 centimeters long.* In later grades, students learn to record measurements more precisely using intervals with upper and lower boundaries and how to determine the accuracy of a measure using relative errors.

Activity

Tangram Discoveries

Objective: compare measurements of perimeter and area using nonstandard units.

Materials: a seven-piece tangram puzzle.

Take the two small triangles and the one medium triangle. Using just these three pieces (but all three), make five different (that is, noncongruent) polygons: square, rectangle, triangle, parallelogram, and trapezoid. Trace each figure and determine which polygon has the greatest perimeter, the least perimeter, the greatest area, and the least area. As you work with the tangram pieces, think about how you are using your understanding of conservation, transitivity, units, unit iteration, and estimation to help you answer the questions.

Things to Think About

The first part of this task highlights the role spatial visualization plays in some measurement activities (see Chapter 11). If you haven't had much experience combining and recombining shapes into new shapes, you may have found the task of building the five polygons frustrating. One way to begin is to place the medium triangle and one small triangle so that they form the configuration below:

Keeping the position of these two shapes constant, place the remaining small triangle in different locations. You can create four of the five shapes from this starting position. Your ability to visualize how shapes fit together is affected by experiences—using shapes to make new shapes helps you become better at this sort of visualization activity. Try making the five polygons again. Was it easier?

Why aren't the areas of the polygons different? Each polygon is made using one medium and two small triangles; because their component parts are identical, their areas are as well. Even though we adults understand the conservation of area, visual cues sometimes override our logical reasoning. The perimeters of the shapes, however, are not the same. When looking at the shapes, some people may focus on their perimeters and therefore erroneously conclude that their areas are different.

Is there a way to determine which perimeter is greatest and which is least without using a ruler? Notice that all three triangles are isosceles right triangles. In isosceles right triangles, the two legs are congruent (the same length) and the hypotenuse (the side opposite the right angle) is longer than the legs. There are some convenient relationships between these triangular pieces in the tangram puzzle: one side of the medium triangle is the same length as the hypotenuse of the small triangle, and one side of the small triangle is equal in length to half of the hypotenuse of the medium triangle. These relationships enable us to measure the perimeters of the five polygons in terms of two units: a side of the small triangle and a side of the medium triangle.

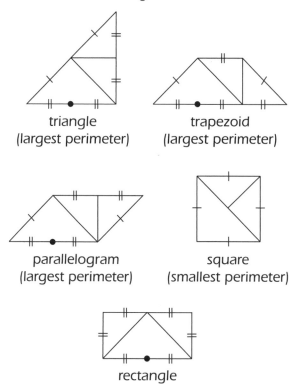

triangle
(largest perimeter)

trapezoid
(largest perimeter)

parallelogram
(largest perimeter)

square
(smallest perimeter)

rectangle

Which polygon has the greatest perimeter? As it turns out, the greatest perimeter is shared by three of the polygons: the triangle, trapezoid, and parallelogram have a perimeter of two medium-triangle sides and four small-triangle sides. The square's perimeter, equivalent to four medium-triangle sides, is the smallest. ▲

Even when students understand conservation, transitivity, units, and unit iteration, they may have difficulty with measurement concepts and skills. Certain aspects of measurement make it a complex school topic. First, there are many kinds of units, and some units have the same name (e.g., ounces that measure weight and ounces that measure capacity). Second, students must become competent users of two measurement systems (the English or U.S. customary system and the metric system) that are built on very different relationships. Finally, some measurements are additive (e.g., length, area, time) in that the measures can be combined. For example, the distance around a window frame is the sum of the length of the parts. Other measures cannot be meaningfully added (e.g., rates). A trip in which you drive 40 mph to work and 30 mph home does not imply you went 70 mph! Helping students make correct generalizations with regard to all three considerations is challenging.

Measurement materials and instructional activities are different from those that support the development of number concepts in part because of the type of data. Numerical information or data that have only whole number values are referred to as *discrete*, or countable, data. Discrete data are used to describe sets of objects such as the number of people sitting at a table or the number of home runs hit during a baseball game. When counting discrete items, students form a one-to-one correspondence between numeral and item. On the other hand, *continuous* data can have any value, including fractional values. By its nature, measurement deals with continuous data—$7\frac{1}{2}$ inches; 12.8 pounds; and 1 hour, 13 minutes, 25 seconds. But in order to measure, we divide continuous quantities into discrete units. Understanding and interpreting measurements can be problematic because the units in continuous data (e.g., a length of 4.5 meters) run together on our measurement tools—they are not distinctly separate.

2. The Metric Measurement System

The metric system was developed by the French Academy of Sciences in 1791. A single, universally accepted system of measurement was needed because commerce among countries had increased substantially. Interestingly, Thomas Jefferson tried to convince the United States Congress at that time to adopt the base ten system of measurement, but his proposal was rejected. Today the United States is the only major nation that does not use the metric system extensively.

Changes have occurred in the metric system over time because of advances in technology. What has evolved is the International System of Units, which is abbreviated as SI. The units in the SI system are based on scientific formulas and natural constants. Strictly speaking there are differences between the metric system and the SI system. However, because there are so many similarities and the differences are slight from a nonscientific point of view, the SI system is often called the "metric system."

The metric system defines standard units for length, mass, temperature, area, and volume. Those units are meter (length), kilogram (mass), degrees Celsius (temperature), square meter (area), and cubic meter (volume). Larger and smaller units are obtained by multiplying or dividing the standard units by powers of ten. The ease with which conversions can be made (by moving a decimal point) within this measurement system are one of the reasons it has been adopted so universally. Greek prefixes indicate units larger than the standard unit—multiples of 10 (deka-), 100 (hecto-), and 1,000 (kilo-). Latin prefixes indicate units smaller than the standard unit—0.1 (deci-), 0.01 (centi-), and 0.001 (milli-). These relationships are summarized below:

Metric Prefixes	Equivalent Units
kilo (k)	1,000 basic units
hecto (h)	100 basic units
deka (da)	10 basic units
deci (d)	0.1 basic unit
centi (c)	0.01 basic unit
milli (m)	0.001 basic unit

Measuring Length

The standard unit of length is the meter (m). It was originally established as one ten-millionth of the distance from the equator to the north pole, but since 1960 has been defined to be precisely 1,650,763.73 wavelengths, in a vacuum, of the radiation corresponding to the transition between two electronic energy levels of the krypton-86 atom. Applying some of the prefixes mentioned earlier, a kilometer is equivalent to 1,000 meters; a dekameter is 10 meters; a decimeter is $\frac{1}{10}$ of a meter; a centimeter is $\frac{1}{100}$ of a meter; and a millimeter is $\frac{1}{1000}$ of a meter.

Many Americans do not have a strong intuitive sense of metric lengths. This may be due, in part, to our limited experience in using metric measures to estimate and measure.

Activity

Exploring Centimeters, Meters, and Kilometers

Objective: develop measurement referents and benchmarks for metric lengths.

Materials: centimeter tape measure.

Measurement tasks are much easier when you have referents for units and sub-units. Find an object that is one centimeter in length (check the width of your pinkie finger). Now use this measure (your referent) to find three additional objects that each measure approximately one centimeter.

Determine the length of your hand span in centimeters and use your hand span to approximate different measures such as the width of a desk or the circumference of a bottle to the nearest centimeter. Try iterating your hand span. Check your estimates using a tape measure. You should practice until you feel confident that you can estimate short lengths in centimeters.

Find a common object or a body measurement that is about one meter long. (The height of a doorknob from the floor and measurements such as your waist, arm length, and distance from hip to floor are possible referents.) Use your referent measure to help identify three other objects that are each one meter long. Check by measuring the objects. What is the ceiling height in meters in the room in which you are sitting?

Determine the length of your normal walking pace in meters. Pace out the dimensions of a large room. How long is the room? How wide? Use the length of your pace to determine a 100-meter distance (one tenth of a kilometer). Use this distance to estimate the length of 1 kilometer. If possible, walk that far. How long did it take you to walk 1 kilometer?

Things to Think About

Linking body measures such as the width of a finger or the size of a normal step to metric units helps you internalize the size of the metric units. In addition, nonstandard units can be used to estimate lengths as long as you know the equivalent standard measures. For example, if you know that your hand span is twenty centimeters, you can use this information both to estimate lengths and informally verify measurements. Common objects can also be used as referents.

How do you determine the length of your walking pace in meters? Measure out a distance of at least ten meters. Conduct an experiment and count the number of normal steps it takes to walk this distance. Conduct three or four trials and then find the average number of paces. If you conduct an experiment only once (no matter how simple it is) your data may not be representative. For example, the first time you walked the ten-meter distance you may have taken longer or shorter steps than normal; this number of paces would not be representative of your normal walking pace. However, by collecting data from a number of trials it is more likely that the average will be representative.

How do you determine the time it takes to walk a kilometer? One method is to use a watch with a second hand to find your walking speed for a shorter distance (10 meters or 100 meters). If it takes 45 seconds (0.75 minute) to walk 100 meters, you can multiply 0.75×10 to determine that it will take about 7.5 minutes to walk a kilometer. (This is a fast walking pace; it takes most adults 9 to 12 minutes to walk a kilometer.)

Somewhere your school may have a trundle wheel, an instrument that measures longer distances more accurately. A trundle wheel has a long handle that allows you to wheel it along with you as you walk. Each time the wheel completes a revolution, a click is heard. A metric trundle wheel typically has a circumference of one meter, so counting the number of clicks tells you the number of meters traveled. You can also determine the length of one kilometer using the speedometer of your car: a kilometer is approximately 0.6 mile. ▲

Measuring Area

The standard metric unit for area is the square meter (m^2). This unit is a square that is one meter in length on each side. Square meters are used to measure the amount of carpeting for a room. Smaller units such as square centimeters are used to measure the amount of gift wrap for a present, and larger units (hectares) are used when estimating the land area of a forest. A hectare is a standard metric unit that is equivalent to 10,000 square meters.

In order to solve problems that involve area measurements, students must understand the concepts of conservation, transitivity, and unit iteration as they apply to area. In addition, they must understand that:

▲ Area is an expression of how much surface is covered, not a length.
▲ Some shapes cover the plane (a flat surface) more completely than others.
▲ The size of the unit used to designate how much surface is covered determines the number of units.
▲ Areas of regular and irregular shapes can be determined by counting square units or using formulas.

Conversions between units of area are not as straightforward as conversions between units of length. The effect of changing the dimensions of a shape on that shape's subsequent area can be perplexing.

Activity

Exploring Square Meters and Square Centimeters

Objective: explore the relationship between linear and area measure.

Construct a square meter from sheets of newsprint. Place meter sticks showing centimeters along two sides of the square meter. Draw one square centimeter on the paper. Imagine covering the square meter with square centimeters. How many square centimeters are needed to cover the square meter? What is the relationship between a square meter and square centimeters? Use this relationship to determine the area, in square centimeters, of a rectangular room that measures 3.2 meters by 5.5 meters.

Things to Think About

In order to convert square meters to square centimeters you have to consider that two dimensions—length and width—contribute to making a square. Each of the dimensions of a square meter is equivalent to 10 decimeters or 100 centimeters. These two dimensions must be multiplied in order to cover the surface. Thus, 1 square meter is equivalent to 100 square decimeters or 10,000 square centimeters. Visualizing the smaller units may help you understand why there are so many square centimeters in a square meter.

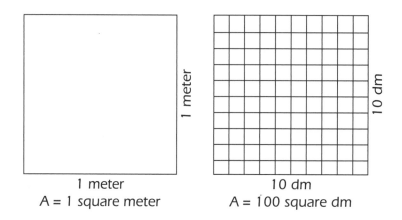

1 meter
A = 1 square meter

10 dm
A = 100 square dm

How do you determine the area of the room? Using the formula $l \times w$, the size of the room can first be determined in square meters ($3.2 \times 5.5 = 17.6$ m²). Since there are 10,000 square centimeters in a square meter, the number of square meters (17.6) must be multiplied by 10,000 (not 100). The area of the room is 176,000 cm². The area could also be found by converting the dimensions of the room to centimeters and then calculating the area (320 cm $\times$ 550 cm = 176,000 cm²). A common error when converting one unit of area to another is to disregard one of the dimensions and only multiply (or divide) by one set of equivalent units (that is, multiply 17.6 m² by 100 instead of 10,000, because there are 100 cm in a meter). When students have created a model of a square meter with square centimeters drawn on it and discussed the relationship between these two units, they are much less likely to make this type of error. ▲

The relationship between the dimensions of a figure and the area of that figure is *analogous* to the relationship that occurs when one square unit of measurement is converted to another. One square meter is equivalent in size to a square that is 100 centimeters per side. Since a smaller unit of measurement is used to determine the length of each side, the numerical value of the area based on these smaller square units will be greater—10,000 (100 $\times$ 100) times greater! The area of the original square meter doesn't change, but the size of the unit used to measure the area does.

Measuring Volume and Capacity

Volume is the measure of three-dimensional objects; it tells us the amount of space something takes up. We also think of volume as the amount an object will hold or the number of units needed to fill the object. The volume of objects can be found using liquid measures such as liters and gallons and solid measures such as cubic centimeters and cubic yards. Often when measuring liquids or describing the size of containers that hold liquids, we refer to volume as *capacity*. However, people use both terms, readily switching between them.

The standard metric unit for volume is the cubic meter—a cube that is one meter on each size. This unit is used to measure the volume of very large objects. Cubic decimeters and cubic centimeters are used when finding smaller volumes. A cubic decimeter (dm³) is a cube 10 centimeters per edge. It is the same size as a 1,000 block

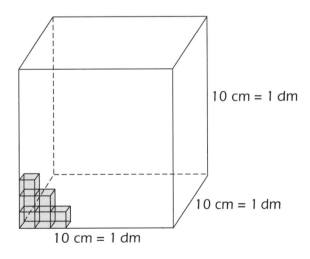

10 cm = 1 dm

10 cm = 1 dm

10 cm = 1 dm

from a set of base ten blocks. A cubic decimeter is equivalent in size to 1,000 cubic centimeters (cm³).

Imagine filling an "open top" cubic decimeter with water. The amount it holds (or its capacity) is a liter (L). There is no international standard regarding when to use liters and when to use cubic meters (or cubic decimeters, etc.). In practice, liters are most commonly used for items measured by the size of their container (such as fluids and berries), whereas cubic meters are most commonly used for items measured by their dimensions. Since 1,000 cubic centimeters are equivalent to a cubic decimeter, it takes 1,000 cubic centimeter containers to fill a liter; the capacity of one cubic centimeter is called one milliliter (mL). Because one cubic decimeter (1,000 cubic centimeters) is equivalent to one liter, we can also state that one cubic centimeter is equivalent to one milliliter. This relationship is one of the many connections that relate units in the metric system.

Measuring Mass and Weight

The terms *weight* and *mass* are often incorrectly used interchangeably. The distinction is that weight is the measure of the gravitational force exerted on an object whereas mass is the amount of material in an object. More technically, mass is the property of an object that resists acceleration. To measure mass we use a balance and compare the object to be measured with a standard unit. To measure weight we use a spring scale and observe how much pull is exerted on the object. A 120-pound astronaut has the same mass when on Earth or when on the moon, but her weight on the moon is one sixth of her weight on Earth because of the difference in gravity (that is, the astronaut's mass remains the same regardless of her location whereas her weight changes). Most elementary school textbooks refer only to weight, not mass; in middle school students are asked to find the mass of objects when using the metric system and the weight of objects when using the English or U.S. customary system. It is not until middle school and high school science classes that students are introduced to the difference between mass and weight.

The standard unit of mass in the metric system is the kilogram (kg). A kilogram is equal to the mass of one cubic decimeter (also known as one liter) of water at 4° Celsius (when it is most dense). If you have access to a balance scale, a one-kilogram standard weight, and a liter container of water (or a hollow cubic decimeter that you can fill with water), you can test this relationship for yourself. Remember that the accuracy of the measure will be affected by the balance used, the temperature of water, and the amount of water used.

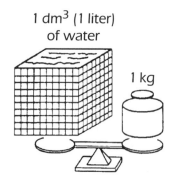

1 dm³ (1 liter)
of water

1 kg

One kilogram is equivalent to 1,000 grams. Since 1 kilogram has the same mass as 1 liter of water, then 1,000 grams have the same mass as 1,000 milliliters. Thus, there is a simple relationship between the measures for volume, capacity, and mass. One cubic centimeter of water is equivalent to 1 milliliter of water and weighs 1 gram. (This relationship holds for water but not for other materials—1 cubic centimeter of gold does not weigh 1 gram!)

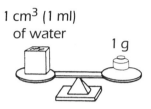

The interrelatedness of the measures in the metric system and the simple method of converting these measures has made the metric system the preferred measurement system in science and commerce. It is important that students have opportunities to use metric units in elementary school before they are asked to use them in upper-level science courses.

3. The English Measurement System

The English system of measures is also known as the U.S. customary system. The system arose from nonstandard units and isn't as easy to use as the metric system: the conversion units need to be memorized, and the calculations are often cumbersome.

The foot at one point was the length of the king's foot and a yard was originally the distance from the tip of the king's nose to the tip of his extended arm. Today the foot is defined by a prototype platinum bar and the other units of length are based on the foot; an inch is one twelfth of a foot, a yard is equivalent to 3 feet, and a mile is 5,280 feet in length. Units of area include the square inch, square foot, square yard, acre (43,560 sq. ft), and the square mile.

Units of volume in the English system are the cubic inch (in³), cubic foot (ft³), cubic yard (yd³), and cubic mile (mi³). Topsoil and cement are often sold by the cubic yard. Everyday units of volume in the English system are often referred to as measures of capacity as well. Capacity can be expressed in cubic inches, cubic feet, or cubic yards, but other units are also used for measuring liquids. These common units of capacity include the teaspoon, tablespoon, fluid ounce, cup (eight fluid ounces), pint (two cups), quart (two pints), and gallon (four quarts). One aspect of the English system that tends to be confusing is that some of the measures of capacity (e.g., teaspoon, cup) are used both with fluids (milk) and dry materials (sugar). In addition, there are specific dry measures of capacity—the bushel and the peck—but these are not used extensively.

The units of weight in the English system are the ounce and the pound. There are two types of measures of weight—troy ounces and pounds and avoirdupois ounces and pounds. The first of these units is used to measure precious metals such as gold, while the latter are the units used to measure the weight of common goods. There are 16 avoirdupois ounces (usually referred to simply as ounces) in 1 pound and

2,000 pounds in an English ton. Very small quantities are measured using grains and drams (a dram equals $27\frac{11}{32}$ grains). As with the other measures in the English system, there is no consistent ratio between consecutive units of weight.

Temperature in the English system is measured using degrees Fahrenheit. The Fahrenheit scale is based on the freezing point (32° F) and the boiling point (212° F) of water. This gives an interval of 180 degrees from freezing to boiling. The metric system of degrees Celsius uses the same two reference points—the freezing point of water (0° C) and the boiling point of water (100° C)—but the interval between these two points is 100 degrees. Temperature in the United States is now commonly reported using both the Fahrenheit and Celsius scales.

4. Measurement Relationships

Students will gain competence with measurement ideas and skills by engaging in many and varied measurement tasks. However, these tasks must be meaningful— they must require students to gather measurement data for a purpose or in connection with clarifying important ideas—not simply provide practice out of context. Giving students problems to solve or situations to investigate that call for measuring is one way to make measuring meaningful. For example, have your students determine how much ribbon you will need to have available for a class art project or how much paint you will need to buy in order to paint the classroom bookshelf. Practical tasks such as designing the cover of a book report to fit certain specifications (title must be four inches from the top of the page, lettering must be one inch high) enable students both to clarify and to refine the measurement process.

Sometimes instructional tasks that use measurement, while not practical per se, help students think about important mathematical relationships. The relationship might be within one measure (e.g., between the dimensions of a shape and its area) or between two different measures (e.g., between the area and the perimeter of a shape). Once students have learned how to measure and are using standard units to solve problems, they need to examine the relationships between measures and units.

Activity

Do Figures with the Same Area Have the Same Perimeter?

Objective: explore area and perimeter relationships.

Materials: square tiles or graph paper.

Using square tiles or graph paper, make as many figures as you can that have an area of 12 square units. Squares must touch on a whole side. Determine the perimeter of each figure. Compare the figures having large perimeters with those having smaller perimeters. What do you notice about the shapes?

Things to Think About

Figures with the same area do not have to have the same perimeter. In fact, you may have found perimeters ranging from 14 units to 26 units. Examine the two groups of figures. What do all the figures with smaller perimeters have in common? What do all the figures with large perimeters have in common? The figures with smaller perimeters are more condensed and compact. The shape of these figures is more closely related to a square. The figures with larger perimeters are elongated. Most of the square tiles are adjacent to another square tile only on one side.

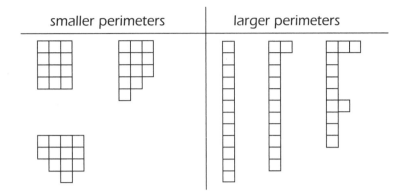

smaller perimeters | larger perimeters

Activity

Do Figures with the Same Perimeter Have the Same Area?

Objective: explore area and perimeter relationships.

Materials: graph paper.

Imagine that you have just purchased 36 yards of fencing and want to fence in a playground area for children. You want to provide the most play space for the children. If the play area is rectangular, what dimensions of the rectangle give the greatest area? Sketch possible rectangular play areas on graph paper. Remember to use all 36 yards of fencing to enclose the playground.

Things to Think About

The playground must have a perimeter of 36 yards, because we want to use all the available fencing. Thus, the two lengths and two widths of the rectangle must sum to 36. Your sketches of rectangular play areas can be placed into an organized list. Listing the rectangles in an orderly fashion, starting with the smallest length possible, may help you see patterns and notice relationships.

$L \times W$ (YDS)	PERIMETER (YDS)	AREA (SQ. YDS)
1 by 17	36	17
2 by 16	36	32
3 by 15	36	45
4 by 14	36	56
5 by 13	36	65
6 by 12	36	72
7 by 11	36	77
8 by 10	36	80
9 by 9	36	81

Using 36 yards of fencing, a square-shaped play space (9 yards by 9 yards) provides the largest area (81 square yards). The results of Activities 4 and 5 show that among rectangular figures, squares have the smallest perimeters and the largest areas. Are there other shapes that have the same perimeter (36 yards) but have an even larger area? Let's consider a circular play area. *Circumference* is the standard name for the perimeter of a circle. The formula for circumference is $C = \pi d$ (d = diameter). Using this formula, we can find the approximate diameter of a circle with a circumference of 36 yards:

$$C = \pi d$$
$$36 = 3.14d$$
$$d = 36 \div 3.14$$
$$d \approx 11.46 \text{ yards}$$

The formula for area of a circle is $A = \pi r^2$. We need to determine the radius of the circle before finding area—since $d = 2r$ we can divide the diameter by two. The radius is approximately 5.73 yards. The area of a circle with a circumference of 36 yards is about 103.1 square yards:

$$A = \pi r^2$$
$$A = 3.14(5.73)^2$$
$$A \approx 103.1$$

Thus a circle provides even greater area for the play space than the square. ▲

Measurement Formulas

There are many area formulas that students are expected to recall by the end of middle school. Many times students try to commit these formulas to memory and then apply them when needed. Students who simply memorize these formulas frequently confuse them, and have to review them every year because they have forgotten one or more. In addition, it is difficult for students to tell from their answers when they have used an incorrect formula. Furthermore, since students rarely engage in activities in which they estimate the areas of figures, and since most figures are drawn to scale, there are few contextual clues to whether or not a student's answer is correct. Students are better served when they understand the formulas and their origins and can reason about the appropriateness of their choice of formulas and calculations.

Very young students learn how to find the area of a rectangle by relating a rectangle to an array; the picture below depicts a 3-by-2 array. It also represents a rectangle with side lengths 2 and 3. Students can count squares to find that the area of the rectangle is 6 square units.

The labels for the dimensions of quadrilaterals can be confusing: *length*, *width*, *height*, *base*. Which of these are correct and why are there so many different names? *Length* and *width* are dimension names that we most often associate with the sides of rectangles. These labels go with the two side lengths that meet at a common vertex.

Which side length is given which label is totally arbitrary. The longer side does not have to be the length, though this is often the case. We can also label the side lengths of a rectangle as base and height. Any side can serve as a base but the height is always perpendicular to the side chosen as base. When we label the dimensions of parallelograms, we always use base and height because the sides of parallelograms do not have to be perpendicular to each other.

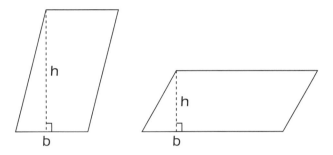

The area formulas for various quadrilaterals can be developed from the area formula of a rectangle. Instead of referring to the dimensions as length and width, we will use base and height, because they generalize more readily to other figures. The area formula for a rectangle is $A = b \times h$.

Consider how to find the area of a parallelogram. When the parallelogram is cut by a segment that is perpendicular to both sides, the two resulting parts may be rearranged to form a rectangle:

The parallelogram and the rectangle have the same area. Thus, we can use the same formula to find the area of a parallelogram: $A = b \times h$.

Activity

Developing the Formula for the Area of a Triangle

Objective: relate the area formulas of a triangle and a parallelogram.

Draw two congruent triangles and cut them out. Form a parallelogram by putting the two triangles together. Use the resulting parallelogram to develop a formula for the area of one of the original triangles. Will this approach work with any type of triangle?

Things to Think About

Any two congruent triangles can be joined to form a parallelogram. In the diagram on the next page, the resulting parallelogram has two times the area of the original triangle.

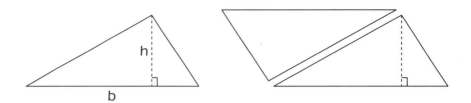

Notice that the base of the triangle and the base of the resulting parallelogram are the same length. The heights of both figures are also the same length. Since the formula for the area of the parallelogram is $A = b \times h$, then the formula for the area of the triangle is $A = \frac{1}{2}(b \times h)$, because the area of one triangle is one half the area of the parallelogram. We can create parallelograms using two right triangles, two acute triangles, or two obtuse triangles; the same relationship holds no matter what type of triangle is used. Thus, the area of any triangle is $A = \frac{1}{2}bh$. ▲

Activity

Developing the Formula for the Area of a Trapezoid

Objective: connect the area formulas of parallelograms and trapezoids.

Using a template or pattern blocks, trace and cut out two copies of the same trapezoid. Red pattern block trapezoids or trapezoids from other shape sets can be used. Rearrange the two trapezoids to form a parallelogram. Use the area formula of a parallelogram to develop a formula for the area of a trapezoid. If available, construct parallelograms using more than one kind of trapezoid (e.g., two isosceles trapezoids, two right trapezoids).

Things to Think About

Were you able to form a parallelogram using the two trapezoids? Any pair of congruent trapezoids may be joined to form a parallelogram.

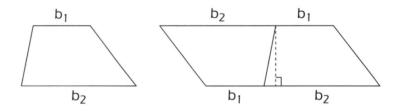

Notice that the resulting parallelogram has a base length that is composed of the sum of the two bases of the parallel sides of the original trapezoid. By convention, we refer to these bases as b_1 and b_2 in order to distinguish between them. What do you notice about the heights of the figures? The height of the original trapezoid and the resulting parallelogram are the same length. Since the area of the resulting parallelogram is twice the area of the original trapezoid, we can use this information to help us make sense of the area formula of a trapezoid. The area formula for any parallelogram is $A = bh$. But the base of this new parallelogram is the sum of the two parallel bases of the trapezoid, b_1 and b_2. We substitute this new base into the formula for the area of the parallelogram: $A = (b_1 + b_2)h$. Finally, although we used two congruent trapezoids to form the parallelogram, we want to find the area of only one. Because the area of the parallelogram is twice the area of the trapezoid, we divide by 2. However, since multiplying by $\frac{1}{2}$ is equivalent to dividing by 2 (why?), by convention we record the formula of a trapezoid as: $A = \frac{1}{2}(b_1 + b_2)h$. ▲

Another common figure that students study is the circle. The circle formulas for circumference and area are challenging for students for a number of reasons. First, the formulas often are not understood and are simply memorized. Second, π, an important component of both formulas, is also often misunderstood. Students generally memorize the value of π to be 3.14, or $\frac{22}{7}$; they do not understand that π is irrational and cannot be represented as a quotient of two numbers and that these two values (3.14 and $\frac{22}{7}$) are approximations. In fact, the value of π has been calculated to more than 1 trillion decimal places, without terminating or displaying any decimal pattern, and it still continues! Because π is an irrational number, the "exact" circumference or area of a circle can only be expressed using the symbol for π. For example, $A = 22\pi$ units or $C = 6.2\pi$ units, in which a value for π is not given, are exact answers. Sometimes, however, we want to solve real problems and find an approximate value for a circumference or area, such as the distance around a bicycle tire or the area of a dinner plate. In these cases, we must use one of the approximations for π.

Activity

Investigating Circumference and π

Objective: derive an approximation for π.

Materials: tape measure and a variety of circular shapes such as container lids, disks, cans, coins.

Measure the diameters and the circumferences of at least eight circular regions. If you use three-dimensional objects such as cans, you may want to first trace the circular bases and then measure the circles. Keep a record of your values and complete the data table. Record the ratios of circumference to diameter as a single number by dividing. Next find the average of the circumference-to-diameter ratios. What do you notice about the average of the values in the last column of the data table? What is π?

NAME OF CIRCULAR OBJECT	DIAMETER IN MM	CIRCUMFERENCE IN MM	CIRCUMFERENCE/ DIAMETER RATIO
plate			
half-dollar			

Things to Think About

For every circular object, the last column in the data table should have a value of approximately 3. If any of your ratios are not close to 3, measure again! Furthermore, depending on the accuracy of your measurements, the values in the last column most likely will be between 3.1 and 3.2. Does this number look familiar? Yes, this is the approximate value for π. When you average all of these values, it is even more likely that your approximation will be the value of π to the hundredths place—about 3.14. The length of the diameter of any circle will fit around the circumference a little more than three times. The exact number of times the diameter will fit around the circumference is precisely π times. This can be expressed as follows:

$$\frac{C}{d} = \pi$$

Pi is a constant ratio. This means that no matter what the size of the circle, the ratio comparing circumference to diameter will always be π. That there is a constant value that relates circumference and diameter has been recognized since ancient times, but it took many centuries for mathematicians to refine techniques in order to achieve more accurate approximations. In 1635 Ludolph van Ceulen computed the value of π to 35 places. W. Shanks holds the record for computing π by hand. In 1853 he computed π to 707 places! It wasn't until 1945 that an electronic calculator was used to check his work. Shanks had made a mistake in the 527th place!

Another form of the equation above is $C = \pi d$, the formula for computing the circumference of any circle. You can use 3 as the value of π for rough estimations of the circumference of circles. For example, the diameter of the world's largest clock (in Beauvais, France) is 40 feet. A rough approximation of its circumference is 120 feet (3 × 40 feet). A more precise circumference can be computed using more exact approximations of π. However, no matter how precise a value for π you use, the solution will still be an approximation. In addition, the measure of the diameter (40 feet) is also only an approximate value. You can see why all physical measures are approximations! ▲

Activity

Developing the Formula for the Area of a Circle

Objective: relate the area formulas of parallelograms and circles.

Materials: scissors, paper circles.

Pi is also used in the formula to calculate the area of a circle. In this activity we will use the area of a parallelogram to develop the area formula for a circle. First draw a circle on a piece of paper and cut it out. Next fold the circle in half. Fold that result in half to form a quarter circle. Finally fold each piece in half once again. Now, unfold the circle and cut it up into the eight pieces suggested by the crease lines from your folding. (If possible, cut each of the wedges in half in order to have sixteenths.) Rearrange these eight pieces to form a parallelogram. What are the base and height of this parallelogram? Use these results to help you develop the formula for the area of a circle.

Things to Think About

The eight (or sixteen) pieces of the circle may be rearranged to form a parallelogram.

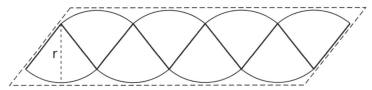

Actually, this figure only resembles a parallelogram, because the bases are not straight lines, but are composed of arcs of the circle. If you did make sixteen wedges, the sixteen rearranged pieces would more closely resemble a parallelogram. The greater the number of wedges, the closer the resulting figure will be to a parallelogram. In fact, it is mathematically correct to say that with an infinite number of wedges, the resulting figure will be a parallelogram.

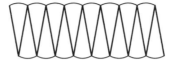

The area of the resulting parallelogram is equal to the area of the circle. The formula for the area of the parallelogram is $A = bh$. How are the base and height of the parallelogram related to the circle? The height of the parallelogram is equal to the radius of the circle, or half the diameter. Thus the formula can be changed to $A = br$. What about the base length? The base is equal to half the circumference of the circle, or $\frac{1}{2}\pi d$. Because the diameter is equal to twice the radius, we can write the base length as $b = \frac{1}{2}\pi 2r$, which simplifies to $b = \pi r$.

Because the area of a parallelogram is: $A = br$
And the base of this parallelogram is: $b = \pi r$
By substitution $A = \pi rr$ or πr^2.
Thus the formula for the area of a circle is $A = \pi r^2$. ▲

Volume Formulas and Relationships

In order to calculate the volume of three-dimensional figures, we need to know the dimensions of the solids under investigation. The dimensions—length, width, height—are commonly used in the elementary grades. Alternatively, the volume can sometimes be calculated using the area of the base of the solid along with its height.

Just as the areas of some common polygons are related, so are the volumes of common three-dimensional figures. Consider a series of 1-inch blocks arranged in a 2-by-3 array, as shown here. The dimensions of this block structure are 1 inch by 2 inches by 3 inches.

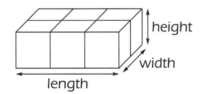

The volume of this solid is 6 cubic inches. The number of cubes is the same as the squares in a 3×2 array. Suppose we add another layer of cubes? and another? and another? What happens to the volume?

Activity

Developing Volume Formulas

Objective: develop an understanding of the formula for determining the volume of prisms.

Materials: cubes.

Build a $3 \times 2 \times 1$ rectangular prism. Continue to increase the height by 1 centimeter by adding layers of cubes to the first level of the structure. Record your results in a table. After building several layers, predict the volume of a figure with 10 layers of cubes; with 32 layers of cubes. Generalize a formula for determining the volume of a rectangular prism. Would your generalized formula work for a triangular prism? a cube? a hexagonal prism? a cylinder?

LENGTH IN CM	WIDTH IN CM	HEIGHT IN CM	VOLUME IN CUBIC CM
3	2	1	6
3	2	2	

Things to Think About

The volume of the rectangular prism with a height of 10 cm is 60 cubic centimeters; with a height of 32 cm, it is 192 cm³. Did you notice that every time the height of the prism increased by 1 centimeter, the volume increased by 6 cubic centimeters? How come? One way to think about the volume is in terms of layers. Each increase in 1 cm of height is equivalent to adding a full layer of blocks. There are 6 cubes in each layer, so multiplying the height by 6 gives the volume of each prism. These layers help us generalize formulas for the volume of rectangular prisms: $V = lwh$ or $V = Bh$.

In this formula V represents volume, B represents the *area* of the base (6), and h represents the height or number of layers in the figure. Notice that by using B for the area of the base instead of $l \times w$, we focus on the layers. You can use this formula to compute the volume of any solid that has identical layers or cross sections for the entire height of the figure, such as a cube, triangular prism, or hexagonal prism. Regardless of the shape of the base, as long as the cross sections all along the height are congruent to the base, $V = Bh$ will compute the volume. This formula can even be used with cylinders, because a cylinder has congruent circles as cross sections along its entire height.

Pyramids and cones are related to the solids discussed above. Cones have circular bases, and pyramids have bases in the shape of polygons. The volumes of these solids are related to the volumes of cylinders and prisms. We can use a cone for an example. If a cone has the same base area and height as a cylinder, then the volume of the cone is $\frac{1}{3}$ the volume of the cylinder. This suggests the following volume formula for cones:

$$V = \frac{1}{3}Bh$$

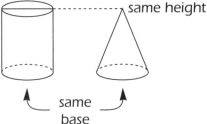

Students can verify this relationship by building cones and cylinders with the same base area and height. Students can then fill the cylinder with dry material and empty it into the cylinder three times to verify the volume formula.

Similarly, students can use prisms and pyramids with the same heights and the same base areas to show that $V = \frac{1}{3}Bh$ is the volume formula for a pyramid. ▲

Teaching Measurement

Students in the United States must become proficient in using both the English system and the metric system of measurement. They will use English units in daily measurement tasks and metric units in science and commerce. Students' understanding of the key features of measurement systems and their facility with measurement concepts form the basis for future understanding. Many of the measurement concepts and skills that students acquire in the elementary grades are applied to more sophisticated problems in middle school. For example, whereas young children may explore the relationship between meters and centimeters, middle grade students are expected to use this relationship flexibly and become proficient with conversions among a wide variety of metric units. By high school, instruction increasingly focuses on the relationships between measures and requires students to use symbols and graphs to represent these relationships. Formulas are used to solve application problems such as comparing the volumes of two containers. In order to prepare elementary students to use measurement in a variety of ways, we must provide them with many opportunities to engage in meaningful measurement tasks—tasks that promote understanding of concepts and facility with measurement units.

Questions for Discussion

1. There are many underlying concepts that contribute to being able to measure. Describe these concepts.
2. Since the United States uses the U.S. customary system, is it important for students to be proficient in the metric system? Why or why not?
3. What relationships exist between the perimeters and areas of figures? Synthesize the information presented in this chapter.
4. Teachers always worry about having enough time to teach all of the mathematics at a particular grade level. What do you say to a teacher who has decided to tell his students formulas rather than asking students to derive (or figure out) formulas as a time-saving measure?

13

Statistics

We're always hearing about averages: the average life expectancy for an American is seventy-five years, the average amount of rainfall per month this year is much lower than last year, a student's average on her math quizzes is 93.4, and the average hat size for men is size 7. An average is a *statistic*—a number used to summarize or describe a data set. Data are collections of information, numbers, or pairs of numbers. Data usually are measurements of some sort.

We are also regularly presented with graphical displays of statistical data. The newspaper *USA Today* has popularized colorful histograms, line graphs, pictographs, and other visual depictions of data. Displays like this are meant to convey meaningful data in a concise way. However, the graphical display of data is a two-edged sword. On the one hand, it allows complex or confusing statistics to be presented in an easy-to-understand way. On the other hand, graphs can be difficult to interpret and even misleading.

We need to be able to understand and interpret statistics if we are to deal with complex issues and make decisions in today's world. As a result, the topic of statistics, which is the science of collecting, organizing, and interpreting information, now appears in school curriculums as early as first grade. Young children collect data by counting and measuring and then learn to represent the data in graphs, charts, pictures, and tables. Older elementary school students encounter some of the statistical terminology related to data sets, such as *range*, *median*, and *mean*. They must also interpret data and develop hypotheses and theories based on the data. In middle and high school, students engage in data analysis. In order to become more discerning citizens, students at all levels need experience in collecting, displaying, and analyzing data.

1. Descriptive Statistics

The Three Kinds of Average

Mean, *median*, and *mode*, the three measures used to describe a "typical" item in a set of data, are introduced in elementary school. All of these averages are represented by numerical data (data in the form of numbers versus data based on categories) and are sometimes referred to as *measures of center* or *measures of central tendency* because they all indicate something that is "common" or "central" to the data set. However, the three measures can be quite different, even for the same set of data. In addition, some data sets are best represented by only one of these "averages." Tests given to seventh graders have shown that although they can compute these three different measures, they lack a fundamental understanding of each measure and have difficulty interpreting the mean, median, and mode in real life (Bright and Hoeffner 1993). It is therefore critical to provide students with experiences in determining and analyzing the mean, median, and mode in many different settings, sometimes using data they have gathered themselves.

The Mean

The mean, sometimes referred to as the *arithmetic mean*, is what people most often think of when they hear the word *average*. The algorithm for determining the mean involves adding the numbers in a data set and then dividing the sum by the number of items in the data set. For example, for the test scores 100, 88, 96, and 92, the mean is 94:

$$\frac{100 + 88 + 96 + 92}{4}, \quad \text{or} \quad \frac{376}{4}, \quad \text{or} \quad 94$$

Many students memorize the mean algorithm ("add and divide") without understanding what the mean represents. However, the goal is for students to understand averages so that they can use them to answer questions of interest.

There are two different ways to think about the mean. One is as the pivot point on a balance scale, or as a central balance point. In this interpretation, the distances from each data point above and below the mean to the mean are equal. The second is based on the idea of equal distribution. In this second interpretation, the data are all leveled out or have the same value and the mean represents that "leveled" value. Activities in which data are gathered and evaluated without using an algorithm can strengthen students' conceptual understanding of the mean. The following two activities will help you become comfortable with both interpretations.

Activity

Finding the Mean

Objective: understand the mean as a balance point.

Without using the add-and-divide algorithm for figuring the mean, draw a horizontal line to indicate what you think is the mean height of the columns pictured below. (The horizontal line is called the *mean line*.)

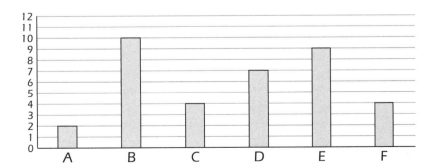

Things to Think About

How did you decide where to draw your mean line? One way to solve this problem is to think about how to "even up" the six columns—that is, take some units off the tall columns and add them to the short columns (you could do this by constructing the columns with interlocking blocks). For these six columns, you know the mean line is somewhere between the height of the highest column (B) and the height of the lowest column (A); just by looking, you can also assume that it is most likely between seven units and four units. Taking four from column B and adding them to column A gives you two columns six units high. Taking two from column E and adding them to column F gives you another column of six units. Now taking one each from columns E and D and adding them to column C makes all the columns even, at six units. That's where the mean line should be drawn:

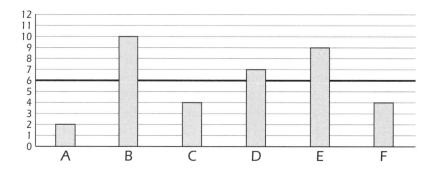

How close was your mean line to the one shown above? We can verify the mean line by computing the mean height using the algorithm. The mean is six units. Another means of verification is to compare the sum of the units in columns that are above the mean line to the sum of missing units in columns below the mean line. Column B is four units above the mean line, column D is one unit above, and column E is three units above, for a total of eight. Column A is four units below the mean line, column C is two units below, and column F is also two units below, again for a total of eight. The two sums are the same. ▲

Is this always true of the mean? For any set of data, is the sum of the amounts by which individual items exceed (or are greater than) the mean always equal to the sum of the amounts by which individual items fall below (or are less than) the mean? Let's try it using the set of test scores mentioned at the beginning of this section—100, 88, 96, and 92. The scores and the mean line (94) are displayed on the graph on the next page.

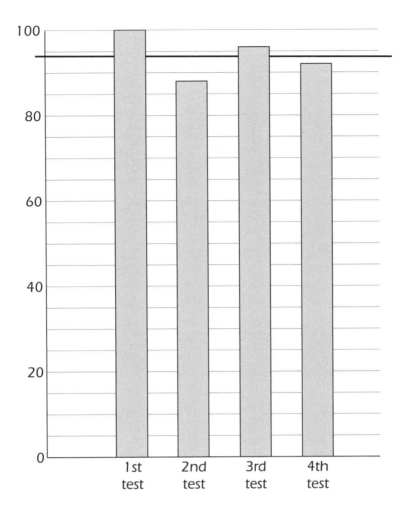

Compare the sum of points by which individual grades exceed the mean (6 + 2) to the sum of points by which individual grades fall below the mean (6 + 2). They are equal. The equality of data above and below the mean is a fundamental property of the mean. The mean value is always such that the sum of the amounts by which individual values exceed (are greater than) the mean is equal to the sum of the amounts by which individual values fall below (are less than) the mean. Or put another way, the distances of data from the mean (above and below) must balance. For many students this basic principle—that the mean of two numbers is a number located halfway between them—gets lost in the algorithm. In the two examples so far, there have been the same number of data points above and below the mean line. However, this does not always have to be the case.

Let's work backward from a given mean in order to explore this further. The following line plot shows the number of cups of coffee people in one office drink each day. There are four squares on the 4. Each square represents one person—the mean amount of coffee drunk by the four office workers is 4 cups.

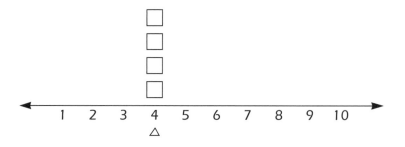

Keeping the mean at 4, move one square to 10. Imagine that one person drinks 10 cups of coffee a day. This data point now exceeds the mean (4) by 6.

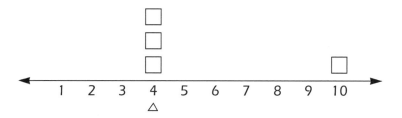

To keep the balance point at 4 (the mean) we need to have other data points 6 units below 4. One possibility is shown below.

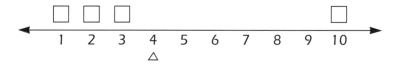

There are two interesting things about this data set. First, even though 4 is the mean, it is not a data point. Students find this possibility a bit confusing and benefit from creating and discussing data sets where the mean is not one of the actual numbers. Second, the *total* number of points above and below the mean are equal but there is only one data point above the mean (10) and three data points below the mean (1, 2, 3). Four is the center or balance point of the data set.

Try creating a balanced data set yourself. Imagine there are 8 people in the office drinking coffee. If the mean for the group is 4 cups of coffee a day, explore two different ways to distribute the data points equally above and below 4. You can keep some squares on 4 if you want!

The other way we think about the mean involves leveling or evening off data. Let's use this interpretation to determine the mean number of letters in the names of students in a class. The diagrams on the next page show trains of interlocking blocks representing the number of letters in students' names.

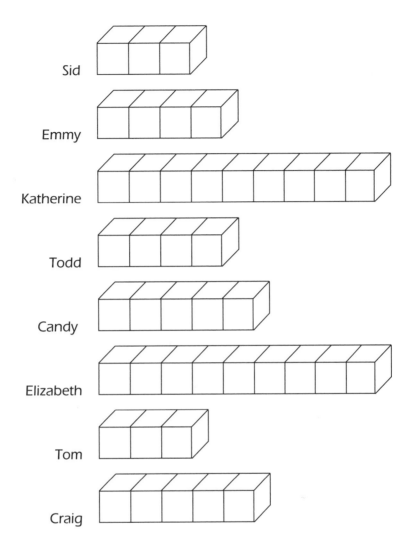

When students build the trains and then try to "even them off" by switching blocks among the trains, they eventually end up with eight trains having five blocks each and two trains having six blocks each. With younger children this result might be expressed thus: the mean number of letters in these names is between five and six letters. Another possibility is simply to consider the mean number of letters as five, since most of the names have five letters in them. Older students might be led to consider that all eight names have five letters and that there are two "extras" that need to be apportioned among all the names equally. This is then expressed in the following ratio:

$$\frac{2 \text{ blocks}}{8 \text{ names}} = \frac{2}{8} \quad (\text{or } \tfrac{1}{4} \text{ or } .25)$$

Thus, the mean number of letters per name for this group of students is 5.25 letters.

Students in elementary grades can display data sets using tiles, blocks, and other manipulatives. They can then physically move objects to "even out" the data by taking items from the larger groupings and adding them to the smaller groupings until all the groupings are equal. Activities like this foreshadow the algorithm to compute the mean and provide students with an intuitive grasp of the mean that will support the application of the algorithm in the middle grades. But if students are really to understand the symbolic algorithm, instruction must ask students to explicitly link the symbols with their actions on materials.

Activity

Averaging Averages

Objective: investigate what happens when we find the mean of means.

The ages of the teachers in Winston Elementary School are 24, 33, 42, 40, 36, 40, 35, and 22. Estimate the mean age of these teachers and then graph the ages and draw a mean line. Now imagine that this school hires four new faculty members whose ages are 51, 55, 49, and 53. Find the mean for these new members. What is the mean age of all twelve faculty members?

Things to Think About

The mean age for the first eight teachers is 34. How close was your estimate? How close were you to the mean age of 52 for the four newly hired teachers? How did you find the mean age of all twelve teachers?

   All means are not created equal. A common misunderstanding many students have is that they can find the mean age for all the teachers in the school by finding the mean of the two means. In other words, the mean for all twelve faculty members is

$$\frac{34 + 52}{2}, \quad \text{or} \quad \frac{86}{2}, \quad \text{or} \quad 43$$

Is this correct? Does 43 seem a reasonable mean age? Make a rough estimate of the years by which ages exceed and fall below this mean value to see if the sums are equal. You should find they are not. The computed mean is too high to be the mean age for the entire data set. Therefore, the two means cannot be used to compute a mean for the entire set of faculty members. Although they are both means, they do not carry the same weight: the first mean is based on eight teachers and the second mean is based on only four teachers.

   We can compute the mean age of all the teachers using the algorithm; add their ages and divide by 12. The mean age for the entire set of faculty members is less than 40 (39.2). ▲

The Median

When a set of numbers is arranged in order of magnitude, either greatest to least or least to greatest, the median is the middle number of the set. In the set 1, 3, 5, 5, 7, 10, 12, 13, 15 the median is 7 because it is the fifth number in order out of nine numbers in the set. Four of the numbers of the set are less than 7 and four numbers of the set are greater than 7. Suppose there were an even number of items in the set, so there was no single number in the middle: 5, 6, 8, 10, 12, 12, for example. In situations like this, the median is the mean of the two middle numbers: in this case, (8 + 10) ÷ 2, or 9. Another way to think about the median here is as the point halfway between the 8 and 10, or 9. Although 9 is not a member of the data set, 9 is the median for the set.

The median is frequently used when referring to the average selling price of a house or the average salary for a corporation. If there are a few high or low values in a data set, the median or middle value may be the best one to describe the set as a whole. Depending on the size and the range of the data set, the mean and the median can be identical, but they do not have to be.

Activity

Mean or Median?

Objective: examine how very high values in a data set affect the mean and median.

Find the mean and median for the following ages of employees at a fast-food restaurant: 20, 16, 18, 22, 19, 19, 20, 30, 23. Compare your results. Which is the better average for this set of data?

Things to Think About

You should have found that the mean is 21 and the median is 20. Since they are so close in value, either the mean or the median gives a good sense of a typical item for the data set. However, suppose the restaurant hires an additional assistant manager who is 63 years old. Compute the new mean and median for the restaurant.

The mean is now 25, but the median is unchanged; it is still 20. The mean age 25 is no longer a good representation of a *typical value* for this data set because most of the work crew are younger than 25. The new assistant manager is much older than the other workers. A data item that is considerably more or less than the other items in a data set generally has a greater effect on the mean than on the median. For this reason the median is used to describe the typical measure of data sets that might contain one or more extreme values. ▲

Real estate listings use the median to indicate the average price of a house in a specific community because a few extremely expensive houses will distort the mean house value, much as the assistant manager's age distorted the mean for the employees' ages. Half the houses in a community are priced below the median value and half the houses are more expensive than the median value. The median is therefore a more reliable and stable indication of average house prices.

Here is another example of how an extreme value can distort the mean: in 1998 the postgraduate mean annual salary of geology majors from the University of North Carolina was more than $500,000. Who knew that geology majors were in such demand? Actually, they're not. Michael Jordan, an NBA basketball star, was a geology major at UNC, and in 1998 his yearly income was over $50 million! His salary was far outside the range of most geology majors' salaries. Extreme values such as this are known as *outliers*. As you can see, outliers distort the mean in a very big way!

As soon as elementary school students are able to count and rank numbers by magnitude, they can begin to find the median of a set. Activities that involve estimating and then determining the median can help lay the basis for an intuitive understanding of the median, which students can then use in middle school to help them differentiate the median from the mean. Students also benefit from building different data sets with the same median in order to broaden their understanding of this concept.

The Mode

The mode of a set of numbers is the number or numbers that appear in the set most often. For example:

1 3 2 12 7 3 8 3	The mode is 3.
1 2 7 5 6 9 12	There is no mode.
2 6 8 2 8 3 5 2 8 3 6	Both 2 and 8 are modes. (When there are two values that appear the same number of times, we state that the set is *bimodal*.)
5 5 6 6 7 7 1 2	When there are three or more values that appear the same number of times, we state there is no mode in the data set.

The mode is a useful average for some sets of data. For example, suppose a sports store sold the following sizes of athletic shoes in a day:

8 9 12 9 5 8 8 9 8 11 9 9 8 8 7 9 7 7 8 9

The two modes for this data set, 8 and 9, provide helpful information for ordering more shoes from the manufacturer. The mean for this set is 8.4, a meaningless number for a shoe size. The median for this set is 8, a value that hides the popularity of 9 as a shoe size. Although the mean and the median are reasonable "averages," they don't tell us what sizes are the most popular, a most important piece of data for reordering purposes. According to the manager of one store in a national chain of women's shoe stores, the most popular shoe sizes (modes) are 6, 8, and 9. When ordering shoes for a new fashion season, the manager always orders more of these sizes.

By introducing activities that focus on the differences between mean, median, and mode, teachers can help students use these measures and interpret them properly. The mode represents the most common value or data point in a data set, such as dress or shirt size. The median is best used for very large data sets or ones that may have one or more extreme values, or outliers. The mean is best used for a data set with a range of numbers where none are very high or very low in comparison with the rest of the data set, such as the amount of daily rainfall over a thirty-day period in New York City. When working with students, teachers should introduce the three types of averages in the order they are understood. The mode is the average that young students tend to recognize first and understand when analyzing data sets. The median is also very understandable when students are able to engage in activities that involve placing data values in numerical order and determining the middle value. The mean is the most complicated average to truly understand, so should be introduced last and explored using a variety of problems. Unfortunately, some textbooks introduce these averages in the reverse order and in an algorithmic manner, which is not the way to make sense of them.

Activity

What's Average?

Objective: determine which of the three measures of center best describes specific data sets.

Each of the three kinds of average has strengths that make it a better typical measure for a given set of data than the other two. Decide which average, the mean, the median, or the mode, is best used for each data set shown below. Explain your choice.

1. Average salary in a large company.
2. Average test score for a student.
3. Average size of a cereal box in a grocery store.
4. Average price of a room in a hotel.
5. Average year of a car in a used-car lot.
6. Average monthly electric bill.

Things to Think About

How did you decide which typical measure to use? Perhaps you decided those activities that use the mode were easiest to identify. The mode might be used for 3, 4, and 5. For 3, the most popular size of cereal box (mode) is the average size carried by the grocery store. Median or mean box size would have little or no meaning here. In 4, the price of a hotel room for a specific hotel is best indicated by the price of most of the rooms. Every hotel has a few expensive rooms, like suites and penthouses, that affect the price of the mean. The majority of hotel rooms are rented out at the same rate, the mode. For 5, "average year" essentially refers to the typical car in the lot, which would be the most popular car year, the mode. The median would be the best average figure for 1. Extreme values like the salary of top officials can affect the mean salary in a large company; also, there are generally a number of different salary structures in a large company, which makes the mode ineffective as a typical measure as well. For 2 and 6, the mean is the most logical average. Both these data sets are generally immune to outliers and in most cases neither data set would contain a mode.

Different, competing groups often use a particular kind of average to promote their own interests. For example, in labor negotiations, management might use the mean salary, which includes top executives' high salaries, while the labor union might instead use the median or mode. Both sides, however, could truthfully be calling their figure the "average salary." ▲

How Spread Out Are the Data?

We have seen how when describing a set of data, the average tells us something about the set. Other descriptive statistics, often referred to as measures of variability or variance, tell us how the data in that set are dispersed. One number telling us how spread out the data are—the *range*—is especially useful. The range is the difference between the greatest and least values in a data set. For example, in the set 19, 21, 21, 22, 23, 26, the range is 7 (26 − 19 = 7). In the set 2, 5, 9, 22, 35, 59, the range is 57 (59 − 2 = 57); and in the set 22, 22, 22, 22, 22, 22, the range is 0. The greater the range, the more spread out, or *dispersed*, the data. The range helps us interpret the mean. For example, the mean of all three of the data sets above is 22 yet they are quite different. It is the range that lets us know that the values in the first set are clustered near the mean, that the numbers in the second set are quite spread out, and the values in the third set are all 22!

Another measure of variability that we commonly hear about is the *standard deviation* of a data set. The standard deviation, like the range, gives us information on whether the measurements are bunched together or scattered apart. Thus, the standard deviation tells us how tightly a set of values is clustered around the mean of those same values. If the set of numbers is close to the mean of those values, the standard deviation will be low. In contrast, if the set of numbers is spread out across a greater range, the standard deviation will be higher. Standard deviation is calculated following specific algorithms and along with the mean is used in the computation of other statistics. It is a high school and college mathematics topic.

2. The Graphical Display of Data

Newspapers, magazines, and television news programs commonly use graphical displays of data to convey important information visually, in very little space. There are two types of graphs encountered in the elementary and middle school curriculum: one-variable graphs and two-variable graphs. Pictographs, circle graphs (pie charts), line plots, bar graphs, stem-and-leaf plots, histograms, and box-and-whisker plots are all examples of one-variable graphs because they represent data in which one trait or quantity is measured. These one-variable data displays are used to explore a wide range of topics: categories such as car types, flag colors, and favorite ice cream flavors and numbers such as successive rolls of a pair of dice, salaries, and ages. There are many ways to graph and summarize one-variable data.

Two-variable graphs represent and display two different variables, such as weight and heart rate or time and distance, on the same graph. Two-variable data are graphed in order to help identify and generalize relationships (if they exist) between the two variables. Scatter plots and line graphs are examples of two-variable graphs.

Pictograph

A pictograph uses a picture or icon to symbolize the quantities being represented. It is often the first type of graph that children create and interpret in the early elementary grades. Pictographs are especially accessible to young learners when one symbol represents one item in the data set. Pictographs enable us to make quick comparisons among similar situations. The pictograph below uses ice cream cones to represent the number of ice cream cones, by flavor, that were sold during a school's home football games:

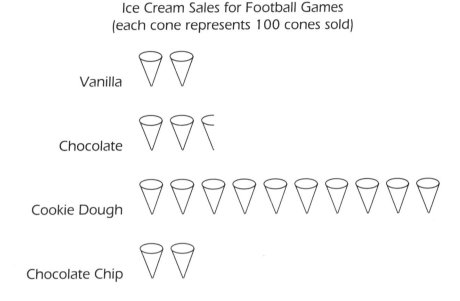

Ice Cream Sales for Football Games
(each cone represents 100 cones sold)

Circle Graph

A circle graph, or pie chart, summarizes data in categories and is used to show the size of each category relative to the whole. It provides visual comparisons of the relative sizes of fractional parts. Often the data in a circle graph are presented as percentages. The circle graph below shows student preferences for the background color of a new school flag:

Student Preferences for Flag Color

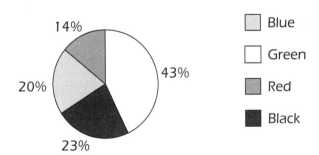

We can easily see that a green background is clearly the favorite, with black, then blue, as the next favorite colors. The convention for making a circle graph is that the category with the largest value begins at the top of the graph—with a vertical line from the center of the circle to the top of the circle. The sections are then ordered by size moving clockwise.

Line Plot

A line plot, sometimes referred to as a dot plot, is an informal means of recording and displaying numerical data. Each item of numerical data is shown as an X or a dot above a number line or horizontal axis. Line plots show the range of the data and how the data are distributed or clustered over that range. They are most appropriate for small data sets in which the range also is small. They let us create a quick visual representation of the distribution. Line plots are one of the first types of graphs that elementary school children use.

The line plot below displays the data from an experiment in which the sums of each roll of a pair of dice were recorded. In this example, an X is used to represent each data point, but other symbols such as dots can be used.

```
                        X
                        X
                        X
                  X     X
                  X     X     X
                  X     X     X     X
            X     X     X     X     X
            X     X     X     X     X
      X     X     X     X     X     X
X     X     X     X     X     X     X     X     X
X     X     X     X     X     X     X     X     X     X
─────────────────────────────────────────────────────────
2     3     4     5     6     7     8     9     10    11    12
```

As we see, this line plot gives a quick overview of the data set: most of the sums were between 5 and 9, a sum of 7 was rolled most frequently (eleven times), sums of 2 and 12 were least frequent.

Bar Graph

A bar graph is often used to compare amounts. The bars, which can be horizontal or vertical, each represent one value and enable you to make direct visual comparisons. Bar graphs are best used to display data that are grouped by category or attribute, called *categorical* data. Bars tend to be separated so that the categories are clearly displayed. For example, the first bar graph on page 307 displays information about how many cars made by particular manufacturers are in a parking lot at the mall. The bar graph underneath it shows the amount of school funding for a district over a four-year period. Notice that on each bar graph, one axis displays the categories and the other axis uses a numerical scale by which the bars can be compared.

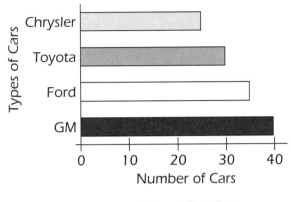

Automobiles in the Parking Lot of a Local Strip Mall

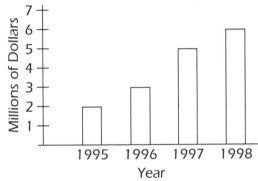

School Funding

Activity

5

Misleading Bar Graphs

Objective: show that graphs can be misused to convey incorrect impressions about the data.

Examine the bar graph below. How do the ice cream sales of company A compare with those of company B?

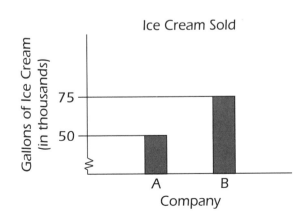

Ice Cream Sold

Things to Think About

Did you notice that the scale showing gallons of ice cream does not begin at zero? How does that affect the data display? At first, it probably appeared to you that company A sold twice as much ice cream as company B. However, when you examine the data display more closely, the ratio of ice cream gallons sold by the two companies is $\frac{75,000}{50,000}$, or $\frac{3}{2}$. Although this graph does not display erroneous data, it is certainly misleading. Graphs that have a break in the numerical scale must be examined closely. Although they may not be intentionally misleading, the impressions gained from such a graph are nevertheless incorrect. A graph that better shows the actual relationships between the sales of the two ice cream companies would have the scale on the *y*-axis start at zero. ▲

Stem-and-Leaf Plots

A recent graphic display innovation is the stem-and-leaf plot. You can think of a stem-and-leaf plot as a combination of a table and a graph. Its shape is similar to a horizontal bar graph, but each data value is shown. The stem-and-leaf plot below represents the following test scores of a mathematics class: 90, 83, 76, 92, 87, 48, 83, 92, 83, 86, 85, 92, 98, 73, 76, 85, 75. In this case, the tens digit acts as the stem and is recorded on the left—the stem side—of the vertical line. The ones digit is the leaf; each ones digit is recorded, in order, on the right—the leaf side—of the vertical line. For example, 7 | 3 represents a score of 73, and 4 | 8 represents a score of 48.

Stems	Leaves
9	0 2 2 2 8
8	3 3 3 5 5 6 7
7	3 5 6 6
6	
5	
4	8
3	
2	
1	

The stem-and-leaf plot above clearly shows where the majority of test scores lie for this class. Notice too that this display preserves all the original data. In other words, all of the test scores can be derived from this stem-and-leaf plot.

Activity

Stem-and-Leaf Plots

Objective: construct and analyze a stem-and-leaf plot.

Use a stem-and-leaf plot to display the following ages of workers in a restaurant: 22, 26, 25, 19, 21, 25, 24, 32, 42, 33, 23, 22, 54, 21, 57, 23, 31.

Things to Think About

How did you go about constructing the stem-and-leaf plot? One way might be to list all the "stem" digits in a column—1, 2, 3, 4, and 5—record the "leaf" digits in the appropriate rows, and then order the values in each row:

Stems	Leaves
1	9
2	1 1 2 2 3 3 4 5 5 6
3	1 2 3
4	2
5	4 7

One advantage of the stem-and-leaf plot is that it is very fast and simple to construct. We can quickly make sure we have included all the data by comparing the number of items in the plot with the number of data items.

What information does this stem-and-leaf plot provide? We can see that the range of ages is 38 (from 19 to 57 years) and that the majority of workers are in their twenties. Stem-and-leaf plots work well when displaying small data sets but become unwieldy when working with very large data sets. ▲

Histogram

A histogram is related to a line plot but is more useful when the data set is large. It reminds us of a bar graph but it uses numerical instead of categorical data. The numerical data are grouped in intervals, called *bins*, that are ordered along the horizontal axis. For example, we can use a histogram to graph the ages at which U.S. presidents were inaugurated. First, we decide on a bin width. Too many bins creates information overload, but too few bins can hide features of the data. A general rule of thumb is to have five to ten bins. Let's group the ages into five-year intervals—40–44, 45–49, 50–54, 55–59, 60–64, and 65–69. The frequency (the number of times a value occurs) in each interval is indicated by the height of the column.

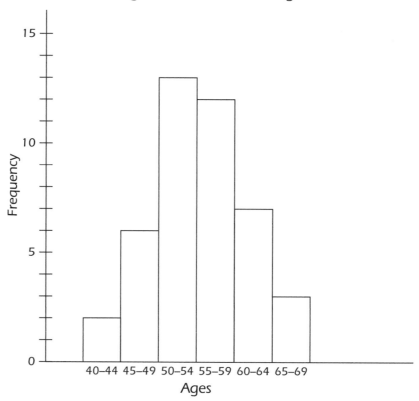

Ages of Presidents at Inauguration

Looking at the histogram above, we see that two presidents were in the 40-to-44 age range (T. Roosevelt and J. F. Kennedy), six were in the 45-to-49 interval, three were in the 65-to-69 bin (R. Reagan was our oldest president at inauguration at 69 years), and the majority (twenty-five) were 50 to 59 years of age when they were inaugurated.

The size of the bins in a histogram should be the same; that is, if the range of one interval is 5, then all of the intervals in that histogram should have a range of 5. Occasionally, however, the interval size does not divide evenly into the range of the data. For example, test scores are often grouped by tens (0–9, 10–19, etc.), but the last interval is eleven (90–100). The columns in a histogram should be right next to each other without any space between them.

A gap between columns indicates that there are no data items with those values. For example, if there were no presidents inaugurated in the interval of 55–59, we would leave a gap between the 50–54 bin and the 60–64 bin.

Can you find individual values in a histogram? That is, from the one above can you determine how many presidents were 56 years old when inaugurated? Histograms summarize data but do not provide information about specific data points. Can you determine the total number of data items from a histogram? Use what you know about the total number of presidents (43) to figure out how.

Box-and-Whisker Plots

Box-and-whisker plots, also known simply as box plots, are used to graphically display and compare large data sets. Typically introduced in upper elementary or middle school, box plots reveal some numerical information about a data set and help us get an overall impression of the features of the data but provide very little information about individual data points within the set nor the total number of data points used to construct the plot. The display has two components, the "box," which is a rectangle that represents the middle 50 percent of the data set, and the "whiskers," which represent the bottom 25 percent and the top 25 percent of the data set.

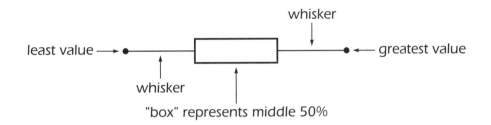

Examine the data in the table below from the U.S. Department of Labor on the 2004 median weekly earnings for different healthcare practitioners. Although this is not a large data set, it can be used to illustrate the power of a box plot display.

Median Weekly Earnings, 2004

OCCUPATION	WEEKLY EARNINGS IN $
Pharmacists	$1,578
Dietitians	669
Physicians	1,660
Registered nurses	904
Occupational therapists	923
Physical therapists	925
Paramedics	690
Lab technicians	727
Speech pathologists	879
Physician's assistants	901
Health information technicians	501

Box plots divide the data set into four equal parts using five data points, known as the *five number summary*: minimum value, first quartile, median, third quartile, and maximum value. To construct a box plot, place the values in the data set in numerical order, and identify the minimum (501) and maximum (1,660) values. Next determine the median (901). Finally, examine the lower half of the data set (501, 669, 690, 727, 879) and find the median of this subset (690). Do the same thing with the upper half of the data, and find the median (925). The lower median is called the first quartile (690), labeled Q1, and the upper median is called the third quartile (925), labeled Q3. Note that the quartiles are not quarters but the boundary values of the quarters, which divide the data set into four parts with approximately the same number of data values in each part.

501 669 | 690 | 727 879 | 901 | 904 923 | 925 | 1,578 1,660

min.   Q1   median   Q3   max.

The five number summary is then used to construct the box plot. This type of graph helps us understand the spread of the data and compare it to other data sets.

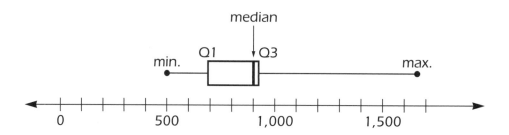

As can be seen from the plot, the upper 25 percent of the data set is quite spread out, whereas 50 percent of the median salary data is concentrated from $690 to $925. The difference between the first quartile and the third quartile (925 − 690 = 235) is called the interquartile range, or IQR. The IQR helps describe the spread of the middle 50 percent of the data. The placement of the line representing the median value indicates that one fourth of the data falls within a very narrow range.

Statisticians use the IQR to decide if a data point qualifies as an outlier. If the distance of a data point from either the first or third quartile is 1.5 times the interquartile range, than it is classified as an outlier. Let's use the healthcare salaries to explore outliers:

▲ The five number summary is 501, 690, 901, 925, 1,660.
▲ The IQR is 235 (925 − 690). Multiply 235 × 1.5. The IQR times 1.5 is 352.5.
▲ The difference between the first quartile and 352.5 is 337.5 (690 − 352.5 = 337.5). Any data points less than 337.5 would be classified as outliers.
▲ The sum of the third quartile and 352.5 is 1,277.5 (925 + 352.5 = 1,277.5). Any data points above 1,277.5 are also outliers.

Two of the healthcare data points are considered outliers: 1,578 and 1,660. These values are considerably above the range of the rest of the data. In other words, physicians' and pharmacists' salaries are so much higher than the salaries of other healthcare practitioners that we may not want to include them when describing the set. Outliers are either eliminated from a data set or are shown on box plots as isolated points, with the whiskers covering the distance from the box to the next highest or lowest point.

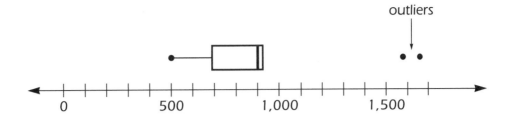

Not all data sets have two whiskers and two parts to the box. In the healthcare salary box plot, for example, the right whisker has been "squeezed" since there are no values between the third quartile and the outliers. Create a data set in which the median and the lower quartile have the same value. What will the box plot of your data set look like?

Activity

Interpreting Box-and-Whisker Plots

Objective: create and compare data represented by box plots.

Do you ever have a small box of raisins for lunch? How are the brands different? How are they similar? Below are data about the number of raisins in 12 boxes of SunMaid Raisins and 12 boxes of Dole Raisins. Each of the boxes weighs the same amount. Make a box plot for each set of data and place them on the same number line. Compare the brands using statistics.

SunMaid Raisins

| 80 | 85 | 86 | 88 | 88 | 88 | 89 | 90 | 91 | 94 | 96 | 100 |

Dole Raisins

| 74 | 93 | 94 | 95 | 96 | 97 | 100 | 101 | 103 | 105 | 107 | 107 |

74 76 78 80 82 84 86 88 90 92 94 96 98 100 102 104 106 108

Things to Think About

The five number summary for SunMaid is 80, 87, 88.5, 92.5, and 100. Fifty percent of the data are from 87 to 92.5. The mean is 88.5. The IQR is 5.5 (92.5 − 87 = 5.5). Notice the box is relatively short, indicating that half of the data are clustered close together. We can check for outliers by multiplying 5.5 by 1.5 (5.5 × 1.5 = 8.25). Quartile 1 (87) minus 8.25 is 78.75 and quartile 3 (92.5) plus 8.25 is 100.75. Since none of the data points is below 78.75 or above 100.75, there are no outliers in this data set.

The five point summary for Dole is 74, 94.5, 98.5, 104, and 107. The IQR is 9.5 (104 − 94.5 = 9.5). The spread of the middle 50 percent of the data set is larger than the other set (9.5 versus 5.5) and the mean is 10 greater (98.5 versus 88.5). This difference in spread and mean can be seen when we compare the "box" part of the plots. Is there an outlier in this set? Multiplying 9.5 by 1.5 equals 14.25. Subtracting 14.25 from Q1 and adding 14.25 to Q3, we find that the outliers are less than 80.25 and greater than 118.25. This means that 74 is an outlier. It is an unusually low value and we should not expect to find this few raisins in a Dole box (though it can occur!). The outlier is shown with a point.

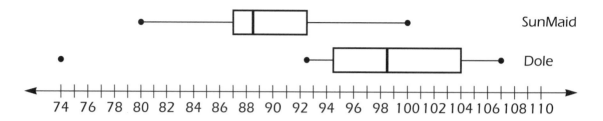

Which brand would you buy? Do you want lots of raisins in a box, or fewer but presumably larger raisins in a box? The box-and-whisker plots indicate that about 75 percent of the time there were fewer raisins in a SunMaid box. Notice that Q3 of SunMaid and Q1 of Dole are approximately the same. In addition, because the data in SunMaid are clustered closer together, we can better predict the number of raisins in future boxes of SunMaid. ▲

Each of the one-variable graphs we've discussed so far can effectively portray data, although some data sets are better portrayed with a specific type of graph. If the data are numerical, then we can choose among line plots, histograms, stem-and-leaf plots, and box-and-whisker plots. If the data are categorical, then pictographs, circle graphs, or bar graphs can be used. Students have a great deal of difficulty determining whether data are categorical or numerical, because we use numbers to count or somehow record the categorical data. For example, in a pictograph we use pictures to represent the number of occurrences in each category. Pictographs have a natural appeal to students. The images in a pictograph usually depict the objects they represent—cars, books, people. Younger students can easily understand pictographs when each image represents a single item. However, when an image represents more than a single item, interpreting a pictograph becomes more difficult. For example, if a single image of a car represents sales of 1,000 cars, then half a car would represent sales of 500 cars. To help students begin to understand that there doesn't have to be a one-to-one correspondence between a picture of an item and one instance of the item, we can ask students to construct pictographs of large data sets. When trying to represent hundreds of ice cream cones, for example, students are forced to let one cone represent a set of cones.

A circle graph displays categories in "wedges" but indicates the size of wedges using percents, which are numbers. For example, if the categories are television networks, a circle graph can be used to show the percent of television sets tuned to specific networks on a given evening. And since the numerical data are percents, it is best to use a circle graph because a percent is a form of a fraction and a circle can be divided into fractional parts. Younger students who do not fully comprehend percents can nevertheless compare the areas of different categories or percentages of a data set in a circle graph, and thus order the data subsets according to relative amounts.

A bar graph has categories (types of dogs, brands of cars, types of music) on one axis and numerical data (the frequency of the category, how many) on the other axis.

One feature of numerical data is that we can determine the mean, median, and mode, but with categorical data we can only find the mode. Students sometimes confuse bar graphs and histograms, because they look very similar, but also because of the type of data used. Note the differences in the two graphs below:

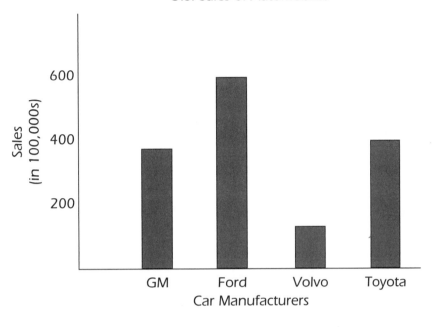

BAR GRAPH

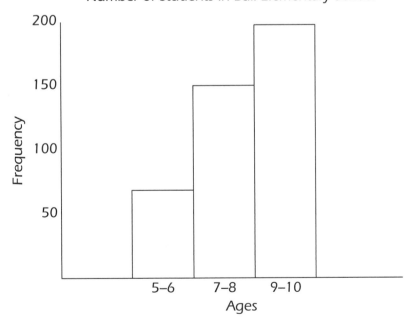

HISTOGRAM

The major difference is that a bar graph displays categorical data and a histogram displays numerical data. In addition, a bar graph displays the bars with spaces in between, and the histogram shows the bars or columns adjacent, or touching. This is because a bar graph shows independent categories of data, and there may be other data or bars that are not displayed. In the previous bar graph, for example, sales from other automobile manufacturers are not included. The numerical data in a histogram involve intervals and include all the data subsets of a given data set. In the histogram shown on the previous page, the intervals represented by the bars encompass all the students in one elementary school. Thus, in a histogram the bars are drawn adjacent to show that where the interval of one data set ends, the next data set begins. There is no such relationship in a bar graph.

Students often do not realize that particular data sets can be represented using some graphs but not all graphs (students tend to want to use bar graphs exclusively). Furthermore, different kinds of graphs emphasize different aspects of the data. For example, if we ask students about the *number* of pets they own, we are collecting numerical data (versus if we asked them the *type* of pet they own, which would be categorical data). However, displaying the number-of-pets data set in a histogram doesn't make any sense since the range of the data is most likely small (most people have less than 10 pets) and does not lend itself to placing data into intervals. A line plot might be a better choice of graphical representation. What other graphs could be used to display the number of pets owned by a group of students?

Stem-and-leaf plots are an intermediary between bar graphs and histograms. They use numerical data, but the visual display is similar to that of horizontal bars on a bar graph. Stem-and-leaf plots work best with small data sets where it is important to note each of the individual data points.

Box-and-whisker plots are especially useful for graphing large numerical data sets. For example, data involving the lengths of hundreds of arrowheads found in one location might be compared to the lengths of hundreds of arrowheads at another site. Anthropologists use the fact that arrowheads made by different tribes tend to have distinctive characteristics and that arrowheads made by the same native American tribes tend to have similar characteristics. Thus, one way to begin to see if arrowheads were made by the same group of native people is to see if the box plots are similar.

In order to graph large categorical data sets, we need to group data into subcategories. Students need experience classifying and categorizing data. For example, a survey that asks forty students to name their favorite cereal may result in more than twenty different responses. A bar graph with twenty categories is not helpful. The cereals need to be grouped to make better sense of the data. One possible set of categories could be hot cereals, unsweetened cold cereals, and sweetened cold cereals. What about a data set that includes fifty different vehicles? One grouping possibility might be trucks, SUVs, and automobiles. Another is domestic vehicles and foreign vehicles. What if the data were favorite games? The games might be categorized into board games, sports games, electronic games, and card games.

Scatter Plots

A scatter plot is a two-variable data display in which values on the horizontal axis (*x*-axis) representing one variable and values on the vertical axis (*y*-axis) representing the second variable are paired and plotted as (*x*,*y*) points. These points are known as ordered pairs. Scatter plots are graphed on the coordinate plane, otherwise known as the *xy*-axis. In the graph below, the weight of small animals in grams is represented on the *x*-axis and number of heartbeats per minute is represented on the *y*-axis. The point (50, 400) represents a weight of 50 grams that is associated with 400 beats per minute (average for chicks). There appears to be a relationship between weight and heartbeats (the hearts of heavier animals beat less often than the hearts of lighter animals). However, just because there appears to be a relationship, or *correlation*, between the variables of weight and heart rate, this does not imply that there is a cause-effect relationship. There could be some outside variable influencing both of the variables we are considering.

Average Heart Rates of Small Animals

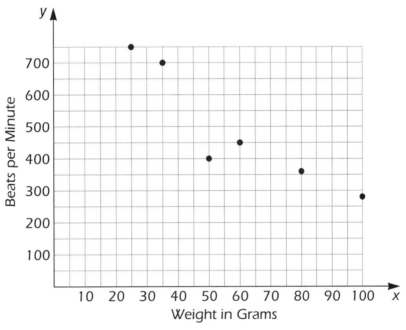

ANIMAL	WEIGHT IN GRAMS	HEART RATE (BEATS PER MINUTE)
Bat	25	750
Chick	50	400
Guinea pig	100	280
Hamster	60	450
Mouse	35	700
Gerbil	80	360

Line Graphs

A line graph is another statistical graph that is used when plotting data to indicate change of some sort between two variables. Sometimes line graphs (e.g., graph of mean daily temperatures during the month of May) are called broken-line graphs to distinguish them from line graphs used in algebra that represent functional relationships and can be represented with an equation. However, the distinction is not always clear and the term *line graph* is used to mean both types of graph.

Generally one of the scales on a line graph uses measurement data or measurements such as temperatures, distances, or times. Both line graphs and scatter plots are used to display the relationship between two variables; therefore, students easily confuse these two types of graphs, reasoning that they are interchangeable. They are not. Scatter plots are used to display discrete data. Discrete data are composed of independent and distinct data units such as the number of students, the number of cars, or the number of houses. Discrete data units cannot be subdivided into smaller units. Discrete data cannot include 2.33 students, $5\frac{1}{3}$ cars, or 3.99834 houses. A line graph is used to show how continuous data change. Continuous data may be subdivided into increasingly smaller units. Examples of continuous data are weight, temperature, distance, and area, which may be divided into smaller units (1.5 lb., 55.4°F, 4.456 miles, or 33.89 square feet). Thus, the type of data represented determines whether to use a scatter plot with distinct points or a line graph where the points are connected. Students often incorrectly connect points on a graph that represent discrete data.

It becomes even more complicated because sometimes the points on a line graph are connected in order to observe trends when technically the points should be separate. For example, teachers often have students graph experimental data such as the number of jumping jacks they can complete in two minutes. The graph below shows the number of jumping jacks one student did. The x-axis is labeled *seconds*, which is a continuous variable—time can be divided into smaller and smaller subunits and used to look at change. The number of jumping jacks—the label on the y-axis—is a discrete variable since the number of jumping jacks must be a whole number, something we count. It does not make sense to think of 30.2 jumping jacks. But the points are connected and this does help us see that while the total number of jumping jacks increases over time, the number of jumping jacks in a ten-second interval decreases over time. Namely, the student slowed down as she became tired.

Jumping Jack Data

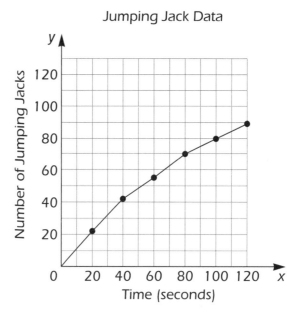

When graphing two-variable data, students need to regularly discuss whether or not it makes sense to connect the points. Students should be aware that connected discrete points help us to observe trends and patterns in the data.

The line graph below shows the average weight of boys between the ages of 2 and 9. Notice that the variables on both axes (weight and age) are represented with continuous data and the points are connected. In comparison, in the scatter plot on page 317, one of the variables is continuous (weight) but the other variable (heartbeat) is discrete. We cannot measure a portion of a heartbeat. Thus, the points cannot be connected.

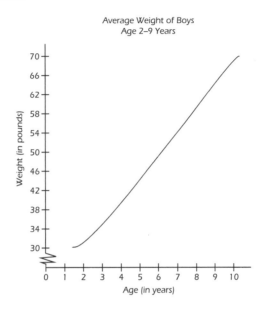

Average Weight of Boys
Age 2–9 Years

Activity

Selecting the Best Graph

Objective: show that graphs may be designed to convey a specific impression about the data.

Which of the two graphs below would you choose to convince a prospective client to invest in your company?

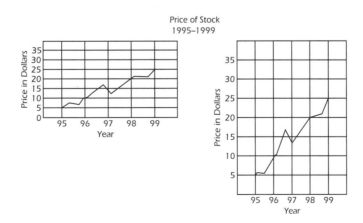

Price of Stock
1995–1999

Things to Think About

Which graph did you select? They both display the same two-variable data, but the displays convey different impressions. The first graph gives the impression that the stock is growing slowly but steadily. The second graph gives the impression that the stock is experiencing rapid, pronounced growth. The scales used on the horizontal axis and on the vertical axis affect the appearance of the company's success. Graphs must be interpreted carefully by synthesizing information from the scales and the data points.

Another common misleading graph is a pictograph whose images are improperly scaled to represent the data. Look at the graph below, which uses two safes to represent the accrued value of two savings banks:

Bank Holdings

$50,000,000
First National Bank

$25,000,000
Second National Bank

Each side of the larger safe is twice as long as each side of the smaller safe. These linear dimensions match the ratio of the bank holdings, 2:1. But doesn't it appear that the First National Bank safe is more than twice the size of the Second National Bank safe? That's because the face of each safe forms a square, and the ratio of the areas of the two faces is not 2:1 but 4:1. The face of the First National Bank safe is four times greater in area than the face of the Second National Bank. A casual observer might conclude that the First National Bank has much more than twice the assets of the Second National Bank. The data displayed is correct, but it is presented in a misleading fashion. ▲

British Prime Minister Benjamin Disraeli once said, "There are lies, damned lies, and statisticians." He was probably thinking of how statistics can be used to create wrong impressions. By providing students with examples of graphical displays to interpret, analyze, and construct, teachers can help students become alert to improper or misleading displays of data, whether intended or not.

Teaching Statistics

Students first learn about the three types of averages and see examples of graphs in elementary school. In middle school, students develop a fuller understanding of the three types of averages and also consider the spread of a data set when interpreting these statistics. They learn to distinguish among the mean, median, and mode in various real-world situations (surveys, data sets, polls, and the like) and to select the most appropriate average to describe a typical item of a data set. They also learn more advanced ways of portraying graphical data: box and whisker plots, double line graphs, and double bar graphs, for example. In high school, students further refine their understanding of typical measures, including standard deviation and variance. As adults, students will use their statistical literacy to analyze commercials, political programs, and medical claims.

Technology plays an increasingly important role in average measures as well as in graphical displays of data. Students at all levels use computers and graphing calculators to generate statistics and to create all sorts of graphs.

Questions for Discussion

1. How do we decide which type of average to use to describe a data set? Give examples of each type.
2. In the early elementary grades, students make a lot of graphs and are asked to identify information on graphs. Find examples of graphing activities and questions in first- and second-grade textbooks. Write questions that go beyond identification and instead ask students to summarize, analyze, and synthesize the information.
3. What are the major similarities and differences among histograms, stem-and-leaf plots, and box-and-whisker plots? What information can be gleaned from each of the graphs and what information is unavailable?
4. How much instructional time should be devoted to data analysis and statistics? Read the section in *Principles and Standards for School Mathematics* (NCTM 2000) for a specific grade level to gain insights into this question.
5. Data are categorized in a number of ways. Discuss the different types of data and how data type dicates our choice of graphical displays.

14
Probability

It's a rare day that passes during which we are not exposed to chance or probability—the weather forecaster predicts a 70 percent chance of rain, you turn a certain age and your insurance rates go up, a sports reporter declares the home team is the favorite in Sunday's big game, your physician recommends an operation with a 95 percent success rate, or you buy a lottery ticket.

As common as these events are, the study of probability can present a challenge to students and teachers alike. One reason is that the probability that certain events will occur is counterintuitive—some things we think are likely to happen actually are not at all likely. Second, probability has only in recent years received significant attention in the elementary and middle school curriculums and may not have been studied in teacher preparation programs. Finally, many adults have not had the opportunity to analyze situations involving probability thoroughly enough to make sense of the likelihood of events.

1. What Is Probability?

Probability is the mathematics of chance. Mathematicians use numerical values to indicate the likelihood that things will happen over the long term. We refer to the "things that happen" as events. The probability of any event's occurrence is expressed as a value ranging from zero (will never happen) to one (will always happen) and can be recorded using a fraction, a decimal, or a percent. An event with a probability of zero is the sun's rising in the west or a person on Earth jumping forty feet off the ground. Events with a probability of one are that in the Northern Hemisphere the days will grow colder in winter and that a face with either one, two, three, four, five, or six dots will appear when we roll a single die. Events with probabilities of zero or one are easy to predict. However, most events have a probability between zero and one. The likelihood of any event's happening can be represented on a number line, like this:

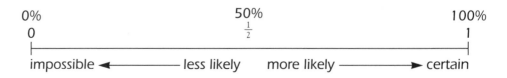

The probability of an event that has an equal chance of happening or not happening can be represented by a point halfway, or 50 percent, between zero and one. The chance of flipping a single coin and getting heads, for instance, is 50 percent, since there is an equal chance that it will come up either heads or tails. It is important to understand, however, that this probability is a prediction of the outcome of a series of coin tosses over a long period, not a prediction of the outcome for any single coin toss. That is, over an extended number of tosses, we can expect heads to come up about one half, or 50 percent, of the time. As the chance of an event's happening increases above 50 percent, it becomes more likely to occur. Conversely, as the chance of an event's happening decreases below 50 percent, it becomes less likely to occur.

Where would you place the following events on the probability number line?

1. Seeing a friend when you are shopping at the mall.
2. Rolling a sum greater than three with a pair of dice.
3. Winning the lottery.
4. Having rain for five days in a row.
5. Hearing a favorite song on the car radio.

How did you decide where to locate each event? Did you first decide whether the event was more likely (more than 0.5) or less likely (less than 0.5) to happen? If you did, you could then position the event more precisely on the probability number line. For example, when you roll a pair of dice you are much more likely to roll a sum greater than three than less than three. Perhaps your experience with games that use dice helped you locate this event closer to one than to one half. However, the chance of rolling a sum greater than three is not one (or 100 percent), because you could roll a sum of two or three.

Probabilistic thinking begins when children start to differentiate between whether an event will always happen, sometimes happen, or never happen. When a glass is knocked off a table, it will always fall toward the floor. Sometimes a glass breaks when it hits the floor. The glass will never fall toward the ceiling. Yet while young children are aware of the range of outcomes to events, they often lack the ability to distinguish between definite events (probability of one) and possible events. Many children think that likely events will always happen and that unlikely events will never happen (Shaughnessy 1992).

Students also may make predictions about the likelihood of an event based on facts that do not directly affect the event. Familiarity causes both children and adults to think an event is more likely to happen. If there have been several recent automobile accidents in a neighboring town, you might conclude that the town has a very high accident rate even if there have been very few accidents over the past ten years. Similarly, if you have won several raffles, you will probably think your chance of winning a raffle is higher than someone who has never won a raffle. Although the probability of a fatal airplane crash is quite low, when one does happen, people tend to overestimate the chance that another will, in part because of the emotional component surrounding any tragedy.

To better understand the likelihood of events, students need to investigate probabilities firsthand through data collection and experimentation. When students collect data, they often are faced with results that do not correspond with their preconceived notions. One of our roles as teachers is to help students resolve discrepancies between what they thought might happen and what actually happens in probabilistic situations. Students need to confront their misconceptions if we are to help them make sense of mathematics.

Probability events are classified in a number of ways that can help us make sense of different types of situations. Two such classifications are independent and dependent events. An *independent event* is an event that is not affected by previous events or events that follow. A single flip of a coin, for example, is not affected by any previous or subsequent coin tosses. *Dependent events* are affected by the outcome of preceding events. The probability or chance that a child will be color-blind is affected by his or her gender—boys are more likely to be color-blind than girls.

A common misconception about probability, called the *gambler's fallacy*, involves confusing dependent and independent events. Imagine tossing a coin five times and having heads come up every time. What is the probability that heads will come up on the sixth toss? Many of us think the probability will be very low, but it's the same as for any other individual toss of a coin, 50 percent. The misconception here is that the sixth flip is somehow related to or dependent on the preceding five flips. But it isn't. Each coin toss is independent. Suppose you rolled a single die three times and a six occurred each time. Are your chances of rolling a six on the next throw higher, lower, or the same as for any other roll of the die? The gambler's fallacy would lead many of us to predict that it is harder to roll a six on the next roll than on the earlier rolls. Again, this is not true. Every roll of a die carries the same probability of rolling a six.

2. Independent Events

We can gather data from a number of independent events and use these data to describe the probability of the event.

Activity

Tossing Tacks

Objective: determine the probability of an event by collecting data and comparing the number of specific outcomes to the total number of outcomes.

Materials: thumbtacks.

When tossed, do thumbtacks land point up or on their side, point tilted down? Predict out of 100 tosses the number of tacks that you think will land both ways. Now toss 10 thumbtacks onto a flat surface and record the number of tacks that land point up. Repeat this experiment ten times. How many of the 100 tacks landed point up? on their side?

Things to Think About

Did your prediction match your results? If you've had no previous experience tossing thumbtacks, you likely made your prediction based on a hunch. There are only two possibilities or outcomes for this experiment—tacks land point up or on their side. If both outcomes were equally likely, then the chance of a tack's landing point up would be one out of two, or 0.5. Are the outcomes equally likely? It is hard to predict without more information. In a situation like this, we can collect data and use these data to make a prediction about future events. What did your data show? Did more of the tacks land point up or on their side? If a majority of the tacks landed point up, you could predict that any tack you toss is more likely to land point up than on its side.

In order to make predictions about future tack tosses, we need to find the relative frequency of that event. *Relative frequency* is a ratio that indicates how often the tack landed point up or sideways (the frequency) compared with the number of times it was tossed. This comparison is relative since it varies depending on the number of tosses. For example, if you toss the tack only 10 times, it might land point up 8 times. The relative frequency is 8 compared to 10, or $\frac{8}{10}$. But if you toss the tack 100 times, the total number of times the tack lands point up might be 62. Now the relative frequency is $\frac{62}{100}$. The relative frequency that an event occurs based on collected data is called its *experimental* or *empirical probability*. Notice that the experimental probability might or might not change every time new data are collected.

When conducting a probability experiment we often talk about "trials." A trial is a single event in any probability experiment—in this case each toss of a tack. We use the total number of trials to determine the relative frequency. More formally, we state that the experimental probability of an event is calculated by forming a part-whole ratio:

$$\frac{\text{frequency of the specified event}}{\text{total number of all trials}} \quad \textit{or in this case} \quad \frac{\text{number of tacks landing point up}}{\text{total number of tossed tacks}}$$

The experimental probability of a tossed tack's landing point up based on these data is 62 out of 100, or $\frac{62}{100}$ (notice that $\frac{62}{100}$ is a number between zero and one). Based on these same data, what is the experimental probability that a tossed tack will land on its side? If 62 tacks landed point up, then 38 landed on their side and the probability is $\frac{38}{100}$. What is the sum of these two probabilities? For any probability situation, the sum of the probability of an event's happening and the probability of the same event's not happening is always one (in this case, $\frac{62}{100} + \frac{38}{100} = 1$). ▲

Experimental probability is used to predict the probability of many situations that are difficult to analyze without data, such as the likelihood that a teenager will be involved in an automobile accident compared with an adult, or the life expectancy of a cigarette smoker compared with a nonsmoker. Insurance companies use collected data to determine the probability that a policy holder will make a claim and then set their premium rates accordingly. In situations like those just mentioned, experimental probabilities are based on a large number of occurrences of a surveyed event and are used to estimate the probability of the same event's happening in the future. When only a small number of trials are conducted, experimental probabilities are not a good predictor of what might happen. For example, although we know that the probability of a coin's landing heads up is $\frac{1}{2}$, this doesn't mean that if you toss a coin twelve times, exactly six will be heads. Laws of probability predict only what will happen based on a large number of trials (if a coin is tossed 1,200 times, about 600 of them will be heads; but if a coin is only tossed 6 times, we cannot predict the number of heads with any certainty).

In some probability situations the frequency of an event's occurring can be determined mathematically, without gathering any data. The relative frequency that an event will occur based on computed results is called its *theoretical probability*. When all possible outcomes are equally likely, the theoretical probability of an event is determined by the following ratio:

$$\text{probability (event A)} = \frac{\text{number of outcomes that result in event A}}{\text{number of all possible outcomes}}$$

For example, a normal die has six faces, with the designations one through six—there are six possible outcomes when you roll it. Each of these outcomes is equally likely to occur. The theoretical probability of the event of rolling a three is $\frac{1}{6}$ since there is only one outcome on the die that results in a three. The theoretical probability of the event of rolling an even number is $\frac{3}{6}$, or $\frac{1}{2}$, since there are three outcomes that are even (two, four, or six) out of six possible outcomes. Whereas some adults make sense of the likelihood of events by determining theoretical probabilities (by analyzing the situations), research suggests that many of us, including students, do not have enough prior experiences to make sense of the mathematics of chance solely on an abstract level. People's understanding of probabilistic situations are enhanced when they have the opportunity to collect and analyze data from experiments and to calculate experimental probabilities, because it helps them develop some intuitions about outcomes. For this reason, instructional materials often direct students to conduct experiments before thinking about the situations abstractly or theoretically. The next two activities ask you to gather data and compare experimental probabilities with theoretical probabilities you can determine by considering outcomes.

Activity

Dropping Pennies

Objective: explore equally likely events and learn about the Law of Large Numbers.

Materials: penny.

Create a target by folding a piece of paper into fourths and labeling them as shown below. Hold a penny at varying heights above the center point and drop the penny onto the paper. Record the number of times the penny lands (stops moving) in each numbered section. Do not count any penny that lands off the target. Repeat twenty times.

1	3
2	4

Things to Think About

Before you begin, predict how often a penny will land in each section. Will the penny land in each of the sections the same number of times? Probability is based on the assumption that every event has an equal probability of occurring in a randomly performed experiment. The act of dropping a penny over the paper is a random event if you drop the penny on the center point in a way that is neutral—that is, in a way that favors no one section over another section. In this case, the paper is divided into four equal sections, and we can assume that the chance that the penny will land on any part of the paper is the same. There are four possible outcomes for each drop, the four sections. The chance the penny will land in section 1 is one out of four, or $\frac{1}{4}$. With twenty drops or trials, the predicted number of times the penny will land in each section is $\frac{1}{4} \times 20 = 5$, or five times each.

Did your experimental data match the theoretical prediction? Why not? One reason may be due to human error in terms of conducting the experiment. But the other reason our experimental data don't match the theoretical prediction is because the predicted results are true only for a large number of drops or trials. The phenomenon that the relative frequency (in this case, the proportion of times the penny lands in each section) gets closer to the theoretical probability as the number of trials increases is known as the *Law of Large Numbers*. The penny activity involved twenty trials. These few trials may or may not produce the predicted results. An activity involving hundreds of drops or trials, however, will produce results that more closely match the theoretical prediction. Even with many trials, the results may not be an exact match of the predicted results, but any differences will be very small. The greater the number of trials, the closer the results will be to the theoretical predictions. ▲

A large number of trials is critical. Children often attempt to generalize an experiment with a few trials. For example, if students conduct an experiment to find the sum of two dice but only perform ten trials, they may get the following sums: 6, 5, 8, 5, 9, 10, 4, 5, 5, and 7. They might conclude that a sum of 5 occurs the most often when rolling two dice. They might further conclude that because the experimental probability of rolling a sum of 5 was $\frac{4}{10}$ in this experiment, in 100 rolls of the dice the sum of 5 will occur about forty times. This seems a reasonable conclusion based on these data, but it is incorrect, as another 20 rolls of the dice are likely to show. Another way to illustrate the Law of Large Numbers is by comparing a survey of only 4 students to a survey of 1,000 students. Which survey is more compelling and reliable? The one with the larger number of respondents is more reliable because the results are based on a larger number of people, or trials. The larger the number of trials, the more meaningful the data. In experimental probability, the larger the number of trials, the more confident you can be of your results. The results of Activity 1 may be different if you toss 1,000 tacks. Which data would be more trustworthy?

In Activity 2, what if the paper is divided differently, as shown below? How does this target affect your predictions about where the penny will land?

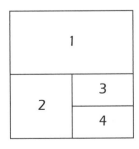

For this paper target, a dropped penny is still going to land randomly anywhere on the paper as long as it is held above the center point and dropped straight down. However, since the four sections are no longer equal in size, the probability that the penny will land in any one of the sections is different and is found by comparing the areas of each section to the area of the entire target. For example, section 1 makes up $\frac{1}{2}$ of the target. The probability that a dropped penny will land in section 1 is

$$\frac{\text{area of section 1}}{\text{area of entire target}} \quad \text{or} \quad \frac{1}{2}$$

What are the probabilities that the penny will land in each of the other sections? One way to determine the probabilities is to compare the areas of each of the sections with the overall area of the paper target. The probability that a penny will land in section 2 is $\frac{1}{4}$. For both sections 3 and 4 the probability is $\frac{1}{8}$. Since in this game there is a 100 percent chance that all recorded pennies landed in one of the four sections, the sum of the four probabilities must be 1 ($\frac{1}{2} + \frac{1}{4} + \frac{1}{8} + \frac{1}{8} = 1$). Can you explain why?

When all outcomes in an experiment or situation are equally likely to occur, as with the first target, we can state that the chance of any one outcome occurring is fair. The concept of fairness is very important in games. Fair games are ones in which all players have an equally likely chance of winning. Students often equate "fairness" with equal turns—that is, if everyone gets the same number of turns, regardless of the rules for winning, the game or situation is fair. Helping students understand that fairness is based on the mathematics underlying the game requires students to gather and/or analyze data. For example, if four people are each assigned one of the sections in the last penny toss, and each gets to keep the pennies that land in her or his section, we quickly conclude that the person assigned section 1 has a considerable advantage. There is not an equally likely chance of winning pennies, since the areas of the four sections are not equivalent in size.

Some situations have only a few possible outcomes and are fairly straightforward to analyze. Other situations involve many more possible outcomes. The more complex the situation, the more valuable it is for students to first collect data to explore that situation. Our familiarity with a problem context contributes to our being able to make sense of the relationships within the problem. Thus, approaching probability from an experimental perspective not only helps students intuitively understand the laws of chance, it better enables them to analyze the situations using a mathematical lens.

Activity

A Dice Game

Objective: show how experimental data contribute to our being able to make sense of theoretical probabilities.

Materials: pair of dice.

Two people, players A and B, roll a pair of dice and calculate the sum. Player A wins if the sum on the dice is 4, 5, 6, 7, or 8. Player B wins if the sum of the dice is 2, 3, 9, 10, 11, or 12. Keep track of the number of wins for each player. Roll the dice at least thirty-six times. Based on the experimental data, do you think this game is fair?

Things to Think About

How did you decide which player you would rather be? Many people choose to be player B, because player B seems to have more chances to roll a winning sum. How did you keep track of the wins for each player? One way is to record the wins on a line plot (see Chapter 13, page 306) using Xs for player A and Os for player B. In the example below, each X or O represents one sum from a toss of the dice. This line plot has a range of 2 through 12 because these are the sums possible when rolling two dice. The players rolled the dice 40 times, or had 40 trials. If you had this information before playing the dice game would you still choose to be player B?

```
                        X
                        X
                        X   X
                        X   X
                        X   X           O
                        X   X           O
                        X   X       O   O
                X       X   X   X   O   O
    O           X   X   X   X   X   O   O
    O   O   X   X   X   X   X   O   O           O
_____
    2   3   4   5   6   7   8   9   10  11  12
```

Looking at the line plot, we can see at once that player A won a lot more often than player B. The experimental probability for player A's winning was $\frac{26}{40}$ and the experimental probability for player B's winning was $\frac{14}{40}$. Remember that experimental probabilities are ratios formed using the collected data:

$$\frac{\text{number of wins for that player}}{\text{number of all trials}}$$

Are these results what you expected? If not, why not?

We can use theoretical probability to try to make better sense of our data. At first glance, since there are eleven possible sums (2 through 12), it would appear that player A has a probability of $\frac{5}{11}$ of winning and player B has a probability of $\frac{6}{11}$ of winning. Yet in theoretical probability we must determine *all* possible outcomes, or in this case, sums. The complication in this situation is that while there are eleven possible sums for any roll of a pair of dice, some sums may be found in more than one way. For example, a sum of 7 may be rolled several different ways, while a sum of 12 may be rolled in only one way. The following table shows all possible sums of a roll of a pair of dice. This is actually an addition table for the addends of one through six, showing the results that occur when we roll two dice and add the numbers that appear. Some sums come up in more than one way. For example, a sum of 6 appears five times on the chart because it can be rolled with 4 and 2, 2 and 4, 1 and 5, 5 and 1, and 3 and 3.

+	1	2	3	4	5	6
1	2	3	4	5	6	7
2	3	4	5	6	7	8
3	4	5	6	7	8	9
4	5	6	7	8	9	10
5	6	7	8	9	10	11
6	7	8	9	10	11	12

DIE NUMBER 2

Use the table to determine how many different combinations of the dice sum to seven. There are six possible combinations: 1 and 6, 2 and 5, 3 and 4, 4 and 3, 5 and 2, and 6 and 1. The combinations for the other sums are listed in the table below.

SUM	NO. OF COMBINATIONS	ACTUAL COMBINATIONS (DIE 1, DIE 2)
2	1	(1,1)
3	2	(1,2), (2,1)
4	3	(1,3), (2,2), (3, 1)
5	4	(1,4), (2,3), (3,2), (4,1)
6	5	(1,5), (2,4), (3,3), (4,2), (5,1)
7	6	(1,6), (2,5), (3,4), (4,3), (5,2), (6,1)
8	5	(2,6), (3,5), (4,4), (5,3), (6,2)
9	4	(3,6), (4,5), (5,4), (6,3)
10	3	(4,6), (5,5), (6,4)
11	2	(5,6), (6,5)
12	1	(6,6)

There are thirty-six possible outcomes, rather than eleven! These data can be used to form theoretical probabilities to predict which player is likely to win the game when a large number of trials are conducted. Since player A wins when sums of 4, 5, 6, 7, and 8 occur, there are twenty-three different winning combinations for player A, or $\frac{23}{36}$ of the total number of outcomes. Player B wins with sums of 2, 3, 9, 10, 11, or 12. Player B has thirteen winning combinations, or $\frac{13}{36}$ of the total number of outcomes. Even though player A has more chances of winning, in a game with a few rolls player B could be the winner. Nevertheless, player A is more likely to win this dice game if it involves a large number of tosses (trials). Thus, this is not a fair game, because the chances (or theoretical probability) of player A's or player B's winning are not equal.

The total number of outcomes when tossing two dice can be determined using what is known in mathematics as the *Fundamental Counting Principle*. The Counting Principle, as it is also known, enables us to count the number of ways a task can occur given a series of events. It states that the number of outcomes of an event is the product of the number of outcomes of each stage of the event. Therefore, because there are six possible outcomes on one die and six possible outcomes on the second die, the product of 6 and 6, or 36, is the number of possible outcomes when tossing two dice. The Counting Principle is usually introduced to students in middle school. ▲

Activity

Fairness: Primes and Composites

Objective: determine if a situation is fair using theoretical probability.

Two roommates, Catherine and Elizabeth, decide who does the dishes each evening by rolling two dice. If the sum of the two dice is a prime number, Catherine washes; if the sum is a composite number, Elizabeth is on dish duty! Is this a fair way to determine who washes the dishes? If it is, explain why. If not, change the rules to make it fair. Explain your reasoning.

Things to Think About

It is difficult to determine on the surface if this situation is fair or unfair. One way would be to collect a lot of data and examine the relative frequency that a prime number sum occurs. Another way is to analyze the situation. Using the Counting Principle—see the addition table in Activity 3 that shows the sums of two dice—we see that there are 36 ways to create sums. However, there aren't 36 different sums, only 11. So how do we figure out the theoretical probability of rolling a sum that is a prime number? By identifying the outcomes of rolling two dice where the sum is a prime number! The numbers 2, 3, 5, 7, and 11 are prime; the numbers 4, 6, 8, 9, 10, and 12 are composite. The prime numbers are circled in the table below.

DIE NUMBER 1

+	1	2	3	4	5	6
1	②	③	4	⑤	6	⑦
2	③	4	⑤	6	⑦	8
3	4	⑤	6	⑦	8	9
4	⑤	6	⑦	8	9	10
5	6	⑦	8	9	10	⑪
6	⑦	8	9	10	⑪	12

DIE NUMBER 2

Notice that there are 15 occurrences of a prime sum out of a total of 36 possible outcomes. Thus, the theoretical probability of rolling a prime sum is $\frac{15}{36}$ or $\frac{5}{12}$. That means that the theoretical probability of rolling a composite sum is $\frac{21}{36}$, or $\frac{7}{12}$. This method of determining who does the dishes is not fair because the probability of rolling a prime or a composite sum are not equally likely.

How do we make the situation fair? First, if we assume the roommates plan to use sums from two dice to decide, then each option should have a theoretical probability of one half, or $\frac{18}{36}$. One solution is that Catherine washes the dishes when a sum of 4, 5, 6, or 7 occurs and Elizabeth washes when any other sum is rolled. Another solution would have Catherine washing when a sum under 7 is rolled and Elizabeth washing when a sum greater than 7 is rolled. (Sums of 7 don't count; they roll again.) Can you explain why each of these rules makes the situation fair? ▲

Activity

Tossing Coins

Objective: use the Counting Principle to determine probabilities of linked events.
Materials: coin.

The probability of tossing a coin and getting tails is $\frac{1}{2}$. If you toss the coin four times, the probability of getting tails on any one of the tosses is still $\frac{1}{2}$. But what is the probability of tossing four tails in a row? Toss a coin four times in a row and record your results in terms of the number of heads and tails (or you can toss four coins at the same time and record the number of heads and tails). How often do you think four tails occur in a row? Repeat this experiment sixteen times. Calculate the experimental and the theoretical probability that four tails will occur in a row.

Things to Think About

Based on your experimental data, you probably found that tossing four tails in a row does not happen all that often. Since each toss is an independent event, each heads or tails has an equally likely chance of happening on each toss. What, then, is the probability that tails will occur on the first toss *and* on the second toss *and* on the third toss *and* on the fourth toss? A tree diagram can help us visualize all possible outcomes for tossing four coins (see next page). We can then examine the outcomes to determine how many of the outcomes show four tails.

The first toss can be either heads or tails and is shown as toss 1. Each of these results is followed by another toss that will be either heads or tails (see the "branches" on the tree diagram). Start at the left and continue to follow the branches to find all possible outcomes of heads and tails when tossing four coins. How many possible outcomes are there? How many result in four tails? Since there are sixteen possible outcomes and only one of them results in four tails, the chance of tossing four tails in a row is $\frac{1}{16}$.

The probability that one event and another event will occur together generally decreases the probability of a particular outcome. If you consider tossing two coins, the probability of two heads appearing is $\frac{1}{4}$, since there are four possible outcomes (e.g., HH, HT, TH, TT). Likewise, when tossing four coins there are many more possible outcomes because of the ways heads and tails can be combined. We can again use the Fundamental Counting Principle to find the total number of outcomes. Since there are two possible outcomes for each toss of a coin, there are sixteen possible outcomes for four coins tossed in a row

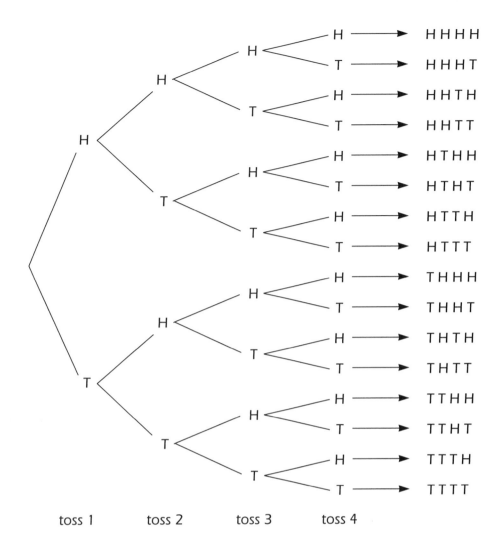

toss 1   toss 2   toss 3   toss 4

$(2 \times 2 \times 2 \times 2 = 16)$. Multiplication can also be used to show that the probability of four tails is $\frac{1}{16}$.

| $\frac{1}{2}$ | $\times$ | $\frac{1}{2}$ | $\times$ | $\frac{1}{2}$ | $\times$ | $\frac{1}{2}$ | $=$ | $\frac{1}{16}$ |
| probability of tails on toss 1 | | probability of tails on toss 2 | | probability of tails on toss 3 | | probability of tails on toss 4 | | probability of tails on four tosses in a row |

What is the probability of tossing five tails in a row? Another toss of the coin will double the possible outcomes (can you explain why?), but only one outcome will result in five tails, so the chance of tossing five tails is $\frac{1}{32}$. It is important to note that the $\frac{1}{16}$ probability ratio is true for a large number of coin tosses. You might toss four tails in a row with the first set of coin tosses, or you may need 100 or more sets of tosses before tossing four tails in a row. As with all probability ratios, $\frac{1}{16}$ predicts that in a large number of coin tosses, four tails in a row should come up close to $\frac{1}{16}$ of the time. The probability ratio cannot predict the result of a single set of tosses. ▲

In each of these activities the chance that an event will happen is written as the ratio of the number of particular outcomes compared with the total number of all possible outcomes. Another way to think about the probability ratio is as a part-to-whole ratio, or fraction (Chapter 5 discusses the different meanings of fractions). Thinking of probability as a fraction helps children link probability concepts to their early understanding of what fractions are. However, probability experiments and probability ratios need not depend on students' understanding of part-to-whole relationships. Research shows that children who cannot reason with part-whole relationships may nevertheless be able to perform probability experiments, collect data, and interpret the data (Shaughnessy 1992). In fact, the use of fractions in a different context may help establish students' understanding of the part-to-whole meaning of fractions.

Not all probability situations are reported using part-to-whole ratios. The mathematical odds of an event's occurring is described using part-to-part ratios. But what are odds? Odds in favor of an event predict the chance of an event's occurring compared with the chance of the event's *not* occurring. Likewise, odds against an event predict the chance of the event's not happening compared with the chance of the event's occurring.

odds in favor of (event) = number of outcomes resulting in the event : number of outcomes not resulting in the event

For example, what are the odds that when you roll two dice the sum of the dice will not be 7? In Activity 3 we found that there are 6 ways to roll a sum of 7 [(1,6), (2,5), (3,4), (4,3), (5,2), (6,1)]. Since there are 36 possible sums, that leaves 30 ways (36 − 6) not to roll a 7. The part-to-part ratio that describes the odds is:

odds (of not rolling a 7) = 30:6, or 5:1 (which we read as "30 to 6" or "5 to 1")

We can state that the odds are 5 to 1 that a sum of 7 will not be rolled. What are the odds that a sum greater than 10 will be rolled? There are 3 ways to roll a sum greater than 10 [(5,6), (6,5), (6,6)] compared with 33 ways not to roll a sum greater than 10. The odds of rolling a sum greater than 10 are 3:33, or 1 to 11. While odds are most often associated with gambling, the application of these ideas to fields such as law and medicine is significant.

Probability instruction for students in the elementary and middle grades should be experimentally based. Probabilities that are calculated as the result of investigating simple questions and gathering data to answer these questions further students' understanding of the mathematics of chance and provide situations in which they might confront intuitive misconceptions about probability. However, it is essential that we as teachers remember the principles inherent in the Law of Large Numbers and make sure that a sufficient number of trials are conducted in order to use experimental probability to make confident predictions.

3. Dependent Events

Dependent events are linked to previous events. A dependent event may be illustrated using a bag containing three red marbles, two green marbles, and one black marble. Suppose you select two marbles from the bag, one at a time, replacing the first marble after you choose it. The probability of picking a red marble on the first pick is $\frac{3}{6}$, or $\frac{1}{2}$, because three of the outcomes are red out of a total of six marbles. The probability of getting a red marble on the second pick is also $\frac{3}{6}$, or $\frac{1}{2}$. But suppose you were to select two marbles from the bag, one after the other, without replacing the first marble. The probability of selecting a red marble with the second pick would depend on what color marble you picked first. If you picked a green or a black marble first, the chance of next picking a red marble is $\frac{3}{5}$, because three of the five marbles left in the bag are red. But suppose you picked a red marble first. Then only two of the five marbles left in the bag would be red. The probability of selecting a red marble with the second pick would therefore be $\frac{2}{5}$. The probability of selecting a specific-color marble on the second pick changes according to the color selected on the first pick, because the first marble is not replaced in the bag. (And because the first marble isn't put back into the bag, the total number of outcomes for the second pick is five, not six.) The probability of the second pick depends on the first pick.

Activity

Investigating Dependent Events

Objective: investigate a dependent event by collecting data and analyzing the situation.

Take three identical sheets of paper. On one sheet write the word *blue* on both sides (blue/blue); on another sheet write *blue* on one side and *white* on the reverse (blue/white); on the remaining piece of paper write *white* on both sides (white/white). Imagine that you've closed your eyes, thrown the three sheets of paper into the air, and selected one of the sheets. You see that the color facing you is blue. Without looking at the back of the sheet or at either of the other sheets, can you determine whether the color on the back of the sheet you are holding is more likely to be blue or white? In particular, what is the probability that the color on the other side of the sheet is blue? Collect data to find the experimental probability and then analyze the situation and determine the theoretical probability. Do your two probabilities agree?

Things to Think About

The set condition here that makes this a dependent event is that you know one side of the paper is blue. Knowing that the color of the paper facing you is blue, however, complicates determining the probability that the other side of the paper is also blue. Many people's initial hunch is that the probability is either $\frac{1}{3}$ or $\frac{1}{2}$. The reasoning behind $\frac{1}{3}$ is that because the word *blue* appears three times, the chance is one out of three. The reasoning behind $\frac{1}{2}$ is that because there are only two pieces of paper with blue on one or both sides, the chance is one out of two. Both of these hunches are incorrect. If you conducted a large number of trials, your experimental probability would not support these ratios. Let's see if we can understand why.

   To find the theoretical probability we must determine all possible outcomes. Keeping in mind that we are looking at a blue side, make a list of the total possible colors that could be on the reverse side. Next, consider the number of times you wrote the word *blue* when you created the papers for the experiment. You wrote the word *blue* three times, so we must account for all three. Since a blue side is showing, the paper could be the blue/blue sheet, with either blue side facing upward. Let's differentiate the two blue sides on the blue/blue sheet as $blue_1$ and $blue_2$. The paper could also be the blue/white sheet, with the blue side, $blue_3$, showing. Thus, the set of possible papers includes only three possibilities:

$$\frac{B_2}{B_1} \quad \frac{B_1}{B_2} \quad \frac{B_3}{W_1}$$

Notice that while all three of these outcomes have blue on the upward side, only two of the three outcomes have blue on the downward side. Thus, the probability that the second side is blue given the first side is blue is $\frac{2}{3}$. ▲

Dependent events are sometimes referred to as conditional events, since one event depends on a set condition of another event. There are formulas for calculating conditional probabilities, and you may wish to investigate them. However, situations that involve dependent events can also be explored using experimental probability.

A related topic studied in middle school is *permutations*. Permutations specifically count the number of ways a task can be arranged or ordered. In other words, when you need to know the number of ways you can arrange items when order is important, you can use a permutation to count them. For example, you may want to know how many ways first-, second-, and third-place winners might occur within a field of ten contestants. Or you want to know how many different ways a group of four students completing a project could be assigned the tasks of recorder, responder, researcher, and calculator. Permutations can be derived theoretically using the Fundamental Counting Principle. When the values are small, permutations can also be determined using a variety of listing strategies and counting.

Let's explore an example. Every August, the New London Hospital sponsors a mini-triathlon as a way to raise money. There are three activities in the triathlon: a quarter-mile swim, a twelve-mile bicycle ride, and a five-mile run. Each year there are discussions about the order of the activities: should competitors first swim, run, or bike? What activity should come next? How many different ways are there for the triathlon committee to order the three activities?

Since we are interested in the arrangement of three activities (swim, bike, ride) and order does matter, we can find the permutations of a series of three events. Let's represent the swim with an *s*, the bike ride with a *b*, and the run with an *r*, and arrange the letters in different orders:

s-b-r

s-r-b

b-s-r

b-r-s

r-s-b

r-b-s

There are six different ways to arrange the three triathlon activities. More formally we say that there are 6 permutations of 3. How do we use the Counting Principle to find the number of permutations? Think about how you listed the activities. For the first activity, you can choose any one of the three options. But as soon as you choose the first activity (e.g., swim), you are limited in your choice for what can come second. Namely, you have just two activities to choose between (bike or ride). Finally, once you pick the second activity, you are left with only one option for the third event. The Counting Principle enables us to determine how many ways we can arrange the three activities (3 choices for the first event times 2 choices for the second event times 1 choice for the third event; $3 \bullet 2 \bullet 1 = 6$), but does not provide information about the actual arrangements. Notice that subsequent choices depend on the earlier choices—the number of options is reduced each time something is chosen! This is why some permutations are related to dependent events (other types of permutations involve independent choices). When there are more than a few items to be ordered, counting permutations becomes laborious and the use of the Counting Principle and other formulas becomes essential.

The process of multiplying a whole number, n, by every positive whole number less than itself is abbreviated using the factorial symbol $n!$. For example, $3!$ is read as "three factorial" and indicates the product of the positive integers less than or equal to 3, namely, $3 \times 2 \times 1$, or 6. We use factorial notation to answer many permutation questions. Let's say we want to arrange 8 books in order on a bookshelf. How many different ways can we arrange 8 books on the shelf (or what is the number of permutations of 8 different books in a row of 8 books)? Take a minute and see if you can explain why the number of ways is $8!$, or $8 \bullet 7 \bullet 6 \bullet 5 \bullet 4 \bullet 3 \bullet 2 \bullet 1$, or 40,320. Remember that we have 8 choices for which book to place first in the row, 7 choices for the second place, and so on.

It is possible to make permutations without using all of the items in each permutation. For example, 12 friends decide to enter the New London triathlon. Teams need to consist of contestants willing to be the designated swimmer, bike rider, and runner, in that order. The order of the contestants on each team will indicate their designated sport. How many permutations of 3 contestants are possible when choosing among 12 different people? When there are 12 people, there are 12 possibilities for the first contestant (the swimmer). There are then 11 choices for the second contestant, and 10 choices for the third contestant. Using the Counting Principle we find that there are $12 \times 11 \times 10$, or 1,320 permutations or different teams of three people where order matters.

Some of the 1,320 teams will consist of the same 3 people (but in different orders). For example, Andrea, Ben, and Chris are contestants that are one team out of the 1,320, in that order. But they also are on another team with their names listed in a different order—Chris, Ben, and Andrea—where they each have a different event in the triathlon. In fact there are 6 instances where these 3 people are listed but in different orders!

Andrea, Ben, Chris	Andrea, Chris, Ben
Ben, Andrea, Chris	Ben, Chris, Andrea
Chris, Andrea, Ben	Chris, Ben, Andrea

When we aren't interested in order, but just how many different groups of 3 people can be made, we are considering the number of possible *combinations* of 12 people when placed into groups of 3. Calculating the number of combinations involves removing ways that repeat groupings. Since every group of 3 people can be arranged 6 ways (see the listing below of how Andrea, Ben, and Chris are arranged), we divide by 6 to find the number of unique groups of 3 people formed using the 12 people. There are $1,320 \div 6$, or 220, unique groups or combinations of 3 people.

You may wish to investigate the specific formulas for calculating the number of combinations and permutations depending on the number of items and size of groups desired. This topic is sometimes studied in middle school but more often in high school and college.

Activity

Telephone Madness!

Objective: learn more about permutations of an event.

To make a telephone call to most places in the United States you need to dial the area code followed by the city code followed by the actual number. Why do we need all those numbers? How many different phone numbers are there in the 508 area code? In the 415 and the 919 area codes? Potentially, how many distinct phone numbers are possible? With the increase in cell phones, do you think this will be enough?

Things to Think About

The order of the numbers in a telephone number is important—we all know from experience that misdialing one digit gives us a wrong number! How many people can have different telephone numbers in the 508 area code region? To answer this we need to use permutations and the fact that based on experience we know that digits can be repeated in a telephone number. Consider each place in the telephone number below, and ask yourself, "How many digits can be used?"

$$508 - \_\_\_ - \_\_\_\_$$

By convention city codes do not begin with 0, so in the first blank place above we can place the digits 1 through 9—there are 9 choices. But in all of the other places we can place any of the 10 digits (0, 1, 2, 3, . . . , 9) so there are 10 choices. Thus there are $9 \times 10 \times 10 \times 10 \times 10 \times 10 \times 10$ or 9,000,000 different phone numbers in the 508 area code. Using the same reasoning, we can generalize that the area codes of 415 or 919 each have nine million different numbers associated with them. Is this enough? No! New area codes pop up in regions with lots of people every few years because the demand in these areas is for more than nine million telephone numbers.

How many different 10-digit telephone numbers are possible? First, let's disregard the fact that certain area codes such as 800 and 866 are designated as toll-free numbers. The number of possible digits for each place is:

$$9 \times 10 \times 10 \times 9 \times 10 \times 10 \times 10 \times 10 \times 10 \times 10$$

Both area codes and city codes do not begin with zero so there are only 9 choices of digits for those places. That leaves 81×10^8—or 8,100,000,000 possible telephone numbers. Now remove the toll-free telephone numbers that have area codes of 800, 866, 877, and 888. We discovered earlier that each of those area codes has 9 million numbers associated with it, so presently there are 36 million numbers reserved for toll-free usage. That leaves over 8 billion phone numbers (8,064,000,000)! As the need for telephone numbers has increased, so has the requirement of dialing many digits. As the number of people in the world increases, we may one day be dialing 12 or more digits to call our neighbors! ▲

Teaching Probability

Elementary school students have difficulty thinking about probabilistic situations. For this reason young students benefit more from exploring probability situations and examining the data from various events than from learning probability formulas and algorithms. By doing so they can build an intuitive foundation for probabilistic thinking. In the middle grades, students continue to perform experiments and gather the resulting data. They learn to present their data in increasingly sophisticated ways, using spreadsheets and graphs. As their intuitive grasp of probability increases, middle school students can be asked to develop and apply formulas and algorithms to determine the theoretical probability of specific events. In high school, students increasingly study theoretical probability, concentrating less on experimental probability. Their experiments or data gathering will use existing and emerging technologies to simulate real situations. After their formal schooling is completed, students should be able to use their understanding of probability to make informed choices as consumers and citizens.

Questions for Discussion

1. Many Americans think that buying 100 tickets instead of 1 ticket in their state lottery game significantly improves their chances of winning. Explain why this line of reasoning is flawed.

2. What do the NCTM Standards suggest should be the focus regarding instruction in probability to students in grades PreK–2? grades 3–5? grades 6–8?

3. A number of laws and principles were discussed in this chapter. What are they, how are they applied to probabilistic situations, and how are they connected to other topics in mathematics?

4. There are many phrases and terms specific to probability. What is the difference between independent and dependent events? between experimental and theoretical probability? Give examples.

5. Write three problems for middle school students that use either permutations, combinations, or both in the solution process. Prepare detailed solutions for each problem. Explain how your problems will support students' developing understanding of these concepts.

Materials List

base ten blocks
calculator
chips, two colors (red and black)
clay or Plasticine
coffee stirrers
coins
cubes
Cuisenaire rods
dice
geoboard and rubber bands
geometric shapes
graph paper
hollow plastic tube
meter sticks
metric tape measure
mini-marshmallows or gumdrops
multilink cubes
newspaper
paper clips
pattern blocks
protractor
scissors
square tiles (graph paper can be substituted)
straws
tangram puzzle
thumbtacks
toothpicks (flat)
tracing paper

Web Sites

Chapter 1

For interactive Web sites that focus on number sense go to:

http://nlvm.usu.edu/en/nav/vlibrary.html (3–5 Number & Operations; see base blocks; number line.)

www.fi.uu.nl/rekenweb/en (See number line.)

http://illuminations.nctm.org/tool/index.aspx (See Bobbie Bear Activity, Counting Strategies.)

Chapter 2

For interactive Web sites that focus on computation go to:

www.fi.uu.nl/rekenweb/en (See number factory.)

http://illuminations.nctm.org/tools/index.aspx (See Bobbie bear; ten frame.)

Chapter 3

For interactive Web sites that focus on addition and subtraction go to:

http://nlvm.usu.edu/en/nav/vlibrary.html (3–5 Number & Operations; see base blocks addition; base blocks subtraction; color chips addition; number line arithmetic.)

www.fi.uu.nl/rekenweb/en (See make three.)

Chapter 4

For interactive Web sites that focus on multiplication and division go to:

http://nlvm.usu.edu/en/nav/vlibrary.html (6–8 Number & Operations; see rectangle multiplication.)

www.fi.uu.nl/rekenweb/en (See make three [negative numbers].)

http://illuminations.nctm.org/tools/index.aspx (See factor game; product game.)

Chapter 5

For interactive Web sites that focus on fractions go to:

www.visualfractions.com/

http://nlvm.usu.edu/en/nav/vlibrary.html (6–8 Number & Operations; see fractions [several].)
http://illuminations.nctm.org/tools/index.aspx (See fractions [several].)

Chapter 6

For interactive Web sites that focus on decimals go to:

http://nlvm.usu.edu/en/nav/vlibrary.html (6–8 Number & Operations; see base blocks, decimals.)
www.bbc.co.uk/education/mathsfile/ (See builder Ted; rounding off.)

Chapter 7

For interactive Web sites that focus on percent go to:

http://nlvm.usu.edu/en/nav/vlibrary.html (6–8 Number & Operations; see percentages.)
www.bbc.co.uk/education/mathsfile/ (See saloon snap.)
www.explorelearning.com/ (See middle school numbers and operations [ratios, proportions, and percents].)

Chapter 8

For interactive Web sites that focus on ratio and proportion go to:

www.explorelearning.com (6–8 Number and Operations; see ratio, proportion, and percents.)
http://nlvm.usu.edu/en/nav/vlibrary.html (See transformations: dilations.)
www.visualfractions.com/

NCTM also provides a wide range of engaging and effective applets for members only at its site www.nctm.org.

Chapter 9

For interactive Web sites that focus on algebra go to:

http://nlvm.usu.edu/en/nav/vlibrary.html (Algebra 3–5; see pattern blocks.)
http://nlvm.usu.edu/en/nav/vlibrary.html (Algebra 6–8; see algebra tiles; algebra balance scales.)
http://illuminations.nctm.org/tools/index.aspx (See pan balance [numbers].)

Chapter 10

For interactive Web sites that focus on geometry go to:

http//:nlvm.usu.edu/en/nav/vlibrary.html (6–8 Geometry; see Pythagorean theorem; geoboard [several]; congruent triangles.)
http//:illuminations.nctm.org/tools/index.aspx (See proof without words [Pythagorean theorem]; interactive geometry dictionary; shape sorter.)
http//:nlvm.usu.edu/en/nav/vlibrary.html (Geometry 6–8; see platonic solids.)

Chapter 11

For interactive Web sites that focus on spatial sense go to:

www.learner.org/teacherslab/math/geometry/space/index.html (See *I Took a Train;* plot plan and silhouettes.)

http//:nlvm.usu.edu/en/nav/vlibrary.html (6–8 Geometry; see ladybug mazes; platonic solids [slicing]; space blocks; transformations.)

www.fi.uu.nl/rekenweb/en (See coloring sides 1, 2; build free; houses with heights 1, 2; rotating houses; rebuild.)

http//:illuminations.nctm.org/tools/index.aspx (See cubes; tools [isometric drawing tool].)

www.bbc.co.uk/education/mathsfile/ (See bathroom tiles.)

Chapter 12

For interactive Web sites that focus on measurement go to:

nlvm.usu.edu/en/nav/vlibrary.html (6–8 Geometry; see volume and shape.)

www.shodor.org/interactivate/activities/index.html (See Geometry and Measurement Concepts [surface area and volume].)

www.bbc.co.uk/education/mathsfile/ (See Shape, Space, & Measure [Estimation].)

www.mste.uiuc.edu/carvell/3dbox/default.html

www.mste.uiuc.edu/carvell/rectperim/RectPerim2.html

http//:arcytech.org/java/pi/measuring.html

Chapter 13

For interactive Web sites that focus on statistics go to:

http://nlvm.usu.edu/en/nav/vlibrary.html (6–8 Data & Probability; see pie chart; coin tossing.)

http://illuminations.nctm.org/tools/index.aspx (See box plotter; circle grapher.)

Chapter 14

For interactive Web sites that focus on probability go to:

http://nlvm.usu.edu/en/nav/vlibrary.html (6–8 Data & Probability; see spinners; box plot.)

http://illuminations.nctm.org/tools/index.aspx (See adjustable spinner.)

Resources

Anno, M. 1995. *Anno's Magic Seeds*. New York: Philomel.

Baroody, A. 1993. *Problem Solving, Reasoning, and Communicating, K–8*. New York: Merrill.

Barry, D. 1994. *The Rajah's Rice: A Mathematical Folktale from India*. New York: W. H. Freeman.

Behr, M., G. Harel, T. Post, and R. Lesh. 1992. "Rational Number, Ratio and Proportion." In *Handbook of Research on Mathematics Teaching and Learning*, edited by D. Grouws, 296–333. New York: Macmillan.

Beilin, H. 1975. *Studies in the Cognitive Basis of Language Development*. New York: Academic Press.

Ben-Chaim, D., G. Lappan, and R. T. Houang. 1988. "The Effect of Instruction on Spatial Visualization Skills of Middle School Boys and Girls." *American Educational Research Journal* 25: 51–71.

Bezuk, N. S., and M. Bieck. 1993. "Current Research in Rational Numbers and Common Fractions: Summary and Implications for Teachers." In *Research Ideas for the Classroom: Middle Grades Mathematics*, edited by D. T. Owens, 118–36. Reston, VA: National Council of Teachers of Mathematics.

Birch, D. 1994. *The King's Chessboard*. New York: Puffin Pied Piper.

Bransford, J., A. Brown, and R. Cocking, eds. 1999. *How People Learn: Brain, Mind, Experience, and School*. Washington: National Academy Press.

Bright, G., and K. Hoeffner. 1993. "Measurement, Probability, Statistics, and Graphing." In *Research Ideas for the Classroom: Middle Grades Mathematics*, edited by D. T. Owens, 78–98. Reston, VA: National Council of Teachers of Mathematics.

Burns, M. 1994a. "Arithmetic: The Last Holdout." *Phi Delta Kappan* 75: 471–76.

———. 1994b. "Four Great Math Games." *Instructor* 103 (7): 44–46.

Carpenter, T., E. Fennema, and M. L. Franke. 1994. *Cognitively Guided Instruction: Children's Thinking About Whole Numbers*. Madison: Wisconsin Center for Education Research, School of Education, University of Wisconsin–Madison.

Carpenter, T., E. Fennema, M. L. Franke, L. Levi, and S. Empson. 1999. *Children's Mathematics: Cognitively Guided Instruction*. Portsmouth, NH: Heinemann.

Carpenter, T., M. L. Franke, and L. Levi. 2003. *Thinking Mathematically: Integrating Arithmetic and Algebra in Elementary School*. Portsmouth, NH: Heinemann.

Carroll, W. M., and D. Porter. 1997. "Invented Strategies Can Develop Meaningful Mathematical Procedures." *Teaching Children Mathematics* 3: 370–74.

———. 1998. "Alternative Algorithms for Whole Number Operations." In *The Teaching and Learning of Algorithms in School Mathematics*, edited by L. Morrow and M. Kenney, 106–14. Reston, VA: National Council of Teachers of Mathematics.

Chapin, S., C. O'Connor, and N. C. Anderson. 2003. *Classroom Discussions: Using Math Talk to Help Students Learn, Grades 1–6*. Sausalito, CA: Math Solutions Publications.

Charles, R. I., and F. K. Lester. 1982. *Teaching Problem Solving: What, Why, and How*. Palo Alto, CA: Dale Seymour.

Charles, R. I., and J. Lobato. 1998. *Future Basics: Developing Numerical Power*. A Monograph of the National Council of Supervisors of Mathematics. Golden, CO: The National Council of Supervisors of Mathematics.

Clements, D., and M. Battista. 1992. "Geometry and Spatial Sense." In *Handbook of Research on Mathematics Teaching and Learning*, edited by D. Grouws, 420–64. New York: Macmillan.

Clements, D., and G. Bright, eds. 2003. *Learning and Teaching Measurement*. Reston: VA: National Council of Teachers of Mathematics.

Coburn, T. 1993. *Patterns*. Addenda Series, Grades K–6. Reston, VA: National Council of Teachers of Mathematics.

Cramer, K., and N. S. Bezuk. 1991. "Multiplication of Fractions: Teaching for Understanding." *Arithmetic Teacher* 39 (3): 34–37.

Cramer, K., and T. Post. 1993. "Proportional Reasoning: Connecting Research to Teaching." *Mathematics Teacher* 86: 404–7.

Cramer, K., T. Post, and S. Currier. 1993. "Learning and Teaching Ratio and Proportion." In *Research Ideas for the Classroom: Middle Grades Mathematics*, edited by D. T. Owens, 159–78. Reston, VA: National Council of Teachers of Mathematics.

Cuevas, G., and K. Yeatts. 2001. *Navigating Through Algebra in Grades 3–5*. Reston: VA: National Council of Teachers of Mathematics.

Cuoco, A., and F. Curcio, eds. *The Roles of Representation in School Mathematics*. Reston: VA: National Council of Teachers of Mathematics.

Del Grande, J. 1993. *Geometry and Spatial Sense*. Addenda Series, Grades K–6. Reston, VA: National Council of Teachers of Mathematics.

Donovan, M. S., and J. Bransford, eds. 2005. *How Students Learn: Mathematics in the Classroom*. Washington: National Academy Press.

Donovan, M. S., J. Bransford, and J. Pellegrino, eds. 1999. *How People Learn: Bridging Research and Practice*. Washington: National Academy Press.

Dowker, A. 1992. "Computational Estimation Strategies of Professional Mathematicians." *Journal for Research in Mathematics Education* 23(1): 45–55.

Driscoll, M. 1999. *Fostering Algebraic Thinking*. Portsmouth, NH: Heinemann.

Edwards, E., ed. 1990. *Algebra for Everyone*. Reston, VA: National Council of Teachers of Mathematics.

Falkner, K., L. Levi, and T. Carpenter. 1999. "Children's Understanding of Equality: A Foundation for Algebra." *Teaching Children Mathematics* 6: 232–36.

Fischbein, E., M. Deri, A. Nello, and M. Marino. 1985. "The Role of Implicit Models in Solving Verbal Problems in Multiplication and Division." *Journal for Research in Mathematics Education* 16 (1): 3–17.

Fosnot, C. T., and M. Dolk. 2001a. *Young Mathematicians at Work: Constructing Multiplication and Division*. Portsmouth, NH: Heinemann.

———. 2001b. *Young Mathematicians at Work: Constructing Number Sense, Addition, and Subtraction*. Portsmouth, NH: Heinemann.

———. 2002. *Young Mathematicians at Work: Constructing Fractions, Decimals, and Percents*. Portsmouth, NH: Heinemann.

Fuson, K. 1992. "Research on Whole Number Addition and Subtraction." In *Handbook of Research on Mathematics Teaching and Learning*, edited by D. Grouws, 243–75. New York: Macmillan.

Fuson, K., and J. W. Hall. 1983. "The Acquisition of Early Number Word Meanings: A Conceptual Analysis and Review." In *The Development of Mathematical Thinking*, edited by H. P. Ginsburg, 49–107. New York: Academic Press.

Fuson, K., D. Wearne, J. Hiebert, H. Murray, P. Human, A. Olivier, T. Carpenter, and E. Fennema. 1997. "Children's Conceptual Structures for Multidigit Numbers and Methods of Multidigit Addition and Subtraction." *Journal for Research in Mathematics Education* 28 (2): 130–62.

Fuys, D., D. Geddes, and R. Tischler. 1988. *The van Hiele Model of Thinking in Geometry Among Adolescents*. Journal for Research in Mathematics Education Monograph Series, no. 3. Reston, VA: National Council of Teachers of Mathematics.

Gardner, M. 1982. *Aha! Gotcha: Paradoxes to Puzzle and Delight*. New York: W. H. Freeman.

Garland, T. H. 1987. *Fascinating Fibonaccis*. Palo Alto, CA: Dale Seymour.

Geddes, D. 1992. *Geometry in the Middle Grades*. Addenda Series, Grades 5–8. Reston, VA: National Council of Teachers of Mathematics.

Geddes, D., and I Fortunato. 1993. "Geometry: Research and Classroom Activities." In *Research Ideas for the Classroom: Middle Grades Mathematics*, edited by D. T. Owens, 199–222. New York: Macmillan.

Ginsburg, H. 1989. *Children's Arithmetic: How They Learn It and How You Teach It*. Austin, TX: Pro-Ed.

Goldman, P. 1990. "Averaging: An Activity Approach." *Arithmetic Teacher* 37 (7): 38–43.

Graeber, A. 1993. "Misconceptions About Multiplication and Division." *Arithmetic Teacher* 40: 408–11.

Greenes, C., L. Schulman, R. Spungin, S. Chapin, and C. Findell. 1990. *Mathletics: Gold Medal Problems*. Dedham, MA: Janson.

Greenes, C., L. Schulman, R. Spungin, S. Chapin, C. Findell, and A. Johnson. 1996. *Math Explorations and Group Activity Projects*. Palo Alto, CA: Dale Seymour.

Harel, G., and J. Confrey, eds. 1994. *The Development of Multiplicative Reasoning in the Learning of Mathematics*. Albany: State University of New York Press.

Harrison, B., S. Brindley, and M. Bye. 1989. "Allowing for Student Cognitive Levels in the Teaching of Fractions and Ratios." *Journal for Research in Mathematics Education* 20 (3): 288–99.

Hembree, R., and H. Marsh. 1993. "Problem Solving in Early Childhood: Building Foundations." In *Research Ideas for the Classroom: Early Childhood Mathematics*, edited by R. J. Jensen, 151–70. New York: Macmillan.

Hiebert, J., T. Carpenter, E. Fennema, K. Fuson, D. Wearne, H. Murray, A. Oliver, and P. Human. 1997. *Making Sense: Teaching and Learning Mathematics with Understanding*. Portsmouth, NH: Heinemann.

Illingworth, M. 1996. *Real-Life Math Problem Solving*. New York: Scholastic Professional.

Jensen, R., ed. 1993. *Research Ideas for the Classroom: Early Childhood Mathematics*. New York: Macmillan.

Johnson, A. 1997. *Building Geometry: Activities for Polydron Frameworks*. Palo Alto, CA: Dale Seymour.

Kamii, C. 1994. *Young Children Continue to Reinvent Arithmetic, 3rd Grade*. New York: Teachers College Press.

Kamii, C., and A. Dominick. 1998. "The Harmful Effects of Algorithms in Grades 1–4." In *The Teaching and Learning of Algorithms in School Mathematics*, edited by L. Morrow and M. Kenney, 130–40. Reston, VA: The National Council of Teachers of Mathematics.

Kasner, E., and J. Newman. 1940. *Mathematics and the Imagination*. New York: Simon and Shuster.

Kieran, C., and L. Chalouh. 1993. "Prealgebra: The Transition from Arithmetic to Algebra." In *Research Ideas for the Classroom: Middle Grades Mathematics*, edited by D. T. Owens, 179–98. Reston, VA: National Council of Teachers of Mathematics.

Kieren, T. 1988. "Personal Knowledge of Rational Numbers: Its Intuitive and Formal Development." In *Number Concepts and Operations in the Middle Grades*, edited by J. Hiebert and M. Behr, 162–81. Reston, VA: National Council of Teachers of Mathematics.

Kilpatrick, J., J. Swafford, and B. Findell, eds. 2001. *Adding It Up: Helping Children Learn Mathematics*. Washington: National Academy Press.

Lamon, S. 1996. "The Development of Unitizing: Its Role in Children's Partitioning Strategies." *Journal for Research in Mathematics Education* 27 (2): 170–93.

———. 1999. *Teaching Fractions and Ratios for Understanding*. Mahwah, NJ: Lawrence Erlbaum.

Lawrence, A., and C. Hennessy. 2002. *Lessons for Algebraic Thinking, Grades 6–8*. Sausalito, CA: Math Solutions Publications.

Lindquist, M., ed. 1987. *Learning and Teaching Geometry K–12*. 1987 Yearbook. Reston, VA: National Council of Teachers of Mathematics.

Litwiller, B., and G. Bright, eds. 2002. *Making Sense of Fractions, Ratios, and Proportions*. Reston, VA: National Council of Teachers of Mathematics.

Mack, N. 1990. "Learning Fractions with Understanding: Building on Informal Knowledge." *Journal for Research in Mathematics Education* 21 (1): 16–31.

———. 1993. "Making Connections to Understand Fractions." *Arithmetic Teacher* 40: 362–64.

McBride, J., and C. Lamb. 1986. "Using Concrete Materials to Teach Basic Fraction Concepts." *School Science and Mathematics* 86: 480–88.

McKillip, W., and J. Wilson. 1990. *University of Georgia Geometry and Measurement Project*. Athens, GA: University of Georgia.

Meiring, S., R. Rubinstein, J. Schultz, J. Lange, and D. Chambers. 1992. *A Core Curriculum: Making Mathematics Count for Everyone*. Reston, VA: National Council of Teachers of Mathematics.

Narode, R., J. Board, and L. Davenport. 1993. "Algorithms Supplant Understanding: Case Studies of Primary Students' Strategies for Double-Digit Addition and Subtraction." In *Proceedings of the Fifteenth Annual Meeting, North American Chapter of the International Group for the Psychology of Mathematics Education*, edited by J. Becker and B. Pence, 254–60. San Jose, CA: Center for Mathematics and Computer Science Education, San Jose State University.

National Center for Improving Student Learning and Achievement in Mathematics and Science (NCISLA). 2003. "Algebraic Skills and Strategies for Elementary Teachers and Students." *In Brief*. www.wcer.wisc.edu/ncisla/publications.

National Council of Teachers of Mathematics. 1989. *Curriculum and Evaluation Standards for School Mathematics*. Reston, VA: National Council of Teachers of Mathematics.

———. 1991. *Professional Standards for Teaching Mathematics*. Reston, VA: National Council of Teachers of Mathematics.

———. 1995. *Assessment Standards for School Mathematics*. Reston, VA: National Council of Teachers of Mathematics.

———. 2000. *Principles and Standards for School Mathematics*. Reston, VA: National Council of Teachers of Mathematics.

Owens, D. T., ed. 1993. *Research Ideas for the Classroom: Middle Grades Mathematics*. New York: Macmillan.

Patriarca, L., M. Scheffel, and S. Hedeman. 1997. *Developing Decimal Concepts: Building Bridges Between Whole Numbers and Decimals*. White Plains, NY: Cuisenaire.

Payne, J., and D. Huinker. 1993. "Early Number and Numeration." In *Research Ideas for the Classroom: Early Childhood Mathematics*, edited by R. J. Jensen, 43–71. New York: Macmillan.

Peck, D., and S. Jencks. 1988. "Reality, Arithmetic, Algebra." *Journal of Mathematical Behavior* 7 (1): 85–91.

Phillips, E. 1991. *Patterns and Functions*. Addenda Series, Grades 5–8. Reston, VA: National Council of Teachers of Mathematics.

Pittman, H. C. 1986. *A Grain of Rice*. New York: Bantam Skylark.

Ranucci, E. R., and J. L. Teeters. 1977. *Creating Escher-Type Drawings*. Palo Alto, CA: Creative.

Reys, B. J. 1991. *Developing Number Sense in the Middle Grades*. Addenda Series, Grades 5–8. Reston, VA: National Council of Teachers of Mathematics.

Reys, B. J., and R. E. Reys. 1971. "Competencies of Entering Kindergartners in Geometry, Number, Money, and Measurement." *School Science and Mathematics* 71: 389–402.

Schifter, D. 1999. "Reasoning About Operations: Early Algebraic Thinking in Grades K–6." In *Developing Mathematical Reasoning in Grades K–12*, edited by L. Stiff and F. Curcio, 62–81. Reston, VA: National Council of Teachers of Mathematics.

Schoenfeld, A. 1992. "Learning to Think Mathematically: Problem Solving, Metacognition, and Sense Making in Mathematics." In *Handbook of Research on Mathematics Teaching and Learning*, edited by D. Grouws, 334–70. New York: Macmillan.

Schoenfeld, A., ed. 1994. *Mathematical Thinking and Problem Solving*. Hillsdale, NJ: Lawrence Erlbaum.

Scott, W. 1981. "Fractions Taught by Folding Paper Strips." *Arithmetic Teacher* 28 (5): 18–22.

Seymour, D., and J. Britton. 1989. *Introduction to Escher-Type Tessellations*. Palo Alto, CA: Dale Seymour.

Shaughnessy, M. 1992. "Research in Probability and Statistics: Reflections and Directions." In *Handbook of Research on Mathematics Teaching and Learning*, edited by D. Grouws, 465–94. New York: Macmillan.

Shaughnessy, M., and B. Bergman. 1993. "Thinking About Uncertainty: Probability and Statistics." In *Research Ideas for the Classroom: High School Mathematics*, edited by P. Wilson, 177–97. New York: Macmillan.

Shell Centre for Mathematics Education. 1982. *The Language of Functions and Graphs*. Nottingham, UK: Shell Centre.

Shulte, A., ed. 1981. *Teaching Statistics and Probability*. 1981 Yearbook. Reston, VA: National Council of Teachers of Mathematics.

Shulte, A., and J. Smart, eds. 1992. *Teaching Statistics and Probability*. Reston, VA: National Council of Teachers of Mathematics.

Silver, E. A. 1997. "Algebra for All." *Mathematics Teaching in the Middle School* 2 (4): 204–7.

Sinicrope, R., and H. Mick. 1992. "Multiplication of Fractions Through Paper Folding." *Arithmetic Teacher* 40: 116–21.

Sowder, J. 1992. "Making Sense of Numbers in School Mathematics." In *Analysis of Arithmetic for Mathematics Teaching*, edited by G. Leinhardt, R. Putnam, and R. Hattrup, 1–52. Hillsdale, NJ: Lawrence Erlbaum.

Sweetland, R. 1984. "Understanding Multiplication of Fractions." *Arithmetic Teacher* 32: 48–52.

Usiskin, Z. 1988. "Conceptions of School Algebra and Uses of Variables." In *The Ideas of Algebra, K–12*, edited by A. Coxford and A. Schulte. Reston, VA: National Council of Teachers of Mathematics.

Van Dyke, F. 1994. "Relating Graphs to Introductory Algebra." *The Mathematics Teacher* 87: 427–33.

Vergnaud, G. 1994. "Multiplicative Conceptual Field: What and Why?" In *The Development of Multiplicative Reasoning in the Learning of Mathematics*, edited by G. Harel and J. Confrey. Albany, NY: SUNY Press.

von Rotz, L., and M. Burns. 2002. *Lessons for Algebraic Thinking, Grades 3–5*. Sausalito, CA: Math Solutions Publications.

Wagner, S., and C. Kieran, eds. 1989. *Research Issues in the Learning and Teaching of Algebra*. Reston, VA: National Council of Teachers of Mathematics.

Wearne, D., and J. Hiebert. 1994. "Place Value and Addition and Subtraction." *Arithmetic Teacher* 41: 272–74.

Wickett, M., K. Kharas, and M. Burns. 2002. *Lessons for Algebraic Thinking, Grades K–2*. Sausalito, CA: Math Solutions Publications.

Witherspoon, M. 1993. "Fractions: In Search of Meaning." *Arithmetic Teacher* 40: 482–85.

Yakimanskaya, I. S. 1991. *The Development of Spatial Thinking in Schoolchildren*. Soviet Studies in Mathematics Education, vol. 3. Reston, VA: National Council of Teachers of Mathematics.

Index

polyhedrons, 243–44
    Euler's Formula and, 245
positive numbers, 22–25
    addition and subtraction of, 68–74
    multiplication and division of, 95–97
power, in exponential notation, 203
precision, in measurement, 275
prime factors, 20–22
    teaching multiplication and division
        with, 88
prime numbers
    prime/composite number probability
        activity, 331–32
    rectangular dimensions and factors,
        activity, 12–14
prisms, 244
    formula for determining volume,
        developing, 291–93
probability, 322–39
    defined, 322–24
    dependent events (see dependent events)
    experimental, 325
    independent events (see independent
        events)
    teaching, 339
    theoretical, 325–26
products
    in multiplication equations, 77
    with prime factors, 20–22
proper factors, 14
proper fractions, 102
properties, mathematical, 31–41
    associative property, 36–40
    commutative property, 32–36
    distributive property, 40–41
proportion, 172
    distance, rate, and time with, 187–88
    percent, proportion approach to, 157–58
    ratios, 172–74, 175
    in similarity, 175
proportional reasoning, 165, 174
protractors, 227–28
pyramids, 244
Pythagoras, 237, 238
Pythagorean Theorem, 6–7, 237–43
    identifying triangles with, 241–43
    proving the, 238–40
Pythagorean triple, 241

Rajah's Rice, The, 205
range, in functions, 193
range, of data, 304
rates, 165
    applications of, 174–88
    defined, 166
    distance, rate, and time, 185–88
    rate problems, 79
    unit rates, 182–85
rational counting, 2–3
rational numbers, 4–5, 99
    density property of, 139
    ratios as, 168–69

ratios, 165–89
    applications of, 174–88
    comparisons, types of, 166–68
    defined, 165–74
    equivalence and, 169–72
    Fibonacci, 213–14
    fractions as ratios of two quantities, 100,
        107–8
    percent as a ratio, 156–57
    proportions, 172–74
    rates (see rates)
    as rational numbers, 168–69
    scale models used with, 177–80
    similarity, 174–82
    teaching, 189
ratio tables, 171–72
rays, 223
Reagan, Ronald (president, U.S.), 310
real numbers, 5–6
reciprocals, 130–31
recognition, in van Hiele levels, 220–21
rectangles
    areas of, 286–87
    doubling dimensions, effect of,
        178–80
    measurement activity, 275–77
    as polygons, 234
    properties of, 234–37
rectangular array problems, 80
rectangular prisms, 244
recurring remainders, 90–91
recursive procedures, 200, 201–2
reduction, of dilation, 257
referents, 136
reflections, 249
    on the coordinate plane, 258–60
    with spatial visualization, 250–54
reflective symmetry, 235–36
relational symbols, 195
relative frequency, 325
remainders
    in division equations, 77
    interpreting, 91–92
    recurring, 90–91
repeated addition/subtraction model,
        78–79, 85
repeating decimals, 140, 142–43
repeating patterns, 198–99
representation, in algebra, 214–18
representational symbols, 194
rhombi, 231
    as polygons, 234
    properties of, 234–37
    rotational symmetry, 255–56
right angles, 228
right triangle
    identifying, 241–43
    Pythagorean Theorem used to compute
        third side, 240–41
rigid transformations, 256
rigor, in van Hiele levels, 220–21
Roosevelt, Theodore (president, U.S.),
        310
rotational symmetry, 235–36, 255–56
rotations, 249
    on the coordinate plane, 260
    with spatial visualization, 254–56
rote counting, 2
rules
    in algebra, 198, 205–14
    functions, 206, 207–10

scaffold algorithm, 52
scalar problems, 79–80
scale drawings, 178
scale factors, 173, 178, 179–80
    with coordinate planes, 260–61
scalene triangles, 229
scatter plots, 316–17
segments, line, 223
separate word problems, 56–57, 59–60
separating from subtraction strategy,
        61–62
separating to subtraction strategy, 62
sequences, 199–205
sets
    classifying numbers by, 4–6
    determining percents based on, 154
    fractions as parts of, 100, 101–5
    illustrating multiplication with, 87
sides, in polyhedrons, 244
signed numbers, 23–24
    addition and subtraction of, 68–74
    multiplication and division of, 95–97
similarity, 174–75
    coordinate grid, activity for exploring
        similar figures on a, 176–77
    effect of scale factor on areas of similar
        figures, activity, 179–80
    patterns in areas and perimeters of similar
        squares, activity, 178–79
    ratios and, 174–82
    volumes and scale factors of similar
        figures, relationship between,
        181–82
skew lines, 226, 227
solids. *See* three-dimensional structures
"Solve for x," 191
spans, 272
spatial orientation, 248–49, 263–69
    block structures, analyzing, 266
    building block structures from two-
        dimensional vues, 266–68
    cross sections, 268–69
    translating between dimensions,
        264–68
spatial sense, 248–69
    defined, 248–49
    teaching, 269
    transformations on the coordinate plane
        (*see* transformations on the
        coordinate plane)
spatial visualization, 248–57
    dilations, 256–57
    reflections, 250–54
    rotations, 254–56
    translations, 249
square numbers
    patterns, exploring square number,
        210–12
    rectangular dimensions and factors,
        activity, 12–14
square root, 7–8
squares
    effect of scale factors on, 178–80
    measurement activity, 275–77
    as polygons, 234
    properties of, 234–37
    rotational symmetry, 255
    sum of angles in, 231
squaring a number, 13
standard algorithms, 43, 44
standard deviation, 304